Foreword by Dr. W. F. Albright

OUR LIVING BIBLE .

*Text by Michael Avi-Yonah
and Emil G. Kraeling*

With 400 illustrations from
The Illustrated World of the Bible Library

The Bible, with its enduring message for men of every age, is the most important collection of writings in the whole of world literature. In view of the all but incredible archaeological discoveries in recent years, vast new dimensions in our understanding of Biblical lands, the people of the Bible, and the Bible itself have been opened to us.

Our Living Bible was conceived as a work that would tell the story of the Book of Books in the light of these ancient treasures unearthed in modern times and meticulously studied. Such visual records, drawings, ritual objects, and monuments, described as they are in this volume, provide valuable aids to a full appreciation of the Bible. In addition, they offer a fascinating reconstruction of the life and culture of Biblical times—knowledge previously accessible to specialists, but now given comprehensive treatment for the general reader.

The editors have drawn on the multi-volume *Illustrated World of the Bible Library,* so widely acclaimed on publication, for the 400 full-color illustrations used here to give the book an unrivaled visual impact as it recounts the story of the world of the Hebrew people and of the early Christians. Page by page, the Biblical world unfolds, faithfully recreated in a way that would have been impossible for artists and writers in earlier centuries. Photographs, drawings, and maps—some especially prepared, and others collected from libraries and museums—accompany the reader's journey through the dramatic and awe-inspiring events of two and three thousand years ago.

Our Living Bible will be welcome in every home—Jewish or Christian—where the Bible is read. It is an incomparable gift book for anyone, at any season, and an ideal addition to the church or home library. Non-theological in its approach, it is an enlightening "living commentary" that will be read and re-read for many years to come by those who know and love the Bible.

OUR LIVING BIBLE

OUR

LIVING

BIBLE

Old Testament text by Michael Avi-Yonah

New Testament text by Emil G. Kraeling

McGRAW-HILL BOOK COMPANY, INC.

New York · Toronto · London

Foreword

IT IS JUST 125 years since the foundations of Biblical archaeology were laid by Edward Robinson's brilliant explorations of Palestine. This American achievement was followed by an extraordinary decade during which a German, Richard Lepsius, created scientific Egyptology, and the French and English began excavating in Assyria and deciphering cuneiform. It was nearly a century before there was again such an archaeological decade as 1837–47, and this was the decade 1929–39, which saw epoch-making French work at Ugarit and Mari, as well as the expeditions of the Oriental Institute of the University of Chicago throughout the Middle East.

In spite of Robinson's fine beginning, it was not until 1890 that scientific excavation in Palestine was inaugurated by Flinders Petrie, who had discovered while digging in Egypt that ordinary unpainted pottery could be used in dating. Following up Heinrich Schliemann's recognition that the mound of Hissarlik (Troy) consisted of stratified layers of town occupation, one on top of another, he not only distinguished the strata of Tell el-Hesi but also dated them by pottery. Since then Palestine has become the parade example of stratigraphically fixed pottery chronology—partly, to be sure, because of the lack of sensational finds to distract interest from more basic matters. Miss Kathleen Kenyon's work at Jericho represents the high-water mark in stratigraphic method, thanks to her brilliant application of the improved trenching methods of Sir Mortimer Wheeler. With the aid of radiocarbon she has pushed the date of the walled city of Jericho back into the early seventh millennium B.C. Radiocarbon has fixed Palestinian chronology back to the Lower Middle Palaeolithic, some 40,000 years ago, and has enabled us to date the first permanent villages in Palestine about 10,000 years ago. Less sensationally, pottery dating now enables us to describe the material culture of Palestine in all Biblical periods from Abraham down to Roman times.

No account of Palestinian archaeology, no matter how brief, can omit the Dead Sea Scrolls, which have revolutionized our knowledge of the textual history of the Old Testament and the religious background of the New Testament. Though only a small fraction of the manuscripts, extensive and fragmentary, found since 1947 has yet been published, we know that every aspect of Biblical research has received an infusion of fresh vitality, and that no Biblical problem remains unaffected in some way.

Since Wilhelm Gesenius published his decipherment of the Phoenician inscriptions, also in the eventful year 1837, work in Phoenicia and Syria has become increasingly important for the Bible. Where Palestine has been exceedingly niggardly with inscriptions from Old Testament times, Syria has been lavish—and most of the early texts found in Syria are written in dialects so closely related to Hebrew that we can use them to clarify Biblical vocabulary, grammar, and style. The Ugaritic religious tablets from the fourteenth and thirteenth centuries B.C. (just before and just after the Exodus of Israel from Egypt) are revolutionizing our approach to the dating and interpretation of Early Hebrew poetry.

While the progress of Egyptology has slowed up in recent years, specialists now have more time to organize and synthesize the vast body of material accumulated since the days of Napoleon. Biblical scholars are coming increasingly to appreciate the value of Egyptology for the better understanding of the Bible. Nowhere have we remotely comparable pictorial material, from the walls of temples and tombs, with which we can illustrate all aspects of ancient Biblical life. Since Egypt was so near and was for such long periods in control of Palestine, it exerted a very great cultural and even literary influence on Hebrews and Israelites. The dry climate of Egypt has preserved many thousands of Greek books and documents dating from the fourth century B.C. to the seventh century A.D., which have thrown a vast amount of light on New Testament language and culture. Not least are the Aramaic documents from Jewish colonies settled in Egypt since the sixth century B.C. and the epoch-making find of Early Gnostic treatises at Chenoboskion in Upper Egypt. Thanks to Qumran and Chenoboskion we can place the New Testament squarely between the pre-Christian Essenes and the post-Christian Gnostics, from the standpoint of the history of religious ideas, thus disproving many of the "assured conclusions" of radical criticism.

Babylonia and Assyria continue to yield an unceasing flow of priceless cuneiform tablets, not only from current excavations but also from the stores of museums and from innumerable small private collections. Since clay tablets are relatively indestructible, there is no reason to foresee any diminution in the flow, barring a major act of God. During the past two decades we have seen the recovery of a substantial part of Early Sumerian religious texts and belles-lettres, thanks to the untiring efforts of S. N. Kramer and his pupils. Throughout Old Testament times Sumero-Akkadian civilization remained dominant in most of Southwestern Asia and exerted a cultural influence radiating in all directions. The better we know ancient Babylonia and Assyria the more we shall know about the civilization of Israel and its basic pattern of thought and behavior.

When we turn to the lands most directly under Mesopotamian influence, such as Iran, Armenia, and Asia Minor (Anatolia, modern Turkey in Asia), we come upon the Elamites, Urartians, Hurrians (Biblical Horites), and Hittites. All are important for Biblical research, especially the Horites and Hittites, who play a role intermediate between the Sumero-Akkadians, the Northwestern Semites (Hebrews, Canaanites, Phoenicians), and the Greeks. Now that both cuneiform and hieroglyphic Hittite have been deciphered, their importance for the student of Biblical institutions has become extremely important.

Throughout these areas and far beyond are scattered remains of the Graeco-Roman civilization which dominated the world for a thousand years. Not only are most of its leading centers mentioned—sometimes repeatedly—in the New Testament, but excavations in them have already illuminated many aspects of early Christianity. One can never tell when an apparently insignificant find may clear up a moot point in the Gospels or Acts, or when a datable inscription may explain a problem elsewhere in the New Testament.

The five-volume set, called The Illustrated World of the Bible Library, gives laymen as well as specialists easy access to this fascinating area. It is, however, expensive, so the publishers have arranged with one of its principal compilers, Professor Michael Avi-Yonah, to select the most useful illustrations, which are explained in the text supplied by him and Dr. Emil G. Kraeling, and to publish this material in a one-volume edition at a more popular price. Our Living Bible is in no sense a mere picture-book; it combines the most interesting and authentic illustrations with a text which utilizes them in Bible interpretation without taking a sectarian position where different religious views are involved. If the book makes the Bible seem more real in a world of flesh and blood, like ourselves, publishers and authors will feel that their labors have been rewarded.

April 20, 1962   W. F. ALBRIGHT

Preface

THE BIBLE, BEARING an enduring message for men of every age, is the most important collection of writings in the whole of world literature. As the source of two great religions—Judaism and Christianity—it has provided spiritual guidance for a large part of the human race in the past and continues to do so for a large and influential body of men and women in the present. As a record of history, it casts invaluable light upon the darkness of the ancient Oriental world from which our Western civilization ultimately derives its culture, its science, and its ideals. As a work of literary art, the Bible is accounted second to none; even in translation, one is conscious of the sparse economy of the original Hebrew of the Old Testament, enlivened by the beauty and power of its imagery, as well as of the straightforward dignity of the Greek of the New Testament. The stories of the Bible have caught the imagination of men's minds. Its psychological insights are original and profound. Its moral appeal has the same pungent urgency as when first proclaimed.

Information of any kind which aids in a fuller understanding of the Bible necessarily helps its readers both to appreciate and to attain the high goals of religious and ethical living which it sets. In the last 150 years archaeological discovery has contributed more than any other activity toward opening new dimensions in that understanding, enhancing our appreciation of the moral and spiritual values of the Scriptures quite as much as providing us with a better knowledge of its material and cultural setting.

One by one, the ancient treasures of the East, saved from destruction through thousands of years of turmoil by their protective layers of debris, have been brought to light and subjected to long and meticulous study. Many excavations have been carried out on the very sites on which the Biblical scenes were enacted. Remains have been found of cities in which people lived during the period of the Bible, providing insight into their patterns of existence. Tablets have been discovered with primitive writing—the hieroglyphics of Egypt and the Babylonian-Assyrian cuneiform—which, when deciphered, shed light on much that was obscure in the Biblical text. Upon ancient vessels, monuments, and walls in temples and palaces can now be seen drawings, paintings, and reliefs depicting people, ritual ceremonies, battles, and contemporary scenes of daily life which parallel the characters and incidents in the Biblical narratives. These visual records serve as an invaluable aid to a full appreciation of the Book of Books.

These are the kinds of illustrations which are reproduced in the condensed edition of *The Illustrated World of the Bible Library*. When studied in the light of contemporary writings by men skilled in the sciences of archaeology and epigraphy, they make possible the reconstruction of much of the life and culture of Biblical times.

This new knowledge has long been accessible to specialists. Along with a few general works, numerous scholarly monographs have appeared which made use of ancient illustrations to illuminate details of the Biblical text. For the general reader, however, a more comprehensive treatment was needed which would cover all the Books of the Bible, include all the most significant discoveries of archaeological research, and be as up-to-date as humanly possible. Such is the purpose of this book.

In the present work, the geographical and archaeological pictures are brought into direct relationship with the text of the Old and New Testament Books in their familiar order.

These pictures are very different from the works of art which have been used to illustrate the Scriptures throughout most of the post-Biblical period. Each age has had its own conception of the personalities of the Bible and the episodes in which they played a part. In an effort to make the Bible live, some of the world's greatest artists have produced paintings, statues, and stained-glass windows devoted to Biblical themes. But these works, magnificent as some of them are, belong to the history of art, not to the world of Biblical scholarship. All reflect the time of the artist rather than that of the Bible. None brings us into authentic relationship with the Biblical world.

With the discoveries of the archaeologist, however, we are for the first time able to establish such an authentic relationship, and it is this fact which gives to the present volume its distinctive character and value. "Authenticity" has been the key-word in making the selections of materials it contains; the aim has been to make it possible for the reader to visualize the Biblical stories in their original context. Only those illustrations have been used which are known to belong to the period dealt with in the text, or to a period which is reasonably near. The commentary describes the illustration and notes its date, its place of discovery, and the enlightenment it offers to the Biblical text. Where necessary, there is included a scientific explanation of the Biblical passage itself. In all of this we have had the general reader rather than the specialist in mind.

The emphasis has been on man and his activities rather than on inanimate artifacts. He is shown engaged in the arts of peace and of war, in earning his bread and in his moments of relaxation. The religious side of his life, of central importance in the case of Biblical man, is illuminated by material drawn from the pagan world, showing the forces against which the Law and the prophets of the Bible directed their moral and religious struggle.

The idea of presenting *The Illustrated World of the Bible Library* was conceived by the Israeli publisher, Mr. Y. Makavy. Work on four volumes of the Old Testament was begun in 1955 under the editorship of Professor Michael Avi-Yonah and Dr. Abraham Malamat of the Hebrew University, Jerusalem, with Professor Benjamin Mazar as Chairman of an Editorial Board consisting of the leading scholars in Israel in the fields of Biblical research, archaeology, history, rabbinics, zoology, botany, geography, geology, ancient weapons and warfare, cults, and arts and crafts. The fourth volume was completed in 1960. In 1961, a fifth volume, on the New Testament, was prepared by Professor Avi-Yonah.

This condensed edition offers a rich selection of the pictorial resources which appeared in the five-volume edition, but in less elaborate form. Where there have been excisions in the larger work, they have been replaced in this edition by a running text which has been prepared by Professor Avi-Yonah for the Old Testament, and by Dr. Emil G. Kraeling of New York for the New Testament. Both have based themselves on the full text of the parent-work.

We tender a special word of thanks to Professor Robert C. Dentan, General Theological Seminary, New York; Professor P. R. Ackroyd, Samuel Davidson Chair of Old Testament Studies, London University; and Mr. Merton Dagut, Haifa, whose advice and devoted labors on behalf of this book have been invaluable.

Contents

In the Beginning

GENESIS

THE FIRST BOOK of the Old Testament, often referred to as the "First Book of Moses" or the "First Book of the Law," is known in the English translation as *Genesis*, which is the Greek rendering of the first word of the Hebrew original—*Bereshit*, "In the beginning". Thus it takes us back as far as human thought can reach in relation to the world as we know it. In its opening chapter God the omnipotent Creator is depicted as bringing the whole visible universe into being by eight majestic divine commands, no sooner uttered than fulfilled. The stupendous miracle of the creation was accomplished in six days: on the first light was formed, on the second the heavens, on the third the earth and the seas, on the fourth the sun and the moon, on the fifth the creatures of the seas and the birds of the air, and on the sixth and last day the land animals, and finally man. There followed a day of rest, the first Sabbath.

After this prologue the book of Genesis proceeds to unfold the story of man, starting from his blissful sojourn in the Garden of Eden with its four rivers. Here we meet the first identifiable names in the Bible: the Tigris and the Euphrates, the twin rivers of Mesopotamia,

A river flowed out of Eden to water the garden, and there it divided and became four rivers. The name of the first is Pison; it is the one which flows around the whole land of Havilah, where there is gold; . . . The name of the second river is Gihon; it is the one which flows around the whole land of Cush. And the name of the third river is Hiddekel, which flows east of Assyria. And the fourth river is the Euphrates.

(GEN. 2: 10–14)

A bone handle from Hazor, c. eighth cent. B.C., showing a Tree of Life depicted as a young date palm.

He drove out the man; and at the east of the garden of Eden He placed the cherubim and a flaming sword which turned every way, to guard the way to the tree of life. (GEN. 3 : 24)

are still flowing today through the fertile plains of what were once Assyria and Babylonia. About the location of Eden itself, however, and about the identification of its two other rivers, the Gihon and Pison, there is no such certainty. The narrative continues with the creation of Eve from the rib of Adam, the first man, followed by the temptation and fall of Adam and the expulsion of the guilty couple, together with their tempter, the serpent, from Paradise.

So far the Biblical narrative moves on a plane that transcends any mundane evaluation. From the moment, however, that Adam is commanded to till the earth from which he was formed, we may at least attempt to correlate the story of Genesis with what we know of the early history of mankind.

The two sons of Adam, Cain and Abel, represent the great division of humanity, dating back to the remote past, into settled cultivators and nomadic sheep-rearers. The problem of obtaining the food necessary to sustain life was shared by the first primitive men with the animals; it was only when man learned to make and use tools and weapons for the satisfaction of his basic needs that he raised himself above all other creatures. In the earliest times he had to obtain what food he could by hunting and by gathering such edible plants as grew wild; but in the Middle Stone Age, about twelve to fifteen thousand years ago, a momentous revolution occurred. Some men took advantage of the annual flooding of certain lands in the vicinity of the great rivers to introduce hoe-agriculture; scratched just deep enough for seeding, the soil yielded a regular crop sufficient for the sustenance of the cultivator. The subsequent selection of the right type of plants for cultivation was the beginning of systematic farming. Parallel with this process went the domestication of such animals as the cow and the sheep, which provided early man with both nourishment and clothing.

This division of early society into two great classes of producers, the farmers and the shepherds, as it appears in the first pages of the Old Testament, is thus indeed as old as human history. The deep-rooted antagonism between the two groups is typified by the story of Cain and Abel, the two sons of Adam. Such conflicts must have been of great antiquity, since the farmer by working the soil restricted the nomadic shepherd's grazing-grounds, while the shepherd's flocks constituted a menace to the farmer's crops. Both Cain, "the tiller of the ground", and Abel, "the keeper of sheep", made an offering of their produce to God. This episode in the Biblical story also corresponds to a definite stage of human culture.

Before both farming and animal-raising comes the primitive hunter, who depended on the luck of the chase, and naturally had recourse to homoeopathic magic. (The numerous slain animals portrayed in the prehistoric cave-paintings may well have been intended to make the scenes represented come true.) The farmer and the shepherd on the contrary, being at the

Now Abel was a keeper of sheep and Cain a tiller of the ground. In the course of time Cain brought to the LORD an offering of the fruit of the ground, and Abel brought the firstlings of his flock and of their fat portions... (GEN. 4 : 2–4)

Dresden Museum—Sumerian cylinder seal. 3500–3000 B.C.

mercy of natural forces and in particular the weather, understandably attributed the control of these forces to supernatural beings that had to be propitiated by offerings of the first-fruit of their labors. Offerings of animals and of agricultural produce are to be found portrayed on the very early seals made by the Sumerians, a people that inhabited the lower valley of the Tigris and the Euphrates, whose history goes back to the fifth millennium. But whereas in the Sumerian representations both kinds of offerings are accepted, in the Biblical story clear preference is given to the shepherd, Abel, for whose offering God had regard, while Cain and his offering were rejected. This stand in favor of the shepherd and his produce faithfully reflects the attitude of the early Hebrews. They were semi-nomadic shepherds moving with their flocks along the steppes which separated the cultivated land of the peasants from the desert proper where roamed the full nomads, the hunters and warriors "whose hand be against every man". As we see from the story of Cain, Ishmael and Esau both the farmer and the nomadic hunter were regarded with equal disfavor. There is a parallel to the story of Cain and Abel in the Sumerian mythological conflict between the shepherd-god and the farmer-god. But in the Biblical version the economic implications of the struggle are completely overshadowed by the moral lesson of the divine punishment meted out to the fratricide.

The historical background of the Biblical story is further characteristically revealed in the fact that it is to the descendants of the outlawed murderer, Cain, that most of the arts and crafts of civilization are attributed. It was Cain who built the first city which he called by the name of his son, Enoch; and it was the descendants of Cain in the sixth and seventh generations, the sons of Lamech the son of Methusael, who were the reputed inventors of musical instruments and of "artifices in brass and iron". It is also interesting to note that in Hebrew the name "Cain" is derived from the same root as that of the tribe of the Kenites, who were famous ancient smiths.

The use of musical instruments undoubtedly goes very far back in human history. We may assume that the Biblical story refers to the professional musicians "those who play the lyre and pipe" (Gen. 4: 21) since such artists were more likely to be found in the service of the temples which from the beginning formed the nuclei of urban agglomerations. As early as the third millennium B.C. we find the representation of an orchestra on a steatite bas-relief from Adab in Sumer. It consists of two harpists, each playing an instrument with a different number of strings, a drummer and a trumpeter, the whole ensemble being led by a conductor with a leafy baton.

Much more important than the "invention" of music, was the discovery that certain natural rocks containing copper ore could be melted in the moderate heat which man could generate in the fourth millennium B.C.; and that, once melted, the ore could be cast in clay molds into any desired form. This made possible the fashioning of weapons and tools which were much superior to those of stone: they were stronger and less brittle, and if damaged could be recast at will. The Biblical era of "bronze and iron" corresponds to the

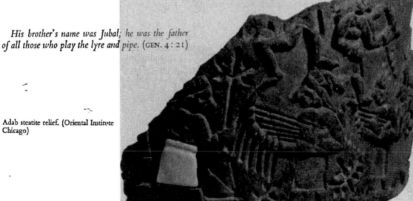

His brother's name was Jubal; he was the father of all those who play the lyre and pipe. (GEN. 4: 21)

Adab steatite relief. (Oriental Institute Chicago)

Mace-heads of copper, from Beersheba. (Israel Dept. of Antiquities)

archaeological findings. Copper, the main component of bronze, was mined and used before iron; the Bronze Age precedes the Iron Age in Palestine and other countries.

Actually the earliest known copper articles are those found in the excavations of the underground houses in the vicinity of Beersheba, dated to the end of the fourth millennium B.C. These objects are mace-heads, cast in molds and fashioned from the pure copper of the Araba (the great rift stretching from the Dead Sea to the Red Sea), where the metal was being mined already in these early times. Since the spread of copper did not supersede the use of stone but developed side by side with it, scholars designate this period as the Chalcolithic Age (from the Greek words *chalkos*=copper and *lithos*=stone). The extraction and use of metals was one of the decisive technical breakthroughs in the history of civilization.

THE GREAT FLOOD

MANKIND IS ALSO described as continuing through Seth, the third son of Adam and Eve, and his descendants. Since in normal times the products of farming and sheep-rearing were more than enough to satisfy early man's immediate needs, he was able to set aside a store sufficient to ensure the preservation of life in lean years too. The human race, whose numbers throughout all the phases of the Stone Age had been very small, now began to multiply. Its increasingly intensive occupation of the Sumerian plain was, however, more than once interrupted by great floods, evidence of which has been brought to light by the archaeologists. Two levels of settlement have been found, separated by layers of sediment several meters high and entirely devoid of human remains. The memory of these cataclysms has come down to us in the "flood stories" which formed

So the LORD said, "I will blot out man whom I have created from the face of the ground. . . ." (GEN. 6: 7)

Babylonian deluge tablet. (British Museum)

part of the traditional lore of many ancient nations, including the Babylonians whose version of them is recorded on the tablets of the epic poem about Gilgamesh, the primeval Babylonian hero. In this version the flood was decreed by the gods because humanity was increasing at such a rate as to threaten their supremacy. The Biblical story, by contrast, while retaining the same basic elements, characteristically stresses the moral aspect of the catastrophe. It was because humanity had become corrupt, because "the wickedness of man was great in the earth", that God decided to "destroy man from the face of the earth". In the Babylonian story one man named Utnapishtim was saved by the grace of the gods: in the Bible Noah was singled out from his contemporaries as being "a just man and perfect in his generation". The details of the Babylonian story are borne out by what we know of the highly developed ancient techniques of boat-building in a country traversed by two great rivers, where watermanship was a necessity of life. Boats of various types are represented on many archaeological finds from Babylonia, including seals. One of these seals depicts a wooden craft, manned by two sailors and carrying a shrine at which a bearded man is worshiping.

17

Make yourself an ark of gopher wood; make rooms in the
ark, and cover it inside and out with pitch. This is how you
are to make it: the length of the ark three hundred cubits, its
breadth fifty cubits and its height thirty cubits. (GEN. 6: 14–15)

Such river-craft, however, were tiny when compared with the huge ark, made of gopher wood and pitched inside and out, which, in the Biblical Story, Noah constructed at the LORD's command. Into this ark Noah gathered his family and representatives of the different kinds of animals and birds. The rest of mankind, together with all the other beasts and birds, perished when the rising waters blotted out the whole surface of the earth, leaving even the highest peaks deeply submerged.

At last the waters began to recede and the ark came to rest on the mountains of Ararat. These mountains are mentioned again in the Bible, in the Hebrew text of Isaiah 37: 38, as the place to which the assassins of Sennacherib, king of Assyria, fled. The mountains of what is today Eastern Turkey were well known to the Assyrians by the name "Urartu", as comprising one of the hostile kingdoms which they had difficulty in conquering. Later Babylonian and Jewish traditions attempted to locate the spot where the ark had come to rest on one of the peaks of the Ararat range, which rises to a height of 17,000 feet.

Once safely aground, Noah began to send out birds to ascertain the extent of the dry land. His first messenger, a raven, did not return at all; his second, a dove, at first found no resting-place and returned to the ark. But when, a week later, the dove came back carrying an olive leaf in her beak, Noah knew that he would soon be able to leave the ark. When the patriarch and his family at last stepped out on to dry land, they made a thank-offering to God and were promised that life on earth would never again be destroyed by a great flood. In confirmation of this solemn covenant the rainbow with its gorgeous hues was to serve as a constant reminder of God's mercy towards His creatures.

After leaving the ark Noah began to cultivate the ground; he also began to plant vines and to make wine from their grapes. Modern scientific investigations seem to confirm that viticulture started in Asia Minor, not far from Mount Ararat. The veneration of the grape, which is of very early origin in this part of the world, continued under the Hittites whose law code extended special protection to vineyards. They also represented their god of fertility with a cluster of grapes in his hand as a symbol of plenty.

18

THE DESCENDANTS OF NOAH

AFTER PLANTING HIS vineyard Noah drank of its fruit. The Biblical narrative relates that once, when the patriarch was lying naked in a drunken stupor,
he was treated as an object of ribaldry by one of his sons, Ham, but shown true filial respect
by the eldest and youngest, Shem and Japheth. The reprehensible conduct of Ham on this
occasion is evidently a story designed to explain the Israelites' sense of superiority to his
descendants, especially to the Canaanites.

· The "Table of Nations" or "The Generations of Noah" (Gen. 10) is an attempt at
drawing up a systematic racial genealogy of the peoples of the ancient world as known
to the Biblical author. Broadly speaking, the Japhethites are thought of as inhabiting the
lands north and west of Israel, the Semites those to the east and southeast, and the
Hamites those to the southwest. However, this geographical order is not strictly observed,
nor can we discern any grouping by language or by race. The classification of the
various peoples, supposedly "after their families, after their tongues, in their lands, after
their nations", seems rather to be dictated mainly by historical and political considerations.

The descendants of Japheth comprise, almost without exception, peoples of Indo-Germanic
stock. Their lands begin in the west with *Tarshish*, which can perhaps be identified with the
island of Sardinia, and *Tiras*, which some
scholars consider to denote the Etruscans who
first appear in history as a nation established in
the center of Italy north of Rome. They were
probably migrants from Asia Minor, since their
language is not related to the Indo-Germanic
group. Their power reached its height in the
sixth century B.C. and lasted throughout the
fifth, when the Gallic invasion of Italy and
the growing power of Rome spelt their doom.
Culturally, as is shown by the paintings in
their tombs, the Etruscans were under strong

*Noah was the first tiller of the soil. He
planted a vineyard.* (GEN. 9: 20)

Rock-cut relief, Ivriz, Turkey; Fertility god
holding bunch of grapes.

The sons of Japheth: Gomer, Magog, Madai, Javan, Tubal, Meshech, and Tiras. The sons of Gomer: Ashkenaz, Riphath, and Togarmah. The sons of Javan: Elishah, Tarshish, Kittim, and Dodanim. From these the coastland peoples spread. . . . (GEN. 10 : 2–5)

(*Above left*) "Javan" (GEN. 20 : 2). Attic marble head. Seventh century B.C. (National Museum Athens)

(*Below left*) "Elishah" (GEN. 10 : 4). Pottery head from Aiya Irini, Cyprus. Sixth century B.C. (Museum, Nicosia, Cyprus)

(*Above right*) "Tiras" (GEN. 10 : 2). Etruscan couple in Tarquinii tomb fresco. Third century B.C.

Greek influence. They imported Greek vases and tried to imitate Greek dress and customs, though with some significant changes, such as giving greater equality to women.

A second group of Japhethites—in the geographical, if not genealogical, sense—includes the Greeks (Javan, i.e. the Ionians, the Greek inhabitants of Asia Minor), who were the most familiar to the Oriental peoples and the Hebrew form of whose name is consequently used in the Bible for all Hellenic tribes. To later generations of Hebrews the Greeks, whose culture had spread throughout the East, became the typical representatives of the Japhethites. Beside the Greeks we can list the *Kittim*, a people mentioned several times in the Bible in connection with "the islands" or "the sea", and perhaps stemming from the Mycenean Greeks, who established themselves in Crete on the ruins of an earlier Minoan civilization, only to be conquered in their turn by the invading Dorians. The name of the next people in the Japhethite group, *Dodanim*, is read by most scholars *Rodanim* (R and D are easily interchanged in the square Hebrew script) and referred to the people of Rhodes, one of the larger Aegean islands off the shore of Asia Minor which was inhabited by Dorian Greeks. It had commercial and military relations with Egypt in the seventh century B.C., and in the Hellenistic period the Rhodians dominated maritime commerce in the Eastern Mediterranean. After the Rhodians come the Cypriotes (*Elishah* was the ancient name of this copper-bearing island). Throughout its history in antiquity, Cyprus lay on the dividing-line of the Greek and the Semitic civilizations, its population partly Phoenician and partly Greek. The Bible apparently includes it in the Greek world, since the Greeks had established their colonies on this island as early as the thirteenth century B.C.

A third group of Japhethites comprises various peoples of Asia Minor: *Meshech, Magog, Tubal* and *Togarmah*. These nations, which are far less known in history than the Greeks and their kindred, formed the submerged lower stratum of the population of this region and provided the labor force that worked its natural resources, especially the iron mines. They were dominated by later arrivals, the Lydians and the Hittites, who are linked in the Biblical table to other sons of Noah.

Lastly there are two more Japhethite peoples which are the furthest of all from the Mediterranean: *Gomer* and *Ashkenaz*. These dwelt on the northeastern shores of the Black Sea. Ashkenaz is identified with the Scythians and Gomer with the Cimmerians who, in the eighth century, were displaced by the Scythians. From the seventh century B.C. onwards the Scythians had relations with the Greeks: we find them represented on Greek works of art, and Greek imports are found in large quantities in their country. The Scythians were especially famous as archers and withstood even the armed might of the Persian king, Darius I. They were conquered in the second century B.C. by the Sarmatians.

The Medes (*Madai*)—who must include their kinsfolk and historical partners, the Persians—

(*Above*) "Dodanim" (GEN. 10 : 4). Rhodian plate. Sixth century B.C. (British Museum)

(*Below*) "Ashkenaz" (GEN. 10 : 3). A Scythian on gold vase from Kul Oba, Crimea. *c.* fourth century B.C. (Hermitage Museum, Leningrad)

The sons of Ham: Cush, Egypt, Put, and Canaan . . . Egypt became the father of Ludim, Anamim, Lehabim, Naphtuhim, Pathrusim, Casluhim (whence came the Philistines), and Captorim. Canaan became the father of Sidon, his first-born, and Heth, and. . . . (GEN. 10: 6–16)

Egyptians, Canaanites, Nubians and Lybians on fresco in tomb of Seti. c. 1300 B.C.

were the inhabitants of the Iranian plateau. They were instrumental in destroying the Assyrian empire in the seventh century B.C. In the sixth century the Medes were subdued by the Persians under Cyrus, who then proceeded to unite the two peoples so thoroughly that the Greeks usually called the Persians "Medes".

In comparison with the Japhethites the sons of Ham constitute a heterogeneous group, the nucleus of which seems to be formed by Egypt (*Mizraim*) and its vassal states: the Libyans (*Put*), the Nubians (*Cush*), and *Canaan*, a collective term for the inhabitants of what later became the land of Israel. The four appear together on Egyptian works of art representing the peoples subject to Pharaoh. They are distinguished from each other by the color of their skins and by their dress, in accordance with the stylized conventions of Egyptian painting. Thus, beginning at the left in the illustration, the Egyptians have red skins (the name for Egypt in their language being *Kemi*, "the red earth", made fertile by the Nile floods and contrasting strongly with the yellow sands of the desert). The Canaanites have brown complexions and wear long beards. The Egyptians included all Asiatics with whom they came into contact with the "wretched Ketenu" as they called the Canaanites. The Nubians, being related to the Negro stock of Africa, are black. The Libyans are white in color and are further identified by their feathered headdress.

Egyptian rule over Canaan began with the consolidation of the Egyptian kingdom under the Pharaoh Narmer in the fourth millennium B.C. and continued, with various ups and downs, almost to the eve of the Israelite conquest. As Canaan was naturally the land best known to the author of the Biblical "Table of Nations", its peoples are listed in the greatest detail. The Canaanites were a branch of the Western Semites, or Amorites; thus "Canaan" was the name by which the Phoenicians used to designate themselves. The Bible (Gen. 10: 15) shows cognizance of this fact by making Sidon (the eponymous founder of the foremost Phoenician city) the firstborn of Canaan, and listing a series of Phoenician towns as his brothers. The Jebusite inhabitants of Jerusalem and the Hittites of Asia Minor are then added for good measure; and in v. 19 the border of Canaan, i.e. of the Egyptian province of that name in Asia, is again defined.

Included amongst the various peoples of Egyptian stock in the list of the descendants of Ham are the *Caphtorim* or Cretans (*Caphtor* being Crete), and the *Casluhim* (inhabitants of northern Asia Minor) who are described as the ancestors of the *Pelishtim* or Philistines. These Philistines were actually part of the "Sea Peoples" who swept down on Egypt at the end of the thirteenth century B.C., and the remains of whose culture point to their affiliations with Cretan civilization of the Minoan era. Having been repulsed from Egypt, the Philistines settled in southwest Canaan, apparently with the consent of the Pharaoh Rameses III, whom they continued to serve as mercenaries. As such they came into conflict with the Israelites and were thus associated by them with Egypt, as here. The remainder of the sons of Ham consists of various groups of South Arabian peoples of mixed Nubian (i.e. Negro) and Semitic stock.

The sons of Shem, Noah's first-born and "the elder brother of Japheth", are the last

(*Top left*) "Egypt became the father of ... Aphtorim." (GEN. 10: 14). Cretan from fresco in palace at Knossos. Fourteenth century B.C.

(*Top right*) Philistine on relief at Medinat Habu, Egypt. Early twelfth century B.C.

(*Bottom left*) "And Canaan Heth" (GEN. 10: 15). Relief at Boghazkoy, Turkey. Fifteenth–fourteenth century B.C.

(*Bottom right*) "Canaan" (GEN. 10: 6). Potsherd from Bethshean. Fourteenth century B.C. (Palestine Archaeological Museum)

The sons of Shem: Elam, Asshur, Arpachshad, Lud, and Aram. . . . Arpachshad became the father of Shelah; and Shelah became the father of Eber. To Eber were born two sons: the name of the one was Peleg . . . and his brother's name was Joktan. (GEN. 10: 22–5)

(*Reading from left to right, above and below*) Eber-Mari fresco, eighteenth century B.C.; Aram—King Bar Rakab, eighth century B.C. (Berlin Museum); Asshur, eighth or seventh century B.C. relief (Louvre); Elamite soldier "Frieze of Archers" Susa, fifth century B.C. (Louvre); "Shem" Adab head, 2000 B.C. (Oriental Institute, Chicago)

group to be listed. Their position at the end of the genealogical table, rounding it off, is meant to emphasize the supremacy of the "father of all the children of Eber", i.e. of the Hebrews from whom the Israelites were descended. Once again the list includes peoples that cannot be considered "Semitic" either by race or language in the modern, scientific sense of the term. Thus the *Elamites*, who lived in the region of Susa to the east of Babylonia, formed a special group; and the *Ludites* (Lydians) were settled in historical times at the far western end of Asia Minor. The Lydians were not Semites, but neither were they of Indo-Germanic stock, though in their hey-day (seventh century B.C.) they were strongly influenced by the Greeks.

The descendants of Shem fall into two main groups: *Asshur* (the Assyrians, the inhabitants of the Land of the Two Rivers, the Tigris and Euphrates, who formed the eastern branch of the Semites); and *Aram*, the Western Semites, with whom are associated a number of small tribes living on the borders of the desert. Besides these two great historical divisions of the Semitic race the Bible also mentions a third one, fathered by *Arpachshad* (Arphaxad) a mysterious name which has not yet been satisfactorily explained by scholars. Some would connect the last part of the word with the *Casdim* or Chaldeans, the Hebrew name for the inhabitants of Babylonia, including Ur, Abraham's birthplace. Arpachshad's grandson was Eber, manifestly the ancestor of the Hebrews; and one of Eber's sons was *Joktan*, the ancestor of a series of South Arabian tribes, some of them identical with the descendants of Ham who lived in the same area. Whether this duplication indicates a corresponding mixture of blood in these tribes, we cannot say at present. Five generations after Peleg, the son of Eber, we come to Terah, the son of Nahor and the father of Abraham.

THE TOWER OF BABEL

BEFORE THE BIBLICAL story focuses down on to Abraham, his family and descendants, there is one more episode concerning mankind as a whole. Starting from the assumption that at one time the human race had only one language, this story relates how a group of men, migrating from the East, came to Babylonia, the Biblical land of Shinar. There they started using brick instead of stone and pitch instead of mortar; and there they decided to build a tower, the top of which was to reach heaven. God, however, confounded (in Hebrew *balal*) their language so that they could not understand one

Then they said, "Come, let us build ourselves a city and a tower with its top in the heavens, and let us make a name for ourselves, lest we be scattered abroad upon the face of the whole earth." (GEN. 11 : 4)

Sumerian seal, 2000 B.C. showing building of a *ziggurat* or huge tower.

another's speech. This is the Biblical author's etymological explanation of the city-name of Babel (which is actually the Accadian *bab-ilu*, meaning the "gate of god"). The whole account appears to be a legendary echo of the penetrations of the Sumerians (coming from the east) into the marshlands of Babylonia. In their former lands they had built with stones and mortar, but now they had to learn to use the different building materials available in rockless Mesopotamia. Moreover, to maintain their ancestral mountain-top worship of the gods even in the flat, level plain of Babylonia, they erected man-made "mountains", the huge pyramidal towers known as *ziggurat* which were attached to their temples. The name given to the great temple of Marduk in Babylon—*Esagila*, "the house which lifts its head" —at once brings to mind the story of the Tower of Babel. The construction of the sky-scraper-like *ziggurat* is represented on many seals from the third millennium onwards.

25

ABRAHAM, HAGAR AND ISHMAEL

THE VAST SWEEP of the Bible, covering the whole early story of mankind, now narrows down to the story of a single family, that of Abraham. Terah, with his son Abram (later to be called Abraham, the "father of many nations") and their wives, migrated to Haran in Northern Mesopotamia. One reason for the choice of the latter dwelling place might be that both Ur of the Chaldees, their original dwelling place, and Haran had famous sanctuaries of the moon good. Abram was then commanded by the LORD to move on to Canaan. Living as a semi-nomad with his great flocks and many slaves, and occasionally tilling a piece of ground in the vicinity of such cities as were friendly, he passed slowly along the watershed of the country west of the Jordan, by way of Shechem, Bethel, Hebron and the south. In years of famine Egypt served him as a refuge.

On one of these visits to Egypt, Abraham acquired for his wife Sarai (later to be called Sarah) an Egyptian maidservant, Hagar. According to the usual Oriental custom, Hagar became his second wife and bore him a son named Ishmael. When in fulfillment of a divine promise Sarah herself bore Abraham a son, Isaac, in his hundredth year, there arose a conflict between the right of the first-born, Ishmael, the child of a slave-wife, and that of the later-born son of a wife of superior social status. Hagar herself, as an Egyptian, was apparently regarded as the representative of a higher civilization: Egyptian slaves were highly prized for their good breeding by Canaanite chieftains and presumably by Abraham too. On the other hand, from marriage contracts executed at Nuzu in Mesopotamia in which the customs and manners of the patriarchal age are reflected in many details, we learn that if a man—with his wife's consent, of course—took a slave-wife and later on had a son by his original spouse, the birthright passed to this son. Certainly in this case Abraham had to allow the claims of Sarah and to expel Hagar. The story is related twice in Genesis (chapters 16 and 21), but in each case the setting is the same.

Semitic nomad with water bottle on his shoulder. Beni Hassan, Egypt. Early nineteenth century B.C.

So Abraham rose early in the morning, and took bread and a skin of water, and gave it to Hagar, putting it on her shoulder.... (GEN. 21:14)

Sarai, Abram's wife, bore him no children. She had an Egyptian maid whose name was Hagar.
(GEN. 16: 1)

Leaving Abraham's encampment near Beer-sheba, Hagar set out on foot to return to her homeland, Egypt, by way of the wilderness leading to Shur (a Hebrew word which means "wall" and in all probability refers to the chain of Egyptian border fortresses running from the Mediterranean to the Red Sea). She made her way from one to the other of the sparse wells which form natural wayside halts for travelers through the nearly waterless Negeb desert. For this journey Abraham had provided Hagar with a "water bottle", most probably a skin container such as is still used by the Beduin to the present day. Such "bottles" are not breakable like earthenware vessels and can be conveniently folded up when empty. In antiquity they were part of the regular equipment of travelers in the desert, as well as of the armies which passed through its barren wastes. Obviously, the quantity of water in Hagar's bottle was totally insufficient for her long journey, and only the miraculous appearance of a well, when she was almost at her last gasp, saved both mother and child from dying of thirst. The early Jewish commentators regarded Ishmael as the ancestor of the Arab tribes, thus explaining the similarity of the Hebrew and Arab tongues. Ishmael lived a precarious life in the desert, depending for his existence on his trusty bow made from wood, animal sinews, and strips of bone. It was the possession of this long-range weapon, used both for hunting and warfare, that ensured the survival of the desert tribes.

Model statue of Egyptian handmaid. c. 2000 B.C. From tomb of Meketre, Thebes. (Metropolitan Museum, New York)

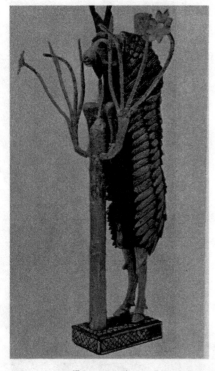

Figurine from royal tomb, Ur. (University Museum, Philadelphia)

And Abraham lifted up his eyes and looked, and behold behind him was a ram, caught in a thicket by his horns. . . .
(GEN. 22 : 13)

THE SACRIFICE OF ISAAC

ABRAHAM'S FAITH IN God was put to a most terrible test when he was ordered to sacrifice his son Isaac on Mount Moriah. Such sacrifices of the first-born child, who was regarded as the special property of the deity, occurred in early times in the East, but were gradually replaced by animal offerings as civilization spread and beliefs became less savage. Abraham traveled to the place appointed by divine decree for the sacrifice of Isaac in the usual manner of ancient Semitic dignitaries: he himself rode in front on an ass, while his son and his servants followed behind him on foot. Such an "order of the road" is portrayed on various monuments in the Sinai peninsula and elsewhere. When the group neared its destination, the servants were left behind and Isaac himself carried the wood. Just as the sacrifice was about to be performed, Abraham's hand was stayed by divine intervention, and "a ram caught in a thicket by its horns" was substituted for the human victim. The ram played an important part in the sacrificial ritual of the Ancient East. We find conventional representations of it, ringed by the branches of a symbolical tree, in the royal tombs of Ur from the middle of the third millennium B.C.

THE PURCHASE OF THE CAVE OF MACHPELAH

SOON AFTER THIS harrowing test Abraham suffered the loss of his wife Sarah, who passed away in Kirjath-arba, the old name of Hebron. In accordance with the customs of the time her body had to be buried on the same day; however, as a "stranger and a sojourner" in the land, Abraham possessed no plot which he could use for this purpose. In his distress he appealed to the Hittite community at Hebron, since they, presumably settlers in the land from the North and strangers in the country like himself, were more likely to give him a favorable hearing. Ephron the Hittite was the possessor of a cave (a double one, hence the name *Machpelah* (Heb. *Kapel*=to double over)) at the end of a field. The bargaining followed the usual Oriental pattern. At first Ephron declared himself ready to make Abraham a present of the cave and field alone; but when it came to the question of an actual purchase, the whole property had to be taken. (According to the Hittite code a partial sale would not discharge the obligations of the owner in the same way as a transfer of the whole property). As usual in such bargaining the seller made light of the not inconsiderable price ("Four hundred shekels, what is that between you and me?"), the equivalent of 4,650 grams of silver. The terms of the sale were finally arranged and the objects sold (the field and the cave in it and all the trees in the field) specified in the agreement. The price was weighed out in "money current among the merchants"; in the absence of coined money (which did not come into use for another twelve hundred years) precious metals were made up into bars or rings, and payments were effected by weighing them in large scales with weights having the shape of animals.

Once acquired, the cave of Machpelah became the family vault of Abraham and his descendants; thus the bones of his grandson Jacob who died in Egypt, were brought to Hebron for burial. Exceptions to this custom were made only in the case of Rachel, who was buried near Bethlehem, and of Joseph who was laid to rest near Shechem. The location of the cave of Machpelah has been traditionally identified within the confines of the sanctuary (*Haram*) of "el-Khalil" (Arabic for "the Friend of God"—i.e. Abraham) inside the town of Hebron. This sanctuary, which was sacred to Jews (and later on to Christians and Moslems alike), is encircled by a high wall the lower part of which was built by Herod the Elder. The cave itself is situated below the mosque (originally a Crusader church in part) and has not been entered for many centuries.

Abraham agreed with Ephron; and Abraham weighed out for Ephron the silver which he had named in the hearing of the Hittites, four hundred shekels of silver, according to the weights current among the merchants. (GEN. 23 : 16)

Weighing gold and silver rings, tomb of Rekhmire, Thebes, Egypt. Fifteenth century B.C.

29

JACOB AND ESAU

AFTER ABRAHAM'S DEATH, Isaac his first-born became the head of the family. One of Abraham's last acts had been to arrange for the marriage of Isaac with Rebekah, the daughter of Bethuel, Abraham's nephew. The girl was fetched from her native Haran by Eliezer, the "eldest servant of his (Abraham's) house". Rebekah bore Isaac twin sons, the elder of whom was Esau and the younger Jacob. In these two children of Isaac the ancient conflict between Cain and Abel broke out again. This time Esau, or Edom, is the hunter who roams far and wide armed with the weapons of his calling, and Jacob the peaceful, harmless shepherd. In the course of their life together in the tribal encampment it was Jacob who followed the pursuits of his father and grandfather and thus qualified himself to be their successor, while Esau adopted the way of life of the desert nomads, the descendants of Ishmael. The formal transfer of the birthright was effected in two ways: first of all, Esau "sold" it to Jacob for a mess of red pottage; then Isaac was tricked into confirming the transfer by giving his solemn blessing to the second-born son, who had been disguised in "the skin of the kids of the goats" to pass for his hirsute brother. The Biblical story represents Rebekah as the instigator of this imposture. She apparently recognized that the future of the tribe of Abraham depended on the continuation of the now traditional patriarchal mode of life; and besides as the descendant of a civilized family living in Mesopotamian Haran, she must have found Esau's ways abhorrent. The documents of Nuzu, which have contributed so much to our understanding of the customs and manners of the patriarchs, also help to corroborate the story of Esau and Jacob. Thus, we know of a person in Nuzu who transferred his heritage (an orchard) to his brother for the price of three sheep; and the validity of death-bed blessings and of the dispositions contained therein was upheld by the courts of that city.

Hunter, from Assyrian relief. Eighth century B.C.

Esau was a cunning hunter, a man of the field, while Jacob was a quiet man, dwelling in tents.

(GEN. 25 : 27)

Rebekah had yet another reason for preferring Jacob: Esau had formed marriage ties with various Canaanite families, and she feared that Jacob might do likewise and take a wife from the daughters of Heth. Hence to preserve the purity of the family of Terah she sent Jacob away to her own family where he would also be safe from the wrath of the tricked Esau. After an adventurous journey, in which he saw at Bethel the famous vision of the ladder stretching between earth and heaven, Jacob reached Haran and was received into the

Then Rebekah said to Isaac, "I am weary of my life because of the Hittite women. If Jacob marries one of the Hittite women such as these, one of the women of the land, what good will my life be to me?" (GEN. 27: 46)

Carchemish relief, showing Hittite priestesses. (Ankara Museum)

family of Laban, Rebekah's brother. On his arrival Jacob met Rachel, Laban's younger daughter, at the well; he fell in love with her and served seven years to obtain her hand. When Laban palmed off Leah, Rachel's elder sister, on him, Jacob served a further seven years to win his true love. After that he remained with Laban as manager of his flocks and amassed great wealth in livestock and servants. Finally Jacob left Laban and returned to his own country, making peace with Esau on his way. After a mysterious encounter with an angel at Penuel he received the symbolical name of Israel, by which his descendants are designated to this day. The Sons of Israel became a distinct group within the larger framework of the Hebrews, the descendants of Eber.

With Jacob the family of Abraham, which till then had numbered only a few members in direct line of descent, branched out into a flourishing clan. Leah and her handmaid—who was a wife of inferior status—bore Jacob altogether eight sons, the heads of eight of the future tribes of Israel, and one daughter; Rachel, after long years of barrenness, at last gave him one son, Joseph, and then another, Benjamin, and two more were born of her slave, Bilhah. With this family Jacob continued to live as his fathers had lived before him, roving up and down the country with his flocks in search of pasture.

JOSEPH AND HIS BROTHERS

As THE FIRST child of the beloved Rachel, Joseph was given preference over his brothers. Thus his father had a long robe with sleeves made for him, a costly garment usually worn only by high-ranking and wealthy Canaanites who are often represented in it on Egyptian paintings. It was made of pieces of embroidered cloth stitched together, and was usually fastened to the body by a band of the same color wound spirally round the waist. Sometimes the inside of the coat was of a different hue from the outside, thus giving it a multicolored appearance when worn in folds (it is called a "coat of many colors" in the Authorized Version).

Such blatantly preferential treatment naturally aroused a strong feeling of jealousy in Joseph's brothers, and Joseph made them still more angry by relating how, in his dreams, his future high destiny as ruler of Egypt and savior of his family had been revealed to him. In the first of these dreams the symbolism was taken from the harvest; hence we may deduce that, although Jacob and his family were predominantly cattle-raisers, they apparently—like the Beduin of the present day—also engaged in some kind of agriculture. Joseph dreamt that he and his brethren were making sheaves and that suddenly his sheaf stood upright and lorded it over the others, which formed a circle round it and did obeisance to it. The tenor of the second dream, in which the symbols were this time the sun, moon and the stars, was the same.

Enraged by what they regarded as Joseph's unwarranted insolence, his brothers waited for the right moment to take their revenge. The opportunity presented itself when Joseph left the protection of his father and came to visit their camp at Dothan. He was seized, placed in an empty well, and then taken out and sold to a group of passing traders on their way from Gilead to Egypt, their camel-caravan loaded with the exotic produce of the former land: spices, balm and myrrh. The camel is the ideal pack-animal for countries with scanty and sparse sources of water, as its hump and stomach can store all the water, food and fat it requires for many days. The domestication of the camel therefore opened up routes through the deserts of the Near East which were shorter than the circuitous regular roads followed by Abraham and other nomads relying on donkeys. The

Now Israel loved Joseph . . . ; and he made him a long robe with sleeves.   (GEN. 37: 3)

Canaanite wearing long-sleeved coat. From painting in Egyptian tomb. Fourteenth century B.C.

Relief from tomb of Akhhotep,
Sakkarah, Egypt. 2500–2000 B.C.

*Now Joseph had a dream. . . .
"Behold, we were binding sheaves
in the field, and lo, my sheaf arose
and stood upright; and behold, your
sheaves gathered round it and
bowed down to my sheaf".*

(GEN. 37: 5–7)

forerunners of the modern Beduin Arabs traversed these desert routes with the sureness of the sailor crossing the expanses of the sea. Coming from Gilead they followed the *via maris*, or "way of the sea" which ran across the Jordan and through the Valley of Jezreel (on the fringe of which Dothan is situated), and continued by one of the passes of the Carmel range to the coastal plain and thence southwards to Egypt. By selling Joseph to traders bound for a distant country, his brothers hoped to get rid of him for good, whereas in fact they were unknowingly ensuring his subsequent high destiny.

Having, as they believed, finally settled their account with Joseph, the brothers had to think of some way of explaining to their father the disappearance of his favorite son. They hit on the simple device of dipping Joseph's "coat of many colors" in a kid's blood and sending it to Jacob. The grief-stricken father naturally assumed that Joseph had been devoured by a wild beast; he knew of the constant danger to which shepherds were exposed from ferocious, man-eating animals, much more numerous in antiquity in the Near East than they are at present. The ancients had to protect themselves as best they could with bows, spears and swords. Representations of people being attacked and torn to pieces by wild beasts abound in ancient art.

33

JOSEPH IN EGYPT

O N BEING BROUGHT to Egypt Joseph was sold to a high officer at the Pharaoh's court, a captain of the royal guard called Potiphar. Thanks to his pleasing presence and innate capabilities, he quickly rose to the post of "overseer of the house", with absolute control of his master's estate. Included in his domain were, in all probability, both the house itself, with its elaborate complex of workshops for women (spinning and weaving), stores, granary, kitchens, etc., and also the country estate which supplied the master's town residence with the necessary produce. Pictures from Egyptian tombs show such estates, with the overseer (or the master of the house himself) supervising the plowing and sowing which were done after the yearly flooding of the Nile had restored the fertility of the soil. Signs of the recent inundation can be clearly seen. Where the soil is still moist, it is worked by the hoe; where it is already dry, teams of oxen are used for plowing. The work in the fields was physically exhausting, and food and drink had to be provided for the refreshment of the workmen.

While working for Potiphar, Joseph was tempted by his master's wife. Infuriated at finding all her enticements steadfastly resisted, she falsely denounced him to her husband for assaulting her and had him thrown into prison. There he again proved his worth, this time

On the third day which was Pharaoh's birthday, he made a feast for all his servants . . . He restored the chief butler to his butlership and he placed the cup in Pharaoh's hand.

(GEN. 40: 20-1)

Reliefs showing the Pharaoh Eye as Akhenaton's butler. Fourteenth century B.C. (Berlin Museum)

And behold, there came up out of the Nile seven cows, sleek and fat, and they fed in the reed grass. (GEN. 41 : 2)

Painting from tomb of Queen Nefertari. Thirteenth century B.C.

to the keeper of the prison, and was given custody of two high officials, the king of Egypt's butler and baker.

These two were among the highest-ranking courtiers. The pre-eminence of the post of chief butler is strikingly illustrated by the fact that the Pharaoh Eye (middle of the fourteenth century B.C.) was, before his own accession to the throne, chief butler to the Pharaoh Akhenaton (Amenophis IV). He is represented on reliefs from his tomb as waiting on Akhenaton and pouring wine into his cup; on another relief the two Pharaohs are shown feasting together like friends. Such festivities were held especially on the occasion of royal birthdays, when a general amnesty was also proclaimed. Joseph, who had correctly interpreted the dreams of his charges (foretelling that the baker would be executed and the butler pardoned), was forgotten for a time, until another turn of events raised him to a new height of glory. The king of Egypt dreamt two dreams: in the one, seven "fatfleshed kine" came out of the river Nile, only to be devoured by seven lean ones; in the other, seven full ears of corn were devoured by seven blighted ones. When the "wise men" of his court were unable to interpret the dreams, the butler, now pardoned and reinstated in his former position, remembered his imprisonment and Joseph's true predictions. The Hebrew slave was forthwith brought, by royal summons, to the court, having first been hurriedly shaved and clothed in fresh raiment to make him presentable. Called before the king, he explained the two dreams as really one, of which the meaning was that, after seven fat years in which the Nile would rise higher than before and make the soil of Egypt bear plentiful harvests, there would come seven years of floods and famine. The Egyptians were all the more ready to accept this interpretation as they used to worship the god of the Nile in the shape of a bull and therefore saw in the cows a symbol of their soil. Such a symbolical representation of seven cows and a bull appears in the tomb of Queen Nefertari

So Joseph found favor in his sight, and attended him, and he made him overseer of his house.... The blessing of the LORD was upon all that he had in house and field.

(GEN. 39: 4-5)

Painting from the tomb of Nakht. Fifteenth century B.C.

(thirteenth century B.C.). The cows have full udders and stand before troughs, with their names (such as "the beloved, the great, the red one") written above their heads. Behind them stands a powerful black bull.

Joseph's advice to Pharaoh was that he should appoint a "discreet and wise" man over the whole land of Egypt with absolute powers to gather in the plentiful harvests and to prepare for the bad years to come. As might have been expected, Pharaoh chose Joseph for this task and nominated him as his viceroy "over the house". A foreigner could presumably enforce the strict measures required and was less likely to yield to the pressure of local demands.

In accordance with Egyptian custom, the new vizier was arrayed in a gold chain (or rather necklet) and fine white linen, and was handed the Pharaoh's gold ring. This last act, symbolical of the transfer of full powers, is illustrated here in the picture of the Pharaoh Tutankhamon handing over his signet ring to the nobleman Huy, whom he has just appointed viceroy of Nubia. Huy had the scene reproduced in his tomb (fourteenth century B.C.) as a visual reminder of the high honor bestowed on him. In ancient society, where comparatively few people could read and write or even sign their name, letters and orders

were authenticated by seal impressions made with a signet ring. The use of the latter therefore invested the document in question with the full weight of the authority of its possessor.

Acting vigorously, Joseph for seven years collected one-fifth of the total yield of Egypt

Then Pharaoh took his signet ring from his hand and put it on Joseph's hand and arrayed him in garments of fine linen, and put a gold chain about his neck. (GEN. 41: 42)

Painting from tomb of Huy. Fourteenth century B.C.

And Joseph stored up grain in great abundance, like the sand of the sea until he ceased to measure it, for it could not be measured. (GEN. 41 : 49)

Model set of granaries, from the tomb of Kamena.
c. 2500 B.C. (Ashmolean Museum, Oxford)

and stored it in royal granaries, each located in the chief city of a district. Granaries were plentiful in a land so full of produce as Egypt; we find them represented in models dating from the time of the Fourth Dynasty, i.e. the middle of the third millennium B.C. Joseph also prospered personally during this time; he married and his wife bore him the two sons who later on became the eponymous ancestors of the two great tribes of Ephraim and Manasseh.

When the years of famine came, Joseph was able to feed the people of Egypt by selling them the stored grain in return for their land, thus extending the royal estates. This is the Biblical explanation of the well-known fact that in Egypt all the land (except that of the temples) belonged to the king. Outside Egypt, where there was no Nile to fructify the fields annually and to permit the accumulation of provision against years of drought, the famine was much more grievous. As we know from Egyptian sources, the riches of the Nile Valley were used to extend the Pharaoh's power over the neighboring countries. Among those affected by the famine were Jacob and his sons, Joseph's own nearest kin. Ten of the brothers (all except the youngest, Benjamin, Rachel's second son) were sent down to Egypt to buy grain.

ISRAEL GOES DOWN TO EGYPT

IT WAS NOTHING unusual for wandering Semites to enter the Nile Valley, although their influx was, naturally, controlled by the Egyptians manning the chain of forts which separated Egypt from Asia along the line now followed by the Suez Canal. Egyptian documents, as well as tomb paintings of the early nineteenth century B.C. (found at Beni Hasan) provide evidence of such entries of nomads from Canaan. In the painting reproduced here, for example, a group of them are represented armed with bows and arrows, their sturdy womenfolk accompanying the men on foot and their children on donkeys or marching along too. In addition to their bows the men hold spears and

Canaanite delegation presented to Tutankhamon. Painting
in tomb near Thebes. Fourteenth century B.C.

musical instruments, and on the back of one of the donkeys there is a portable smithy with
its bellows, which was probably the economic mainstay of the tribe. They are shown being
introduced into Egypt by a powerful official and bringing with them gifts of the desert,
including gazelles. They are an organized clan, headed by one Abisha.

Such was the picture presented by Joseph's brothers when they came before the Egyptian
official in charge of selling grain to all the people—who was none other than Joseph himself.
The brothers did not recognize Joseph, whom they remembered only as a boy sold into
bondage. But Joseph, of course, recognized them and began to play a double game, being
generous to them but at the same time taking revenge for the wrong they had done him.
He first accused them of spying. When they indignantly denied this charge and described
their family and their status, he agreed to let them depart with the grain on condition that
they return, bringing with them their youngest brother, Benjamin. Simeon, one of their
number, was kept back as a hostage to ensure that this was done.

Arrivals of Semites in
Egypt. Beni Hasan
painting.

And from among his brothers he took five men and presented them to Pharaoh. (GEN. 47 : 2)

At first Jacob was unwilling to let the one remaining child of his beloved Rachel leave for Egypt; but as the famine became more severe and the sons more insistent, he finally gave way. On their second appearance Joseph received them kindly, but when they were about to return home he had his silver cup hidden in Benjamin's baggage. After their departure he sent his steward in pursuit of them, had them brought back, and by threatening to punish Benjamin, forced Judah, the brothers' spokesman, to confess the wrong done to him years before. Then at last Joseph made himself known to his brethren and sent them back to bring his father Jacob down to Egypt.

Jacob's entry into Egypt with all his family and dependants, seventy strong, marks an important turning-point in the history of Israel. From this moment they ceased to be merely a clan and became a people, small at first but growing larger with time. The patriarch and his entourage were welcomed with much pomp by Pharaoh. We can easily conjure up the scene from the many representations in Egyptian tombs of foreign, especially Canaanite, delegations being received by the king of Egypt. As usual in Egyptian paintings, the persons portrayed are differentiated in size according to their social importance. The Pharaoh, wearing the high blue helmet-crown with the golden uraeus snake over his brow, is a giant. In his right hand he holds the *ankh*, the symbol of life, and in his left the flail of Osiris as a sign of his divinity. Before him, drawn on a slightly smaller scale, stands an official dressed in fine white linen, as Joseph was, and holding his emblems of office. Other chamberlains introduce the Canaanites who are wearing their "coats of many colors". They are proferring gifts and raising their hands in veneration before the king. Their followers are depicted on a still smaller scale than the leaders; some fall down and kiss the ground before the Pharaoh, while others carry the produce of their country or lead in its animals. A similar scene must

And the sons of Israel carried Jacob their father, their little ones and their wives in the wagons which Pharaoh had sent to carry him. They also took their cattle and their goods, which they had gained in the land of Canaan, and came into Egypt, Jacob and all his offspring with him. (GEN. 46 : 5-6)

Head of Tutankhamon. (Cairo Museum)   Amenhotep IVth—or Akhenaton. (Berlin Museum)   Amenhotep III. (British Museum)

have been enacted at the court when Joseph presented his father and five of his brothers to the king. Hearing that they were cattle breeders and shepherds, Pharaoh allowed them to settle in the land of Goshen, the eastern part of the Nile delta, where there were good pastures. The reason given in the Bible for the separation of the newcomers from the rest of the Egyptians, viz: that shepherds were an abomination to the Egyptians, may show that the sojourn in Egypt started after the expulsion of the Hyksos, the so-called "Shepherd Kings", foreign invaders (eighteenth to sixteenth century B.C.) who were greatly hated by the Egyptians.

The Book of Genesis ends with the death and burial of Jacob. Before he died the patriarch blessed his sons in turn, in a series of prophecies foreshadowing the historical role of the descendants of each, and thus marking their transition from a clan to a people composed of many tribal groups. After Jacob's death, his body was mummified by the Egyptian embalmers and borne in a solemn funeral procession to the cave of Machpelah, where it was buried.

Now there arose a new king over Egypt, who did not know Joseph. (EXOD. I : 8)

Statue of Rameses II. (Turin Museum)

*The time that the people of Israel dwelt in Egypt
was four hundred and thirty years.* (EXOD. 12: 40)

(*Top*) Thutmosis III. (British Museum)

(*Below*) Hatshepsut. (Metropolitan
Museum, New York)

EXODUS

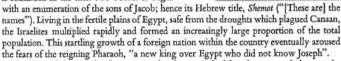

THE SECOND OF the five "books
of Moses" deals with the Exodus
of the Israelites from Egypt and with the
events which befell them during their long
journey through the Sinai Desert. This story
is continued in the next two books. It begin
with an enumeration of the sons of Jacob; hence its Hebrew title, *Shemot* ("[These are] the
names"). Living in the fertile plains of Egypt, safe from the droughts which plagued Canaan,
the Israelites multiplied rapidly and formed an increasingly large proportion of the total
population. This startling growth of a foreign nation within the country eventually aroused
the fears of the reigning Pharaoh, "a new king over Egypt who did not know Joseph".

The date of the Exodus from Egypt has been much debated among scholars, as the
Bible does not specifically name the Pharaoh in question. Archaeological evidence places
the main events of the Israelite conquest of Canaan in the thirteenth century B.C. Allowing for the period of wandering in the wilderness, this would date the Exodus to the end of
the fourteenth or the beginning of the thirteenth century. According to the usually accepted
computation, the Israelites' sojourn in Egypt lasted several hundred years; one view is
that they entered the country in the wake of the Hyksos invasion, but this particular
point is disputed. However that may be, the most likely time for the Exodus would seem
to be during the crisis between the end of the XVIIIth Dynasty (1570-1305 B.C.)
and the rise of the XIXth (1305-1205 B.C.). Among the great rulers of the XVIIIth
Dynasty, under whose scepter the Hebrews lived in Egypt, were the following: Hatshepsut
(1486-1468 B.C.), the only woman to reign as Pharaoh; her husband and successor Thutmosis
III (1490-1436 B.C.), the greatest of the Egyptian conquerors, whose armies reached
the River Euphrates; Amenhotep (Amenophis) III (1398-1371 B.C.), during whose reign
Egypt reached the peak of its cultural and material development in the period of the New
Kingdom; his son and successor Amenhotep IV (1369-1353 B.C.), the religious reformer,
who adopted the name of Akhenaton and worshiped Aton, the sun god, as the only deity,
and whose policy brought Egypt to the brink of anarchy. Akhenaton's son-in-law and
second successor Tutankhamon (1352-1344 B.C.) was himself an undistinguished ruler; but
by a strange quirk of fate he is the only Pharaoh whose tomb has been preserved to our
times with all its splendors untouched, thus providing visible and tangible evidence of the
fabulous wealth and luxury of the ancient kings of Egypt, in sharp contrast to the abysmal
poverty of their exploited subjects.

Merneptah (c. 1232 B.C.), one of the kings of the XIXth Dynasty, mentions Israel as a people living in Canaan; moreover, the Israelites are described in the Bible as providing the forced labor for the building of the store-city of Raamses (probably Pi-Ramese, the ancient name of Zoan or Tanis, the capital of the later Pharaohs). These two references taken together have led many scholars to assume that the Pharaoh of the oppression was Rameses II, Merneptah's predecessor. This Rameses was a very powerful monarch who, in the course of a long reign (1298–1232 B.C.), fought a series of wars against the Hittites to restore Egyptian influence in Asia and erected great public monuments covered with reliefs and inscriptions boasting of his victories. In actual fact, however, his greatest battle with the Hittites, at Kadesh, ended indecisively and he was forced to conclude a treaty with them dividing Syria between the two great powers. Possibly this setback made him suspicious of all foreigners residing in Egypt. On the other hand, the fact that certain of the tribes of Israel are already mentioned in Canaan in the days of Seti I (1308–1298 B.C.), militates against the identification of Rameses II with the Pharaoh who was humbled by Moses. The many extant statues of Rameses represent him wearing the blue crown of Lower Egypt, the war helmet of the Pharaohs, protected by the uraeus snake and holding the emblems of sovereignty.

(Below) Reeds painting from tomb of Kenamon, Thebes, Egypt. Fifteenth century B.C.

She took for him a basket made of bulrushes; ... and she put the child in it and placed it among the reeds at the river's brink. (EXOD. 2 : 3)

(Above) Basket. (Metropolitan Museum, New York)

And made their lives bitter with hard service, in mortar and brick. (EXOD. 1 : 14)

Painting from tomb of Rekhmire. Fifteenth century B.C.

THE YOUNG MOSES

THE NEW RULER began a systematic oppression of the Israelites. They were conscripted as laborers and set to work on great construction schemes under the lash of Egyptian taskmasters to whom their own foremen, "the officers of the children of Israel", were responsible. This forced labor was also the lot of the Egyptians themselves, who were at all times compelled to provide Pharaoh with manpower. The great public works of Egypt—the pyramids and fortresses, as well as the various installations regulating the flow of the Nile—depended for their execution on the *corvée* system. But as far as possible foreign slaves and prisoners-of-war were used for this backbreaking work. Thus in the tomb of Rekhmire, the vizier of Thutmosis III (fifteenth century B.C.), we find lighter-skinned Semites among the workmen making bricks for the restoration of the temple of Amon at Thebes. The men are shown taking water from a pool, mixing it with mud, pouring the mixture into molds, and carrying the bricks up to the temple structures. They are supervised by a taskmaster who stands ready with his staves to force them to work without the slightest slackening of effort. Such must have been the harsh fate of the Hebrews enslaved by the Egyptians. This hard labor, however, weakened only the adult males; there was still a danger that Israelites would continue to increase in numbers because of their high birth-rate. Pharaoh therefore decided to order that every male Hebrew child should be killed at birth; but it was, in fact, from among the babes born in that dark time of oppression that the future deliverer of Israel came.

The Biblical story relates that, when a son was born to Amram of the tribe of Levi, the mother hid the child as long as she could. When this was no longer possible she made an "ark" of the bulrushes which abounded on the banks of the Nile and set it down among the

43

And he saw an Egyptian beating a Hebrew, one of his people. (EXOD. 2: 11)

"flags by the river's brink". The ark was probably a kind of basket, protected against the water by pitch, a raw material easily available in Egypt and constantly used for the making of mummies. Baskets skillfully woven out of reeds have been found preserved in many of the Egyptian tombs and give us a clear idea of the shape of the ark. Moreover, many of the tomb-paintings (such as that of Kenamon at Thebes) show plants, mostly lotus or papyrus, growing in profusion along the banks of the Nile, with birds perching on the thickets. In such places the ark could have remained unobserved for a long time. In this particular case, however, it was noticed by the daughter of Pharaoh while she was walking with her maids along the riverside. The princess had compassion on the babe and unknowingly called in its own mother to be its foster-nurse. When the child grew up he was adopted into her household and called Moses, from the Egyptian word *Mose* meaning "son", but which in the Bible is interpreted as being from a Hebrew root and meaning "drawn out of the water".

Although Moses grew up as a young Egyptian, he was conscious of his true descent. Once happening to see a Hebrew being mercilessly beaten by an Egyptian taskmaster, he became so enraged that he slew the Egyptian. Such brutal oppression might have been an unusual sight to a young man delicately brought up at the court, but in everyday life in Egypt, especially among the lower classes, the use of physical force was a regular occurrence. This was the method by which taxes were extracted from the peasants and slaves driven on to greater efforts. In a painting from the tomb of Puyemre at Thebes, for example, we see slaves making wine, a bearded Semite driving cattle, and one of the other workers being beaten by an overseer.

Fearing royal retribution as soon as his deed became known to the Pharaoh through tale-bearers among his own people, Moses fled to the eternal safe retreat of outcasts from ancient

44

Painting from tomb of Puyemre,
Thebes, Egypt. Fifteenth century B.C.

EXODUS

society and of those in revolt against authority—the wilderness. In this case it was in the
desert of Sinai, inhabited by the Midianites who were of Semitic stock like himself, that
young Moses found refuge. Having helped the daughters of Jethro, or Reuel, the priest of
Midian, who were tending the flocks of their father, he was adopted into the family and
married one of them. Moving from place to place in search of pasture with the flocks of
his father-in-law, Moses eventually penetrated into the mountains of the central Sinai range
(one of which, today called Jebel Serbal, is a majestic, towering mass of granite with three
soaring peaks) where vegetation survives in the Sinai summer longer than in the more
parched plains. It was there that he saw the vision of the burning bush in which he was
ordered by God to return to Egypt, deliver his people from the bondage of the Pharaoh, and
lead them to their promised land of Canaan. In this theophany God also revealed to Moses
His true name and recalled the solemn covenant He had made with Abraham, Isaac and
Jacob, the patriarchal ancestors of the people of Israel. In obedience to the divine command
Moses returned to Egypt, where a new king had in the meantime succeeded to the throne.

THE PLAGUES OF EGYPT

Now Moses was keeping the flock of
his father-in-law, Jethro, the priest of
Midian; and he led his flock to the west side
of the wilderness and came to Horeb, the
mountain of God. (EXOD. 3 : 1)

Jebel Serbal, Sinai.

THE TASK ASSIGNED to Moses,
even when assisted by his more
eloquent brother Aaron, was indeed formidable. He had first to persuade the people of
Israel that the time of their deliverance had
come; and as if that were not difficult enough,
he then had to prevail upon Pharaoh to give up
his bondslaves, a severe blow at once to the
latter's pride and to his material interests.
Indeed, the first appeals addressed by Moses

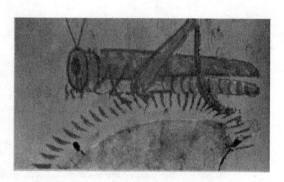

Behold, I will plague all your country with frogs . . . behold, tomorrow I will bring locusts into your country and they shall cover the face of the land.

(EXOD. 8 : 2; 10 : 4–5)

Locust in painting from tomb of Horemheb, Thebes, Egypt. Fifteenth century B.C.

and Aaron to the king of Egypt evoked only still harder oppressive measures; the Israelites were no longer supplied with straw to make the bricks, but had the additional toil of finding this binding material for themselves. It took a succession of ten natural disasters, the "Plagues of Egypt", finally to convince Pharaoh that his struggle against the will of God was in vain. Nine times he agreed to the Exodus and nine times went back on his consent. The plagues were of various kinds, most of them an abnormal increase and intensification of minor afflictions endemic in the unsanitary living conditions of the Egyptian masses. Thus frogs always abounded in the vicinity of the Nile and its canals and ponds, so much so that the Egyptians venerated them as symbols of Hekat, the goddess of fertility; hence a hieroglyphic sign in the shape of a tadpole means "a hundred thousand". But now the frogs multiplied far beyond all normal bounds. Similarly, the locust is a plague which strikes the Middle East every few years. The breeding ground of these devouring insects is in the Arabian desert where they form vast swarms which then migrate and destroy the vegetation of the neighboring countries. Locusts are frequently represented on Egyptian paintings, as for example in the tomb of Horemheb. They are depicted with the minute exactitude of observation the Egyptian artists brought to bear on all natural phenomena.

It was the death of the first-born, human and animal alike, that finally broke down the

resistance of Pharaoh. Although in the polygamous Egyptian court the ruling monarch usually had many sons, the first-born of the legitimate queen nevertheless took pride of place in his father's affections and was often associated with him on the throne, so as to make the succession easier and more secure. Thus in our reproduction here, Rameses III is shown with his first-born, the crown-prince, standing before the goddess Isis, who is

Fresco from tomb of Amenherkopshef, Thebes, Egypt. Twelfth century B.C.

And all the first-born in the land of Egypt shall die, from the first-born of Pharaoh who sits upon his throne, even to the first-born of the maidservant who is behind the mill. (EXOD. 11: 5)

Statue from Gizeh. (Metropolitan Museum, New York)

promising both father and son a long and prosperous life. At the other end of the social scale, far removed from "the first-born of Pharaoh that sitteth upon his throne", was the lowest of the low, the "first-born of the maidservant that is behind the mill". The grinding of grain was a back-breaking task with the primitive hand-mills of the Egyptians. These usually consisted of two stones, a flat one on which the grain was placed, and a round one which was rotated over the grains until they were all crushed. In Egyptian tombs, especially those of the Middle Kingdom, originally human servants were sacrificed, so as to accompany their lord into the nether world, there to supply his needs. In more humane later times models were used instead. Among these we also find figurines of maidservants in a crouching position behind a hand-mill. They are simply dressed, with a cloth over their heads to keep the dust from the mill out of their hair.

THE EXODUS

THE LAST AND most devastating plague finally broke Pharaoh's stubborn will, at least for a time. The Israelites, who had in the meantime made preparations for the journey, having provided themselves with unleavened bread and offered up a

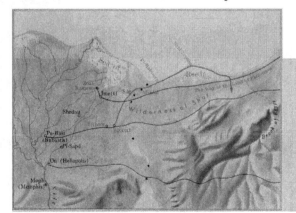

Tell the people of Israel to turn back and encamp in front of Pihahiroth, between Migdol and the sea, in front of Baal-Zephon; you shall encamp over against it by the sea.
(EXOD. 14: 2)

Map showing first stage of the Exodus.

*The Egyptians pursued and went in after
them into the midst of the sea, all Pharaoh's
horses, his chariots, and his horsemen.*

(EXOD. 14 : 23)

Cover painting of chest from the tomb of
Tutankhamon. Fourteenth century B.C.

sacrifice of lambs, set out on the road to freedom. Their starting-point was Succoth, in the
vicinity of those same store-cities of Pithom
and Raamses that they had built. The first
problem confronting this unarmed host was
how to make their way unmolested through
the chain of Egyptian frontier posts built along
the line of natural lakes in the depression
between the Mediterranean and the Red Sea.
There are different theories about the route
they followed. One very ancient view places the route southeastwards towards the northern
tip of the Red Sea. Here we follow an alternative suggestion. This supposes that they
turned north and passed at Pi-Hahiroth between the fortress of Midgal (later on called Pelu-
sium) and the sea. Having thus rounded the Egyptian line alongside the marshy lake known
today as Bahr Bardawil, they had perforce to traverse the spit of land which separates this
lagoon from the Mediterranean proper. It was probably during this passage that the famous
miracle of the Reed Sea (thus in the Hebrew original and not the "Red Sea") took place
Pharaoh had in the meantime recovered from his dazed stupor and decided to give chase to
his escaping slaves. Collecting his force of chariots and foot-soldiers (the "horsemen" of
the Biblical text must refer to the chariots, since the use of cavalry was unknown at that

time in the Ancient East, and was to remain so for many centuries to come), he advanced along the same spit of land in hot pursuit of the slow-moving Israelites. We can form a clear mental picture of the appearance of Pharaoh's army from contemporary representations like that reproduced here from a chest found in the tomb of Tutankhamon. The king, of superhuman size as usual in Egyptian art, is seen riding at full gallop, his bow drawn, in front of three columns of troops, chariots to the right and left and infantry in the centre. Behind him stand two Nubian slaves with high fans made of ostrich feathers. Various divine emblems protect him from above. In real life there would have been a charioteer accompanying the king in his chariot, and the slaves and other paraphernalia of courtly pomp would have been missing.

To understand what happened at the Crossing of the Sea, we must bear in mind that

Then they came to Elim, where there were
twelve springs of water and seventy palm trees;
they encamped there by the water. (EXOD. 15:27)

occasionally, with a strong east wind blowing, the narrow tongue of land on which the drama was enacted can be suddenly swamped by the angry waves of the Mediterranean. Apparently the Israelites had just safely reached the far side when such a violent inundation occurred, overwhelming the Egyptian hosts who had drawn close behind them. Small wonder that this timely and awe-inspiring deliverance seemed a miracle to the terror-stricken mass of refugees.

Having skirted the Bahr Bardawil, the Israelites were on the high road to Canaan, which in the Biblical narrative is anachronistically called the "Way of the Land of the Philistines", for the Philistines arrived in Canaan after the Israelites. However, Moses and Aaron were admonished not to lead the people by this road; it was so heavily fortified and so frequently traversed by Egyptian armies that to continue along it was to court certain destruction. Instead they turned off into the heart of the Sinai peninsula.

THE WILDERNESS

THE SINAI DESERT is divided into three parallel geographical belts, running from west to east. The northernmost of them, verging on the Mediterranean coast, consists of sand-dunes. To the south of these there extends a scree-covered, undulating plateau, the desert of Tih. Still further to the south, occupying the tip of the Sinai peninsula, is a mass of granite mountains.

In all three of these regions natural supplies of water are extremely meager. Their monstrous, barren wastes are enlivened by only a few sparse oases, and even in them the water is as often brackish as sweet. In these harsh desert conditions the provision of food and drink for such a large multitude as the Israelites must have been (even if their numbers fell far short of the million or so reported in later sources) an ever-pressing problem. Moses therefore led his people from oasis to oasis, starting from Elim with its twelve springs and seventy palm trees. Other water sources are found along the Wadi el-Arish (the Biblical "Brook of Egypt"), on the eastern coast of the peninsula at Nuweib and Dhabab, and even in the granite mountain massif of southern Sinai, in Wadi Feiran. All these oases are fed by the flood waters of the brief winter rains which continue to flow underground beneath the

. . . now the house of Israel called its name manna; it was like coriander seed white, and the taste of it was like wafers made with honey.
(EXOD. 16: 13, 31)

Female of *Trabutina manipara* in egg sac; egg sac excreted by female of *Majococus cerpentinus*; female secreting drops of manna; dried grains of manna.

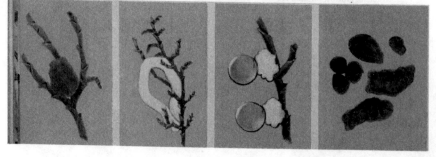

[. . . I am the LORD your God that [brought] you out of the land of E[gypt.]
[You shall not hav]e other gods be[fore] Me. You shall not make [for yourself an image]
[or any likeness] that is in the heavens above or that is in the earth [beneath]
[or that is in the water]s beneath the earth. You shall not bow down to them [nor]
[serve them, for] I am the LORD your [God, a jealous God visiting the iniquity]
[of fathers upon son]s to the third and to the fourth generation unto them that hate Me, [and doing]
[kindness unto thousands] unto them that love Me and keep My commandments. You shall [not]
[take up the name of the LORD] your God in vain for the LORD will not hold guiltless [him that]
[takes up His na]me in vain. Remember the day of the Shabbath [to hallow it.]
[six day]s you shall work and do all your business, and on the [seventh day]
a Shabbath for the LORD your God; you shall not do therein any business, [you,]
[and your son and your daughter], your slave and your handmaid, your ox and your ass and all your [cattle]
[and the stranger that is] in your gates. For six days did the LO[RD make]
[the heaven]s and the earth, the sea and all th[at is therein,]
and rested [on the] seventh day; therefore The LORD blessed the
seventh day and hallowed it. Honour your father and your moth[er, that]
it may be well with you and that you be long upon the ground [that]
the LORD your God gives you. You shall not do adultery. You shall not do murder. You shall [not]
[st]eal. You shall not [bear] against your neighbour vain witness. You shall not covet [the]
[wife of your neighbour. You shall] not desire the house of your neighbour, his fie[ld, or his slave]
[or his handmaid, or his o]x or his ass, or anything, that is your neighbour's.
[(?) And these are the statute]s and the judgements that Moses commanded the [sons of]
[Israel] in the wilderness, when they went forth from the land of Egypt. Hear
[O Isra]el, the LORD our God, the LORD is one; and you shall l[ove]
[the LORD your G]o[d with al]l y[our heart . . .]

Papyrus Nash, with Decalogue. Second century B.C.

And God spoke all these words, saying, "I am the LORD your God, who brought you out of the land of Egypt out of the house of bondage."
(EXOD. 20 : 1-2)

dried-up river beds even through the summer. Palm trees, which provide fuel, food and clothing, grow plentifully in such well-watered spots.

Another source of food for the Israelites in their desert wanderings were migratory flocks of quails. These birds pass over Sinai in spring and autumn on their seasonal journeying from the Sudan to southern and western Europe and back again. The Exodus coincided with the spring migration. Occasionally groups of exhausted birds land on some piece of ground where they can be caught with ease.

The *manna* is now understood to have been the sweet edible drops of fluid secreted by two kinds of tiny insects living on tamarisk trees. The drops are secreted in the spring, then dry and fall to the ground where they are to this day collected as food by the Beduin Arabs. The Arabs still call such dry pellets *man* or *man min sama* ("Manna from heaven").

But it was not enough to overcome the malignity of nature: there was also the malice of man to contend with. The Amalekites, bands of desert brigands, added greatly to the hardships of the marching column by their harassing attacks, and not till they had been resoundingly defeated could the Israelites continue their long trek unmolested. Since they had already on several occasions shown themselves to be an unruly people, Moses, acting on the advice of his father-in-law Jethro, now imposed some kind of political organization on them under seventy elders who were henceforth to be their judges.

AT MOUNT SINAI

AFTER THREE WEARY months of wandering the Israelites completed the first stage of their journey when they arrived at the foot of Mount Sinai. The location of this mountain has been much disputed. Some scholars would place it in the vicinity of Kadesh Barnea, the Israelites' main camping place in the wilderness; others prefer one of the mountains in the land of Seir, beyond the Jordan and the Dead Sea, while still others identify it with the peak in the southern Sinai massif traditionally known as Jebel Musa ("Mount Moses"), though here too the rival claims of Jebel Serbal have been advanced. The only serious argument against this traditional identification is the presumable difficulty of explaining the feeding of a large multitude in the heart of the desert. But if the number of the Israelites is reduced to what seems to be the true meaning of the Biblical text, this difficulty is greatly diminished.

The events connected with the lawgiving on Mount Sinai have left an indelible impression on the consciousness of the people of Israel and probably did more than any other single event to mold it into a nation. The most important of the laws were those contained in the Decalogue or the Ten Commandments which, opening with a solemn affirmation of Israelite monotheism and a stern prohibition of idolatry, go on to ordain the keeping of the Sabbath and the honoring of parents, and to forbid murder, adultery and theft, bearing false witness and covetousness. The fundamental significance of these precepts (which appear twice in the Bible, Exod. 20 and Deut. 5) for the faith of Judaism was fully appreciated in later times; they formed the nucleus of Jewish prayers and were inscribed on the phylacteries. One of the earliest surviving papyri with a Biblical text, the so-called Nash Papyrus, contains the Ten Commandments.

Commentators once found it difficult to explain how the divine commandments could have been written down. But there is really no problem here. Apart from the fact that Moses must have been fully conversant with Egyptian hieroglyphs, we now have evidence that a kind of alphabetical script, based on the Egyptian signs, was developed in these early times in the Sinai peninsula, probably among the Semitic slaves employed by the Egyptians

And Moses wrote all the words of the LORD. . . . (EXOD. 24: 4)

Proto-Sinaitic writing. Fifteenth century B.C.

Reconstruction of tabernacle.

And let them make me a sanctuary, that I may dwell in their midst. According to all that I show you concerning the pattern of the tabernacle, and of all its furniture, so you shall make it.
(EXOD. 25 : 8–9)

in the copper and turquoise mines of that region. Remains of this script have been discovered at Serabit el-Khadem and elsewhere, and scholars are generally of the opinion that it represents the prototype of the later Semitic alphabets.

The Ten Commandments are followed in the Bible by various laws and ordinances of a mainly penal character, with some social legislation for the protection of the resident alien and the widow added to them.

THE TABERNACLE

THE REMAINDER OF the book of Exodus is taken up by the description of the Tabernacle which was constructed by the Israelites under the inspired direction of Bezalel the son of Uri, according to the detailed instructions given by God to Moses. This portable shrine was of the utmost importance, since it created a religious

You shall make the court of the tabernacle . . . a hundred cubits long for one side. . . . And likewise for its length on the north side there shall be hangings a hundred cubits long. . . . And for the breadth of the court on the west side there shall be hangings for fifty cubits. . . . The breadth of the court on the front to the east shall be fifty cubits. (EXOD. 27 : 9–13)

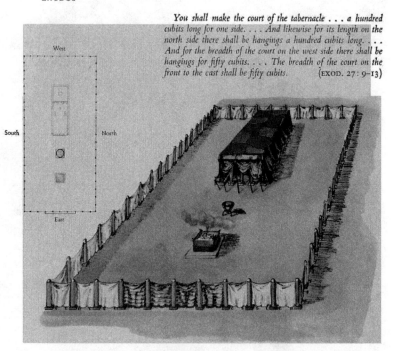

rallying-centre for the tribes. It thus kept them united during the long years of wandering in the desert and made concerted action possible. Many scholars believe that the eventual form of the description of the Tabernacle and everything connected with it was written out to provide a basis for a restoration of the religion, possibly after the exile in Babylon. But it seems clear that much ancient tradition is preserved in the account.

The Tabernacle was made of acacia wood and consisted of two main parts, the shrine and the Holy of Holies. The whole had walls made of boards, which could be taken down and packed for transport. They were covered with gold inside and out and had bars and rings to hold them together when erected. A veil, hung on four acacia-wood posts, separated the Holy of Holies from the rest of the shrine. Behind this veil stood the Ark containing the stone tables inscribed with the Ten Commandments; above it was the "mercy seat" of gold, flanked by two gold cherubim, winged figures with human heads. The part of the shrine in front of the Holy of Holies was occupied by the table of shewbread, an incense altar, and a gold candelabrum with seven arms. A screen, supported on five acacia-wood posts, was placed over the entrance to the tent. The whole shrine was hung with curtains of fine twined linen and of blue, purple and scarlet stuffs, embroidered with cherubim in gold thread. These curtains were protected by an outer covering of goat's hair. The whole structure was thus created from a combination of materials to be found in the desert, together with the gold objects and finely woven linen which the Israelites had learnt to make in Egypt. The absence of any image of the deity, such as was usually placed in the temples and shrines of the Ancient East, distinguished it as the sanctuary of a new type of religion.

The Tabernacle was set up within a larger court enclosed by curtainings of linen, except for the hangings on either side of its entrance which were made of fine twined linen embroidered with needlework in blue, purple and scarlet. The curtains which surrounded the court were hung on brass pillars with silver hooks and bands. Inside the court, which was about 150 feet long and about 75 feet wide, were the altar for burnt offerings and a laver for the priests. The Tabernacle stood at its eastern side, opposite the entrance to it.

Together with the making of the Tabernacle special ceremonial vestments were prepared for the high priest, Aaron, and for his sons, the priests. The dress of the high priest was especially magnificent. Next to his body he wore linen breeches and a tunic of fine linen, with a girdle in the three sacred colors. Over this came a blue robe with a fringe of golden bells alternating with pomegranates; and over this again was placed the ephod, a stiff coat of gold, colored wool and linen, held in position by two shoulder-pieces on which there were two onyx stones engraved with the names of the tribes of Israel. Suspended from these shoulder-pieces there was a breastplate of gold, inset with twelve precious or semi-precious stones, in a prescribed order, each with the name of a different tribe incised on it. On his head the high priest wore a miter, probably a high white conical cap of the type regularly worn by priests in the Orient; and on the front of this fastened there by a blue lace, there was a plate of solid gold engraved with the words "Holy to the LORD".

Reconstruction of the garments of the high priest.

And you shall make holy garments for Aaron your brother for glory and for beauty. (EXOD. 28 : 2)

The twelve stones of the breast-
piece according to the late Dr.
N. Shalem. They were: (*First
row*) Sard-Carnelian, Plasma,
Jasper-Agate; (*Second row*) Tur-
quoise, Lazurite, Chalcedony;
(*Third row*) Amber, Agate,
Amethyst; (*Fourth row*) Mother
of Pearl, Black Onyx and Jasper-
Onyx.

The twelve stones of the breastplate have for generations been the subject of special
studies. They were arranged in four rows of three, having been selected to give the greatest
possible variety of colors from among the stones available in the desert. According to the
latest identifications there were: first row: sard-carnelian, plasma, jasper-agate; second row:
turquoise, lazurite, and chalcedony; third row: amber, agate, amethyst; fourth row: mother
of pearl, black onyx, jasper-onyx.

Apart from the tent itself and the robes for the high priest and priests, the work on the
Tabernacle involved a multitude of other skilled activities, none of which could have been
performed by the Israelites if they had not received some schooling in the arts and crafts of
Egypt. Egyptian art abounds in illustrations of the craftsmanship that went into the making
of various ritual accessories. The carpentry work on the boards of the Tabernacle and its
furnishings, as also on the ark and the other wooden fittings, must have been of the highest
standard and precision, especially if we consider that these objects were continually being

transported from place to place and had therefore to be strong and well-fitting, as well as decorative. Egyptian carpentry of a similar standard is often represented in tomb-paintings. Thus in the tomb of Apy (thirteenth century B.C.) we see craftsmen completing a shrine. They are working with the usual carpenter's tools, which have hardly changed down to our time: the saw, the chisel, the drill, and the hammer. Above, a foreman is seen reproving a negligent workman. The whole shrine is made of wood, with inlaid emblems of the Egyptian gods.

But it was not only the permanent cultic appurtenances that had to be made in connection with the construction of the Tabernacle; there were also the actual materials to be used in the ritual itself, and above all the incense and the anointing oils. These were mixed from special ingredients and prepared with the utmost care. The raw materials for these ingredients were brought from distant lands, mostly from South Arabia and Africa, and had therefore to be used sparingly. A good idea of the painstaking care called for is given us by the portrayal of a similar operation in the Egyptian tomb of one Ammon (c. 1500 B.C.). Aromatic plants are first pounded and then mixed with oils in a big bowl. The resultant unguent is then made up into large balls. Some of the spices are steeped in wines which have been previously strained for this purpose. The ritual materials for the Tabernacle must have required preparations hardly less meticulous than those depicted in the Egyptian painting.

Then he made the upright frames for the tabernacle of acacia wood. . . . (EXOD. 36: 20)

Tomb painting, tomb of Apy, Thebes.
Thirteenth century B.C.

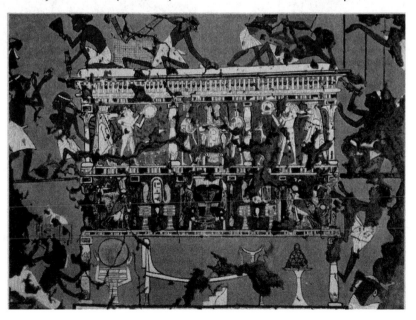

And you shall take on the first day the fruit of goodly trees, branches of palm trees, and boughs of leafy trees, and willows of the brook. . . . (LEV. 23 : 40)

Palm tree; Ethrog; myrtle; and willow trees.

LEVITICUS

THE THIRD "BOOK OF MOSES", called Leviticus (in Hebrew *Wayikra* ("And [he] called"), from its opening verse, "The LORD called Moses") is devoted to the religious prescriptions of the so-called Priestly Code. These concern the various kinds of sacrifices, the clean and unclean meats, the laws of purification and cleansing, the offerings for the priests and the people, the feasts to be observed annually, the penalties for impurity, the blessings for obedience to the LORD's commands and the curses following upon any infringement of His covenant.

One of the greatest blessings is that of the fertility of the Promised Land. Among the many symbols of this fertility are the branches to be taken from four different trees for the rejoicing of the harvest festival of Tabernacles. In the translation of the RSV, these are the "fruit of goodly trees, branches of palm trees, boughs of leafy trees and willows of the brook". Modern research into the Hebrew names, supported by the traditional usage of the Jews, has now identified the four kinds as follows: the fruit of the *ethrog* (*Citrus medica* var. *lageriformis*), the first of the citrus group to reach the Near East; the palm tree (*Phoenix dactylifera* L.), which provided man with building material, clothing and food; the myrtle (*Myrtus communis* L.); and the willow of the brook (*Salix acmophylla*), which grows by the water in the Jordan Valley, the Huleh and throughout Galilee, as well as in the coastal plain. In traditional Jewish usage, the branches of the palm, the willow and the myrtle are bound together into a bunch (*lulab*), while the *ethrog* (citrus) is held separately.

Besides carrying these symbolical objects on the Feast of Tabernacles, the worshipers built themselves huts of branches in commemoration of their forefathers' sojourn in the wilderness, where such "booths" or "tabernacles" were the only shelter available.

NUMBERS

THE FOURTH "BOOK OF MOSES", known in English as "Numbers", after the numbering of the Israelites described in its first chapter, is in Hebrew called *Bamidbar* ("In the wilderness") from its opening words: "And the LORD spoke to Moses in the wilderness". It comprises, in the main, a description of the camp and marching order of the Israelites, followed by a number of supplementary laws and ordinances. But it also continues the story of the desert wanderings, with a recapitulation of the various events that occurred during this long period and a comprehensive list of the halting-places on the circuitous route.

The first and second chapters specify the numbers of the Israelites, tribe by tribe, and describe their organization by "standards". Every male Israelite was required to pitch by his *own standard* (i.e. that of his tribe) with the ensign (symbol) of his father's house

Painting from tomb of Tanuni, Thebes.
Fifteenth century B.C.

The people of Israel shall encamp each by his own standard, with the ensigns of their fathers' houses. (NUM. 2:2)

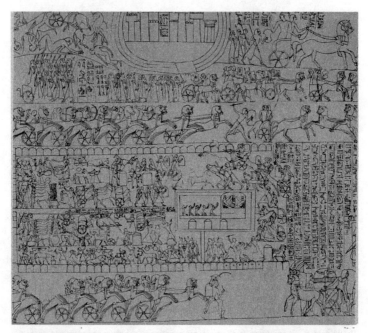

So they encamped by their standards, and so they set up, every one in his family, according to his father's house. (NUM. 2 : 34)

Camp of Rameses II, before Kadesh. Thirteenth century B.C.

(i.e. with the emblem of the ancestor from whom descent was claimed). It is generally assumed that the symbolical animals or objects associated with the tribes in the blessing pronounced by Jacob on his sons (Gen. 49) were also those appearing on the various tribal standards. The use of emblems, carried aloft to serve as rallying-points in the tumult and confusion of battle, became a common military practice in the ancient Orient as early as the third millennium B.C. and has remained so until today. Standards of this kind are represented in Egyptian paintings, such as that in the tomb of Tanuni (fifteenth century B.C.), reproduced on the previous page. A group of Nubian soldiers is seen advancing, armed with throw-sticks; the last in the row is holding a pole with, at the top of it, what looks like a wooden panel, on which are drawn the figures of two wrestlers. This was apparently the unit emblem.

A regular order was established for the Israelite camp, each tribe having a fixed station assigned to it. Only thus could the leaders ensure the coordinated movement of the large host and prevent confusion on its arrival at the next halting-place. The positions of the tribes around the central tabernacle were, for this reason, decided on beforehand, and also with a view to their serving as battle-stations in case of an attack on the camp. As such attacks were most likely to come from the highly mobile desert rovers, fighting might break out at any point on the periphery. According to the traditional order, the position on the east side, towards which the camp would usually move, was taken up by Judah, Issachar, and Zebulun; Reuben, Simeon, and Gad were on the south; Ephraim, Manasseh, and Benjamin on the west; Dan, Asher, and Naphtali on the north. The Levites, as ministrants in the sanctuary, kept watch over their charge and were not included in the battle order.

Representations of camps in Egyptian art, especially that of Rameses II before the battle of Kadesh (1288 B.C.), illustrate the employment of the same principles in camping. The army occupies a rectangle, with a wall formed by the soldiers' shields placed side by side surrounding it. Openings are left in this wall as gateways, and within the enclosure the various troops have their fixed positions, the chariots with their horses in one place, the infantry in another. Some troops guard the entrance while others stand near the royal tent, which is placed like a shrine in the center of the camp. Inside it are the images of the gods and the divine name of the Pharaoh, held by two winged figures. As the king of Egypt was given divine honors, his tent would naturally serve as a shrine for the whole camp. Around this focal point we see some troops preparing their meals, some sharpening their weapons, and others exercising. Spies and other intruders who have been arrested and put in custody within the camp are brought to punishment. Outside the camp troops in battle order advance to attack the fortress of Kadesh, which is surrounded by a deep moat.

And the people of Israel, the whole congregation, came into the wilderness of Zin. . . . (NUM. 20: 1)

View of the desert between Quseima and Nitsana.

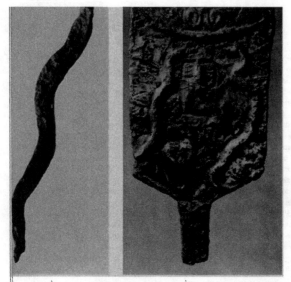

*So Moses made a bronze serpent, and
set it on a pole. . . .* (NUM. 21 : 9)

(*Left*) Bronze snake from Lachish.
Late Bronze Age (Palestine Archaeological Museum); (*Right*) Standard
from Hazor from the same period,
with head of goddess and two snakes
on either side (Hazor Expedition).

LAST DAYS IN THE WILDERNESS

AFTER FORTY YEARS in the desert, thirty-eight of which were apparently
spent in the big oasis of Kadesh Barnea where the people rested after the
lawgiving on Sinai, the Israelites at last moved towards Canaan. According to tradition the
purpose of the long sojourn in the wilderness was to let the generation which had fled
Egypt die out, as being too cowed and warped by their long enslavement to be capable or
worthy of occupying the Promised Land. The march of the Israelites towards Canaan followed a most devious route. A direct attempt to advance from Kadesh Barnea towards
Arad and the foothills of what later became the Judaean mountains was beaten back with
heavy losses. The would-be invaders had therefore no choice but to retreat from the
northern Negeb into the desert of Zin in the southern Negeb, and from there to cross the
Arabah, the great rift valley which runs southwards from the Dead Sea to the Red Sea.
The desert of Zin is composed of a series of small hills, separated by valleys which become
deeper and more difficult to cross as they approach the Arabah which bounds them on the east.

It was while traversing this desert that the children of Israel were afflicted by a plague of
serpents, from which Moses, at God's command, brought them relief by setting up the image
of a brass serpent on a pole. According to the Biblical narrative, this incident occurred near
Punon, the ancient center of copper-mining in the Arabah, where the raw material necessary
for the making of the serpent could be obtained with ease. The whole story reflects the
primitive awe of the snake which, because of its sudden appearance from underground,
was regarded as being endowed with special magical qualities connected with the gods of
the underworld. It was thus both feared and venerated. We find snakes of brass (or copper)
among the ritual objects discovered at Lachish; and a silvered bronze standard from the

Late Canaanite Period, found at Hazor, also bears a representation of a deity flanked by two serpents. Many other cult objects excavated in various sanctuaries also attest to this primitive cult.

The problem facing the Israelites after their repulse at the gates of Arad, which (in punishment for the lack of trust in God shown by ten of the spies sent out to reconnoitre the Promised Land) closed the direct approaches to Canaan to them, was how to reach the Jordan Valley. Once the road through the Negeb had been cleared by the defeat of the Amalekites, the Israelites could pass Mount Hor and descend into the Arabah. Thence, however, the continuation of their route was barred by the two kingdoms of Edom and Moab, which had been established about a hundred years before the Exodus.

These kingdoms, which occupied the southern part of the tableland to the east of the Jordan, the Dead Sea, and the Arabah, represented a new wave of settlement in this area. Archaeological surveys have shown that, in ancient times, the territory between the desert and the River Jordan was alternately settled and abandoned to nomads. One such period of the encroachment of the desert had come to an end just a short time before the Israelite wanderings in the wilderness. Both Moab, whose rule ran from the Jordan to the Zared, and Edom, which extended from the Zared southwards, were relatively strong kingdoms. Their frontiers were well guarded by a chain of fortresses from which the approach of an invader could be signalled in good time and the invasion itself subsequently repulsed. The Israelites made an effort to persuade the rulers of these kingdoms to grant them free passage, promising not to infringe their sovereignty but to keep to the "king's highway", the old Pharaonic road which traversed the lands beyond the

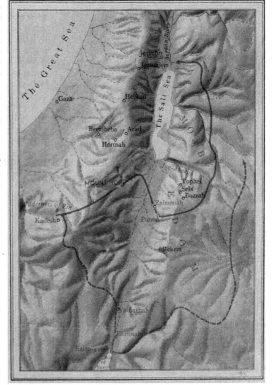

These are the stages of the people of Israel. . . .   (NUM. 33 : 1)

Map showing the last stage of the Israelite wanderings.

*So Balak the son of Zippor, who was king of Moab
at that time. . . .* (NUM. 22 : 4)

Stele from Balua, Moab, showing
Moabite ruler between two deities.
Twelfth or eleventh century B.C. (Am-
man Museum)

Jordan from south to north, joining Elath and
Damascus. However, when the Edomites
refused this request there remained only the
possibility of forcing the passage.

Numbers 33 contains a list of camping sites,
mostly temporary halts which can no longer
be identified. The route taken by the Israelites
from Mount Hor to the Plains of Moab overlooking the Jordan has been described in two
ways. They may have descended the Arabah
to the Red Sea and then by-passed Edom on
the east, following the fringe of the desert. Or,
while perhaps some of them went this way,
the main body may have forced its way
through the northeastern part of Edom, in the
region disputed by the two adjacent kingdoms
of Edom and Moab. A route through that part
of the country would have been easier. On
this view, the Israelites reached the banks of
the Zared by way of Zalmona and Punon,
circled round Moab, and at Yahaz met the
army of Sihon the Amorite, ruler of the
country north of Moab and west of Ammon.
With the defeat of this king and the conquest
of his capital, Heshbon, the way into the
Plains of Moab and to the Jordan beyond was
at last open to the Israelites.

THE STORY OF BALAAM

THE MARCH ROUND the borders of Moab proved hard going for the Israelites. In addition to the natural difficulties of the wild terrain, they had also
to contend with the hostility of Balak the son of Zippor, the then ruler of Moab, who tried
to summon up supernatural forces in support of his armed opposition. The Moabites, like
all the peoples of ancient Canaan, worshiped many gods. We find their kings represented on
steles as raising their hands in gestures of worship toward the images of gods which combine
Semitic and Egyptian features. Furthermore, as members of the Western Semitic groups of
nations the Moabites were racially related to the Mesopotamian tribes: the Bible regards
Moab and Ammon as descendants of Lot, Abraham's nephew, and hence as members of the
same family as the Israelites. Thus we can understand why it was that, when king Balak felt

the need of a particularly potent spell to defeat his Israelite kinsmen, he applied to the seer Balaam, the son of Beor, who lived at Pethor at the confluence of the Sajur and the Euphrates rivers, twelve miles south of Carchemish. Despite the length of the journey involved (twenty days by donkey), Balak thought that it would be well worth his while to wait to have the Israelites cursed by the powerful incantations of so famous and feared a magician.

On his arrival, Balaam at once set about his work in the approved manner of the Mesopotamian *baru* ("prophet") by building seven altars and offering up a bullock and a ram on each. But when the moment for uttering the curse came, the seer had his heart changed by God and, instead, pronounced a poetic blessing on Israel, acclaiming the present might of the invaders, and still more fulsomely extolling their future greatness. In the course of this grandiloquent benediction, couched in the best traditions of extravagant Oriental imagery, he compared Israel to the two mightiest creatures known in the East—the lion and the aurochs. The latter was once common in this region in both the wild and the domesticated state, but today it is almost extinct there. We find many representations of the aurochs in ancient Oriental art, where it is shown rising on its hind legs and making ready to gore with the powerful and majestic horns which are its distinguishing feature.

The lion—king of the animals and most dangerous of the beasts of prey in the Orient—was also used by Balaam to symbolize the military prowess of the Israelites. The sight of this powerful beast rearing up to attack its victim or the hunter pursuing it stirred the imagination of ancient Oriental poets, painters, and sculptors. The lion rampant thus became the symbol of warlike power, and he who could defeat it was shown to be the greatest of hunters.

The aurochs on a stele from Gozan, Mesopotamia. Ninth century B.C. (Berlin Museum)

God brings them out of Egypt; they have as it were the horns of a wild ox.
(NUM. 23 : 22)

*When you enter the land of Canaan (this is the
land that shall fall to you for an inheritance, the land
of Canaan in its full extent).*   (NUM. 34: 2)

Map showing the boundaries of Canaan.

Balaam's mission having failed, there was nothing Balak
could do to prevent the Israelites from passing through the
borders of his land and encamping in the Plain of Moab
opposite Jericho to await the day of the crossing of the river.
While they camped there the tribes of Gad, Reuben, and half
of the tribe of Manasseh were allowed to take possession of
the lands of Sihon the Amorite and of his northern neighbor,
Og, King of Bashan. The latter had been defeated at the
battle of Edrei and his large realm, extending up to the
Hauran, annexed by Israel. The cattle-rearing tribes who
thus received their heritage east of the Jordan undertook to
supply their full quota of fighting men to assist the rest of the
Israelites in occupying the whole of the Promised Land.

THE BOUNDARIES OF THE PROMISED LAND

TOWARDS THE END of the Book of Numbers,
in chapter 34, we find a recapitulation of the
boundaries of the area included in God's promise to Israel.
They correspond, roughly, to those of the Egyptian province
of Canaan as it existed in the thirteenth century B.C., with
the addition of northern Trans-Jordan. But the area of the
Egyptian province did not become entirely Israelite until the
days of David and Solomon. In any case the border delineated
here refers only to the area occupied by the nine and a half
tribes remaining after Gad and Reuben had already settled
east of the Jordan.

The description of the boundaries of the Promised Land
starts from the southern end of the Dead Sea, from where it
first turns south to the Ascent of Akrabbim ("Ascent of the
Scorpions"), the pass leading from the wilderness of the
Arabah into Moab. Continuing westwards into the desert of
Zin, where the Negeb hills give way to the Sinai plateau, the
boundary line crosses the area traversed by the Israelites on
their departure from Kadesh Barnea. This oasis itself is also
included in the Land of Israel, a claim which receives historical

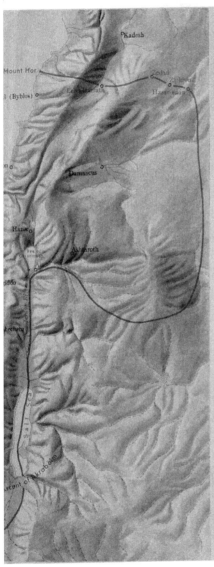

Tell Qudeirat in the Northern Negeb.

Your south side shall be from the
wilderness of Zin along the side of
Edom, and your southern boundary
shall be from the end of the Salt Sea
on the east; and your boundary shall
turn south of the ascent of Akrabbim
and cross to Zin and its end shall
be south of Kadesh-barnea; then it
shall go on to Hazar-addar, and pass
along to Azmon; and the boundary
shall turn from Azmon to the Brook
of Egypt, and its termination shall be
at the Sea.   (NUM. 34: 3-5)

Air-view of "The Ascent of Akrabbim
(Scorpions)" between Kadesh and the Dead
Sea.

View of the Sea of Chinnereth (Sea of Galilee).

This shall be your northern boundary: from the Great Sea you shall mark out your line to Mount Hor; from Mount Hor you shall mark it out to the entrance [Lebo] of Hamath, and the end of the boundary shall be at Zedad; then the boundary shall extend to Ziphron, and its end shall be at Hazar-enan; this shall be your northern boundary. You shall mark out your eastern boundary from Hazar-enan to Shepham; and the boundary shall go down from Shepham to Riblah on the east side of Ain; and the boundary shall go down, and reach to the shoulder of the sea of Chinnereth on the east. (NUM. 34: 7–11)

confirmation from the remains of a fort constructed there by the kings of Judah. Azmon has been identified with a height overlooking the Wadi el Arish, the "Brook of Egypt", which forms the rest of the southern boundary of Canaan until the Mediterranean is reached. This wide river bed is dry in summer; but in winter, when it channels off the rainfall over an extensive area, it is often a raging torrent which, with its numerous tributaries and side channels, forms a natural boundary between the Negeb and the Sinai peninsula.

The western border of the Land of Israel is formed by its Mediterranean seaboard from the Brook of Egypt to north of Gebal (Byblos) on the Phoenician coast. As the country's one and only unchanging geographical limit, the "sea" became, in the Hebrew of the Old Testament, a synonym for "west". The Mediterranean coast here included within Canaan falls into two parts, the more southerly of which, as far as Mount Carmel, is flat and sandy, with no good natural harbors. Only the promontories and bays near Jaffa could offer some sort of safe anchorage; the other ports along this stretch of coast, from Ashkelon in the south to Caesarea in the north, were artificial. Other landing-places were no more than open beaches suitable only for the flat-bottomed boats of the coastal traders. The flatness of this part of the coast served, on the whole, as a natural barrier against sea-borne invasions in antiquity. It was first held by the Canaanites. Then its southern stretch, up to the Yarkon river, fell to the Philistines, while Dor farther north was occupied by some of their allies. Under David and Solomon the Israelite kingdom gained control of this entire coastline and maintained its rule in the northern section until the Assyrian invasion of Tiglath-Pileser III, in the eighth century B.C.

Very different is the configuration of the other part of the Canaanite seaboard, from Haifa Bay northwards. Here the mountains come right down to the sea and form a series of good natural harbors. These were exploited by the Phoenicians from the beginning of the

68

The modern Sedad (Zedad) on the edge of the Syrian desert.

Western Semitic expansion and, although in theory part of the heritage of Israel, were never effectively controlled by it.

The boundary delineated in the Book of Numbers next reaches Mount Hor, a high peak slightly to the north of Gebal. From there it turns inland, crossing the Lebanon ridge and running down into the valley between the Lebanon and the Hermon, to a point called "the entrance (*Lebo*) to Hamath". Modern scholarship considers this a place name rather than merely an indication of direction, and identifies it with Lebwe in the Beqa Valley. The border line then continues to Zedad (modern Sedad) about fifty miles north of Damascus, thus including the whole of the Hermon range within the Promised Land. Bulging outwards so as to include the Hauran mountains, the boundary then runs along the slope of the escarpment on the eastern shore of Lake Chinnereth. The lyre-shaped "Sea of Chinnereth", so named from the town of Chinnereth (Tell el-Oreimeh) on its northwestern shore, is the largest freshwater lake of the Holy Land and a conspicuous landmark. It serves as a natural reservoir for irrigation and as a rich breeding-ground for fish. The idyllic beauty of its soft blue waters is enhanced by the sun-parched barrenness of the surrounding terrain, especially in the heat of summer. From the Sea of Galilee the boundary follows the River Jordan to the Dead Sea, thus closing its circuit.

DEUTERONOMY

AFTER A BRIEF résumé of the history of Israel from the Exodus, through the wanderings in the wilderness, to the first battles and the first conquests to the east of the Jordan, the main theme of the book is introduced by Moses' solemn exhortation to the people to observe faithfully all God's injunctions. After repeating the Ten Commandments to his audience, Moses gives them a stern warning against idolatry and reminds them of the sins committed during their wanderings through disobedience to God's will. Then follows the central part of the book—a code of laws and regulations covering ritual purity, clean and unclean foods, the sabbatical year, and the year of release, the Passover and other annual festivals, the status of the Levites, the cities of refuge, penal offences, family life, warfare, and the protection of animals. After this, Moses enjoins the whole people to come together again after the Conquest in the valley between the mountains of Ebal and Gerizim which flank Shechem, to hear the solemn proclamation of curses from Mount Ebal on those that break the Law and of blessings from Mount Gerizim on those that keep the Law. Then after formally investing Joshua the son of Nun with his authority as the national

A land of wheat and barley, of vines and fig trees and
pomegranates, a land of olive trees and honey.
(DEUT. 8 : 8)

leader, Moses offers up his thanks to the LORD in an eloquent hymn of praise and gives the people his last blessing. The book ends with the vision of the Promised Land granted Moses from Mount Nebo, and his death and burial in a place unknown.

Modern criticism assumes that Deuteronomy, or more probably an earlier form of it, corresponds to the book found in the Temple in the reign of King Josiah, *c.* 622 B.C., but that much of its material goes back further to the time of the Judges or the early Monarchy.

THE BLESSINGS OF THE HOLY LAND

O NE OF THE principal chapters in the first part of Deuteronomy is that which glowingly describes the blessings of the Promised Land to be given by God as a heritage to the Children of Israel in the fulfillment of his covenant with their ancestor Abraham, a covenant renewed in the burning bush and on Mount Sinai.

The land into which God will bring them is "a good land, a land of brooks of water, of fountains and springs, flowing forth in valleys and hills".

By comparison with Egypt, with its single great watercourse, the Nile, and in contrast to the barren and arid desert, Canaan might well be considered a land of abundant rivers and springs. In addition to the many smaller streams and winter torrents, there is the River Jordan which flows through the whole length of the country from north to south, and which could be used for irrigation at least in its upper reaches near the Sea of Galilee.

The good soil and the rich water resources of the Promised Land produced, in antiquity, a plentiful crop of the necessities of life for man and beast. The principal natural products, the "seven kinds" of Jewish tradition, were "wheat and barley, vines and figs and pomegranates, olives and honey". Wild wheat was already growing in Canaan in prehistoric times; the later cultivated variety was of excellent quality and won a name for itself even

outside the borders of the country. Barley was grown in regions unsuitable for the cultivation of wheat because of smaller rainfall; it provided food primarily for animals, but if necessary also for man. The vine, which was known in Canaan from the earliest times, supplied wine, grapes and raisins; some wines from Canaan were also exported to Egypt. The vinestock and the fig tree were the symbols of prosperous husbandry; when a man could live unmolested in their shade, the country was at peace. Figs were eaten fresh, dried or preserved; pomegranates were used both for food and drink. The olive flourished in ancient Israel, and to this day the numerous old gnarled olive-trees, with their grey-green leaves, are a striking feature of the country's landscape. The "honey" mentioned here was in fact syrup from fruit trees, and is therefore included among the products of the soil. It was usually extracted from the dates of the palm tree.

Among the remarkable natural phenomena of the Holy Land are the springs which spurt

forth from the rock in seemingly desert regions. Such apparent miracles are explained by
the accumulation of streams of underground water from the winter rains. The rain perco-
lates down through the porous soil till it meets a level of impermeable rock. Unable to
penetrate farther, it runs along this barrier and gushes out wherever it happens to come to
the surface of the soil again. In their wanderings the Israelites were several times saved
by the sudden appearance of "water out of the flinty rock" and such examples of God's
saving grace were treasured in the memory of later generations.

The fact that rain fell on the Promised Land was astonishing to the Israelites, used as they
were to rainless Egypt, where water had to be obtained from the Nile and its adjacent
channels and ponds, and usually had to be raised from the lower level of the river to the
higher one of the fields and gardens requiring irrigation. Since the primitive machines by
which this process was performed were often worked by leg-power, ancient Egypt might
be described as being "watered with the feet". One such irrigation device consisted of an
upright post, on the end of which a pole was balanced. A bucket suspended from the end of
this sweep was first filled with water by being lowered into the pond; it was then levered
up by means of a counterpoise weight and the water poured out at the place desired. After
years of back-breaking labor on such contraptions the Israelites could now hope for seasonal
rainfall which, though providing poorer crops, at least reduced the peasant's toil.

> For the land which you are entering to take posses-
> sion of it is not like the land of Egypt, from which you
> have come, where you sowed your seed and watered it
> with your feet, like a garden of vegetables.
>
> (DEUT. 11: 10)

Egyptian painting from tomb of Ipui, Thebes,
thirteenth century B.C., showing slave working
an irrigation machine.

History

The ruins of Tell es-Sultan (Biblical Jericho).

JOSHUA

THE FALL OF JERICHO

AFTER THE DEATH of Moses, the leadership of the Israelites passed to Joshua the son of Nun. The host assembled on the banks of the Jordan now made ready to cross the river and to advance into Canaan. Such is the position described at the beginning of the Book of Joshua; by its end most of the country was in the hands of the Israelites. The book relates how the conquest was achieved and the part played in it by the various tribes.

First the Jordan had to be crossed. The section of the river facing the Israelites in the Plains of Moab, opposite Jericho, is not easily fordable; but as in the crossing of the Sea, a natural event—unforeseeable and hence seen as a direct intervention of God—once again came to their aid. As has happened several times in recorded history (the last time in 1927), an earthquake or an undercutting of the river's banks caused a landslide which temporarily dammed the flow of its waters, thus enabling the Israelites to pass over dryshod. Twelve stones, one for each tribe, were taken from the river bed and set up, cairn fashion, at the first camp beyond the passage. This memorial at Gilgal remained a famous landmark for centuries. At this same camp the people were ritually circumcised to ensure that before entering on their promised heritage, they conformed to the terms of God's covenant with Abraham.

The first Canaanite city barring the Israelites' advance was Jericho, which at that time was much reduced from its former greatness. With its copious spring and the fertile soil

Middle Bronze Age wall of Jericho.

around it, the palm-girt town of Jericho (the "City of the Moon") formed an oasis in the otherwise barren Jordan wilderness. Recent excavations have shown that Jericho is one of the most ancient cities in the world, going back to the Neolithic or New Stone Age (seventh millennium B.C.). Even before they knew how to fashion pottery the men of Jericho built huge walls and buried their dead ceremonially. The city flourished in the Early and Middle Bronze Ages but suffered a decline just prior to the Israelite conquest. In fact archaeologists have so far been unable to locate its walls from that period, and some have actually suggested that the older Middle Bronze Age wall was still used, with houses built on to it, as related in the Bible.

The attack on Jericho, the first walled city confronting the Israelites, was carefully prepared. Joshua sent in two spies who were hidden in the house of a prostitute named Rahab. In return for her services she was promised personal safety for herself and her family after the conquest, a promise which was kept.

When the Israelites approached Jericho, the inhabitants shut the city gates and prepared for a siege. At God's command, Joshua ordered his forces to circle the city, accompanied by the priests blowing on the great rams' horns (called in Hebrew *shofar*); at a given signal the whole people were to raise a general shout. The purpose of this stratagem, of which there are other examples in the Bible (Judges 7), was to make as much noise as possible in order to confuse and dismay the enemy. The harsh and penetrating note of the ram's horn led to its employment in various armies in the ancient East. At Jericho the walls fell down and the city was left defenceless. In accordance with the divine commandment that the booty of the conquered city was to be dedicated in its entirety to God, everything found at Jericho was devoted to the ban. When a certain Achan secretly appropriated part of the spoil, he was punished by death.

The priests blowing the trumpets. (JOSHUA 6: 4)

Carchemish relief showing how horns
were blown. Eighth century B.C.
(Ankara Museum)

AI AND THE GIBEONITES

THE FALL OF Jericho secured the Israelites' flank in their advance into the interior; but it did not in itself give them a clear ascent to the ridge of the mountains which form the watershed between the Mediterranean and the Dead Sea and are the backbone of the country. To ensure this one of the cities on the road leading up to the watershed had to be captured, and a firm foothold obtained on this line. The next objective of the Israelites after Jericho was therefore Ai. This site is usually identified with et-Tell ("the ruin", the Arabic equivalent of the Hebrew "ha-Ai") to the east of Bethel. However, although a "king of Ai" and its people are mentioned in the Book of Joshua, the site itself was not settled in the time of the conquest, but only before and afterwards. This difficulty has been explained in various ways. It is possible that the army of some neighboring city, e.g. Bethel, used the ruin as a camp in their war with Joshua. The strategic ability of the Israelites' new leader was brilliantly displayed in this campaign; he organized an ambush, made as if to retreat before the enemy (in itself a manoeuvre not to be attempted with unseasoned troops), and took the city before its inhabitants had become aware of the stratagem. Ai was destroyed and its king hanged.

The fall of Jericho and Ai in quick succession, and the fact that the Israelites had now established themselves in control of part of the central ridge, made a great impression in Canaan. Some of the Amorite kings in that part of the country which was later to be known as Judah, with the king of Jerusalem at their head, realized the threat to their security and prepared for battle. However, the nearest neighbors of Ai to the south, the confederation of

But Joshua made them that day hewers of wood and drawers of water for the congregation and for the altar of the LORD. . . . (JOSHUA 9: 27)

Egyptian model of bakery. On the left is a water-drawer. (Model, Museum of Fine Arts Boston)

Hivite cities with Gibeon as their capital, made peace overtures to Joshua. The Hivites differed from the Canaanites not only ethnically but also politically and socially; they had no kings but were ruled by a Council of elders (Joshua 9: 11). Their confederation consisted of the four cities of Gibeon (modern el-Jib, northwest of Jerusalem), Beeroth (possibly Nabi Samwil, to the south of it), Chephirah (Tell Kefire to the southwest), and Kiriath-jearim (Tell Deir el-Azhar) on the main road from Jerusalem westwards. It thus controlled part of the descent from the watershed ridge westwards and lay across the communications of Jerusalem with the rest of the country. As the Hivites were expressly mentioned among the Canaanite nations whose lands God gave to Israel, Joshua would have refused to make peace with them, had they appeared under their true name. Therefore they had to resort to subterfuge to obtain a peace treaty: they made themselves out to be foreigners from a distant land, and produced circumstantial evidence in the shape of old patched sandals, worn-out garments, moldy bread, and torn and mended wine-bottles. When the fraud was discovered, Joshua and the Israelites could not go back on their word; but the Gibeonites and their allies were made to serve as "hewers of wood and drawers of water", the most menial of the ritual ministrants. They may have first served at the high place which existed at Gibeon; in the reign of Saul they were almost exterminated there. The surviving remnant ministered in the Temple of Solomon and shared with the rest of the Judahites in the Babylonian Exile, where they lost their national identity; their descendants who returned from the Exile were completely assimilated with the rest of the nation. Carrying water from the well was, under ancient conditions of life, a necessary but toilsome chore, often left to the women. Water-carriers are represented in Egyptian models from the time of the Middle Kingdom (some with water jars on their heads and others with two buckets balanced on a yoke across their shoulders). The latter method is also depicted on a painted potsherd found at Megiddo.

The five Amorite kings regarded the submission of the Gibeonite confederation as a piece of rank treason, and forthwith laid siege to the chief of its five cities. The hard-pressed Gibeonites sent out an appeal for help to Joshua at his camp at Gilgal in the Jordan Valley. Realizing how important it was not to let his new allies be defeated, the Israelite leader made a forced march with his army up to Gibeon and in a day-long battle routed the Amorites, pursuing them along the ancient Beth-Horon road into the valley of Aijalon. Here, at the ascent of Beth-Horon, Joshua uttered his epic prayer: "Sun stand thou still upon Gibeon and thou moon in the valley of Aijalon!" By this invocation he sought to prolong the (for him) militarily favorable position of the heavenly bodies at dawn, when the sun rose over Gibeon in the east while the waning moon could still be seen over the valley of Aijalon (Aiyalon). This valley, referred to in the el-Amarna letters as the "field of Yaluna", is still called after the

The valley of Aijalon seen from the west.

Sun, stand thou still at Gibeon, and thou Moon in the valley of Aijalon. (JOSHUA 10: 12)

Reconstruction of Megiddo ivory showing Canaanite troops.

And they came out, with all their troops, a great host, in number like the sand that is upon the seashore, with very many horses and chariots. And all these kings joined their forces, and came and encamped together at the waters of Meron, to fight with Israel. (JOSHUA 11 : 4–5)

nearby Arab village of Yalu. It forms a very convenient route up the Judaean mountains, from the southwest to the northeast, ending in the pass of Beth-Horon.

The victory at Aijalon was followed by attacks on the cities of the allied kings. Although they were defeated in the battle one by one, some of the cities, including Jerusalem, the head of the league, did not actually fall to the Israelites. In one of the cities that were taken, Lachish, the Israelite conquest has been archaeologically confirmed. In the ruins of the fosse temple of that city, dating to Canaanite times, a vessel was found with an inscription probably from the fourth year of the Pharaoh Merneptah (1230 B.C.). As the temple was burnt down soon afterwards, the inscription furnishes a likely date for the Israelite conquest of Lachish.

THE STORMING OF HAZOR

AFTER THE DEFEAT of the Amorite kings, the narrative goes straight on to recount the overthrow of a northern coalition led by the king of Hazor. Scholars have noted that, although after the Conquest a convention of all the tribes was held at Shechem in the central mountains and the Covenant was renewed there as prescribed in Deuteronomy, the Book of Joshua makes no reference to the actual taking of this city, or indeed of any of the other cities on the central ridge. From this strange silence they conclude either that these areas were thickly wooded and sparsely populated—as may also be inferred from the story of the House of Joseph's coming to Joshua to ask for more land and being told to clear the forest and to possess it (Joshua 17: 18)—or that the inhabitants were closely related to the Israelites, being also of Hebrew descent, and merged peacefully with the invading tribes.

The same process of slow infiltration into the wooded areas of the country, which were left relatively unoccupied by the Canaanites, the possessors of the fertile plains, has been

observed in the course of an archaeological survey in Galilee. There too the Israelites apparently seized the forest lands before engaging in a decisive battle with the lords of the cities.

Of these Galilean towns Hazor was by far the largest and most powerful. Recent excavations have shown that it was in fact a double city: the high mound was occupied by a Canaanite acropolis, at the foot of which extended a Lower City of much greater size, protected by its own walls. This city flourished both in the Middle and the Late Bronze Age, and was destroyed some time in the thirteenth century. It covered an area of 200 acres and might well have contained a population of 40,000, by far the largest calculated for any of the cities of Canaan. The trading connections of Hazor stretched from Egypt to the

And Joshua turned back at that time, and took Hazor, and smote its king with the sword; for Hazor formerly was the head of all those kingdoms.
(JOSHUA 11 : 10)

The ancient mound of Hazor in Upper Galilee.

Euphrates, and its kings were proud and independent rulers. For example, it has been noted that one of these kings, Abd-Tarshi, who ruled in the fourteenth century, in writing to the Pharaoh Akhenaton, referred to himself as "king of Hazor" and not as "thy servant", as did all the other local rulers of Canaan.

Jabin, the king of Hazor at the time of the Israelite invasion, collected an imposing force of horses and chariots; the latter operating most effectively in the plains where the Israelites had nothing comparable to oppose them, helped to save most of the Canaanite cities from being conquered. Brought to Egypt by the Hyksos, the Canaanite chariot was adopted by the Egyptians and eventually became the pride of their army. They strengthened the originally light vehicle by providing it with six-spoked wheels. This modification was subsequently copied from the Egyptians by the Canaanites themselves, as is shown by an ivory carving from Megiddo (thirteenth or early twelfth century B.C.) depicting heavy chariots drawn by two horses. Fastened to one side of each chariot are the quiver of arrows and the bow-case of the bowman, the fighting partner of the charioteer who holds the reins. The chariots are escorted by foot-soldiers armed with the round shield and the sickle-sword, characteristic of the Canaanites in that period.

Joshua took the assembled kings by surprise near the waters of Merom, perhaps Tell el-Khirba near Jebel Marun in the Lebanon. After routing the hostile army, which fled in disarray northwards (to Sidon), westwards (to Mishrephoth mi-yam on the sea coast) and eastwards (to Mizpeh), Joshua turned back, stormed the great city of Hazor and razed it to the ground. Although the kingdom of Hazor revived at a later date, the city itself was destroyed for good in its lower part; the Israelite city of Solomon and Ahab was restricted to the upper mound. The defeat of Jabin, king of Hazor "the head of all these kingdoms", sealed the fate of the Canaanites in the north of the country.

THE CONQUEST OF ALL CANAAN

IN HIS SUMMARY of the victorious campaigns in chapters 11–12, the author of the Book of Joshua dwells with pardonable pride on the completeness of the conquest, though in actual fact his account includes notes of large tracts of the country unconquered, as is confirmed by a later recapitulation in the first chapter of the Book of the Judges. The Israelites occupied the whole of the central hill country, all the Negeb (the "south country"), the land of Goshen (the region south of Hebron, called after the city of Goshen there and quite distinct from Goshen in Egypt), the "lowlands" (*Shephelah* in Hebrew, i.e. the foothills of the mountains, called "low" from the point of view of the Israelites perched on the heights), and the "plain" (*Arabah*, the rift valley of the Jordan and the Dead Sea). The Jerusalem enclave, the Valley of Esdraelon, and the whole of the coastal plain remained outside their control. But even so, theirs was a great and memorable military achievement. A group of nomad tribes had possessed itself of a large and potentially fertile area, had taken a fair number of walled cities, dispersed their armies, and put an end to a whole civilization.

The decisive factor in the Israelite victory was the lack of national cohesion among the Canaanites. Each city formed a separate state, nominally ruled by its god or baal ("owner")

Map of the division of Cana
among the tribes.

And these are the inheritances which
the people of Israel received in the land
of Canaan.... Their inheritance was
by lot.... (JOSHUA 14: 1–2)

Canaanite king on Megiddo ivory. (Palestine Archaeological Museum)

The king of Megiddo, one.
(JOSHUA 12 : 21)

and actually governed by a king who was seen as the god's representative on earth. Some of these kings were more powerful than others; and some even headed confederations of a few cities. But Joshua had only twice to contend with such leagues, once in the south and once in the north. For the rest, the kings went down to their defeat separately and alone.

One such local ruler is depicted on an ivory plaque found at Megiddo and belonging to the Late Bronze period, the time of Joshua. On the right he is shown returning victorious from a war, preceded by an armed soldier and followed by his armor-bearer, with two naked captives tied to his chariot. On the left the king is seen feasting: he sits on a throne flanked by cherubim, with the queen waiting upon him; another woman, a player, stands behind the queen, while behind the throne stand two attendants with a jar and offerings. The contrast between the peaceful life at the court, with its luxuries copied from Egyptian and Syrian models, and the violent scene of warfare is striking. The forces of each of these little kingdoms by themselves could hardly have sufficed to oppose a strong tribal army. Even if the latter was deficient in technically developed weapons, its enthusiasm and the military capacities of its leader more than outweighed such defects.

The conquest once accomplished, the land was portioned out amongst the victorious tribes. The Book of Joshua gives a detailed description of the area allotted to each tribe, with its boundaries and principal cities. Some of these descriptions were apparently edited at a later date to conform to the changed circumstances; thus it is generally assumed that the meticulous delineation of the territory of Judah, in the longest chapter devoted to the tribal portions, reflects the situation at the later stage of the divided monarchy. However that may be, chapters 15–21 of the Book of Joshua are certainly our fullest and most detailed geographical treatise concerning the Holy Land in the early Biblical period.

These chapters place four of the tribes—Asher, Naphtali, Zebulun, and Issachar—in the northern mountains later known as Galilee. Asher controlled the hinterland of Tyre and Sidon, Naphtali a large tract of eastern Galilee down to the Sea of Chinnereth. Zebulun occupied a smaller area in western Lower Galilee, and on one or two occasions actually succeeded in gaining a foothold on the shore of the Mediterranean Sea. Issachar was the least independent of these tribes; although its lands were fertile, it was dominated by the Canaanite cities in its midst, as well as by the powerful tribe of Manasseh.

This group of northern tribes was cut off from the rest of the Israelites by the Valleys of Esdraelon and Harod, in which such rich and powerful Canaanite cities as Megiddo and Bethshan kept their independent status.

84

Then the boundary went down to the brook Kanah. The cities here, to the south of the brook, among the cities of Manasseh, belonged to Ephraim. Then the boundary of Manasseh goes on the north side of the brook. . . . (JOSHUA 17 : 9)

The brook Kanah, which rises to the west of Mount Gerizim.

The second group of Israelite tribes comprised the House of Joseph (Ephraim and Manasseh), together with the tribe of Benjamin which was associated with them by virtue of a common descent from Rachel. Manasseh had the largest of all the territorial portions, with half the tribe settled on the east side of the Jordan and half west of the river. But the leading position was occupied by Ephraim, due to its central situation and also to the fact that the city of Shechem and the sanctuary of Shiloh, with the Ark reverenced by all the tribes, were in its territory. Ephraim's portion, which was occupied without much fighting, consisted (like the adjoining lands of Manasseh) mostly of forests. Once these had been cut down the soil could be worked with the help of rain-water stored in lime-covered cisterns, a fairly new device which greatly helped to make the heavily wooded mountains of Ephraim habitable. Thanks to its central position and its security from outside attack, Ephraim was able to take the lead in the following centuries. South of it the small tribe of Benjamin reached down to the Jordan Valley; but the chief city of the area allotted to it, Jerusalem, remained an unconquered Canaanite enclave in Israelite territory, separating the central tribes from the southern ones. The small tribe of Dan was attached to the western border of this central *bloc.*

Put away the gods which your fathers served beyond the River, and in Egypt. . . .
(JOSHUA 24: 14)

The Canaanite goddess, Kadesh, worshiped by the Egyptians.

The third group of tribes comprised Judah and Simeon, the latter of which was soon absorbed into the former. The area of these tribes was only partly fertile and was subject to constant raids by the desert-roving Amalekites. Nevertheless, the military and political potentialities of this group were very great.

The fourth group of tribes was formed by the cattle-raising clans of Reuben, Gad and half of Manasseh settled beyond the Jordan.

All the tribes were associated in a loose confederacy, mainly religious in character and held together by memories of a common past, including the theophany at Mount Sinai and the desert wanderings, and by the central sanctuary at Shiloh, with its priests claiming direct descent from Aaron.

JOSHUA'S DEATH AND BURIAL

AFTER COMPLETING THE conquest of most of the Promised Land, the aged leader of the host retired to his personal estate at Timnath-Heres ("the portion of the sun god", Judges 2: 9) in the mountains of Ephraim where he passed his last days, died, and was buried. The exact locality of Timnath-Serah ("the portion of licentiousness"), as it was afterwards called in contemptuous reference to the idolatrous associations of the place, is unknown. In later tradition the tomb of Joshua is placed at Khirbet Tibnah, about twelve miles northeast of Lod, in the foothills of the mountains of Ephraim. The structure traditionally identified as Joshua's burial place is of far more recent date, but in its general features (a rock-cut tomb cave) it need not differ much from the original edifice. The rabbinical literature records that a sun-disk was placed over Joshua's tomb, probably in memory of the sun-worship connected with the locality.

Joshua the son of Nun . . . died. . . . And they buried him in his own inheritance at Timnath-Serah, which is in the hill country of Ephraim, north of the mountains of Gaash.

(JOSHUA 24 : 29–30)

Traditional tomb of Joshua at Khirbet Tibnah, Mount Ephraim.

JUDGES

THE PERIOD FROM about 1200 to 1010 B.C. was a very difficult two centuries for the Israelites. After the first great wave of military victories the tide of Israelite successes lost its momentum. The neighboring peoples, especially the other warlike tribes in their immediate vicinity, had now taken their measure and were no longer demoralized by the panic which accompanied and facilitated the conquests of Joshua. Once settled in the Promised Land, the Israelites' greatest weakness was their lack of unity in peacetime. Occasionally an energetic leader could rouse the tribes to a joint military effort against some particularly dangerous enemy; but, as soon as the emergency had passed, they relapsed into their usual indifference to each other. Such temporary leaders were called "Judges" and their deeds form the contents of the book named after them. Some of these stories may well be traditions concerned only with some part of the whole group of tribes, but used by the later compilers of the book to give a picture of the fortunes of all Israel.

*So the anger of the LORD was kindled against
Israel, and he gave them over to plunderers. . . .*
(JUDGES 2 : 14)

The Book of Judges contains the stories of six major judges, whose exploits are described
at length, and five minor ones, who are only briefly mentioned. The twelfth judge, Shamgar
ben Anath (Judges 3 : 31), is given only one verse; his name is Canaanite and his enemies
were the Philistines who appear much later in this story.

The Book begins with a description of the state of the country after Joshua's death. Apart
from some successes on the part of the tribe of Judah, which took Hebron, the rest of the
picture is a gloomy one; most of the Canaanite cities of importance in the other tribal areas
continued to hold out. There was no leader of military genius left in Israel comparable
to Joshua. But worse was to come; the Israelites "forsook the LORD and served Baal and
Astaroth". To the editor of the Book of Judges such backsliding was typical of the whole
period of the Judges. In punishment of their repeated relapses into idolatry the Israelites were
again oppressed by some foreign ruler; but as often as they repented a new Judge arose to
deliver them.

THE STORY OF EHUD

ONE OF THE earliest of the oppressors came from the east: Eglon, king of
Moab, in alliance with the Ammonites and the Amalekites, made himself
master of the tribe of Benjamin, his neighbors across the Jordan. The ravages of the
Amalekites were especially grievous, as of all the brigands of the desert none more deserved
the appellation *shosim* ("plunderers") given them by the Biblical narrator. This same word
occurs, in the form *shasu*, in Egyptian records of the Nineteenth and Twentieth Dynasties
to denote nomads. In Egyptian reliefs these *shasu* appear as tall, lean men of the desert, with
long hair and pointed beards, wearing characteristic tight wrappings round their chests and
stomachs. As is usual in Egyptian pictures, they are shown defeated and mostly dead, like the
other foes of Egypt.

The Moabite domination was terminated by the assassination of Eglon, carried out
with great coolness and daring by Ehud, the son of Gera, from the tribe of Benjamin.
First of all Ehud had to prepare a special weapon, suitable for his design. The usual sword of

88

the period was curved, with a cutting edge on the convex side. It could thus be used only for slashing, and could not be concealed on the person of its wearer. Since concealment was the essence of Ehud's plan, he made himself a sword of a new type just then coming into use. This weapon was two-edged, and as such suitable for both slashing and piercing, it was also relatively short and could therefore be concealed by Ehud under his clothes; moreover, once driven into Eglon's stomach it could not easily be pulled out. To gain access to the king, Ehud headed a tribute-bearing delegation, and, after being received into the royal presence, requested a private audience. Eglon evidently encouraged Israelite informers to bring him clandestine reports on the state of the subject nation, so he dismissed his attendants and

And Ehud made for himself a sword with two edges,
a cubit in length. . . .   (JUDGES 3 : 16)

Late Bronze Age sword found at Megiddo.
(Palestine Archaeological Museum)

was left alone with Ehud. The latter had as an additional precaution, concealed his sword on his right side, since usually only the left would be searched for weapons. With a swift movement of his left hand, Ehud drove the sword deep into Eglon's stomach and made good his escape, locking the door on the corpse. By the time the deed was discovered the Israelites, mustered by Ehud, had come down from the mountain of Ephraim and easily discomfited the confused servants of Eglon. Another period of peace followed this assassination and Israelite victory; with the removal of the threat of foreign domination, leadership remained dormant for a time.

THE STORY OF SISERA AND DEBORAH

THE POWER OF a Judge was not absolute nor was his office hereditary. The call to serve was a singular act of divine grace, and might even come to a woman, a remarkable phenomenon in the predominantly masculine society of the ancient Orient. The next danger to Israel appeared in the north, where the power of Hazor (although not the city itself) revived under a king called Jabin. His commander-in-chief, Sisera (a foreign mercenary, to judge by his name), gathered a great force in the mountainous area of Central Galilee and threatened the independence of the northern group of tribes. The people were summoned to battle by the prophetess Deborah, who resided in Ephraim. In contrast to the local affray between Ehud and Eglon, this was a large-scale encounter involving almost the whole of Northern Israel. The commander of the Israelite army was

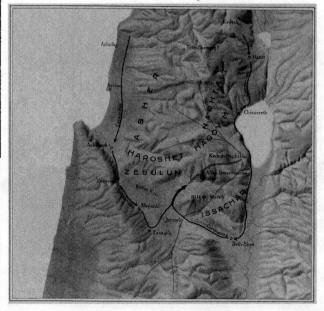

chosen from the tribe most threatened: he was Barak the son of Abinoam, from Kadesh in Naphtali, now identified with Khirbet Kadas southwest of Lake Chinnereth. The northern tribes assembled in force and were supported by warriors from Benjamin and Ephraim who answered the call of the prophetess in their midst. The Israelite army took up its position on Mount Tabor, from the top of which it could look with unconcern on the nine hundred chariots of the enemy massed in the plain below. Ivories from Megiddo show such chariots in action; drawn by two horses charging at a furious gallop, they overwhelmed any enemy bold enough to risk battle on level ground. They could not advance up the slopes of Mount Tabor; but neither could the Israelites manoeuver on their mountain-top. This stalemate ended when the weather came to the Israelites' aid. After Sisera had drawn up his army in battle array, heavy rains so swelled the River Kishon that when the Israelites at last descended from Mount Tabor the Canaanite chariot-charge came to a disastrous end in the flooded fields. "The river of Kishon swept them away, that ancient river" (Judges 5: 21). Sisera, fleeing alone, was killed while taking refuge in the tent of Jael, a Kenite nomad.

The account of the battle of the Kishon is followed in the Book of Judges by a spirited victory ode, one of the oldest extant pieces of ancient Hebrew poetry. After a brief, impassioned opening in praise of God, who had delivered Israel from its state of utter political subjection and dire economic distress caused by the foreign oppression, the song goes on to praise those tribes who assembled to do battle and to taunt the others who held back in cowardice. Next comes a vivid description of the course of the battle, culminating in its dramatic consequences: the flight of Sisera and his death at the hand of a woman. The

Her wisest ladies made answer . . .
"spoil of dyed stuffs for Sisera, spoil
of dyed stuffs embroidered, two pieces
of dyed work embroidered for my neck
as spoil?"   (JUDGES 5 : 29–30)

Canaanite lady on ivory from
Megiddo, thirteenth or twelfth
century B.C. (Oriental Institute,
Chicago); Canaanite on glazed tile,
Medinet Habu, twelfth century B.C.
(Cairo Museum)

poem ends with an ironical description of Sisera's mother waiting for the victorious return of her famous son, while her ladies gloatingly picture to themselves the booty which they are sure he will bring with him: for every man a damsel or two, and a rich assortment of dyed and embroidered cloths for the victors to wear. This is a reference to the costly garments worn by prosperous Canaanites and their womenfolk in the times of the Judges. The men affected long robes, embroidered in many colors, while the women draped their bodies in flowing cloaks, braided at the edges. The ladies of Sisera's entourage confidently expected abundant spoils of this kind, but their hopes were sorely disappointed.

THE STORY OF GIDEON

AFTER ANOTHER INTERVAL of peace, the Israelites began to be harried once more from the eastern desert, this time by the Midianites and their allies, the peoples of the East and the Amalekites, whose great mobility made them a serious menace. The domestication and increasingly widespread use of the camel now enabled the dwellers

For they would come up with their cattle and
their tents, coming like locusts for number; both
they and their camels could not be counted.
(JUDGES 6: 5)

Beduin camels at pasture.

of the desert to appear suddenly from nowhere with "their cattle and their tents . . . and their
camels could not be counted" (Judges 6: 5). They poured through the Beth-shan gap into
the Valley of Esdraelon and plundered the whole of the country as far as the coast. The main
sufferer must have been the tribe of Manasseh, whose lands lay directly across the path of the
invaders. It was only fitting, therefore, that the deliverer should have come from this tribe.
Gideon the son of Joash of Ophrah, a village just to the north of the Valley of Esdraelon and
hence directly affected by the Midianite raids, was the leader chosen by God. After twice
requesting and being granted a sign that his call was indeed divinely inspired, Gideon
demonstrated his zeal for the God of Israel by overturning an altar of Baal belonging to his
father. He then mustered a fighting force from his own tribe and from the three northern
tribes of Asher, Zebulun, and Naphtali.

Gideon assembled his warriors at the foot of Mount Gilboa, near the Well of Harod, a
spring still in existence today. He chose this spot as being suitably situated for a retreat, in
case of need, into the mountains, where the Midianite camels could not follow. The military operation that Gideon had in mind—a night attack—did not require a large force. At
the pool Gideon therefore picked his assault troops by a simple test: of the whole number
only the three hundred "that lapped" of the water with their tongues, "as a dog laps", were
chosen for the attack and the rest dismissed.

The Midianites were encamped on the "Hill of Moreh", a mountain not mentioned elsewhere in the Bible. However, as Ps. 83: 10 states that they "were destroyed at En-dor"
which has been identified with Khirbet Safsafa, near the modern village of Indur, the hill of
Moreh is most probably Jebel Dahi, an eminence rising to 1,550 feet above sea level. The

Then Jerubbaal (that is Gideon) and all the people who were with him rose early and encamped beside the spring of Harod. . . .
(JUDGES 7: 1)

The spring of Harod.

Midianite host, stretching from the Hill of Moreh to Mount Tabor, thus faced the Israelites on the opposite side of the valley.

Gideon based his plan of attack on two facts: the notorious dislike of the nomads for night fighting, and the vulnerability of their tents to fire. Arming his band with torches hidden in jars, he made a surprise night attack, accompanied by trumpet-blasts and wild shouting. In the ensuing confusion his men were able to set light to the Midianite tents and thus spread panic amongst the whole vast and mobile nomad host which fled in disorder by way of Beth Shitta into the Valley of Bethshan eastwards. Clearly, only a small body of men was required for such an operation; a larger number would only have created confusion amongst the Israelites themselves.

Gideon followed up his victory by pursuing the Midianites beyond the Jordan, killing their leaders Zebah and Zalmunna, and punishing the people of Succoth in the Jordan Valley, who had refused him assistance. The spoil taken from the desert robbers was immense, 1,700 shekels of gold went into the making of a golden *ephod* which was set up and consulted as an oracle in the shrine established at Ophrah, now the federal capital. However, despite his undisputed authority, Gideon refused to rule Israel as a king.

*They said to him, "Then say Shibboleth," and he said
"Sibboleth," for he could not pronounce it right; then they
seized him and·slew him at the fords of the Jordan.*

(JUDGES 12: 6)

Assyrian relief
from the palace
of Sennacherib,
Nineveh, show-
ing battle and
surrender at a
ford of a river.

After Gideon's death, Abimelech, his son by a woman of
Shechem, made himself king in his mother's city, killing all
of his brethren but one. On the occasion of Abimelech's
coronation, this single survivor, Jotham, publicly uttered his
famous parable, comparing the choice of the Shechemites to
the bramble, a worthless plant, that ruled because its betters
had refused the crown. The new dynasty did not last long;
Abimelech and the men of Shechem fell out and he captured
and destroyed their city. Soon after, at the siege of Thebez
(modern Tubas, northeast of Shechem), Abimelech was killed by a millstone thrown by
a woman from the city tower and the short-lived kingdom came to an end.

JEPHTHAH'S DAUGHTER

ABIMELECH WAS FOLLOWED by a series of leaders whose names alone are
mentioned in the Book of Judges. After them there was a new oppression
by the Ammonites, from which the people of Gilead beyond the Jordan and north of
Ammon were the chief sufferers. The Ammonites claimed for themselves the tract of land
from the Arnon to the Jabbok and the Jordan, the spoils of Israel's victory over Sihon the
Amorite. In this emergency, the Gileadites recalled a brigand-captain named Jephthah, of
obscure birth, who had formerly fled from his father's house and taken to the desert because
his brothers had refused him a share in the family inheritance. Before going out to battle,
Jephthah vowed to dedicate to the LORD as a burnt-offering "whoever comes forth from the
doors of my house to meet me". When, after the victory, he returned in triumph to Mizpeh,
it was his own daughter that came out to meet him "with timbrels and with dances". This
was in accordance with the ancient oriental custom of returning victors being met by the
women of their tribe or nation, welcoming them with music, song, and dance. This custom
had been observed centuries before Jephthah, after the passage of the Sea (Exod. 15: 21);

and it was observed again in later times, when David and Saul defeated the Philistines (1 Sam. 18 : 7). The timbrels were a small hand drum of the type still very popular in the East to this day. Maidens playing the timbrel are represented in scenes of sacrifice on many ancient monuments and works of art, amongst them an ivory casket from the palace of Calah (ninth century). Unable to revoke his solemn vow Jephthah had no choice but to sacrifice his daughter, in whose memory an annual four-day lamentation was instituted in Israel.

Embittered by his grievous loss, Jephthah dealt harshly with the Ephraimites, who had refused to follow him into battle against Ammon. This inter-tribal encounter was fought somewhere east of the Jordan, and the victorious Gileadites seized the fords of the river before their defeated enemies could escape across them to their own land. The occupation of the Jordan fords was a well-tried stratagem, already employed in the campaign of Ehud and Gideon. By cutting off the enemy's retreat it made certain the complete destruction of his army. Decisive engagements in antiquity were often fought beside rivers. Assyrian battle reliefs show the outcome of such actions: the vanquished submitting to the victors on the bank, while the bodies of their dead and the debris of their chariots float down the river.

As it was impossible at the fords of Jordan to distinguish victors from vanquished by any outward signs, the Ephraimites were singled out by a pronunciation test: whoever said *sibboleth* instead of *shibboleth* ("stream of water") was killed. This detail shows that even two related tribes (the Gileadites being descendants of Manasseh, Ephraim's brother) already spoke different dialects of Hebrew.

And behold, a young lion roared against him; and the Spirit of the LORD came mightily upon him, and he tore the lion asunder as one tears a kid; and he had nothing in his hands. . . . (JUDGES 14 : 5–6)

Gozan relief showing hero fighting lion.
(Berlin Museum)

THE STORY OF SAMSON

FROM THE NORTH and the east the scene shifts to the southwest. There a new enemy began to oppress Israel: the Philistines. The main brunt of their expansive pressure was borne by the small tribe of Dan, established northeast of the Philistine city of Ekron. The Israelite champion was the legendary hero Samson, whose birth had been foretold by an angel and whose superhuman strength enabled him to perform, single-handed, incredible feats of valor and daring. Not all his life, however, was spent in fighting; there were peaceful interludes, such as his marriage to the Philistine beauty at Timnath (possibly Tell el-Batashi in the Sorek Valley), close to Samson's camp between Eshtaol and Zorah. On his way to the wedding Samson was attacked by a young lion which he tore asunder with his bare hands. Lions were found throughout the lands of the East, including Canaan, in Biblical times; they occur in the Old Testament both in the historical narrative and as part of the symbolism of Biblical poetry. Two other heroes besides Samson, David (1 Sam. 17: 35–36) and Benaiah, one of David's "men of valor" (2 Sam. 23 : 20) also overcame lions in single combat. But of the three, Samson performed the most prodigious feat; for he killed his lion without the use of weapons, thereby accomplishing a deed of valor

Now the lords of the Philistines gathered to offer a great sacrifice to Dagon their god. . . . And Samson grasped the two middle pillars upon which the house rested, and he leaned his weight upon them, his right hand on the one and his left hand on the other. (JUDGES 16 : 23, 29)

Columns in staircase of palace at Knossos, Crete. Fifteenth century B.C.

comparable to those of the mythical Gilgamesh, the hero of Mesopotamian epic. Representations of fights with lions, in which the hunter is shown facing the beast as it rears up on its hind legs, abound in the art of the ancient Orient. The one reproduced here was found on a relief at the royal palace of Gozan (tenth or ninth century B.C.).

When the Philistines realized that they could not get the better of Samson in open combat (for he had devastated their fields with foxes carrying torches, killed a thousand of their men with the jawbone of an ass, and bodily lifted up and carried off the gates of Gaza which had been closed upon him when he entered the city), they enlisted the seductive charms of a woman of the Valley of Sorek named Delilah. After several unsuccessful attempts, Delilah at last wormed out of Samson the secret of his strength: following upon the Nazirite vow taken by his mother, Samson was under divine injunction not to cut his hair; once he was shorn his strength would be gone. Thus it came about that the mighty hero was rendered powerless through a woman's wiles. He was seized by the Philistines, blinded and brought in fetters to Gaza, there to work the prison mill. But the day of his revenge came at last, when he was brought to "make sport" for the multitude thronging the temple of Dagon at Bethshan and Ashdod. Running round the central court of the temple at Gaza there was an upper gallery supported on pillars. These pillars were possibly designed on the Cretan pattern since the Philistines were probably connected with the Minoan culture of Crete. The peculiarity of the Cretan column was that it tapered toward the base, being thus less

97

stable than the straight columns of the Greeks. While in prison Samson had regained his strength; led to the two middle pillars of the building he grasped them firmly and, ready to die with the Philistines, pressed on them with all his weight till the whole roof fell in on the mocking crowds of assembled worshipers. "So the dead whom he slew at his death were more than those whom he had slain in his life."

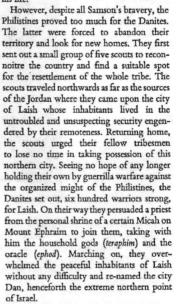

However, despite all Samson's bravery, the Philistines proved too much for the Danites. The latter were forced to abandon their territory and look for new homes. They first sent out a small group of five scouts to reconnoitre the country and find a suitable spot for the resettlement of the whole tribe. The scouts traveled northwards as far as the sources of the Jordan where they came upon the city of Laish whose inhabitants lived in the untroubled and unsuspecting security engendered by their remoteness. Returning home, the scouts urged their fellow tribesmen to lose no time in taking possession of this northern city. Seeing no hope of any longer holding their own by guerrilla warfare against the organized might of the Philistines, the Danites set out, six hundred warriors strong, for Laish. On their way they persuaded a priest from the personal shrine of a certain Micah on Mount Ephraim to join them, taking with him the household gods (*teraphim*) and the oracle (*ephod*). Marching on, they overwhelmed the peaceful inhabitants of Laish without any difficulty and re-named the city Dan, henceforth the extreme northern point of Israel.

And they turned aside here, to go in and spend the night at Gibeah. And he went there and sat down in the open square of the city. . . . (JUDGES 19: 15)

The Damascus Gate of the Old City of Jerusalem, showing a part of the paved square in front of it.

But when the signal began to rise out of the city in a column of smoke, the Benjaminites looked behind them; and behold, the whole of the city went up in smoke to heaven. (JUDGES 20 : 40)

Burning town on bronze relief, Balawat. (British Museum)

THE BENJAMINITES

THE BOOK OF Judges concludes with a story illustrating the lawless character of the period in which "every man did that which was right in his own eyes". A Levite from Mount Ephraim was travelling with his concubine from her home at Bethlehem to his own abode. Being unwilling to stop for the night at Jebusite Jerusalem, he carried on to Gibeah of Benjamin (Tell el-Ful), three miles further north. There the woman was so brutally outraged by some men of the city that she died. In order to avenge this crime, the rest of the Israelites resolved on a punitive campaign against Benjamin, one more instance of the inter-tribal warfare which broke out again and again in the time of the Judges. Gibeah was attacked by a stratagem which recalls that employed at Ai: one group of Israelites retreated before the men of Benjamin while another group, concealed in ambush, entered the city and fired it. In antiquity the capture of a city frequently ended in its being burnt by the conquerors. Written accounts of such burnings are confirmed not only by the thick layers of ash found in many of the artificial mounds in Palestine, but also by reliefs such as that on the palace gates of Shalmaneser III, king of Assyria (ninth century B.C.), found at Balawat. When the pall of smoke which rose from the burning city showed

Wall-painting from tomb of Antefoker, Thebes, showing
dancers, nineteenth or eighteenth century B.C.

And watch; if the daughters of Shiloh come out to
dance in the dances. . . .   (JUDGES 21 : 21)

the "retreating" Israelites that it had been taken, the pursued turned and became the
pursuers.

In addition to killing most of the warriors of the guilty tribe, the Israelites took an oath
not to provide the remnant with wives from among their own daughters, thus apparently
dooming Benjamin to extinction. But on soberer thought they began to be afraid that
there "should be today one tribe lacking in Israel". Some wives were therefore provided
for the surviving Benjaminites from Jabesh Gilead, a city which had refused to join in the
fight against Benjamin. In order to find others a stratagem was used. It was the custom
in Biblical times in Israel and in Egypt as well to celebrate the agricultural festivals with
boisterous merrymaking. The dancing of the daughters of Shiloh at the yearly festival
of the LORD was a popular celebration of this kind, and as such it took place in the vineyards
outside the city, without the participation of the priests. On the instructions of the other
Israelites and with their connivance, the Benjaminites lay in wait in the vineyards and when
the maidens came out for their dance they seized as many of them as they could and took
them as wives. In this way the inviolability of the oath was safeguarded, while at the same
time the continuity of the tribe of Benjamin was ensured. It was in fact from this tribe that
there came the first king in Israel, and with him the termination of the anarchic but colorful
period of the Judges.

THE BOOK OF RUTH

THIS CHARMING PASTORAL idyll is inserted in the English version of the Old Testament between the Books of Judges and First Samuel because it purports to relate events which occurred under the Judges. Its actual composition has been assigned to the time of Ezra and Nehemiah in the fifth century B.C. It is an eloquent plea on behalf of the wives of foreign extraction who were ready to join Israel in that later period. In striking contrast with the mainly warlike atmosphere of the Book of Judges, the conditions described here are so peaceful that a member of the tribe of Judah, a Bethlehemite called Elimelech, could in time of famine emigrate temporarily to Moab with his wife Naomi and his two sons; and his sons could take Moabite wives. One of these was Ruth the heroine of the book.

When the famine eventually passed, the males of this small family were no longer living. Naomi therefore decided to return to Judah, and said farewell to her two daughters-in-law. One of them was ready to stay with her own people; but the other, Ruth, decided to follow Naomi wherever she went: "Thy people shall be my people and thy God my God."

The two lonely women reached Bethlehem at the beginning of the barley harvest. In Palestine this falls in the month of Nisan (March-April) and is closely connected with the Passover festival and the offering of the sheaf (*omer*) (Lev. 23: 9-14). To this day at harvest time whole families of Arab peasants (*fellahin*) leave their houses and go out to the fields, where everyone works as best he can. The grain is either reaped with a sickle or pulled up by hand. The single ears are bound together in sheaves which are then carried to the thresh- ing floor. The head of the family, and sometimes the whole household, sleep on this floor till the end of the threshing, to guard the crop from theft. Although Naomi had inherited from her husband a piece of land which she was later able to sell (Ruth 4: 3), for the moment both she and Ruth were destitute. The Mosaic law had, however, provided for such

Harvest in Israel.

And they came to Beth-
em at the beginning of
ley harvest.
(RUTH 1: 22)

Woman gleaning after man, tomb
of Ramose, Thebes.

cases: the owner of a field was forbidden to glean the occasional ear left behind the reapers,
to harvest his field up to the corners, or to go back for a sheaf that had been forgotten in
the field (Lev. 19: 9, 23: 22); these had to be left for the poor and the "sojourner"—the
foreigner resident in Israel. Nevertheless, an unaccompanied and unprotected woman was
exposed to abuse and molestation by the farm-laborers; and, in any case, gleaning was
back-breaking work. Ruth was lucky enough to find a protector in the person of Boaz,
a rich landowner of Bethlehem, who happened to be a close relative of the deceased Elimelech. When he noticed Ruth, and heard her story, he was touched by her attachment to her
mother-in-law, for the sake of whom she had left her own people and country. He took the
Moabite woman under his protection and allowed her to glean behind his reapers, to take
refreshment and eat with them.

The work of gleaning behind the men was the woman's task in all the countries of the
ancient Orient. Thus in the tomb-painting of Ramese (thirteenth century B.C.) the wife is
shown gathering the fallen ears behind her reaping husband; she is collecting her gleanings
into a basket.

In the course of a whole day Ruth gleaned as much as an *ephah* (eight-tenths of a bushel)
of barley, enough for her own and Naomi's sustenance. In the evening she beat out what she
had gleaned. After arranging the grain in bundles, with all the ears pointing in one direction,
she struck each bundle repeatedly with a stick, thus separating the ears from their straw
stems. She then gathered up the grains, leaving the straw, which could be used for roofing
and plaited work.

With Boaz's permission, Ruth continued gleaning after his men till the end of the harvest.
Then one night, when Boaz was sleeping on his threshing-floor, Ruth, prompted by Naomi,
came to him and humbly asked him to "do the part of the next of kin" for her. Struck by her
devotion, Boaz promised to fulfill her request, if the immediate next of kin, who was
legally bound to marry Ruth "to restore the name of the dead to his inheritance", would
not. Then he sent her away with six measures of barley.

And Ruth the Moabitess said to Naomi, "Let me go to the field, and glean among the ears of grain after him in whose sight I shall find favor." And she said to her, "Go, my daughter."
(RUTH 2: 2)

Next day, in the city gate, the place of judgment, in the presence of ten of the city elders, Boaz called on the next of kin to buy the part of Elimelech's plot of land belonging to Naomi, in order to keep it in the family. This the next of kin was prepared to do. But when it was made clear to him that he would also have to redeem the part that Ruth inherited from her husband and marry Ruth, he waived his right in favor of Boaz, the next nearest relative. Thus Ruth became Boaz's wife.

The Book of Ruth concludes with a list of their descendants: their grandson was Jesse the father of David. A Moabite woman thus had the honor to be one of the direct ancestors of the greatest king of Israel.

THE FIRST BOOK OF SAMUEL

T HE LAST OF the Judges in Israel, accounted the first of the prophets, was Samuel, the son of Elkanah of Ephraim by his wife Hannah. Hannah had remained barren for a long time. One day, when she had almost despaired of bearing children, she prayed to the LORD at the sanctuary of Shiloh and vowed, if a child were given

So she gleaned in the field until evening; then she beat out what she had gleaned, and it was about an ephah of barley. (RUTH 2: 17)

Primitive method of beating out grain.

her, to make him a Nazirite and dedicate him to the service of God. When her prayer was granted she sent her son Samuel to minister at Shiloh. There he witnessed the corrupt practices of the sons of the priest Eli. While Samuel was at Shiloh the Israelites suffered a shattering defeat at the hands of their most dangerous enemies, the Philistines.

The Philistines (the name seems to signify "invaders") were a people of uncertain origin who arrived in Egypt as part of the great migratory movement of nations known as the "Sea Peoples" in the thirteenth century B.C. Their last stay before Egypt seems to have been in Crete (Caphtor). About the end of the century they landed in Egypt and fought several desperate battles by land and sea with the army of the Pharaoh Rameses III. Although unable to defeat the Egyptians, they showed themselves such doughty fighters that the Pharaoh was only too glad to allow them to establish themselves on the southwestern coast of Palestine, where they settled in five cities—Gaza, Ashkelon, Gath, Ekron, and Ashdod, the Philistine pentapolis. They may at first have served as mercenaries of Egypt, but, if so, they became independent with the decline of the Nineteenth Dynasty. They very soon adopted the language and religion of the Canaanites; at least we know nothing of any of their own gods apart from Marnas of Gaza, who was apparently originally a Cretan deity. However, the title of their rulers (*seren*, related to the Greek *tyrannos*) and some of their proper names, as recorded, still indicate their Aegean origin. The same is true of some of the objects associated with them, such as a characteristic type of pottery which seems to be derived from Mycenean ware. Although the Philistines were no more than a fighting aristocracy ruling over a subject population, they had one great military advantage over all their adversaries in Canaan. During their sojourn on the coasts of Asia Minor they seem to have learnt from the Hittites the secret of making iron weapons. Thus armed they were more than a match for both the Canaanites and the Israelites. The former were either subject to the Philistines or allied with them: Philistine garrisons were found as far east as Bethshan.

In the course of their far-ranging forays the Philistines clashed with the Israelites at Ebenezer. This battle, fought in the middle of the eleventh century B.C., was a desperate attempt on the part of the Israelites to check the Philistine advance into the central mountains of Palestine. The Philistines drew up their forces at Aphek (modern Rosh-ha-Ayin), a well-watered locality situated on the edge of the plain at the northeastern corner of the territory held by them. The position of the Israelite camp is uncertain; possibly it was located at Migdal Aphek, the hill-site facing Aphek in the mountains of Ephraim. In order to assure themselves of divine assistance, the Israelites brought with them the most sacred of their

Now Israel went out to battle against the Philistines . . .

(I SAM. 4: I)

Egyptians fighting Philistines and their allies, from relief of Rameses III, early twelfth century B.C., at Medinet Habu, Egypt.

cultic objects, the Ark of the Law. But the battle ended in the headlong rout of the Israelites; the Ark was captured. On hearing the news of the disaster, Eli the priest fell dead and Israel was left leaderless. The triumphant Philistines advanced on Shiloh which they burnt.

There was some consolation for Israel in the fact that the possession of the Ark did not profit the Philistines much. The wrath of the LORD at the sacrilege made itself felt in the devastation of the sanctuary of Dagon at Ashdod, to which the Ark was first brought, and then in a plague of mice. In the end the Philistines were only too glad to get rid of their trophy. They sent it away with all due ceremony in a new cart drawn by two milch cows, which made their way, unguided, straight to Beth Shemesh, the nearest Israelite city. From there the Ark was taken to Kirjathjearim, where it remained until the days of David.

Apart from this fortunate recovery of the Ark, the situation of the Israelites was gloomy enough. The Philistines had occupied the whole of the territory of Benjamin and lorded it over the central mountains. Philistine warriors became a familiar sight to their Israelite subjects. We too know their appearance, both from the Egyptian representations found at Medinet Habu and from the man-shaped clay coffins discovered at Bethshan and elsewhere which, with their head-pieces of horizontal bands with a row of circular bosses (and occasionally with additional vertical bands) are thought to represent the typical feathered

. . . and the Philistines encamped at Aphek.

(I SAM. 4: I)

View of Migdal Aphek, Israel.

So they sent and gathered together all the lords of the Philistines. . . .

(1 SAM. 5: 8)

Sarcophagus coffin-covers from Beth-shan, representing Philistine warriors.

head-dress of the Philistines. Differences in the ornamentation of these head-dresses are supposed to indicate either military rank or clan affiliation.

The Philistines took good care that there should be no Israelite smiths who knew how to forge iron, especially the harder kind of wrought iron obtained by the carbonization of the metal. They supplied the Israelites with finished iron implements, but jealously guarded the secrets of the working of the metal and the methods by which the implements were made and sharpened. The Israelite peasants, who as we know from archaeological finds were using iron tools at that time, thus remained dependent on the Philistine smiths. These latter charged them outrageous prices for any sharpening or repairing.

KING SAUL

IN THESE DIRE straits the Israelites decided to sink their tribal differences and to accept the rule of a king having permanent authority over them, who would be able to bring the full force of the nation (and not only that of some scattered tribes) to bear on the invader. As one of the great strongholds of the Philistines was Gibeah in Benjamin, it was only fitting that the leader of the united nation should come from this tribe. Samuel indeed raised a warning voice against the establishment of the monarchy, taking his stand on the old argument—which Gideon too had advanced

—that only the LORD should rule over Israel. An earthly monarch would conscript his subjects for military service and the manufacture of arms; would set men and women to forced labor on the royal estates and in the palace; would exact a tax of one-tenth of all agricultural produce, and whenever he pleased; would expropriate the individual's property for the benefit of those in authority.

Two of the activities described in this list—the manufacture of arms in royal workshops, and the preparation of perfumes—are found represented in Egyptian paintings and reliefs. Some of these show the making of shields, the finishing of chariot wheels, and the cutting of quivers, and the covering of them with strips of leather. On others the manufacture of bows and arrows is depicted. There are also representations of women gathering lotus-flowers and bringing them in baskets to a press, where other women are squeezing out juices of the flowers into a large jar.

Samuel's warnings were, however, in vain; present necessity prevailed over future fears, and the elders demanded a sovereign ruler to govern them "like all the nations". The man

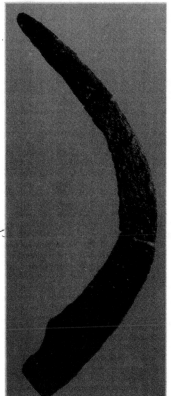

chosen, Saul the son of Kish, was not unworthy of the task: "and there was not among the children of Israel a goodlier person than he; from his shoulders and upward he was higher than any of the people". Sent by his father to recover some lost asses, he found a kingdom instead. When he approached Samuel to ask for his guidance, he was recognized by the seer as the LORD's chosen and anointed by him in secret. Public proclamation was delayed till the new leader could prove himself.

The first opportunity for this presented itself in the east and not against the main enemy, the Philistines. When the city of Jabesh Gilead was besieged by Nahash king of Ammon, Saul mustered an army and came to its rescue, all the Israelite tribes rallying to his call. His success, and the rout of the Ammonites, showed that the people were now ready to become a united nation. After this victory Saul was proclaimed king at

Now there was no smith to be found throughout all the land of Israel; for the Philistines said, "Lest the Hebrews make themselves swords or spears"; but every one of the Israelites went down to the Philistines to sharpen his ploughshare, his mattock, his axe . . . and the charge was a pim for the ploughshares and for the mattocks. . . . (I SAM. 13 : 19–21)

Iron sickle from Tell Jemmeh. Eleventh or tenth century B.C. (Palestine Archaeological Museum)

And Samuel hewed Agag in pieces before the LORD in Gilgal. (I SAM. 15: 33)

Ceremonial axe of the Pharaoh Ahmose
(sixteenth century B.C.), from Thebes.

Gilgal and immediately proceeded to the greater task, that of beating back the Philistines. For this purpose resistance was organized in Benjamin, while at the same time peace was made with the Canaanites ("Amorites" of I Sam. 7: 14); both nations now had a common enemy in their new overlords.

The center of Philistine power in Benjamin was at Gibeah (Jeba), about four miles northeast of the Gibeah of Saul. To check their further advance, Saul disposed his forces at three key-points in the mountains: at Bethel and Michmash under his own command, and at Gibeah of Benjamin under the command of his son, Jonathan. Jonathan attacked first and succeeded in routing the Philistine garrisons at Gibeah. The Philistines reacted by sending out punitive expeditions ("the raiders") against Michmash, while Saul entrenched himself at Gibeah of Benjamin with six hundred men. From there Jonathan made a daring sally against the Philistine camp at Michmash, accompanied only by his armorbearer who "killed after him".

The armor-bearer performed an indispensable function in ancient warfare, following after his lord with the various weapons used by the latter in battle: the bow for long-range shooting, the javelin for fighting at medium range, and the sword and dagger for hand-to-hand combat. Since all these could not be carried by the warrior himself, the principal fighters were accompanied by armor-bearers who handed them the weapon required at the particular moment. The armor-bearer was chosen for his fidelity and trustworthiness; he was not supposed to move from his master's side even in the greatest danger, and often perished with him, as Saul's armor-bearer did on Mount Golboa. On one of the reliefs from Carchemish an armor-bearer is shown, carrying a javelin in his right and a club in his left with a sword buckled to his waist.

Taking advantage of the confusion caused in the enemy's camp by Jonathan's daring assault, Saul suddenly attacked and defeated the main body of Philistines, which was still at Michmash and consisted partly of Hebrew mercenaries. These came over to Saul during the battle and joined his troops in the pursuit of the fleeing Philistines westwards, past Aijalon, and down into the coastal plain. With this great victory the central mountains were freed from the invader, who however still remained powerful in the lowlands.

After the defeat of the Philistines, Saul consolidated the southern border of Israel, incidentally establishing his hold on the tribe of Judah in this region. The constantly troublesome, fast-moving desert rovers, the Amalekites, were caught in an ambush and pursued to the borders of Egypt, but the nomad Kenites, who were bound to Israel by many ties of friendship, were allowed to depart in peace.

After this victory and the capture of the Amalekite king, Agag, a dispute broke out between Saul and Samuel. The prophet, who insisted on applying the full rigor of the old command to destroy Amalek utterly (Deut. 25 : 17–19), was shocked by the king's leniency and solemnly executed Agag with his own hands at Gilgal. The ceremonial execution of a defeated enemy as a symbol of his utter defeat was a regular practice in the ancient East. One such scene is represented on the battle-axe of the Pharaoh Ahmose (sixteenth century B.C.), where Ahmose is seen about to despatch with his sword an enemy whom he is grasping by the hair.

DAVID AND GOLIATH

THE BREACH BETWEEN Samuel and Saul was final. By divine command the aged seer secretly anointed another to reign over Israel in Saul's place. God's new choice was David the son of Jesse, the youngest of a large family from Bethlehem in Judah, and a shepherd by occupation.

Whereas Saul had been anointed from a "vial" of oil, David received the unction from a horn. The horns of animals were sometimes used in antiquity as receptacles for liquids. Usually these were ram's horns, but occasionally a container of this kind has been found made from a whole elephant's tusk, often adorned with gold bands, like the one excavated at Megiddo which dates to the Late Bronze Age. Its wide end was sealed off, and the pointed end pierced with a hole; for anointing it was held with the pointed end downwards so that the oil dripped through the hole.

Soon David was raised from the lowly task of tending his father's sheep to a higher sphere of activity. Saul, who had always been inclined to states of spiritual exaltation, as is attested

Then Samuel took the horn of oil and anointed him. . . .
(1 SAM. 16: 13)

Megiddo horn of ivory and gold. (Palestine Archaeological Museum)

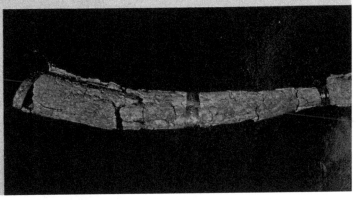

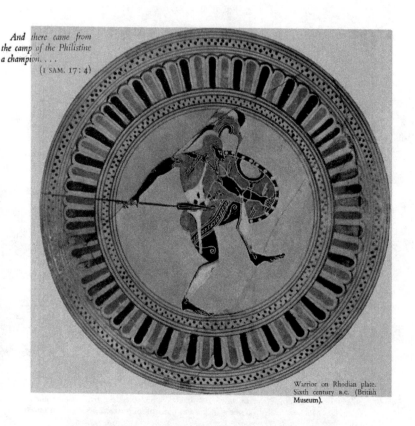

Warrior on Rhodian plate.
Sixth century B.C. (British
Museum).

by two stories of his joining a band of prophets and sharing in their prophetic ecstasy
(I Sam. 10 and 19), now veered to the other extreme and began to suffer from violent attacks
of melancholia. Although devoid of a scientific understanding of human psychology, the
ancients had gained a rough and ready empirical notion of how to combat the symptoms of
such mental depressions. One of the means most favored by them was music. Now it
happened that, like many other shepherds of antiquity, David was a highly skilled musician.
He was accordingly chosen to soothe Saul's spirit with the strains of his instrument. On a jar
of the eleventh century B.C., the very period now under discussion, we find the representation of a man holding a lyre and playing and singing while he walks among a group of
animals, just as David must have walked and played among his flocks.

Intermittent clashes with the Philistines continued throughout Saul's reign, and eventually
there was another full-scale encounter in the Valley of Elah. This valley lies in the foothills

of the Judaean mountains, on the direct road from the Philistine cities into Judah. To check the progress of the invaders, Saul encamped with his forces directly across the Philistine's line of advance, opposite their battle-front from Azekah to Soco.

For a time nothing happened. Then in the manner of the Homeric Greeks to whom they were in some ways akin, the Philistines issued a challenge to single combat between the champions of the warring sides. Such single combat usually preceded and sometimes even decided the battle. The Philistine champion who challenged Israel was a giant, Goliath of Gath. The Biblical text describes in detail his great size and formidable equipment. His protective armor—helmet, breast-plate, shield and greaves—was all made of bronze, while his offensive weapons were of iron. His spear is compared to a weaver's beam, because it had a leather loop like the loops of cord tied to the former. By means of this loop the spear could be thrown to a great distance. A painting on a Rhodian plate (end of the sixth century B.C.) shows a warrior armed very much as Goliath was. His whole body is tensed for throwing the javelin, with his fingers inserted in its looped thong. The poorly armed Israelites shrank back in terror from this towering, bronze-clad giant with his iron-tipped spear.

This was the situation when David came to the Israelite camp from his home in Bethlehem, bringing food for his three older brothers who were serving in Saul's army, and also a special gift of some cheeses for their superior officer. Undaunted by the blood-curdling threats and contemptuous taunts of the Philistine colossus, David took up the challenge. He refused to let himself be encumbered with whatever armor and weapons could be supplied by Saul; for obviously he could not hope to defeat, in a straight fight, an opponent of so much greater size and strength and one so much better trained for single combat. Instead he decided to attack Goliath with the arms with which he was familiar: a sling and five smooth stones taken from the nearby brook. For fighting at short range the sling was a highly effective weapon. It consisted of a sling-strap made of leather or cloth, two thongs to impart momentum to the strap, and a missile of stone or lead. Slingers formed an integral part of ancient armies and are frequently

And David put his hand in his bag and took out a stone and slung it. . . . (I SAM. 17:49)

Gozan relief showing slinger. Tenth or ninth century B.C. (British Museum)

David departed from there and escaped to the cave
of Adullam. . . .   (1 SAM. 22: 1)

Hills and caves in the Adullam region.

represented on reliefs, such as one from Tell Halaf (Gozan) which is contemporary with
David (tenth or ninth century B.C.). Taking aim, David struck the oncoming Goliath square
on his unprotected forehead, either killing or stunning him, and then beheaded the giant
with the latter's own sword. At the sight of their hero's severed head, panic seized the
Philistines and they fled in disorder to their cities. David's renown among the Israelites now
surpassed even that of the king himself.

DAVID HIDES FROM SAUL

DAVID RETURNED TO Saul's court a famous national hero. There he became
linked in an undying friendship to Jonathan, Saul's son, and allied to the
royal family by his marriage to Michal, Saul's daughter. The king himself, however, was
now so morbidly suspicious of his son-in-law that he sought by various means to do away
with him. Once in a mad fit he tried to kill him by flinging a javelin at him. On another
occasion, when Saul sent his servants to assassinate him, David was able to escape into hiding
thanks to a timely warning from Michal, his wife, and with her assistance. Jonathan loyally
took up his friend's cause, but thereby only enraged Saul the more. David remained in
hiding near the court, waiting for a secret meeting with Jonathan; but seeing that his father's
hatred for David was now implacable, Jonathan gave the fugitive a prearranged signal to
make good his escape.

Many and varied were the wanderings of David, now a hunted exile. First he went to the
priests at Nob, whom he persuaded to give him the hallowed shewbread as food and

Goliath's sword as his personal armament. Then he had to pass over to his inveterate foes, the Philistines, taking refuge with Achish king of Gath. There, suspected by those whom he had defeated in so many battles, he had for a time to feign madness to save his life.

Escaping again to Judah, he hid in one of the great caves in the mountains, near the city of Adullam. Here he gathered round him a band of four hundred outlaws, debtors, and other malcontents, whom he organized into a fighting troop with which he made audacious sorties into the surrounding districts. The region of Adullam was very well situated as a base for raids of this kind. First, it was strategically placed, being close to the border between Philistia and Judah and dominating the Valley of Elah; and then its position in the hills made it difficult of access and therefore a safe refuge. Moreover, all round it lay good agricultural land, with fields for crop-growing in the valley and expanses of pasture on the lower slopes of the hills. The outlaw band could thus find there both food and security, or at least be sure of a timely warning of any danger threatening them.

Saul's anger at the support given David by some of his subjects knew no bounds, and he took a terrible revenge on the priests of Nob, who had helped the fugitive. Later when David entered the town of Keilah, in the close neighborhood of Adullam, to provide armed support for the inhabitants who were hard-pressed by the Philistines, Saul thought that he had trapped him there; but the wily outlaw slipped out of the town in time and escaped into the wilderness of Ziph, part of the great Judaean desert. This area, which stretched from the central watershed to the Dead Sea, is geologically different from the rest of the country. The mountains here are mainly composed of soft whitish chalk and their contours are therefore

Go, make yet more sure; know and see the place where
his haunt is, and who has seen him there. . . . See therefore,
and take note of all the lurking places where he hides. . . .

(I SAM. 23 : 22–23)

View of the desert of Judah where David was hiding from Saul.

But take now the spear that is at his head, and the jar of water, and let us go.   (I SAM. 26: 11)

Water flask, found at Gezer, and spearhead. Early Iron Age. (Clark Collection, Y.M.C.A., Jerusalem)

smooth and rounded. They are scored by many valleys which, as they approach the Dead Sea, become deep gorges with craggy sides. In these crags there are numerous caves which afford excellent hiding-places. The rainfall is very scanty, and there is almost no vegetation. Apart from the little rain that collects in a few natural cisterns there is no water to sustain large bodies of troops; neither are there any roads. For these reasons, a small, highly mobile band like David's could hope, in this rocky waste, to evade a larger army by keeping constantly on the move. Saul exhausted his forces in a futile pursuit of David from Ziph to Maon and from Maon to Engedi.

From time to time, when the pursuit slackened, David was able to approach settled areas again and to replenish his supplies. On one such occasion his demand for food was met with a churlish refusal by a rich landowner called Nabal, who lived at Carmel in Judah; however, Abigail, Nabal's clever wife, supplied David in secret and mollified his anger. When later Nabal died, David married Abigail, thus strengthening his hold on the Calebite area southwest of Hebron.

In the course of their marches and countermarches Saul and David were often very close to each other; on two occasions at least David could have taken Saul's life but refrained from doing so. Once he caught Saul sleeping in the wilderness. Leaving the king unmolested, David took away the spear and water-bottle that were lying beside him to show that he had had Saul in his power, but had not touched him. The ancient water-jar, an essential article of equipment for anyone marching through the desert, was usually a clay vessel with a flattened body and two small pierced handles through which a cord could be passed; it could thus be easily slung over the shoulder and carried at the side. Water-jars of this type have been found in most excavated sites in Israel. The spear was the standard weapon of the ancient hunter or warrior; it had a bronze or iron head, fastened to a wooden shaft by a spirally wound ribbon or metal.

THE BATTLE OF GILBOA

ULTIMATELY SAUL'S PRESSURE became too harassing for David and he had again to take refuge with the Philistines at Gath. As a dependant of the king of this city he settled at Ziklag, from where he could effectively protect the whole of southern Judah against the inroads of the Amalekites. The booty taken on these punitive raids he distributed among the elders of the cities in the Negeb, thus strengthening his ties with Judah and gaining many friends.

Though the Philistines now accepted David as an ally they were still somewhat suspicious of him, and this proved fortunate. For when the Philistine army and its allies mustered at Aphek, prior to the fateful engagement with Saul in the Valley of Esdraelon, David was sent home with his troops as unreliable and was thus spared the invidious necessity of having to fight against his own people.

Saul's last battle with the Philistines was fought on the slopes of Mount Gilboa. Baffled

*Now the Philistines gathered all their forces at
Aphek; and the Israelites were encamped by the
fountain which is in Jezreel.* (I SAM. 29: 1)

View of the Jezreel valley.

They put his armor in the temple of Ashtaroth; and they fastened his body to the wall of Beth-Shan. (I SAM. 31: 10)

Heads and bodies of defeated enemies exposed on the walls of Kulisi, from bronze reliefs on the Balawat palace gates. Ninth century B.C. (British Museum)

in their attempts to penetrate into the Mountains of Ephraim and Judah, the Philistines decided to thrust through the flat expanse of the Valley of Esdraelon (Jezreel), where their superior armament would give them a decisive advantage. The strong-points of Megiddo and Bethshan, which were at that time not yet in Israelite hands, would serve them as bases. By advancing into the valley they would cut off the northern tribes from those of the center and the south, and possibly be able to turn the fastnesses of the Ephraim mountains from the north.

To meet this new threat, Saul drew up his army on the slopes of Mount Gilboa, hoping thereby to bar the road into the heart of Israelite territory. But he had now lost his earlier confidence and his spirit was troubled by bitter forebodings; sensing that the divine spirit had departed from him, he had recourse to sorcery, turning in his desperation to a witch of En-Dor, who at his behest conjured up the spirit of the recently dead Samuel. Yet even necromancy gave no hope. The apparition foretold disaster: "To-morrow you and your sons shall be with me."

The outcome of the battle was as predicted. Saul and the Israelites were utterly defeated; Saul's sons fell on the field and the king himself committed suicide to avoid capture. Their bodies were impaled on the walls of Bethshan, a barbarous custom widely practiced by the Assyrians, as is shown by the reliefs on the palace gate of Shalmaneser III, found at Balawat, depicting what this monarch did to the conquered inhabitants of the city of Kulisi on the Upper Tigris in 852 B.C. However, the men of Jabesh Gilead, whom Saul had saved at the beginning of his reign, showed their reverence for his memory by risking their lives to take down the impaled bodies and give them proper burial.

As the Philistine victory had rendered the whole of Israelite territory west of the Jordan unsafe, Abner the son of Ner, the commander-in-chief of the remnants of the army, took Saul's surviving son Ishbaal (called Ishbosheth in the Book of Samuel, a name in which the hated word "baal" has been replaced by one meaning "shame"), and withdrew across the Jordan, setting up a new capital at Mahanaim in Gilead.

116

THE SECOND BOOK
OF SAMUEL

THE WARS OF DAVID

O N HEARING OF the death of Saul, who had raised him to greatness, and of
Jonathan, his dearest friend, David passionately lamented their end in a
famous elegy, one of the finest specimens of early Hebrew poetry. For the moment, however,
he could do nothing to avenge them; his own position first needed consolidation. In the
preceding years he had assured himself of the support of the people of his own tribe, Judah,
by sending gifts to its cities, and by judicious marriages (such as that with Abigail, which
gained him the backing of the Calebite clan). Now, with the house of Saul powerless to
intervene in Judah, the moment had come to take full advantage of this favorable situation.
David accordingly went to Hebron and was there anointed king. For the next seven years
Israel was divided, part owing allegiance to Saul's son Ishbaal, and part to David.

When the Philistine danger had receded, the army of Ishbaal returned from Mahanaim
to Gibeon. One of the many encounters during this period of civil strife, in which "David
grew stronger and stronger, while the house of Saul grew weaker and weaker" (2 Sam. 3:1),
took place at the great rock-cut pool in this old Canaanite city. The recently excavated great

*And Joab the son of Zeruiah,
and the servants of David, went
out and met them at the pool of
Gibeon; and they sat down, the
one on the one side of the pool,
and the other on the other side
of the pool.*   (2 SAM. 2: 13)

View of the recently excavated rock-cut pool at el-Jib.

pool of Gibeon is 36 feet in diameter, with spiral flights of 42 steps descending 52 feet to the bottom of the pool, whence another spiral stairway is tunneled down a further 45 feet to the water level. The whole installation is one of the most magnificent examples of Canaanite rock-cutting technique.

When the two armies, Ishbaal's captained by Abner, and David's led by Joab the son of Zeruiah, met at the pool, there was a series of single combats between the "young men" (Hebrew *ne'arim*, which in the Bible, as in Canaanite, denotes vigorous, well-trained warriors) who were the champions of the respective sides. The "play" of the young men consisted of a duel to the death, "and each caught his opponent by the head and thrust his sword in his opponent's side"—as illustrated on a relief from the time of David, found at Gozan (Tell Halaf in Syria). There were twelve such combatants on each side. In their particular case, the outcome of the battle was not decided by the single fights—"they fell down together"—and a general engagement developed with twenty killed on Joab's side and three hundred and sixty on Abner's. Asahel, Joab's brother, was among those slain. In the end Abner and his troops retreated to Mahanaim again.

After that, Abner fell out with his king and came over to David; hardly had he done so, however, when he was treacherously assassinated by Joab to avenge the death of his brother. To free himself from any suspicion of complicity in Joab's crime, David decreed a public mourning for Abner and himself uttered an elegy over the dead man. The killing of Abner had shown that David was still not strong enough to impose law and order in his kingdom.

With the gifted commander of his army gone over to the enemy, Ishbaal's cause was virtually lost. Even before, he had tried to appease David by returning him Michal, Saul's daughter and David's wife, whom her father had married to another man while David was a fugitive. David was interested in having her as proof of the legitimacy of his claim to inherit Saul's kingdom. Soon after Abner's death, Ishbaal was murdered by two of his captains and David was acknowledged king by all the tribes of Israel.

And Abner said to Joab, "Let the young men arise and play before us. . . ." (2 SAM. 2: 14)

Combat of two warriors on Gozan relief. Tenth or ninth century B.C. (Berlin Museum)

Michal the daughter of Saul looked out of the window. . . .

(2 SAM. 6: 16)

Ivory plaque from Calah, Assyria. Ninth or eighth century B.C.

David could now legitimately regard himself as the "shepherd of all Israel", since his rule was based on a covenant between the king and his people, which was ultimately transformed into a covenant between the king and God. The first practical problem confronting David, however, was to find a capital outside the territory of any of the tribes of Israel, so as to avoid arousing strong feelings of jealousy still latent between the various sections of the nation.

An opportunity soon presented itself of securing such a capital and at the same time of eliminating one of the foreign enclaves still separating the various areas of the country under Israelite control. The Jebusites in Jerusalem had not only kept their independence, but since the arrival of the Philistines they had allied themselves with the latter and thus secured a strongpoint for Israel's main enemy in the heart of the Israelite mountains. Now David suddenly attacked them with a small band of his own personal followers. By thus not being beholden to any tribe for the conquest of Jerusalem, he obtained the city as his own and his descendants' private property, although in terms of the original tribal allocation it lay—in theory at least—within the territory of Benjamin.

The description of the capture of Jerusalem in the Bible is somewhat obscure. Mention is made of an assault up a "gutter" (*sinnor* in Hebrew), possibly a reference to the tunnel by which, in time of siege, the Jebusites obtained water from the spring Gihon situated outside their walls, to the east, in the side of the Kidron valley. By means of a stepped tunnel beginning inside their city they could reach a vertical shaft cut in the rock. Through it water was drawn up by buckets from a channel connected with the spring by a slightly sloping conduit. Once the Jebusites' only source of water had been cut off, their strong walls were no longer of any avail and they had to capitulate. David spared the lives of the inhabitants but transformed the formerly Jebusite city into a fortress called Zion and established his capital on its neutral ground.

On hearing that their allies, the Jebusites, had been conquered, the Philistines made two

119

And the Aramaeans fled before Israel; and David slew of the Aramaeans the men of seven hundred chariots. . . .

(2 SAM. 10: 18)

Relief from Gozan.
(Aleppo Museum)

attempts to re-establish their authority by force of arms. They were soundly beaten both times: once at Baal Perazim in the Rephaim valley, southwest of Jerusalem; and again at Beth-Horon, when they attempted to attack the capital from the north. These two defeats decided the century-old struggle between Israel and the Philistines. Once united, the vigorous Israelite nation was more than a match for the Philistine warrior caste, who had by then largely adopted Canaanite ways and lost their original military superiority. David at first adopted guerrilla tactics but soon he could face the Philistines in the open field and even invade their territory. Defeating them again at Gath or Lachish, he forced them to accept Israelite suzerainty. As his vassals they supplied him with mercenary troops, the Cherethites and Pelethites. All the Sharon north of the Yarkon river now came under David's control and Israel for the first time gained access to the sea. A harbor and store-houses were established at Tell Qasile on the north bank of the Yarkon.

David's next step was to transfer the sacred national emblem, the Ark, from its place at Kiriath-jearim to Jerusalem. Although he was not permitted to build a permanent temple, the temporary tent that he erected to house the Ark was enough to make Jerusalem the religious, no less than the political, capital of the nation. The priests now became royal officials, and the king himself took on the sacral character of the former kings of Jerusalem, one of whom, Melchizedek, is expressly described in Genesis 14 as a priest of God Most High.

From then onwards David went from strength to strength. As there was no further trouble from the Philistine quarter, he could turn all his energies against the other enemies of Israel. The international situation was most favorable to Israelite expansion. Egypt and Assyria were both paralyzed by internal troubles, and in the area between the Euphrates and the Nile there was no military force which could match David's army.

His first conquests brought about the elimination of the remaining foreign enclaves in the Promised Land. The cities of the Valley of Esdraelon, chief among them Megiddo and Bethshan, were finally subdued. Turning farther north, David allied himself with the Phoenicians and attacked the Ammonites and the Aramaeans. Joining forces as usual with the enemies of his enemies, he concluded an alliance with Hamath, whose king Toi (Tou) was, like

120

David, at war with Hadadezer, king of Aram Zobah. After David's victory over Hadadezer, Toi sent him a congratulatory mission headed by his son Joram (perhaps an acknowledgment of David's superior status), and bearing very valuable articles of silver, gold, and bronze as a gift. Fragments of silver plate, apparently from the eighth century B.C., skillfully engraved with braided borders and griffins, show how well the Syrian silversmiths of that time knew their trade.

Strengthened by his new alliances, David next turned against the Ammonites, who had summoned the Aramaeans to their aid. In response to this call, a strong force of Aramaean chariots was sent southwards. In a great battle at Medeba David defeated this joint force. In a second encounter at Helam (in northern Trans-Jordan) seven hundred of the enemy's chariots were destroyed. The appearance of this usually decisive war-vehicle can be studied on reliefs from Gozan dating to the ninth century B.C. The chariots were drawn by two horses, one on either side of a shaft attached to the bottom of the chariot. A twined cord connected the upper part of the chariot with the yoke, thus lessening the danger of the chariot being severed from the shaft; it also prevented the reins from becoming entangled when held loosely. Each chariot was manned by two warriors: the charioteer who is shown holding a whip, and a bowman whose quiver can be seen fastened to the side of the vehicle.

The defeat of their best troops forced the Aramaeans to submit to David. He then proceeded to deal with their allies, the Ammonites. Their capital, Rabbath Ammon, was actually captured by Joab, but he diplomatically waited for the king to complete the conquest. Entering the conquered city, David took possession of the crown worn by "their king" (Hebrew *malkam*). As this weighed more than a talent of gold, i.e. over 80 pounds, it is inconceivable that it should really have been worn by any human being. It has therefore been suggested that the correct reading is *Milkom*, the god of the Ammonites. The meaning would then

And he took the crown of their king from his head; the weight of it was a talent of gold, and in it was a precious stone; and it was placed on David's head. . . .
(2 SAM. 12 : 13)

Limestone head from Amman, Early Iron Age. (Amman Museum)

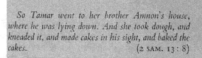

So Tamar went to her brother Amnon's house, where he was lying down. And she took dough, and kneaded it, and made cakes in his sight, and baked the cakes.   (2 SAM. 13 : 8)

Wooden model of the house of an Egyptian farm-steward from the Twelfth Dynasty. Twentieth and nineteenth century B.C.

be that David took the crown off the head of the idol and set the jewel which it contained in his crown. Reproduced on the previous page a limestone head found at Amman, and presumably representing an Ammonite god or king bears the atef crown worn by the god Osiris and by the king of Egypt. The head is from the Early Iron Age and may convey some idea of the shape of the crown captured by David.

Finally David made himself master of Edom and the copper mines of the Arabah. These last conquests gave Israel access to the Red Sea at Elath and made possible the country's integration into the network of the international trade routes of the period. But these commercial possibilities were not fully exploited in David's time. His next task was administrative. First the Canaanites were incorporated into the nation as "sojourners" (*gerim*) living with the Israelites. Then an elaborate bureaucratic machine was set up, based partly on the experience of the court scribes of Jebusite Jerusalem and on Egyptian models. In the conquered nations governors were appointed who acted as the king's representatives. So immense was the growth of the royal estates, partly by the confiscation of the property of the defeated rulers, that special officers were put in charge of the king's many and varied possessions: his treasure in the capital, his storehouses outside Jerusalem, his field laborers, his vineyards, his wine-cellars, his olives and sycamores, his oil-cellars, his herds in the Sharon, his herds in the valleys, his camels, his asses, and his flocks. The king was advised by a council of military and civil officials and princes. In the provinces the Levites now assumed the functions of royal officials and served as judges, teachers, and tax-collectors.

AMNON AND TAMAR

THE OUTWARD SPLENDORS of the Davidic court and state were marred by internal dissensions among the princes born of the king's various wives and by the general corruption of morals following the sudden and unexpected transition from a tribal to a centralized society. David himself was not blameless in this respect; desiring Bathsheba, the wife of Uriah the Hittite, he had the husband sent to his death on a suicidal military mission and married the widow.

The royal princes followed their father's example: when Amnon, one of David's sons, fell in love with his half-sister, Tamar, he resorted to an ignoble trick to lure her into his house. Pretending to be sick he asked that she be sent to make some cakes for him. David acceded to his request because, unlike ordinary meals, a sick man's repast had to be prepared for him by specially trained women. To make the cakes desired by Amnon, Tamar first had to knead and shape the dough in Amnon's sight; this done, she then baked the cakes, apparently outside the room in the open air. An Egyptian model found in a tomb of the Twelfth Dynasty (twentieth and nineteenth centuries B.C.) depicts a similar scene. It shows a house with the owner, a farm-steward, sitting in the upper storey, while a woman is kneading dough on a kind of bench in the lower court.

When Tamar finally brought the cakes to Amnon, he ravished her; and then, when he had satisfied his lust, his love turned to hatred and he thrust her away. Tamar went into mourning; after sprinkling her hair with ashes and rending the royal garment which she wore, she placed her hand on her head and wept loudly and bitterly. Such scenes of female mourning are often found in Egyptian tomb-paintings. An example is the picture of the widow of Nebamon at Thebes (fourteenth century B.C.); she is shown weeping with her hair in disarray, sprinkling ashes on her head and touching the feet of a mummy.

Amnon soon paid the penalty for his evil deed. Absàlom, Tamar's brother,

And Tamar put ashes on her head, and rent the long-sleeved robe which she wore; and she laid her hand on her head, and went away, crying aloud as she went. (2 SAM. 13 : 19)

Reproduction of a painting from the tomb of Ipuki and Nebamon at Thebes. Fourteenth century B.C.

Absalom got himself a chariot and horses, and fifty men to run before him. (2 SAM. 15: 1)

Detail from a painting from Tell el-Amarna.

avenged his sister by having Amnon killed by his servants at a sheep-shearing festivity. After several years David forgave Absalom and he was able to return to the court.

ABSALOM'S REVOLT

DAVID'S LAST YEARS were troubled by revolts; in the general feeling of imminent change contenders for the crown tried to seize power while the old, and now enfeebled king, was still alive. The most serious of these attempts was that made by David's favorite son, Absalom. This rising was carefully planned and had the support of a group of royal counsellors and officers. By flattery and promises Absalom succeeded in gaining a large number of adherents among the people. He also made a great impression by displays of royal pomp. Thus he arrogated to himself one of the prerogatives of royalty by driving in a chariot preceded by runners. Such runners had a twofold function: to display the exalted rank of the man who rode in the chariot; and to clear a way through the narrow and thronged streets of an oriental town. The higher the rank of the owner of the chariot, the greater the number of the runners who preceded it: Absalom ostentatiously chose the maximum of fifty. Runners in front of royal chariots are depicted in a painting from el-Amarna, showing Nefertiti, the famous wife of Akhenaton (fourteenth century B.C.), on an outing with her daughters and retinue.

With many of the courtiers and most of the people adhering to Absalom, David was left no choice but flight. Accompanied by a few faithful supporters he left Jerusalem by the

Kidron valley and went eastwards, crossing the Jordan and taking up his abode in Ishbaal's old capital, Mahanaim. Absalom seized power, with the cunning Ahithophel as his chief adviser; but one of David's friends, Hushai, remained at court and, while counter-plotting, secretly advised David of what was happening in Jerusalem. In his flight, David was assisted by the servant of Mephibaal (Mephibosheth), Saul's grandson, and cursed by one Shimei, another of the members of Saul's family.

While David was gathering his forces at Mahanaim, Absalom's ministers were divided in their counsel. Ahithophel was for marching against David at once, but Hushai played for time to enable David to grow stronger. When Ahithophel's advice was rejected, he committed suicide.

At last Absalom moved against David and the two armies joined battle in Gilead. The decisive engagement took place in wooded terrain where fighting was extremely difficult. In such conditions it was easy to surprise an enemy at close quarters, and the loose boulders amongst which the trees and bushes grew made a treacherous, slippery footing for soldiers advancing at the run. Assyrian reliefs from the palace of Sennacherib at Nineveh depict this type of warfare. The Assyrian soldiers are seen advancing with the help of sticks across wooded and rocky ground; the trees separate them from each other and the battle becomes a series of hand-to-hand single combats. In such terrain David's experienced veterans were better fighters than Absalom's levies. When the latter were put to flight, they had great difficulty in extricating themselves from the tangled woodland: "and the forest devoured

The battle spread over the face of all the country; and the forest devoured more people that day than the sword.
(2 SAM. 18: 8)

Relief from the palace of
Sennacherib at Nineveh.

more people that day than the sword". Absalom himself was caught by his head in the branches of an oak, while attempting to escape on a mule, and left hanging in the air. While still swinging there helpless, he was killed by the ferocious Joab, against David's express orders.

David mourned bitterly over his dead son, who was brought to burial in the monument which he had built himself in the Lower Kidron valley (also called the "King's Valley" because it had a royal garden watered from the Gihon Pool). It was customary for rulers in antiquity, especially the Egyptian Pharaohs, to construct their tombs in their own lifetime, since such edifices took many years to build. The "pillar" erected by Absalom was probably some kind of obelisk to mark the site of the nearby tomb. Popular tradition has identified "Absalom's Tomb" with a prominent monument standing in the Kidron valley and consisting of a rock-cut vault, containing the tombs, and a masonry superstructure.

Now Absalom in his lifetime had taken and set up for himself the pillar which is in the King's Valley . . . and it is called Absalom's monument to this day. (2 SAM. 18: 18)

The edifice in the Kidron valley which by popular tradition is named "Absalom's Tomb".

These are the names of the mighty men whom David had . . .

(2 SAM. 23 : 8)

Fragment of pottery from Megiddo showing armed warriors. Second millennium B.C.

In actual fact this is one of the most magnificent tombs of the Second Temple period, dating to the first century B.C., and hence nearly a thousand years later than Absalom. After crushing Absalom's revolt, David returned to Jerusalem and rewarded those of his subjects who had remained loyal to him. His own tribe, Judah, came to meet him at the Jordan, and this attempt to claim for themselves a privileged position made bad blood between Judah and the rest of Israel. Soon another revolt flared up, this time in Benjamin, led by one Sheba the son of Bichri. Sheba fled to Abel-beth-maachah and was besieged by Joab, until the people of the city were persuaded by a wise woman in their midst to kill Sheba and surrender.

It is also recorded that David ordered a census of Israel. The territory ruled by him and inhabited by his people—apart from the peripheral districts subject to him—now stretched from Aroer on the Arnon and Gilead in the east to Tyre in the north and down to Beersheba in the south. Traditionally connected with the census was the requisition of the threshing floor of Araunah, the Jebusite, who made it over to David. Later tradition (cf. 2 Chron. 3, 1) regarded this as the site of the future Temple.

The history of the kingdoms is found in two works. One of these, the Books of Kings, continues the narrative of the Books of Samuel. The other, composed much later, is found in the Books of Chronicles, and these are continued in Ezra and Nehemiah. In fact, the first Book of Chronicles covers in outline the period from Adam to David, and then deals with David's reign, while the second Book of Chronicles gives the history of Judah from Solomon to the exile. To give the narrative of both these histories here would be too repetitive. What follows therefore is based mainly on the Kings narrative, but occasional reference is made to material contained only in Chronicles. For a proper assessment of this latter work, it would be necessary to discuss its author's viewpoint in detail. While some of his new material is of late origin, there is every indication that some is based on good early sources. In any case it is convenient to illustrate some of the points it makes without artificially combining the two different accounts of the period of the monarchy.

THE BOOKS OF KINGS
AND CHRONICLES

THE FIRST BOOK OF KINGS

DAVID'S REIGN WAS not only a period of political expansion and successful wars. Stimulated by the sudden removal of foreign danger, the poetry and literature of Israel began to flourish as never before. The king himself was a poet, as may be seen from his laments over Saul and Abner. Later tradition ascribed the psalms to him. We see at this period the beginnings of a national historiography. The story of David's life is told coherently and objectively, without any attempt to hide the blemishes on the hero's character, and is much more trustworthy than the boastful annals of the Egyptian and Assyrian kings. The Biblical historian shows an understanding of political cause and effect not found again until the Greek historians in the fifth century B.C.

SOLOMON MADE KING

SHORTLY BEFORE THE death of David the court was split between two rival claimants to the throne. The king's eldest surviving son, Adonijah the son of Haggith, was supported by David's chief captain, Joab, and by Abiathar the priest. But Nathan the prophet, Zadok the priest, and Benaiah the son of Jehoiada, the second-in-command of the army, decided to crown Solomon, David's son by Bathsheba and his father's favorite. With the old king sinking rapidly, arrangements were made by Adonijah's faction for his coronation; but the still conscious David was prevailed upon by their opponents to designate Solomon as his successor.

The coronation of the crown-prince during his father's lifetime was a frequent practice in oriental monarchies, for it ensured a smooth and undisputed transference of power. In such cases the reigning monarch introduced the crown prince chosen by him to the assembled grandees of his court and had him proclaimed king. A scene of this kind appears to be represented on a relief from Carchemish, from the first half of the eighth century B.C. The king, Araras, is shown on the right, with his scepter in his left hand, while with his right he holds the crown prince, Kamanas, by the arm, thus symbolically guiding the latter's steps. The crown prince has a staff in his right hand and a long sword hanging from a shoulder-strap.

Thus for a very short time David and Solomon ruled together. To give this co-regency a religious sanction, Solomon proceeded with his adherents to the spring Gihon and was there anointed by Zadok the priest and Nathan the prophet. The Gihon, which issues from the west side of the Kidron valley, to the east of the City of David, was the only spring in the Jerusalem area and as such was vital for the life of the city. Flowing at an average rate of 25,000 gallons a day it supplied Jerusalem with water as early as the third millennium

· And he shall come and sit upon my throne; for he shall be king in my stead . . .   (I KINGS I : 35)

King Araras and crown-prince Kamanas on a relief from Car- chemish. From the first half of the eighth century B.C.

B.C. Evidently because of its life-and-death importance for the capital, it was chosen as the scene of such public ceremonies as the coronation of Solomon.

In the meantime Adonijah and his supporters were feasting at En-rogel, a smaller spring south of the Gihon. There they heard the people's loud acclamation of the new king and the sound of the trumpets blown in his honor. Seized with panic the revelers hurriedly dis-persed. The pretender to the throne, Adonijah himself, fled to the tent of the tabernacle and seized the horns of the altar, claiming the right of asylum.

Like most of the altars in antiquity, the one erected in Jerusalem in front of the shrine of the Ark was provided with horns to which those seeking its protection could cling. Altars excavated at Megiddo show this traditional form; the one illustrated is made of lime- stone and is one foot and a half high.

Having thus settled the question of the succession, David gave his last charge to Solomon, instructing his son how to treat his various friends and enemies: Joab, Barzillai, Shimei, and others. He then died and was buried in the City of David.

129

And Adonijah feared Solomon; and he arose, and went, and caught hold of the horns of the altar. (I KINGS I: 50)

Iron Age "horned" altar found at Megiddo. (Palestine Archaeological Museum)

Among the various nations of the ancient Middle East, kings were granted the special privilege of being buried within their cities. Usually the burial grounds of antiquity were outside the city walls; thus in Jerusalem the most ancient cemetery was in the Kidron valley, to the east of the city, so that the dead should lie down-wind from the living. The kings of Judah, however, were regularly buried inside the walls until the time of Uzziah. It is generally assumed that the three largest and most impressive of the rock-cut tombs excavated in the City of David were royal burial vaults. One of them, better preserved than the other two, is in the form of a double vaulted tunnel (50 feet long and 8 feet wide). At the far end of the floor, in the upper branch of the tunnel, a niche was hewn out of the rock, apparently to receive a sarcophagus. This was possibly the burial-place of the founder of the dynasty, king David himself.

Within a short time after the death of David, Solomon managed to get rid of his most dangerous enemies: Adonijah and Joab were killed and the priest Abiathar exiled to Anathoth; Shimei was also slain. "So the kingdom was established in the hand of Solomon."

Having thus removed the danger of domestic unrest Solomon engaged in an active and successful foreign policy. He even formed marriage ties with Egypt, receiving the hand of one of the Egyptian princesses who brought with her the city of Gezer as her dowry. He

Rock-cut tombs in the "Ophel" area.

also organized his internal administration with bureaucratic efficiency: the country was divided into twelve tax districts of unequal size but of equal economic importance, each of which had to support the king and his court for one of the months of the year; it is probable, but not certain, that Judah was exempt from this burden, being the "king's house". The king's wisdom and equity, which became proverbial, are exemplified in the famous "Judgment of Solomon" delivered in an apparently insoluble case: two women both claimed to be the mother of the same child, but Solomon discovered which of them was lying by a threat that showed a shrewd understanding of human psychology.

THE BUILDING OF THE TEMPLE

ALTHOUGH DAVID HIMSELF was forbidden by God to build the Temple, the first Book of Chronicles relates that he had made active preparations for the construction of the central sanctuary that was permanently to invest Jerusalem with the hallowed status of the religious capital of the Israelite nation. He had accordingly set masons to work dressing the stones in the prevailing architectural fashion of the time. The use of carefully shaped and well-finished stones was a definite innovation in Israel; special craftsmen

City gate at Megiddo
from Solomon's time.

and stone-cutters had to be engaged from among the "resident aliens", meaning apparently the Canaanites living within the confines of David's kingdom. The distinguishing feature of this type of stone-work was the wide margin cut by the masons along three edges of the block, leaving an undressed boss in the center. Archaeological finds have shown that Solomon used such dressed ashlars not only in the construction of the Temple but in his other public buildings as well.

David is also reported to have drawn up careful plans for the Temple. The royal founders of temples in the ancient East made exact designs of the edifices they proposed to erect and boasted of their generosity to their gods. Thus we find plans of the temples erected by Gudea, ruler of Lagash in Mesopotamia (twenty-first century B.C.), engraved on the knees of the statue of this ruler. Models of secular buildings were also prepared, as we can see from an Assyrian relief dating to the time of Sargon II.

As soon as his rule was firmly established, Solomon proceeded with the actual building of the House of the LORD. Like the ground-plan of the Tabernacle, which corresponded in its general layout to the Canaanite temples found at Hazor and at Tell el-Teinat in Syria, the Temple consisted of three main parts: the vestibule (*ulam*) the nave (*hekhal*), in which the priests performed the principal rites connected with the burning of incense, the offering of bread, and the intoning of liturgical psalms; and, behind this, the Holy of Holies (*debir*), where the Ark stood between its cherubim. The entrance to the vestibule was flanked by two great bronze pillars, Jachin and Boaz. The sanctuary proper was surrounded by a court in which stood the bronze altar of sacrifice and the large bronze basin. The inner walls of the Temple were inlaid with cedar boards, ornamented with carved "gourds and open flowers". Such stylized patterns have been found in many examples of ancient decorative design, such as cosmetic spoons and ivory inlays from Megiddo, dating to the Late Bronze Age, with the repeated palm leaf motif. Some of the work of the Temple required a very high standard of craftsmanship, such as could be supplied only by Solomon's Phoenician allies. Perhaps the most difficult technical feat was the casting of the huge bronze basin known as "the sea". This had a capacity of two thousand *bath*, i.e. a maximum of 13,300 gallons, and apparently weighed about thirty tons, it rested on twelve bronze bulls, and served primarily as a storage tank from which the lavers were filled. Its ritual importance was very great, since the washing of hands and feet was a necessary preliminary to every priestly office performed in the sanctuary.

At the same time, a magnificent palace was erected for Solomon out of cedar and fir trees brought from the Lebanon. The timber was cut down by the skillful foresters of Hiram the king of Tyre, and was then transported by the conscripted labor of thirty thousand Israelites, in relays of ten thousand at a time, each working one month in the Lebanon followed by two months of rest at home.

The royal residence contained a throne hall, a guard-house, large stables, and an interior court for the royal harem. A special palace was built for the most important of the king's wives, the daughter of Pharaoh. The completion of these magnificent undertakings was signalized by a great national assembly at which Solomon uttered a solemn prayer of dedication. For the moment all was glory and splendor, although already the first difficulties were becoming apparent; Solomon had to cede to Hiram the area of Cabul bordering the lands of Tyre in northwestern Galilee, as he was unable to pay the sums for which this area had been pledged.

SOLOMON'S WEALTH

SOLOMON'S BUILDING ACTIVITIES, costly as they were, would have been quite impossible had he not been able to exploit the industrial and commercial potentialities of his kingdom. Ruling over an empire which extended from the Euphrates to the Mediterranean and from there to the Red Sea, he virtually controlled the caravan routes passing between the lands of the Fertile Crescent and Egypt. The tradition that it was he who "built" the caravan city at Tadmor (Palmyra) is an additional proof of his hold

The house which king Solomon built for the LORD was
sixty cubits long, twenty cubits wide, and thirty cubits high.

(I KINGS 6: 2)

Reconstruction of Solomon's Temple.

on the lines of communication through the desert. Hardly less important was his control of the port of Elath on the Red Sea. It was to this that he owed his commercial alliance with the Phoenicians, who were at that time masters of most of the Mediterranean sea-trade. They were vitally interested in extending their maritime activities without having to pass through Egyptian-held territory, and Solomon could offer them, in Elath, a convenient port from which to engage in profitable sailings in the Red Sea and the Indian Ocean. This trading venture was a joint one; Solomon provided the harbor, built the ships, and supplied the rowers, while the Phoenician king furnished skillful sailors, "that had knowledge of the sea". The Phoenician ships, on which Solomon's merchants fleet was modeled, were sturdy, flat bottomed vessels, equipped with strong sails and oars; a specially big oar served as rudder, and stones were used as anchors.

Sailing out into the open seas, the ships carried cargoes of copper supplied by Solomon's big smelting plant at Ezion-geber on the gulf of Elath. The ore was mined in the Arabah and brought down to the refinery, where the prevailing north wind supplied the strong draft necessary to keep the furnaces burning. The labor required for this exhausting work must have been provided by royal slaves.

From Elath the ships sailed to Ophir, a country rich in gold, spices and precious stones, for which their cargoes of copper were bartered. The whole voyage lasted three years. Its destination, the fabulous land of Ophir, has been variously located in India and in East African Somaliland. The name, which in the Bible usually designates a special kind of gold, also occurs in an incised inscription found on a potsherd of the eighth or seventh century B.C.,

Three thousand talents of gold, of the gold of Ophir . . .

(I CHRON. 29: 4)

Tell Qcasile sherd mentioning "Ophir gold". (Israel Department of Antiquities)

Once every three years the fleet of ships of Tarshish used to come bringing gold, silver, ivory, apes, and peacocks. (I KINGS 10: 22)

Monkey—Painting from tomb of Rekhmire, Thebes. Fifteenth century B.C.

excavated at Tell Qasileh on the Yarkon river. The inscription reads: "Gold of Ophir to Beth-horon, thirty shekels." Evidently this is a record of a consignment sent to the well-known settlement on the Jerusalem highroad, probably as payment for exports from the harbor on the Yarkon.

In exchange for their copper, the ships brought back such rare luxury goods as gold and silver, ivory, and apes. Egyptian ships plying to the East African country known as Punt also provided bags of gold, incense, balsam, antimony, and monkeys. One such monkey is depicted in the tomb of the vizier Rekhmire (fifteenth century B.C.).

Besides the maritime trade carried on from Elath, Solomon also profited from the position of his country on the road running along the Mediterranean coast from Asia Minor to Egypt. Through special merchants appointed by himself and trading on his behalf, he organized the export of horses from Kue (Cilicia) in Asia Minor, a country famous for its war-horses bred from pedigree studs. As in the case of the copper-gold exchange with Ophir, this trade too was conducted on a barter basis. In return for the horses of Kue, Solomon's merchants transported northwards the products of the Egyptian chariot industry, which were renowned throught the ancient world for their quality. The typical Anatolian war-horse, with short legs, long tail and shaggy mane, is represented on reliefs of the eighth or seventh century B.C.; Egyptian chariots, made of wood and gilded leather, have been found in tombs of the fourteenth century B.C.

The riches accumulated by Solomon through his trading ventures were used to finance the construction of the Temple and the Palace, and in addition a chariot force for which stables were built at Megiddo, Hazor, and other places. Such strongpoints were guarded by massive high walls with complicated gateways, intended to protect their entrances. At Megiddo, for instance, the only access to the main gate was by a forecourt surrounded by towers, which exposed the attackers to a withering cross-fire. The horses to draw the chariots were kept in stables inside these fortresses; at Megiddo, illustrated on the following page, there was stabling for 450 horses, i.e. enough for a force of 150 chariots, assuming a team of two horses for each chariot and one horse in reserve.

In addition to all these expenses, Solomon had to pay Hiram for the supply of cedar and other wood sent from Tyre to the harbors on the Yarkon. This timber was transported in the form of rafts which were tied together and towed by ships to "the sea of Joppa", from where the separate logs were hauled overland and uphill to Jerusalem by Solomon's laborers.

And Solomon gathered together chariots and horsemen; he had fourteen hundred chariots and twelve thousand horsemen, whom he stationed in the chariot cities . . .
(1 KINGS 10: 26)

Model of Megiddo in the time of the Israelite monarchy.

Rafts of the kind used by Solomon are illustrated on the reliefs of Sargon II, king of Assyria. Six merchant vessels are seen being propelled by oars pulled by slaves sitting in rows on each side of the ship. Two of the vessels are sailing ships, as is clearly indicated by the mast in their center. All of them are towing rafts of logs. The water between the rafts is alive with fishes and other sea-creatures.

Apart from its primary religious function, the Temple also served Solomon as a treasury to be drawn upon in time of need. Bars of silver and gold, and vessels made of these metals were stored in the Temple depositories for use in national emergencies. Because of their sanctity, temples in the ancient East were commonly used as storehouses of various kinds. Thus in the tomb-painting of Rekhmire at Thebes (fifteenth century B.C.), we find a picture of the treasures of the temple of Amon, consisting of gold dust, rings of gold and silver, precious stones, lumps of copper, spices, wines, ivory tusks, ostrich feathers, clothing, and shoes. The treasuries of Solomon's Temple must have presented a similar appearance.

So great was the fame of Solomon's riches and wisdom that the Queen of Sheba paid him a royal visit, bringing with her a caravan of gifts and spices. Situated at the southern tip of Arabia, her kingdom was one of the ports on Solomon's trading route to Ophir.

As a result of these developments a new flourishing urban culture came into being in Israel, fostered by a State-controlled economy and a general feeling of political security. But at the same time, as it was made possible by forced labor, it gave rise to class distinctions in the formerly classless tribal society. Moreover, contact with foreign nations, which began with commerce, opened the way to influences in other spheres as well, including that of religion. The king himself set a bad example by allowing his many foreign wives (married usually for political reasons, in order to cement alliances or consolidate the control of a subjugated province) to practice their native cults in Jerusalem, and by himself participating in such idolatrous worship.

As Solomon grew old his grip on the empire, won by his warlike father David, became steadily feebler. In Egypt, a new and vigorous dynasty, the Twenty-Second, was inaugurated by the Pharaoh Shishak, whose court served as the rallying point of all Solomon's enemies.

A certain Rezon, the son of Eliada, raised a successful revolt in Damascus, and by cutting off the northeastern part of Solomon's empire, inflicted a grievous commercial loss on Israel.

But worse was to come: disaffection among the ten tribes of Israel, and especially in Ephraim, for long the leading tribe, mounted rapidly. The heavy royal exactions, and above all the hardships of the forced labor gangs, often compelled to work far away from their homes, created the conditions for an open breach. A focus for this smouldering discontent was found in Jeroboam the son of Nebat, who, as Solomon's overseer of the conscript labor force supplied by the "House of Joseph" (Ephraim and Manasseh), could learn of the people's suffering at first hand. He was encouraged by the prophet Ahijah the Shilonite. Solomon, learning of the plot, gave orders for Jeroboam to be killed, whereupon the latter fled to Egypt.

When Solomon died in c. 930 B.C. his kingdom was still peaceful on the surface and his son Rehoboam succeeded without dispute. To renew the covenant made by the Israelite tribes with David, the new king went to Shechem to have his succession publicly acclaimed there. He was met, however, with a demand for the abolition of the forced labor and the lightening of the taxes. When foolishly he refused, ten of the tribes seceded and chose Jeroboam as their king. Thus came to an end the united monarchy established by Saul and

And we will cut whatever timber you need from Lebanon, and bring it to you in rafts to the sea of Joppa . . .
(2 CHRON. 2: 16–17)

Assyrian relief (eighth century B.C.) showing transport of logs in rafts. (Louvre, Paris)

And he stored the silver, the gold and all the vessels in the treasuries of the house of God. (2 CHRON. 5: 1)

Temple treasures stored—Painting from the tomb of Rekhmire, Thebes, Fifteenth century B.C.

developed by David and Solomon. Only Judah and the small tribe of Benjamin remained faithful to the house of David.

The war which now broke out between the two separate States of Israel and Judah, and continued on and off for fifty years, was mostly a struggle for the frontier fortresses. Judah was too weak to endanger Israel, even though the latter was plagued by foreign foes and dynastic instability. Religious schism was added to the political breach: in order to undermine the position of the Temple of Jerusalem, which remained in the hands of the Davidic Dynasty, Jeroboam established royal sanctuaries at Dan and Bethel where the God of Israel was symbolized by bull images, and these evidently came to be regarded as objects of worship. Judah too had its own troubles: it was attacked in the south by Shishak of Egypt, who also devastated Israel. But at least Judah kept a stable dynasty.

ELIJAH

IN THE FIRST quarter of the ninth century B.C. a great change occurred. A new and vigorous dynasty arose in Israel, founded by Omri. Having defeated and killed all his rivals, he founded a new capital at Samaria, entered into an alliance with Tyre, reconquered Moab, and in general made such an impression on his contemporaries and on posterity that Israel was henceforth known in Assyrian annals as "The House of Omri" (*bit humri*), regardless of the name of the king actually reigning there. Only over Damascus and its Aramaean king was Omri unable to assert his authority; he even had to concede privileges to the Syrian merchants in his own capital.

Judah was at this time ruled by Jehoshaphat (877–849 B.C.), who according to the Chronicler reorganized the administration and the army and established royal tribunals in the provinces composed of priests and the heads of the local families, with a court of appeal in Jerusalem. Foreign policy was also reoriented: peace was made with Israel, and the two kingdoms, now secure in their rear, could engage in a vigorous policy of expansion. Encouraged by Omri and his Phoenician allies, Jehoshaphat attempted to revive the Elath maritime venture, though with little success.

Omri was succeeded by Ahab (874–852 B.C.) who as crown prince had married Jezebel, the daughter of king Ithbaal of Sidon. Henceforward Phoenician influence in Samaria grew by leaps and bounds. Jezebel had brought with her hundreds of priests and prophets of the Baal of her native town and of his consort, Asherah. With peace and prosperity the material wealth of Israel increased, and signs of luxury and corruption appeared among the upper classes of the kingdom. The old traditions of Israel, based on a simple life and the worship of one God, seemed on the point of extinction.

But the spiritual heritage of Israel found a fearless and uncompromising champion in Elijah the Tishbite, a native of Gilead who suddenly appeared before Ahab and threatened him with the wrath of God, in the form of a prolonged drought. Naturally after such a bold denunciation Elijah's life was not safe; he fled to his native Gilead, where he took refuge in a desolate spot near the brook Cherith (identified by some scholars with the Wadi Yabis, on the assumption that Elijah was a native of Jabesh Gilead, taking Tishbite as a form of Jabeshite). There he was miraculously fed by ravens and provided with water by the brook, which, however, dried up after a time, for the prophesied drought had come. Elijah left the wilderness and went to Zarephath in the vicinity of Sidon. There he met a widow who, with her son, was dying of hunger on account of the drought afflicting the land. A miracle now occurred and all three of them—the widow, her son, and the prophet—found adequate sustenance in a handful of meal and a little oil in a cruse. "And the barrel of meal wasted not, neither did the cruse of oil fail." When the boy fell ill and was given up for dead, Elijah revived him.

The drought increased in intensity and lasted for three years. Only at the end of this period

Depart from here and turn eastward, and hide yourself by the brook Cherith, that is east of the Jordan. (I KINGS 17: 3)

View of Wadi Yabis, east of the Jordan.

But he himself went a day's journey into the wilderness, and came and sat down under a broom tree . . .

(I KINGS. 19: 4)

"The desert broom" blooming in the desert.

did Elijah return to Israel, there to match his faith against the prophets of Baal in a dramatic contest on Mount Carmel. Both parties prepared a sacrifice; but in spite of all the frenzied invocations of the priests of Baal, their god gave no sign of life, whereas the sacrifice of Elijah was kindled by fire from heaven in answer to his prayer. At the prophet's command, the assembled people made the priests of Baal pay with their lives for their idolatry. Elijah's great victory was followed by heavy rain and the end of the drought.

The destruction of her priests roused the proud consort of Ahab to a murderous fury, and Elijah again had to flee from Israel. In keeping with the ascetic tradition which he represented, he sought refuge in the desert, whence had come the spiritual strength of Israel. In the waste land south of Beersheba he rested under "a broom tree". This was no doubt the shrub still called the desert broom (*Retama roetam*), which grows in the gullies of the southern Negeb and in the Sinai peninsula and is sometimes high enough for its shade to provide protection for a human being. Its thick roots are still today, as in ancient times, used for fuel. After being miraculously provided with food and water, Elijah gathered strength to continue his pilgrimage to Horeb, the mountain of God. In thus making his way to the fountainhead of the Israelite religion, Elijah was seeking spiritual comfort. This was afforded to him in an awe-inspiring theophany in which, as at the giving of the Law, God's presence was preceded by tremendous elemental forces, a wind that "rent the mountains and broke in pieces the rocks", followed by earthquake and fire; but finally it was in a still small voice that the divine message was delivered.

On his return to Israel, Elijah took Elisha the son of Shaphat as his disciple. In the meantime important events had occurred. Ben-hadad of Damascus had besieged Ahab's capital, Samaria; the siege was raised and the invaders so resoundingly defeated at Aphek that Ben-hadad had to restore the territories lost by Omri and to concede to the Israelite merchants in Damascus rights equal to those enjoyed by the Damascans at Samaria. Ahab's leniency to the defeated enemy aroused the prophet's anger, but it had political reasons.

The growing might of Assyria was menacing Israel no less than the Aramaean kingdoms. Israel made an alliance with her ancient foes and the coalition attacked the Assyrians at Karkar in 853 B.C. (the first date in the Bible that can be determined exactly from exterior sources). Ahab of Israel supplied only half the number of foot-soldiers mobilized by Ben-hadad of Damascus, but in the more technically developed arm of the chariot-force, his contingent of two thousand was by far the strongest. Although Shalmaneser III boasts of victory, the fact that he henceforward left the allies in peace shows that the battle ended with no decisive advantage to him and effectively checked the Assyrian advance for some time to come.

And he arose, and ate and drank, and went in the
strength of that food forty days and forty nights to Horeb
the mount of God.   (I KINGS 19: 8)   Jebel Musa in the Sinai.

And after this Ahab said to Naboth, "Give me your vineyard, that I may have it for a vegetable garden, because it is near my house ..." (I KINGS 21 : 2)

Egyptian relief in tomb of Mereruka (second half of third millennium B.C.) showing laborers working in lettuce garden.

NABOTH'S VINEYARD

AHAB WAS ALSO involved in a grave act of injustice which has blackened his name with posterity. In consequence of the long drought, many peasants had been forced to sell their plots to the great landlords, who thus increased their properties. The king too had begun to form a large estate in the Jezreel valley, which subsequently passed to successive rulers of the country down to Roman times. As the official capital, Samaria, was situated in the colder central hills, the kings of Israel established a winter capital for themselves in the Valley of Jezreel, in the city of that name. Its strategic importance at the junction of two great roads, and its beautiful surroundings, mild climate, and fertile soil, made it a favorite royal residence.

One of the small proprietors who held out, in spite of all the difficulties which beset the peasants at this time, was a certain Naboth of Jezreel. As his piece of land adjoined the royal palace, Ahab was desirous of acquiring it for his vegetable garden. Such gardens, which were commonly attached to a king's palace, served to supply the royal table with choice products. Those surrounding the palaces of the kings of Egypt and the mansions of the nobles of that country were especially splendid, with their profusion of fruit-bearing and other trees, of vines and aromatic shrubs, their bathing pools and irrigation channels. In the tomb of Mereruka at Sakkarah we see laborers carefully watering the lettuce plants in such a garden.

It speaks well for the power and impartiality of Israelite justice that, once Naboth had refused to sell, Ahab felt powerless to enforce his wishes; it did not apparently befit the king to use high-handed violence to achieve his ends. Jezebel regarded the matter differently and arranged a judicial murder to get rid of Naboth; letters were sent to the elders of Jezreel in the king's name and sealed with the royal seal, to which Jezebel, as the king's wife, had access. On Hittite royal seals the name of the queen appears beside that of the king; but such was not the custom in Israel, and Jezebel had to abuse Ahab's trust. On her instructions two false witnesses were suborned to accuse Naboth of "cursing God and the king". The established legal procedure was carefully observed: first a fast was proclaimed, then the charge was brought by the two supposed witnesses, and finally Naboth, having been condemned, was executed by stoning. By virtue of his royal prerogative the king inherited the property of a felon convicted of blasphemy and lese-majesty. Only Elijah, the living conscience of the nation, did not acquiesce in the crime; he roundly condemned Ahab and Jezebel and predicted the tragic end of their dynasty.

After the successful battle at Karkar the allies fell out again and Ahab fought Ben-hadad for the possession of Ramoth Gilead. As was usual in antiquity the Israelite king led his troops into battle in person, armed in a coat of mail and standing upright in his chariot. A chance arrow struck him between the "scale armour and the breastplate" at a joint in his panoply which was one of the few vulnerable spots in the protective armor of an ancient warrior. A similar wound has been inflicted on a Semitic leader who opposed Thutmose IV (late fifteenth century B.C.) in the scene represented in gilt boss on the leather sides of the royal chariot. Gravely wounded as he was, Ahab knew that if he fell his army would break and run, so he kept himself on his feet to the last and bled to death in his chariot, facing the enemy.

So she wrote letters in Ahab's name and sealed them with his seal.
(I KINGS 21 : 8)

Hittite royal seal impressed on clay tablet. Fourteenth century B.C. (Louvre, Paris)

143

THE SECOND BOOK OF KINGS

THE DEATH OF Ahab was only the beginning of the misfortunes of Israel. His successor Ahaziah died from a fall after a short reign and was succeeded by Jehoram. Elijah's role as the leader of the opposition to the dynasty of Ahab was now taken over by Elisha; according to the Biblical account the elder prophet was carried up to heaven by a fiery chariot. The weakening of the once powerful dynasty of Omri now became so evident that Mesha, king of Moab, dared to revolt.

THE CAMPAIGN AGAINST MOAB

THE REVOLT OF Mesha (c. 852 B.C.) is one of the few Biblical events which are known to us from non-biblical records. A stele found at Dibon and inscribed in Moabite, a dialect closely akin to Hebrew, commemorates the victorious exploits of this king, which are ascribed to the favor of his god, Chemosh. Mesha first recounts the enslavement of Moab to Israel in the reign of Omri and his son, and his country's subsequent liberation after a bitter struggle. After boasting of his conquests and of his savagery to his foes, Mesha goes on to glory in the blessings he has brought upon his land, listing the cities he has built, the gates and towers he has erected, the cisterns he has dug, and the highways he has constructed.

And struck the king of Israel between the scale armour and the breastplate . . . And the king was propped up in his chariot . . . (I KINGS 22: 34–35)

Wounded Semitic charioteer in relief on chariot of Thutmose IV. Late fifteenth century B.C.

The revolt of Moab endangered both Israel and Judah, and their respective kings, Jehoram and Jehoshaphat, therefore joined forces to attack the rebellious vassal. As the Jordan fords were blocked by the enemy, the allies advanced upon Moab from the Judaean desert, through the Arabah, from south of the Dead Sea. They followed the traditional "way of Edom" on which stood various fortresses constructed by the kings of Judah, like the one shown here, dominating the descent along the Wadi el-Qeini (Valley of the Kenites?). The attack on Moab was facilitated by the fact that the king of Edom remained loyal to Judah and accompanied the allied kings. Elisha the prophet also gave the enterprise his blessing and foretold a sudden flooding of the valleys by rain water, an event which did indeed occur after the armies had suffered from a severe shortage of water.

Besieged in Kir of Moab (RSV Kir-hareseth, KJV Kir-haraseth), Mesha was reduced to such dire straits that he resorted to the last desperate expedient of sacrificing his eldest son and designated successor on the wall. The Israelites thereupon withdrew to their own land.

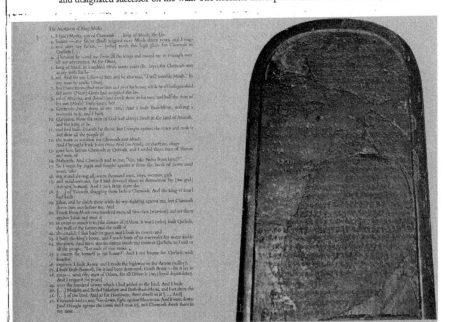

Stele of Mesha, king of Moab.
(Louvre, Paris)

Now Mesha king of Moab was a sheep breeder; and he had to deliver annually to the king of Israel a hundred thousand lambs, and the wool of a hundred thousand rams. But when Ahab died, the king of Moab rebelled against the king of Israel.

(2 KINGS 3 : 4–5)

THE REVOLT OF JEHU

ELISHA'S FAME AS a miracle-worker spread far and wide. He cured Naaman, the Syrian king's commander-in-chief, of leprosy and punished his own servant, Gehazi, for his cupidity by afflicting him with the disease which had just left Naaman. He also healed the child of a pious woman of Shunem who provided him with food and lodging. When Ben-hadad again besieged Samaria and there was a terrible famine, Elisha foretold the panic-stricken flight of the Aramaeans under the illusion that their camp was being attacked by the combined forces of the Hittites and the Egyptians. He was instrumental in bringing about a change of dynasty in Damascus, Hazael replacing the ailing Ben-hadad on the throne. Finally Elisha became the moving spirit in the revolt against the dynasty of Ahab in Israel.

The opportune moment had come: Jehoram of Israel had been wounded in a battle with Hazael at Ramoth-gilead and was convalescing at Jezreel, where Ahaziah of Judah went to visit him. The Israelite army remained in Gilead under the command of Jehu the son of Jehoshaphat, the son of Nimshi. During Jehoram's absence, Jehu was anointed king by Elisha's messenger and the army rose in his support. Jehu at once made for Jezreel in his

*So a man on horseback
went to meet him . . .*
(2 KINGS 9: 18)

Horseman on Gozan relief.
Tenth to ninth century
B.C. (Berlin Museum)

Jezebel heard of it; and she painted her eyes, and adorned her head, and looked out of the window.

(2 KINGS 9 : 30)

Egyptian relief showing hairdresser *c.* 2000 B.C.
(Brooklyn Museum)

chariot, driving furiously. On being informed of Jehu's rapid approach, Jehoram, whose suspicions were aroused, sent a horseman to meet him and find out if his intentions were peaceful. Horses were employed for the carrying of messages in antiquity long before their military use as cavalry, because of the difficulty of managing them on the battlefield: the ancient cavalryman had to control the animal while at the same time holding his shield and handling his offensive weapons, a feat which required long and arduous training. A horseman is shown on a relief from Gozan (tenth to ninth century B.C.) riding bareback, without saddle or spurs. A round shield is slung over his shoulder and he is holding a mace in his right hand and the reins in his left.

When Jehoram's messengers did not return, the king decided to confront the usurper in person. On seeing Jehoram, Jehu loudly denounced him for the wickedness of his mother, Jezebel, and then killed him with a well-aimed bow-shot. Ahaziah of Judah, who accompanied Jehoram, was shot down with him. Then Jehu proceeded to the palace where Jezebel was waiting.

When Jezebel received the news of the killing of Jehoram, she knew that her own doom was near. Proudly determined to betray no sign of fear, she prepared to confront the usurper in a manner worthy of her name, which possibly meant: "My brother (my father) is a prince" ([*Abi*]-*Zebul*). She therefore painted her eyes with antimony to heighten the impression of self-assurance, and adorned her head after the fashion of ladies of noble birth. Egyptian reliefs show the elaborate coiffures given by ancient hairdressers to their aristocratic female patrons. Her preparations completed, Jezebel took her stand at the window, the customary position in the ancient Orient from which to welcome honored guests. Knowing

147

that her fate was sealed, she greeted Jehu with mocking abuse: "Had Zimri peace, who slew
his master?" At a sign from Jehu she was thrown to her death from the window by two
palace servants and her bones left to be eaten by dogs. Thus was Elijah's dire prophecy
fulfilled in literal detail.

The revolt against the dynasty of Omri spread to Samaria. Not only did the whole family
of Ahab perish in it (no fewer than seventy princes were slain by the elders of Samaria in
their eagerness to curry favor with the new king), but the worship favored by the fallen
dynasty was also swept away. The austere sect of the Rechabites who clung to the traditions
of the desert, abstaining from dwelling in houses and from the use of wine, helped Jehu to
wreak vengeance on the priests of Baal. Eighty of them were slaughtered and their shrine
destroyed.

Baalism was thus for the moment eradicated in Israel, though the writers of the Book
of Kings condemn Jehu for not abolishing the national shrines at Bethel and Dan. Moreover, however great the spiritual benefit of his revolt to Israel, its political and economic
consequences were most unfavorable. The alliance with Tyre was abruptly ended by the
killing of Jezebel and her priests. True, the taxes exacted by Ahab were abolished and the
assimilation of Israel to the sophisticated and materialistic pagan environment was halted,
but politically Israel was isolated and weakened. As a result Jehu had to withdraw from the
Syrian confederacy and submit to the power of Shalmaneser III, king of Assyria (859–824
B.C.). It is owing to this unconditional surrender that an image of Jehu has been preserved,
the only one of an Israelite king in existence. On Shalmaneser's black obelisk "Jehu the Son

of Omri", escorted by Assyrian palace officials, is depicted doing obeisance to his suzerain. Behind the king stand tribute bearers carrying vessels of gold, silver, and tin.

JOASH CROWNED KING OF JUDAH

B AALISM TOOK ON a new lease of life in Jerusalem. Taking advantage of the political confusion that followed Jehu's conspiracy, Athaliah, the daughter of Ahab and mother of Ahaziah, king of Judah, made herself queen by wiping out almost all the members of the reigning dynasty. In this violent usurpation of the throne, which she occupied from 842 to 837 B.C., she was aided by the privileged position enjoyed by the Queen Mother in Judah. There were few such women rulers in the ancient Orient. One of them may perhaps be portrayed on a relief from ancient Shamal (Zinjirli), dating to the eighth century B.C., which shows a woman seated before an offering table, holding a cup in her right hand and a flower bud in her left; she wears regal apparel and a round pointed cap. A maidservant with a fly-whisk stands by her. Athaliah may have looked like this.

While Athaliah reigned over the land. (2 KINGS 11 : 3)

Relief from Shamal showing a feasting queen. Eighth century B.C. (Berlin Museum)

Just before Athaliah executed her design of blotting out all her dead son's family, one of his children, a small baby named Joash, was hidden by Jehosheba, the daughter of King Jehoram and wife of the priest Jehoiada. Thus one last scion of the Davidic dynasty was saved. Jehosheba kept the infant secreted with a wet-nurse for six whole years in the bed-chamber of the Temple, to which only the priests had access. The nurse apparently became a kind of foster-mother to Joash, rearing him and giving him his early upbringing.

When the time was ripe a carefully planned and executed conspiracy, led by the priest Jehoiada, was made against Athaliah. Jehoiada was supported by the Levites, the heads of the clans, the captains of the hundreds, and the royal bodyguard on whose co-operation the swift success of the plot depended. At the appointed moment Jehoiada and his aides suddenly brought Joash from his hiding-place and presented him to the assembled people in the Temple, where they crowned him and proclaimed him king. The ceremony was accompanied by hymns of praise, the blowing of trumpets and the playing of pipes. At the end of it the people raised a shout of "Long live the king!"—the traditional expression of a people's loyalty to its sovereign, as illustrated by the Egyptian courtiers' loyal greeting of their new Pharaoh, Horemheb, depicted on a relief of the fourteenth century B.C. Their faces are raised in homage to their sovereign and their hands lifted in reverent submission to his will.

After the ceremony in the Temple, the royal guards took charge and escorted Joash from the House of the LORD, through the guards' gate, to the royal palace. Two units of the army participated in the revolution: first, the "runners" who escorted the sovereign wherever he went, following his chariot and guarding his person, and who also acted as messengers and heralds; as the most trusted troops of all they were quartered next to the palace. The other unit consisted of Carites, probably mercenaries from Asia Minor, who formed a royal bodyguard. Being foreigners, the Carites were thought to be more trustworthy than native Judahite soldiers; but in this case they too sided with the winning cause. Deserted by those who were supposed to protect her, Athaliah was seized, led out of the Temple area and executed. Then Jehoiada made a covenant between God and the king and people, binding the latter to observe the divine commandments. The temple, altars, and images of Baal were completely destroyed, while the long-neglected and by now dilapidated Temple was repaired with the people's donations.

UZZIAH IN THE WILDERNESS

THE VIOLENT INTERNAL struggles which accompanied the rooting out of Baalism left both Israel and Judah so exhausted as to be unable to play any major role on the international stage. The reign of Jehoahaz the son of Jehu (814–798 B.C.) began with military disasters, foreign domination (by Syria), and political decline. It was only when "the LORD gave Israel a saviour"—Adadnirari III, king of Assyria, who crushed Ben-hadad in 805 B.C.—that Jehoahaz was enabled to turn the tables, defeat the Syrians and regain lost territory in Trans-Jordan.

In Judah too things took a turn for the worse before improving. Amaziah, the son of Joash, eventually halted the decline of Judah by a victorious campaign against the Edomites. Presumably his aim was to gain control of the Arabah, through which ran the roads from

Then he brought out the king's son, and put the crown upon him . . . and they said "Long live the king". (2 CHRON. 23: 11)

Judah to Edom, Moab, Elath, and to the copper mines near Punon. He won his victory in the Valley of Salt, which is identified with the barren expanses of the northern Arabah, west of the Dead Sea.

After this, however, Amaziah got himself involved in a foolish war with Israel, which ended in his defeat by king Jehoash and in the breaking down of a large part of the walls of Jerusalem to render the city defenseless. Amaziah was succeeded by his son Uzziah, who remained firm in his alliance with Israel. As in the days of Omri, the two kingdoms again prospered side by side. Jeroboam II, the son of Jehoash, proved himself one of the greatest rulers of the Northern Kingdom. In the course of his long reign (784–744 B.C.) he reconquered all the country from Lebo Hamath, including Damascus, to the Arabah. Uzziah profited by the alliance with Israel to extend his authority over the Negeb right down to the Red Sea. He regained control of the caravan routes; established his dominion over Philistia and dismantled the walls of Jabneh, Ashod, and Gath; defeated the desert brigands; and forced the Ammonites to pay him tribute.

Uzziah's greatness, however, did not lie in military successes alone. He was also renowned for his initiative and drive in executing a large-scale program of construction, ranging from the erection of strongpoints and defensive towers to the establishment of new settlements in Judah and the south. He brought prosperity to the Negeb and the Judaean wilderness by developing agriculture in the districts bordering on the desert, and especially by the encouragement of vine-growing and sheep-rearing, "for he loved husbandry" (2 Chron. 26: 10). One of his great achievements was the restoration of the Judaean outlet to the Red Sea by the rebuilding of Elath. The archaeological discoveries at Tell el Kheleifi confirm that, in the eighth century B.C., there was a renewal of settlement on the ruins of Solomon's old smelting site. With the Arabah mines once more under Judaean control, the copper-smelting and metal-working were resumed at Elath. Attempts were again made to renew Solomon's sea-trade, but without success.

In Jerusalem Uzziah reorganized the army and the defenses of the city. In addition to the "mighty men of valor", he created a regular fighting force "to help the king against the enemy" and fitted it out with a variety of military equipment, including "engines, invented by skillful men, to be on the towers and the corners, to shoot arrows and great stones" (2 Chron. 26: 15).

Emboldened by his successes, Uzziah resumed the struggle with the priesthood that had been begun by his grandfather Joash. Owing his crown to the conspiracy against Athaliah led by the priest Jehoiada, Joash had remained under the tutelage of the priesthood for a long time; so much so that in his reign the Temple began to evolve from the status of a royal chapel to that of an independent sanctuary. But eventually Joash fell out with Zechariah, Jehoiada's son, and had him killed. According to Chronicles, Uzziah tried to re-establish the royal control of the Temple by himself sacrificing incense. Shortly afterwards he was stricken with leprosy and replaced on the throne by his son Jotham, acting as regent. Uzziah lived the rest of his days outside Jerusalem and was buried apart from his royal predecessors. At some time during the period of the Second Temple his bones were disinterred and transferred to another burial place; an inscription in Aramaic was placed over them reading: "Hither were brought the bones of Uzziah king of Judah. Do not open."

THE SAMARIAN EXILE

THE REVIVED POLITICAL glories of both Judah and Israel were soon dimmed by the lengthening shadow of the mighty empire of Assyria. Israel, being in the direct line of the Assyrian advance, was the first to feel its full weight. Jeroboam's son, Zechariah, reigned for only six months. In the following twenty years there were no fewer than five kings in Israel, each one more deeply in trouble with Assyria than his predecessor. The first of the great Assyrian conquerors, Tiglath-Pileser III, also known as Pul (745–727 B.C.), made a series of campaigns into Syria and Palestine. It was he who instituted the systematic policy of annexing the conquered kingdoms and turning them into Assyrian provinces administered by governors, after large-scale deportations of the native populations. These mass expulsions brought about the disintegration of the traditional small states of the ancient Orient and reduced their scattered peoples to helpless servitude to any conqueror, Assyrian, Babylonian or Persian.

> *Pul the king of Assyria came against the land; and Menahem gave Pul a thousand talents of silver, that he might help him to confirm his hold of the royal power.* (2 KINGS 15: 19)

When in 734 B.C. Rezin, king of Aram-Damascus, and Pekah, the son of Remaliah, attempted to throw off the yoke of Tiglath-Pileser III, the Assyrian monarch crushed their revolt in a series of campaigns (733–732 B.C.), in the course of which he annihilated Aram-Damascus and annexed substantial parts of Israel. Tiglath-Pileser was all the more incensed against Pekah, because Menahem, whose son Pekah had murdered in his usurpation of the throne, had paid him tribute, thus formally admitting Assyrian supremacy. Now the Assyrian king lopped off Galilee and the coastal strip from Israel, as well as Gilead. He deported the inhabitants of these areas and imposed a heavy tribute on the rump kingdom left in the mountains of Ephraim. According to Assyrian sources Tiglath-Pileser appointed Hoshea, the son Elah, to rule over the remainder of the population, who had deposed Pekah; according to the Bible Hoshea conspired against Pekah and slew him.

Hoshea too could not, in the end, meet the heavy Assyrian exactions and revolted in 724 B.C. After a prolonged siege his capital, Samaria, fell to Shalmaneser V, king of Assyria (727–722 B.C.), who died before its actual capture. His successor, Sargon II, deported 27,900 people

Tiglath Pileser III ("Pul") on relief from Calah. (British Museum)

In the fourteenth year of King Hezekiah, Sennacherib king of Assyria came up against all the fortified cities of Judah and took them. And Hezekiah king of Judah sent to the king of Assyria at Lachish, saying, "I have done wrong; withdraw from me . . ." . (2 KINGS 18 : 13–14)

The siege of Lachish on reliefs from Sennacherib's palace at Nineveh. Seventh century B.C.

from the city and rebuilt it as the capital of an Assyrian province. Those exiled from Israel were dispersed among the Assyrian provinces and lost all touch with the rest of the nation. On Assyrian reliefs we see the form taken by such deportations: women laden with sacks and girls carrying burdens are shown plodding wearily along on foot, while the men drive carts loaded with corn and drawn by oxen; small children were allowed to ride in the carts.

THE SIEGE OF LACHISH

AHAZ OF JUDAH (743–727 B.C.) saved his kingdom by refusing to join in the coalition against Assyria and by abject submission to the conqueror, even going as far as to adopt the Assyrian ritual. His son Hezekiah (727–698 B.C.) instituted a religious reform. He disregarded the counsel of Isaiah the prophet, however, in joining a coalition of Egypt and various Philistine cities against Sennacherib. In preparation for the possibility of a siege, Hezekiah cut a tunnel under David's city in Jerusalem and channeled the waters of the Gihon spring into the city, blocking the original entrance. This conduit is still in use.

The allied armies were crushed by Sennacherib at Eltekeh in the year 701 B.C. From the coastal plain, in which the decisive battle was fought, Sennacherib advanced against the cities of Judah. The siege and capture of Lachish are shown in detail on a large four-paneled relief from his palace at Nineveh. The Assyrian infantry is assaulting the city in three columns, with the javelin throwers in the van, followed by bow-men operating in pairs; behind these come the slingers whose weapon had the longest range of all. The city of Lachish is seen on the second panel, with its double wall and double gateway towering above it (confirmed by archaeological excavations). The defenders stand on the turrets and pinnacles,

shooting arrows and throwing stones from behind the protection of wooden frames and shields. In the foreground the Assyrian army is seen mounting its assault. Battering rams are brought up against the walls; when the defenders try to set them on fire with blazing torches, the crews protect their engines by pouring water on them. In the compressed manner of Assyrian pictorial representation, the surrender of the city is portrayed as taking place at the same time as the siege. The women and children are leaving by a gate, while the bodies of some of the defenders are being impaled. In the third and fourth panels captives are being led before Sennacherib enthroned outside his tent. Some of the vanquished plead for mercy; others—differently dressed, perhaps Hezekiah's men—are being killed and tortured. The spoils include ritual appurtenances, weapons, and a chariot. Some of the inhabitants are seen being deported at the lower left.

From Lachish the Assyrian army advanced on Jerusalem, spurning Hezekiah's peace overtures. The commanders of the invading force tried to shake the loyalty of the people of Judah by direct appeals over the head of the king. But Isaiah strengthened the people's will to resist, and sudden disaster—possibly a plague—befell the besieging army. Sennacherib had to be content with accepting tribute from Hezekiah and withdrew his forces in haste. Later he was assassinated by two of his sons at Nineveh. Judah was saved from total destruction for the time being.

THE EXILE OF JUDAH

Hezekiah was succeeded by his son Manasseh, who restored the cults of Baal and Astarte, perhaps under Assyrian pressure. Throughout his reign (697–643 B.C.) Manasseh remained the loyal vassal of Esarhaddon and Ashurbanipal, the last great Assyrian rulers, and by his prudence not only saved his kingdom from disaster but was even able to strengthen it somewhat. His son and successor, Amon, followed the same policy, until his life was cut short by assassination. Manasseh's grandson, Josiah, reaped the fruits of his grandfather's political prudence. As the power of Assyria was now visibly waning, he was able to extend his kingdom northwards, annexing the southern parts of

Samaria. In his reign (640–609 B.C.) great reforms were instituted in the religious life of Judah, for "he walked in all the way of David his father and turned not aside to the right hand or the left". The Temple was thoroughly purged of idolatrous rites; a law book, probably an early form of the Book of Deuteronomy, opportunely found in the Temple, was made the law of the land; and the various local sanctuaries scattered about the country, including that of Bethel, were abolished. The Temple at Jerusalem was henceforth to be the one and only place of sacrifice.

Unfortunately, Josiah's political wisdom was not equal to his religious zeal. When the king of Egypt, Pharaoh Neco, advanced into Palestine in 609 B.C. on his way to Nineveh to help his tottering Assyrian ally against the rising power of Babylonia, Josiah barred his way at Megiddo and there lost the battle and his life.

Josiah's son, Jehoahaz, reigned for only three months and was then replaced by his brother Jehoiakim, an Egyptian vassal, who, after the Babylonian victory at Carchemish in 605 B.C., submitted to the new imperial power. Jehoiakim was succeeded by Jehoiachin, who after a reign of only three months was deposed by Nebuchadnezzar and deported, together with his courtiers and ministers, and all the craftsmen, smiths, and military commanders. His captivity was, however, an honorable one: he was kept at the Babylonian court and well cared for.

A newly discovered Babylonian chronicle confirms the Biblical account. According to this source, Nebuchadnezzar king of Babylonia "encamped against the city of Judah (i.e. Jerusalem) and in the month of Adar, on the second day, he captured the city and took the king prisoner. A king of his own choice he set up in its midst; its heavy tribute he received and carried it off to Babylon." The king appointed by Nebuchadnezzar was Jehoiachin's uncle, who reigned under the name of Zedekiah (597–586 B.C.).

After submitting to the Babylonian yoke for nine years, while all the time a war party and a peace party struggled to gain the upper hand at his court, Zedekiah finally revolted, despite the warnings of the prophets Jeremiah and Ezekiel, and was besieged in Jerusalem by the Babylonian army. After a long struggle the Babylonians breached the city wall; Zedekiah attempted to flee but was captured on the road to Jericho and blinded at Riblah. In accordance with the Assyrian and Babylonian policy of razing and burning cities

And Nebuchadnezzar king of Babylon came to the city, while his servants were besieging it; and Jehoiachin the king of Judah gave himself up to the king of Babylon . . . (2 KINGS 24 : 11–12)

Babylonian chronicle of Nebuchadnezzar's reign. (British Museum)

In the first year of Cyrus king of Persia . . . the LORD stirred up the spirit of Cyrus king of Persia so that he made a proclamation throughout all his kingdom and also put it in writing . . . "The LORD the God of Heaven, has given me all the kingdoms of the earth, and he has charged me to build him a house at Jerusalem, which is in Judah." (EZRA I: I-2)

Cylinder of Cyrus proclaiming restoration of the temples. 538 B.C. (British Museum)

taken by assault, Nebuzaradan, the captain of the guard, was entrusted with the work of destroying Jerusalem. He performed his task with systematic thoroughness.

With similar ruthlessness, the Babylonians executed the national leaders and royal ministers of Judah, deported the remaining dignitaries, pillaged the Temple treasury, and reduced parts of the city walls to rubble, burning down the Temple, the palace, and every "great house".

The destruction of Jerusalem put an end to the political independence of Judah, which was turned into a Babylonian province. But the hope of redemption and national revival lived on in the people's hearts.

THE BOOKS OF EZRA
AND NEHEMIAH

THE DESTRUCTION OF Jerusalem did not mark the lowest point in the fortunes of Judah. The Babylonians set up a local administration under Gedaliah the son of Ahikam, a former high royal official and leader of the peace-party at the court of Zedekiah. Gedaliah established himself at Mizpah, north of Jerusalem; but his

157

efforts to ensure some sort of tolerable existence for those of the population left in Judah were cut short by his assassination at the hands of a fanatical political opponent instigated by the Ammonites, who sought to profit from Judah's downfall. Fearing punitive action by Nebuchadnezzar, most of the few leading personalities left in Judah fled to Egypt, taking with them the prophet Jeremiah. In Judah there remained only the "poor of the land to be vinedressers and husbandmen".

The situation looked much less desperate in Babylonia, where successive deportations had concentrated the aristocracy, priests and prophets of Israel—virtually everyone of superior character and ability. Led by priests and prophets like Ezekiel, the exiles resolutely refused to assimilate with the Babylonians, although the commercial classes among them found a large and profitable field of operations. They fervently kept alive the hope of a return, which could not be long delayed, now that the exile had purged the people of their sins. A great prophet of consolation, known to scholars as the Second Isaiah, arose among them. At the same time the priests were busy codifying and collating the various laws and ordinances which should govern the conduct of the nation in the future to make it a truly holy people, and plans were drawn up for a new Temple.

The political situation soon began to favor such hopes. The short-lived Neo-Babylonian empire declined rapidly after the death of its one powerful ruler, Nebuchadnezzar. His weak successors were soon set aside by an energetic usurper, Nabunaid (Nabonidus), a religious reformer of great zeal. He left Babylonia in the hands of his son Belshazzar, and went to live at Teima in the Arabian desert. Babylon was overwhelmed by a new power, that of the united Persians and the Medes under Cyrus, who created a great empire, more efficient, larger and vastly more tolerant than those of Assyria or Babylonia. In 539 B.C. Cyrus occupied Babylon almost without a struggle.

One of his first acts was to order a general restoration of the religious cults that had been brutally suppressed by the Babylonians. Among the measures taken by him in this

With vessels of silver, with gold, with goods, with beasts . . .   (EZRA I : 6)

Babylonians bearing tribute on Persepolis relief. Fifth century B.C.

The province of Judah . . . (EZRA 5: 8)

Seal impression on jar-handle
from Ramet Rahal.

connection was his proclamation to the Jewish people declaring that God "hath charged me to build a house at Jerusalem which is in Judah", and that whoever of the exiles wished should "go up to Jerusalem . . . and build the house of the LORD". This proclamation is not unique. On a cylinder inscribed in cuneiform Cyrus similarly presents himself as the emissary of Marduk the god of Babylon, adding: "For all those whose temples have been in ruins many days, I restored to their places the images of the gods . . . and erected for them everlasting shrines. I gathered together the inhabitants and restored to them their dwelling places."

In spite of the royal decree, the return to Zion was a slow and weary process. The first to make the long and arduous journey was a group, including priests and Levites, led by one Sheshbazzar, a prince of Judah, possibly a descendant of Jehoiachin, king of Judah. Those who decided to remain in exile made contributions to those returning home, in the spirit of Cyrus's proclamation which stipulated that those going should be helped "with silver and gold, with goods, and with beasts".

The choice of the articles listed here was by no means arbitrary, but represented the durable and negotiable objects most likely to be useful to the returning exiles. A similar selection is shown on the reliefs of the palace of the Persian king Darius, at Persepolis. A delegation of Babylonians is seen approaching the royal presence. The first two have bowls of silver or gold in their hands, the third a piece of woven material with tasseled ends, and the last two are leading a hump-backed bull. Cyrus himself ordered that the Temple vessels carried away by Nebuchadnezzar should be restored to their rightful owners.

The difficulties facing the returning exiles became fully apparent only when they reached their goal. The Judah to which they returned had been reduced to a tiny province by the annexations of large areas of its former territory by the neighboring nations. Jerusalem itself was desolate, and the few Judaeans still left there were desperately poor and out of touch with the remainder of the nation. The people of Samaria, descendants of a mixed group of indigenous Israelites and Babylonian settlers established in Samaria by the Assyrians, claimed that Jerusalem was within their domain and demanded to be allowed to share with the Judaeans in the Temple worship, a demand which the latter were not willing to allow. Troubles in the Persian empire after the death of Cyrus's son Cambyses, and denunciations by the officials residing at Samaria further delayed the restoration of the Temple. This was finally completed after the original of Cyrus's decree had been found in the royal archives at Ecbatana. The final steps were taken by a new wave of immigrants, led by a descendant of David, Zerubbabel the son of Shealtiel, and the high priest, Jeshua the son of Jozadak, who were roused to action by the prophets Haggai and Zechariah.

The Second Temple was at last dedictated in 515 B.C., in the presence of some who remembered the First. Although in their eyes the new Temple was "as nothing" in comparison with Solomon's magnificent shrine, Haggai foretold that "the glory of this latter house shall be greater than that of the former" (Haggai 2: 3, 9). In any case with the rebuilding of the Temple a great step forward had been taken, and a new national and religious center had been created.

The work of restoration was greatly facilitated by the large measure of autonomy granted by the Persians to Judah. The Persian empire, stretching from the Mediterranean and the Black Sea to India, was too vast to permit of any close central supervision of the affairs of every province. The Persian kings therefore delegated much of their authority to twenty governors, known as *satraps* (a corruption of a Persian word meaning "over-seer"), each ruling over a territory known as a satrapy. The fifth of these satrapies, called "Beyond the River" (i.e. beyond the Euphrates—from the point of view of the Persian king residing east of it in Susa or Persepolis) included all the lands from Asia Minor to Egypt. The autonomous province of *Yehud* (the Aramaic form of Judah) had its own local governor, who ruled it in consultation with the high priest and the elders of the people. For a time the governor was Zerubbabel. He may have had still higher ambitions, but his name suddenly disappears from the records, and it is not known what actually happened to him. This is the last we hear of the dynasty of David. Henceforward it was the high priests that stood at the head of the Jewish nation.

The governors of the provinces issued their own currency, imitating the contemporary Athenian coinage with the image of an owl, but with the addition of the name of the particular province. Stamp-impressions inscribed "Yehud", followed by the name of a governor or Temple treasurer, have been found on jar-handles on various sites in Palestine. One such handle, excavated at Jericho, has the name "Uria" stamped on it. Some scholars have suggested that this is Uriah the son of Hakkoz, the father of Meremoth (Neh. 3: 4, 21) who was Temple treasurer; apparently the office was hereditary in the family. The jars thus stamped served for the collection of taxes in kind which were stored at district centers (of which Jericho was one).

Although the material condition of Judah continued to improve under the rule of Darius and his successors, the steadily developing community was beset by many spiritual difficulties. The ideals of Judaism elaborated in the Exile by the priests and prophets laid great stress on the strict observance of the Mosaic Law. But the renascent community in Judah disregarded many of the injunctions of this Law, especially as regards intermarriage with persons of the surrounding nations and the commandments concerning priestly purity and the sanctity of the Temple. It was to put an end to this religious laxity that Ezra the scribe—apparently a royal official in charge of Jewish religious affairs, a "ready scribe in the law of Moses"—set out for Judah from Babylonia. He did so with royal consent, being empowered to appoint magistrates and judges, to instruct the people in the Law of God and to enforce it on a par with the law of the king. A large group of priests and Levites joined Ezra on his journey, carrying with them many gifts for the Temple in money and in kind.

Traveling as he was with royal sanction, Ezra was entitled to an escort of Persian soldiers. Enforcing the king's rule in the satrapies and patrolling the vital lines of communication were among the tasks assigned to the Persian army, which contained some of the finest troops in

For I was ashamed to ask the king for a band of soldiers and horsemen to protect us against the enemy on our way . . .
(EZRA 8 : 22)

The frieze of the archers from Susa.
Fifth century B.C. (Louvre, Paris)

antiquity. Some of these soldiers are represented on a frieze, made from glazed bricks, found in the royal palace at Susa.

Safely arrived in Jerusalem, Ezra at once made a powerful appeal to the people assembled in the Temple for the evening sacrifice. So greatly were his hearers moved by his pious eloquence that they agreed to cease their transgressions forthwith. Ezra then called a second special assembly of all the "children of the captivity" and the men of Judah and Benjamin in the "street of the house of God", probably a square in front of the Temple. There the people, trembling in remorse for their sins and chilled to the bone by the heavy winter rain, solemnly renewed their covenant with God, and swore to sin no more. In particular, Ezra insisted on the dissolution of the mixed marriages with the neighboring nations which had been particularly offensive to the priests and the community in exile.

THE STORY OF NEHEMIAH

THE STORY OF Ezra is at this point interrupted in the biblical record by part of the story of Nehemiah. Subsequently it is resumed, and we are told how he read the Law to the people (Neh. 8), and how the people accepted its obligations. Scholars are divided in their opinions about the course of the history. Many believe that Ezra actually followed Nehemiah, either later in the reign of Artaxerxes I or in the reign of Artaxerxes II. The issue is a complex one, and here the stories of the two men are simply narrated side by side without any precise attempt at relating them together.

All Ezra's endeavors in the religious sphere would have been in vain if a solid political basis for a national revival had not already been provided by Nehemiah the son of Hachaliah. In the Book of Nehemiah we have an account, based on Nehemiah's own memoirs, of the events connected with this great man.

Nehemiah was that peculiar combination of politician and visionary which occurs from time to time in Jewish history. His story opens with him serving as cupbearer to the Persian king, Artaxerxes I (465–425 B.C.). Deeply distressed by the news he received from Jerusalem of the abject plight of its inhabitants and of the defenseless state of the city itself, with its broken walls and burnt gates, he succeeded in obtaining the king's authorization to go there on a special mission, accompanied by an escort of Persian cavalry and invested with full powers to requisition materials for the rebuilding of the walls. Nehemiah set out in the twentieth year of Artaxerxes' reign (445 B.C.). Arrived safely at Jerusalem, he quickly apprised himself of the situation and in particular of the opposition he would have to expect from Judah's neighbors. The leading spirit in this opposition was Sanballat, the governor of the province of Samaria, who had till then exercised some form or degree of control over Judah, and, moreover, had relatives among the aristocratic families in Jerusalem; the creation of a new center of authority there would naturally not be at all to his liking. Another enemy was Tobiah, the governor of the district of Ammon, a member of an old Israelite family and a relative by marriage of the high priest Eliashib, who represented the opposition of the rich and influential Jewish circles to any reform that might diminish their power to exploit the poor.

Nehemiah outwitted these formidable opponents by shrewd planning, absolute secrecy, and swift action at the opportune moment. First he reconnoitred the walls of Jerusalem by

*Why should not my face be sad, when the city, the place of
my fathers' sepulchres, lies waste . . .* (NEH. 2: 3)

◀ Part of the ancient cemetery
in the Kidron Valley.

night with a very small body of men. In his account of this reconnaissance, and in the
following chapter describing the actual repairs of the walls, we have the only complete
survey of the extent of the Jerusalem of Old Testament times. Since Nehemiah himself
states that he did not build a new wall but only repaired the breaches in the old, it follows
that the line traced by him is that of the pre-exilic wall reduced to rubble by Nebuchadnezzar.

Ancient Jerusalem was built on a spur running out from the central ridge of mountains
which forms the watershed between the Mediterranean and the Dead Sea. This spur branches
out into two hills at its southern end, where it slopes down into the Valley of Ben-Hinnom.
All scholars are agreed that the City of David (and ancient Jebus before it) stood on the
eastern of these two hills, the one from which the spring Gihon issues. It is also agreed that
Solomon extended the city area by erecting the Temple on the site now occupied by the
Dome of the Rock, and building his palace between the Temple and the City of David. But
there is still no concensus of scholarly opinion as to whether the western hill (now commonly
and erroneously called "Mount Zion") was part of Solomon's city. In the reconstruction
given here the valley between the two hills is included in the city area, but not the western
hill itself.

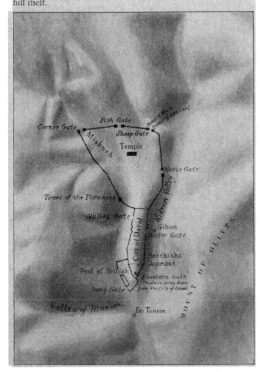

*Then I went up in the night by
the valley and inspected the wall;
and I turned back and entered by
the Valley Gate, and so returned.*
(NEH. 2: 15)

Plan of Jerusalem in Nehemiah's
time.

On his night reconnaissance Nehemiah rode out of the city on its western side by the Valley Gate and made a circuit of the walls until he reached the Fountain Gate at their south-eastern end; here the rubble was heaped so high that he had to dismount and continue on foot across the City of David. Having thus obtained a clear picture of what needed to be done, he next called together "the priests, nobles and officials" and, after producing his royal credentials, had no difficulty in persuading them to "put their necks to the work of the LORD".

The repairs were performed by groups of volunteers, each working on a stretch of wall assigned to it. The description of the various assignments starts from the Sheep Gate north of the Temple and runs anti-clockwise westwards and then southwards, returning to the north to complete the ring of the walls. The different sectors were of unequal length, the determining factors in each case clearly being the equal distribution of labor (since the amount of repair work necessary varied from place to place) and the economic ability of the group responsible for each particular sector. The priests were set to repairing the walls of the Temple Mount, while the merchants were put to work near their shops. Since most of the sectors were distributed among the inhabitants of the various districts of Judah, the list incidentally provides us with a survey of the administrative subdivisions of the province. In a few cases individuals or groups undertook a second stretch of the walls in addition to their original one.

Only a few points in the various sectors can now be indentified with certainty. One of these is in the area repaired by Shallum, the ruler of the district of Mizpah, which included the "Fountain Gate . . . and the wall of the Pool of Shelah by the king's garden, as far as the *stairs that go down from the City of David*". These steps were discovered in 1914 in excavations at the southeastern end of the eastern hill, the site of the City of David. They are cut into the rocks at a very steep angle and run diagonally downwards from the city. The flight, which is 43 feet long and about 6 feet wide, leads to a gate in the wall which apparently was the ancient "gate between the walls".

The whole repair of the walls was completed in the remarkably short time of fifty-two days; the people worked with a will, despite some grumbling, disregarding all threats of their enemies. Throughout this period, every one of the builders "with one hand labored on the work and with the other held his weapon". Nehemiah kept half his labor force armed and ready for defensive action; he himself moved from sector to sector with a trumpeter at his side, ever ready to sound the alarm.

In the meantime, the enemies of Judah were not idle. They well understood that, once the new community was protected by a strong wall, all attempts to wreck the work of restoration and reform would be unavailing. The main center of the opposition to Nehemiah was at Samaria, where Sanballat the Horonite, the leader of the Samaritans, was joined by Tobiah the Ammonite and Geshem (or Gashmu) the Arab. They plotted to assassinate Nehemiah and tried to undermine his standing with the Persian king by accusing him of inciting the

> In it was written, "It is reported among the nations, and Geshem also says it . . ."
>
> (NEH. 6:6)

Silver dish with inscription of "Qainu the son of Geshem the king of Qedar". Fifth to fourth century B.C. (Brooklyn Museum)

Jews to revolt so as to make himself king of Judah. The Geshem mentioned here was probably an early Nabatean ruler, perhaps the one referred to on a dish inscribed "Qainu the son of Geshem the king of Qedar". The Nabateans may then have been allies of the Ammonite ruler Tobiah, who was their neighbor; or Geshem may have been the governor of Edom (Idumaea), i.e. the southern part of Judah, lost since the destruction of the First Temple to the Edomites. These neighbors of Judah who after her defeat had taken over large slices of her former territory were naturally not anxious to see her strengthened again.

Having successfully completed the repair of the walls, Nehemiah had to deal with the social problems of the Judaean community in order to strengthen it internally. Bad harvests and high taxes had caused much social distress. The small peasants had pledged their lands to the rich, and some had even had to give their children in bondage to their creditors. By his energetic intervention and impassioned appeals Nehemiah brought about the cancellation of all such mortgages, thus restoring social stability to Judah. His enemies now tried to get him into their power by luring him to a meeting in the Plain of Ono. Failing in this, they hired "prophets" to speak against him. And when that too produced no effect, they sought to frighten him into taking refuge in the Temple, only to be met with Nehemiah's proud and fearless refusal: "Should such a man as I flee?"

After the completion of the walls Nehemiah took further measures to frustrate the designs of Judah's enemies. He fortified the *birah*, the stronghold situated on the vulnerable northern side of the Temple, appointed a trustworthy governor of Jerusalem, instituted a roster of guard-duty from among the inhabitants, had the gates shut at sunset and kept shut throughout the night, and ordered all the nobles and one-tenth of the common people to take up residence in Jerusalem, for "the city was wide and large, but the people were few therein".

Men of Tyre also, who lived in the city, brought in fish and all kinds of wares and sold them on the Sabbath to the people of Judah, and in Jerusalem.

(NEH. 13 : 16)

Phoenicians on Persepolis relief. Fifth century B.C.

He ensured the proper observation of the prescriptions concerning the payment of tithes and the portions of the Levites. But for himself he was satisfied with the minimal prerogatives of his office, shunning all additional exactions.

When these reforms had been carried through, the new walls were solemnly inaugurated. The people walked along them in two great processions, the one going eastwards and the other westwards from the southernmost point of the walls, until they both met in the north and descended together into the Temple court to give thanks to the LORD.

Nehemiah now paid a brief visit to the Persian court, where his governorship of Judah was renewed for a further term. While he was away, the high priest Eliashib took advantage of his absence to allot his relative, Tobiah "the Ammonite", rooms in the Temple courts. On his return to Jerusalem Nehemiah at once used the full powers in which he had been confirmed by the Persian king to eject Tobiah and his possessions from the Temple chambers.

Nehemiah also had to deal with the problem of the brisk trade plied on the Sabbath, in complete disregard of the holiness of the day, by both the Judaeans and the Tyrians. The latter, because of their close business connections with the Phoenician coastal cities, were in a position to supply the population of Judah with many of its requirements. Moreover, as the mainstays of the Persian navy the Tyrians (and Sidonians) enjoyed the support of the central imperial government, which had already showed its special favor to them by presenting them with large stretches of the Palestinian coast to supplement the meager resources of their own territories. We are familiar with the physical appearance of these traders from the reliefs belonging to the reigns of Darius I or Xerxes; they are shown wearing the characteristic

Syrian caps and bringing the king a gift of two jars, two bowls, and two bracelets. By closing the city gates on the Sabbath and threatening the desecrators of the day of rest with bodily harm, Nehemiah put a stop to this trade.

An unfortunate result of the energetic enforcement of the full rigor of the Law was the deepening schism between the Jews and the Samaritans. One of the sons of Jehoiada, the son of Eliashib, had married the daughter of Sanballat the Horonite; when Nehemiah drove him out of Jerusalem, he went over to Samaria and helped to establish the rival worship on Mount Gerizim which has continued to this day. With the building of the temple on Mount Gerizim somewhat later the two communities were completely and irrevocably sundered. This 1,600 foot eminence is part of the watershed ridge of the mountains of Ephraim; it is covered with olive groves and has numerous springs at its base. In Deuteronomy it appears as the mountain of blessings (in contrast to Mount Ebal opposite), on which the covenant between Israel and the LORD was to be renewed, as was actually done in the days of Joshua. The temple of the Samaritans enjoyed the favor of foreign rulers from Antiochus Ephiphanes (175–164 B.C.) onwards though it was destroyed by the Jewish ruler John Hyrcanus in the later part of the century. Rebuilt subsequently it continued in existence long after its Jerusalem counterpart, being finally destroyed only in the fifth century A.D.

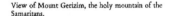

View of Mount Gerizim, the holy mountain of the Samaritans.

THE BOOK OF ESTHER

THE BOOK OF ESTHER is placed in a historical setting contemporary with that of the Book of Nehemiah. It is not, however, history in the strict sense, but rather a vividly told romance about the miraculous deliverance of the Jews from extermination in the days of the Persian Empire. The story begins with a description of the might of "King Ahasuerus", usually identified with Xerxes, the son of Darius (486–465 B.C.), who is represented in Greek sources as a temperamental monarch, much given to sensual pleasures and accustomed to delegating some of his royal powers to his ministers. The Book of Esther opens with an account of a huge banquet supposedly given by this monarch to the grandees of his court, the commanders of the armies of Persia and Media, and the nobles and princes of the provinces.

The guests reclined on sumptuous couches inlaid with gold and silver, in pavilions of white, green, and blue. The drink was served in vessels of gold, each one differing in shape from the next. Many artistically wrought Persian gold vessels have survived the centuries. They include a gold goblet of the sixth or fifth century B.C., ending in the body of a lion, a common decorative motif on the gold vessels and jewels of the Persian kings. Winged lions also appear on a gold cup of the same period, which has handles shaped like double-headed ibexes.

A parallel feast for the women was given by Queen Vashti in her palace. On the seventh day of the banquet the king commanded Vashti to appear before the assembled princes, thus infringing the convention which kept the royal consort within the walls of the palace harem. When Vashti indignantly refused to display herself in public she was forbidden to come any more into the royal presence. After a long search among the beauties of the empire for a suitable successor to the queen the royal choice fell on Esther, the niece of the Jew Mordecai, a descendant of the Benjaminites, who had been exiled together with king Jeconiah (Jehoiachin).

While Esther reigned as Ahasuerus' queen, Mordecai was instrumental in exposing a conspiracy of two of the king's chamberlains, a matter which was recorded in the royal chronicle.

Soon after this the status of the Jews in the Persian Empire was threatened by the rise of Haman the son of Hammedatha, an Amalekite, who had inherited a burning hatred of Israel from his ancestors. When Haman became the all-powerful vizier of Ahasuerus, he prevailed upon the king to issue a decree ordering the extermination of the Jews throughout his empire and the confiscation of their property. The day fixed for the massacre was the thirteenth of Adar. The utter consternation with which the grim news was received by the Jewish community found expression in deep mourning and prolonged fasting.

Acquainted by Mordecai with the disaster threatening her nation, Esther took the extraordinary step of going to the king on her own initiative, well knowing that she did so at the risk of her life; for unless the king extended his scepter to her she would certainly be put to death for her effrontery. Dressed in her full regal attire she stood, trembling with apprehension, in the inner court, opposite the king's regal chamber, from where she could see Ahasuerus sitting on his throne with his golden scepter in his hand. Her life and the fate of her nation hung upon the movement of that scepter.

· How Ahasuerus looked at this critical moment we can infer from a relief at Persepolis, showing King Darius seated upon his throne. He is wearing a wide-sleeved robe and holding a royal scepter, topped by a knob of gold or a precious stone, in his right hand, and

In the third year of his reign he gave a banquet for all his princes and servants, the army chiefs of Persia and Media and the nobles and governors of the provinces being before him. (ESTHER 1 : 3)

Persian and Median nobles on Persepolis relief.
Fifth century B.C.

a lotus flower with two buds in his left. The throne without arms on which he is sitting and the footstool under his feet are both made of wood overlaid with gold; the legs of the throne end in lion's paws. The scepter in the king's hand was also apparently of gilded wood. When held upright it was as tall as a man, so that the king could easily stretch it out to anyone standing at some distance from him in the inner court. This happened now: the king held out the golden scepter to Esther; she touched the tip of it and was saved. Not daring as yet to reveal her real purpose, Esther did no more than invite the king and Haman, his vizier, to a banquet.

At the banquet Esther succeeded in artfully insinuating that Haman had designs on her own person. So incensed was the king by this seemingly brazen affront to his own and his

Seal it with the king's ring...
(ESTHER 8 : 8)

Above: Gold signet ring from Persepolis.

Below: Impression of the seal of Xerxes. Fifth century B.C. (Oriental Institute, Chicago)

queen's honor that he ordered the immediate execution of the fallen minister and all his family. The royal decrees against the Jews were revoked and new ones despatched, written by Esther and Mordecai and signed with the royal seal. The "king's ring" was the signet ring with which official documents were signed to give them royal sanction. In ancient Persia documents were sealed in one of two ways: with a signet ring if they were written on papyrus, or with a cylinder seal if they were written on clay tablets. Among the objects excavated at Persepolis there is a gold ring, engraved with the figure of an antelope. This was the kind of ring used for making an impression on the lump of clay which sealed the knot in the string tied round a folded sheet of papyrus. One such seal-impression, which belonged to King Xerxes and was found on an Elamite tablet in the royal treasury at Persepolis, shows the king standing between two winged bulls, with a winged emblem of the sun (symbolizing the Persian god Ahuramazda) over his head. On the left there is a palm tree, another typical motif on the Persian royal seals of the period.

Armed with unlimited powers, Esther and Mordecai were able to send the new decrees by the swift mules and camels of the royal post, and thereby turn the mourning of the Jews into glad rejoicing. This miraculous salvation is still commemorated annually by the Jewish festival of Purim.

Poetry

Then Job arose and rent his robe, and shaved his head, and fell upon the ground, and worshiped. (JOB I : 20)

Mourning Egyptians. Tomb of Edu, Gizeh, Egypt. Second half of third millennium B.C.

THE BOOK OF JOB

JOB'S DISASTERS AND DESPAIR

WITH THE BOOK OF JOB we leave, for the time being, the historical setting of the books thus far treated. The background of Job is the legendary period of the Patriarchs as seen from the literary viewpoint of the seventh or sixth century B.C. The hero of the book is a patriarchal nomad living in the land of Uz, a just man of exemplary piety, who when the story opens possesses great wealth in cattle and a numerous progeny.

The scene then moves to heaven, where the Satan, "the adversary" (from a Hebrew verb meaning "to accuse"), appears among the "sons of God" attending upon the Divine Presence. When, true to his function, "the adversary" casts doubts on Job's piety as not yet having been tested by misfortune, God agrees to try His servant, first by the loss of all his possessions, and then by the sudden destruction of all his family in a desert hurricane.

When Job experienced this shattering reversal of his fortunes, he rent his garment, shaved his head and fell down upon the ground, thus demonstrating in the traditional way of the Orient his bitter grief at the disasters that had come upon him. Shaving the head and covering it with dust were part of the conventional mourning rites of antiquity. Job's prostrating himself on the ground further symbolizes his resignation to the fate meted out to him by God. The customary ways of expressing grief and mourning were in the main similar throughout the ancient East. They were also a common theme on ancient reliefs and paintings, especially in Egypt. Men and women are there shown lifting their hands to their heads, falling upon the ground, and wailing loudly.

But even this was not the end of Job's calamities for the Satan now suggested that he should be still further proved by bodily suffering, and he was accordingly smitten with boils. Taking a potsherd to scrape himself with, Job sat down on an ash-heap while his wife, in despair, advised him to end his sufferings by cursing God and dying. But Job still patiently accepted his fate. Then three of his friends came to visit him and to bewail his bitter misfortunes.

This first part of the Book of Job is a straightforward prose prologue to the great debate which now follows between the hero and his three friends, and which consists of three cycles of poetic dialogue. In each of them Job speaks first, is answered by his three friends in turn, and finally replies to their answers. The theme of this debate is the age-old philosophical enigma: Why does the just man suffer? To the ancient Hebrews, who had as yet no conception of reward and punishment in another world, but considered that all rewards and punishments were meted out by God on earth, the problem as thus stated appeared insoluble. Hence Job is forced by his sufferings to doubt God's justice; his friends, on the other hand, assume that he must have committed some secret sin which is being punished by the Deity. This suggestion is vehemently and indignantly rejected by the sufferer; he feels himself to be blameless and regards his friends as traitors.

In one of his similes Job compares his "brethren" to the "treacherous" torrent beds. Such seasonal winter torrents are characteristic of all countries with a short period of winter rains, followed by a long, dry summer. They are especially numerous in the Negeb, the southern part of Israel, where normally waterless wadis may be flooded with spectacular suddenness. There are several reasons for this: the large area drained by these watercourses; the absence of vegetation that could retard the flow of water in their upper reaches; the non-porous nature of the limestone, marl rocks, and loess soil of this region, which increases the volume of water; and the fact that the sudden downpours are confined to limited areas. All these factors together are responsible for the remarkable phenomenon of watercourses, which are so completely dry for most of the year that Beduin encamped on their banks almost die of thirst, yet which suddenly fill with a tremendous spate of water. But as these watercourses dry up again as quickly as they are flooded, the hopes raised by them are treacherously disappointed; hence Job compares his friends to such "dry torrents" in the midst of the desert.

Bitterly complaining of his unmerited sufferings, Job compares his fate to that of the wretched and oppressed classes of ancient society, such as the slave toiling in the sun's merciless heat. In the hot climate of the Near East, shade is what everyone toiling in the fields most desires. Outside the cities, in antiquity, natural shade was only sparsely provided by trees; where there were no trees, a booth was sometimes erected. Wayfarers, especially in desert regions, occasionally found protection under a rock. The slave toiling in the fields, to whom Job likens himself, was given no time to rest in the shade; he could only long for the evening with its refreshing shadows and coolness. Those farm-laborers that could take advantage of any available shade never failed to do so; thus shepherds are often represented in Egyptian paintings resting under trees, their crooks in their hands, drinking from a jug, while the animals in their charge nibble at the vegetation.

Like a slave who longs for the shadow, and like a hireling who looks for his wages, so I am allotted months of emptiness, and nights of misery are apportioned to me.

(JOB 7: 2-3)

Relief from the tomb of Ahhotep at Sakkarah, from the end of the Fifth Dynasty, middle of the third millennium B.C.

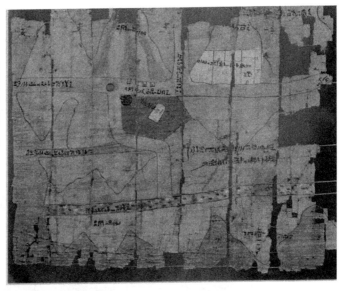

Surely there is a mine for silver, and a place for gold which they refine. Iron is taken out of the earth, and copper is smelted from the ore.

(JOB 28 : 1–2)

Egyptian map drawn on papyrus (from the thirteenth century B.C.) showing the gold-mines in Waddi Hammamat, in the desert east of the Nile.

THE PRAISE OF WISDOM

ONE OF THE gems of the Book of Job is in chapter 28, an impassioned praise of Wisdom, whose source man is incapable of discovering either in the bowels of the earth or at the bottom of the sea, and whose worth he cannot begin to estimate. God, and God alone, "knows its place". This chapter opens with a poetic description of man's ability to mine precious minerals from the depths of the earth. Even though Wisdom eludes man there, too, his technical achievement is still to be admired. In fact this chapter contains the earliest extant descriptions of the mining methods of the ancients: the cutting of underground galleries to get to the ores, and their extraction by washing or smelting. Mining in the Arabah and the Sinai Peninsula began as early as the Chalcolithic Age; at first copper was mined, then iron. The Sinai Peninsula was already being exploited by the Egyptians in the third millennium B.C. In Upper Egypt and in Midian there were gold mines in which the lumps of earth containing the precious ore were burnt out of the rock-face or chipped off with picks made of stone or bronze. The gold was then refined close to the mine by washing in rain water. Special maps were drawn showing the location of gold mines in the desert. Such knowledge was of course extremely valuable; but Wisdom was still harder to find.

Indeed, the poet continues, so great is Wisdom's worth that it is more precious not only than gold but even than glass. The word for glass (Hebrew: *zekhukhit*, "crystal" in the AV) occurs only here in the Old Testament, but is frequent in later Hebrew and the cognate Semitic languages. In the ancient East, glass was an article of great luxury, of even higher value than the most precious of metals, gold. The Egyptians were the first to produce glass-ware,

175

Can you bind the chains of the Pleiades, or loose the cords of Orion? Can you lead forth the Mazzaroth in their season, or can you guide the Bear with its children? (JOB 38 : 31–32)

as early as the fourth millennium B.C. This early glass was not, however, transparent and was used mainly as inlay for jewelry in place of precious stones. Later on, glass vessels were produced which served as cosmetic containers and the like. They were made by stretching semi-liquid glass threads around a core of sand, a process which produced the characteristic "feather" decoration. Glass-making was later taken up by the Phoenicians, who became famous for their products, especially after they had discovered methods of glass-blowing and glass-pressing similar to those used today.

GOD'S WONDERS IN NATURE

WHEN JOB AND his three friends have said all that they have to say, and when another younger man, Elihu the son of Barachel the Buzite, has also tried to answer Job by a justification of God's ways, the Almighty Himself, speaking out of a whirlwind, finally refutes the sufferer's contentions. This He does by a vivid and powerful description of the ineffable marvels of the creation, thus throwing into sharp relief the utter inability of a mere creature like man to judge its omnipotent Creator. The wonders described by God range from the cosmic to the natural. Among the former are the great heavenly constellations that were visible to the naked eye of the ancients, including the Pleiades (Hebrew: *kimah*) and Orion (Hebrew: *ksil*). These terms were part of the general stock of astrological lore in the ancient East. The most important contributions to this knowledge were made by the Babylonians and Egyptians, who for generations compiled tables of constellations based on the division of the skies into "regions", the estimated distance between the stars, and the position of the signs of the Zodiac. Drawings based on ancient originals, which go back to the twelfth century B.C., show imaginary pictures of the moon, the Pleiades, the Bull, Mercury, Virgo, and other constellations.

The second part of God's reply to Job contains descriptions of living creatures whose very existence may be regarded as a miracle, or in whose manner of life there is something beyond human understanding. This sequence of word pictures, all in the form of rhetorical questions, presents Job with a panorama of the transcendental, incomprehensible wisdom out of which the world was created and by which it is controlled. The animals chosen to illustrate this thesis are the lion, the "king of the beasts"; the raven whose young are provided with food by God's abundant mercy; the wild rock-goats, with the miracle of their reproduction, which, because of their extreme wariness, no human eye can behold. Then come the wild asses (*Equus hemi-hippus*) which are exceptional for the lone, untamed existence they

176

Babylonian drawings of constellations.
(Berlin Museum; Louvre, Paris)

lead, roaming the saline steppes and feeding off any and every piece of green vegetation they can find. They therefore occur frequently in the Old Testament as a symbol of the unconstrained and uncivilized life of the desert. The wild ass was difficult to hunt because of its strength and speed, as evidenced in its strong leg muscles and thickset, short neck. For this very reason the Babylonian and Assyrian kings used to hunt the animal for sport, as we learn from their paintings and reliefs.

After a few verses devoted to the wild ox (the "unicorn" of the AV), the poet next describes the ostrich with its fine wings and feathers, dwelling particularly on the two qualities associated by the ancients with this bird: its stupidity and its speed. The ostrich (*Struthio camelus*) today survives only in small numbers in the deserts bordering on Palestine, but in antiquity it was numerous. Its feathers were used as personal adornments by the kings and warriors of Egypt; its eggs were eaten as food and their shells used as receptacles. The bird itself appears in various Egyptian hunting pictures.

Next after the ostrich in the list of nature's marvels comes the horse, followed by the hawk and the eagle. The qualities of the horse singled out for wonder are its strength and valor; apparently this verse was written at a time when cavalry was already being used in warfare, for the poet imaginatively writes of the noble steed that it "saith among the trumpets, ha! ha! and smelleth the battle afar off, the thunder of the captains and the shouting".

Though Job has already been made to feel his own nothingness, the LORD concludes His impressive homily with the description of the two most powerful creatures of all, the Behemoth and the Leviathan. In contrast to the unadorned, naturalistic descriptions of the animals in the first part of the divine reply, the portrayals of these two monsters are colored with flashes of poetic imagination suggestive of ancient myths. At the same time, there is no lack of realistic details. The poet dwells on the Behemoth's enormous strength, its huge bones (like bars of iron), its habit of spreading out its bulk under the river willows, and its power to withstand the force of the river which rushes against its mouth. It is generally assumed that the animal referred to is the hippopotamus, a huge creature which still survives in Upper Egypt and further south; elsewhere it has been exterminated because of the damage it did to cultivation. Hippopotamus hunts are often represented in Egyptian tomb reliefs: the hunters surrounded the animal in their skiffs and plunged harpoons with spiky barbs into its hide, thus causing it to bleed to death. The "Leviathan", probably the crocodile, is described with a similar wealth of imagery.

Crushed by the LORD's arguments, Job repents his presumptuous attempt to judge God's ways and humbles himself. In a prose epilogue, the sufferer is recompensed with renewed prosperity, a larger progeny than before, and long life.

177

Suppliants on relief from tomb of Horemheb. Fourteenth
century B.C. (Leiden Antiquities Museum)

THE BOOK OF PSALMS

THE BOOK OF PSALMS is a collection of one hundred and fifty religious poems
of varying length and content. There are psalms of praise and thanksgiving,
of entreaty and complaint, of lament and repentance. There are also hymns extolling the
people of Israel and its kings, and Zion the City of God and its Temple, as well as didactic
poems. Some psalms seem to be connected with specific ritual acts, such as the dedication
of the Temple, or with specific religious occasions, such as the beginning of the Sabbath or
certain special days of the week. Others reflect political events, such as the coronation of
a king. Almost half of them are attributed to David, and others to Solomon and various
"singers in Israel"; most have musical instructions attached, now obscure in meaning. Like
all the poetry of the ancient East, the psalms followed fixed patterns of thought and expression, suited to certain set themes. Four of such central themes are the ultimate reward of the
just despite all their temporary suffering, the final downfall of the wicked, the omnipotence
of God, and the supremacy on earth of God's anointed, the Davidic king.

THE JUST MAN

THE BOOK OF PSALMS opens with a liturgical poem vividly depicting the
contrast between the just man, favored by God, and his wicked counterpart. The righteous man is poetically compared to the luxuriant tree growing beside streams

of water, which bears its fruits in season and is always green and fresh. This figure of a tree planted by running water is also found in Egyptian and Mesopotamian literature, as is natural in countries where the rivers are the source of life and wealth, and where the most luxuriant forms of vegetation, such as the Jordan tamarisk, the Mesopotamian poplar and the palm, are found on their banks. All these trees are remarkable for the abundance and greenness of their foliage (growing as they do in regions where the annual rainfall is slight), although for ecological reasons they are not tall.

In spite of his assured ultimate success, the path of the just man is beset with tribulations. Surrounded by wicked foes, he is bowed to the dust in anguish and his body cleaves to the earth as he supplicates the LORD to save him. It was customary in the ancient East for anyone presenting an entreaty to go down on his knees, or even to stretch himself full-length on the ground. Foreign suppliants—Canaanites, Libyans, and Ethiopians—are thus represented in Egyptian reliefs. In the el-Amarna letters too we find the expression "(lying) on my belly, on my back I shall hearken to the king's words". Worshipers also used to prostrate themselves in prayer on the paving of the Temple courts, thereby expressing their self-abasement before the Creator and their complete surrender to His will.

Saved by God from his enemies, the just man could fittingly liken himself to the flourishing olive tree, which today as in antiquity is one of the most characteristic features of the landscape of Israel and which once grew in large numbers in the vicinity of the Temple Mount. The olive, a typical Mediterranean tree, is one of the "seven species" for which the Land of Israel was famous. Indeed, a considerable part of the prosperity of the ancient Israelite peasant was derived from the cultivation of this tree, which, once fully grown, yields its fruit year after year with very little tending. It requires neither irrigation nor deep soil, but flourishes even in dry, rocky ground. It supplies oil for cooking and anointing, olives for eating, and wood for fuel. The olive is also one of the most handsome trees of the country; its foliage retains its greenness even in the parched days of summer, when its leafy spreading

He is like a tree planted by streams of water, that
yields its fruit in its season, and its leaf does not wither.
In all that he does, he prospers.   (PSALMS 1: 3)

Palms beside the Jordan.

top is a delight to the heat-weary eye. It is a long-lived tree, sometimes lasting for hundreds of years; its trunk thickens as it grows older, but its vitality is not at all impaired by the passage of time. As longevity and a vigorous old age were regarded as among the principal boons conferred by God on His elect, the olive tree was an especially apt simile for the righteous man.

THE EVILDOER

IN CONTRAST WITH the righteous man, the wicked is compared to chaff blown away by the wind, to symbolize his sudden and complete destruction. In Biblical times the threshing floor on which grain was winnowed usually stood on top of a rocky hillock, from which the wind could blow the chaff away. Winnowing is portrayed in Egyptian tomb paintings, the methods being the same as those employed in ancient Israel.

Nevertheless, before his final destruction, the wicked could cause the righteous much suffering. In the warlike imagery of some of the psalms, he is regularly described as drawing a bow and shooting an arrow at his unsuspecting righteous victim; while, conversely, the upright true believer is portrayed as the hunted worshiper of God. The ancient bow was "bent" preparatory to shooting it. The bowman made his weapon ready for action by fastening the bowstring with a loop to one end of the bow and then curving back the body till he could attach the other loop to the opposite end. To shoot, he placed an arrow in position against the taut string which he pulled back with his right hand—this was the act of "bending" the bow—and then, aiming the arrow at the target by steadying its tip with his left thumb, he let it fly.

For lo, the wicked bend the bow, they have fitted their arrow to the string, to shoot in the dark at the upright in heart. (PSALMS II : 2)

Bowman in Sennacherib's army. Eighth to seventh century B.C. (Museo Baracco, Rome)

*Be not like a horse or a mule, without understanding,
which must be curbed with bit and bridle, else it will not
keep with you.*   (PSALMS 32 : 9)

For all his evil cunning, the wicked man lacks the fundamental wisdom which ensures true, as opposed to fleeting, success. He is therefore likened to a horse or a mule that, being devoid of intelligence, needs to have its wildness restrained by the bit and bridle with which its master curbs it. The horse's head-harness, of which the bit and bridle formed an integral part, was in antiquity often a work of art serving an aesthetic, not less than a practical, purpose. Assyrian reliefs, for example, show elaborately groomed horses' heads encased in ornate harnesses complete with studded ribbons, ornamental tassels, and crescents.

THE OMNIPOTENCE OF GOD

HIGH ABOVE THE suffering righteous man and the scheming evil-doer stands the power of God, shielding the former from the machinations of the latter. The one thing on earth comparable to the divine strength is that of the great kings and their numberless hosts. Hence the psalms are full of poetical images taken from war and the weapons of war. Thus, God is compared to a shield (*magen*) protecting the worshiper from his foes. This small type of shield was intended primarily to guard exposed parts of the body (such as the head) which could hardly be protected by a coat of mail. Though its shape varied from period to period and from nation to nation, it was always carried on the warrior's left arm by means of a special thong attached to its inner side. To make it easier to handle, this small shield was of a light construction, usually consisting of a framework of wood or plaited reeds with a piece of leather stretched over it. As represented on reliefs from the palace of Sennacherib at Niniveh, the *magen* was convex in shape to give protection to the body from the front and from both sides.

Another poetical image expressive of God's protective grace is the "shadow of God's wings" in which the suppliant takes refuge. The origins of this metaphor go back to earlier, non-Israelite, ways of thinking. Thus the concept frequently appears in plastic form in the art of ancient Egypt, where wings are a symbol of divinity and the gods are portrayed as stretching out their wings over the king to shelter him. In a dark grey diorite statue of the

181

*Keep me as the apple of the eye; hide
me in the shadow of thy wings.*

(PSALMS 17: 8)

Horus, the falcon god, covering with his
wings Pharaoh Chephren. First half of third
millennium B.C. (Cairo Museum)

Pharaoh Chephren (Fourth Dynasty, first half of third millennium B.C.) found at Gizeh, the
god Horus is seen standing on the back of the throne in the form of a falcon, with his wings
spread out to cover the back of the king's head. In Israel, of course, the expression had already
lost its primal meaning and had become nothing more than a stock literary phrase.

In some of the psalms, especially in Psalm 78, the omnipotence of God is demonstrated
by a review of the past history of Israel. The purpose of this survey is to assure the congregation of God's power and of His readiness to succor His people, if only they show themselves
worthy of it. One of the many supernatural marvels described in the Pentateuch and recalled
by the poet here is the miracle of Massah and Meribah, when water issued from a rock
struck by Moses in the wilderness and the thirsting people drank their fill. This making of
water to flow from rock is mentioned several times in the poetical books of the Bible as one
of the outstanding marvels of the Exodus. It was naturally regarded as such because the
sources of water in the desert are so sparse and poor; hence the few that are not saline and
therefore fit for human use create islands of life around them, life for man, beast, and plants.
Because of the geological fissures by which the desert of Judaea is traversed, water sometimes
spurts surprisingly from the hard rock above the steep gorges of the canyons, here and there
falling in impressive cascades that resemble "rivers".

The praise of the Creator and of his works is summed up in Psalm 104. While this psalm
was evidently influenced by literary patterns which originated in Egypt, and in particular
by the "Hymn to the Sun" of the Pharaoh Akhenaton, the religious reformer who lived in

the fourteenth century B.C., this purely literary resemblance cannot obscure the vital difference between the religious conception underlying the two poems: in the "Hymn to the Sun" the Egyptian god adored by the Pharaoh is the sun (Aton); whereas, in the psalm, the sun too was created by the God of Israel, who is outside nature and above its laws.

THE PRAISES OF THE KING

THE ATTRIBUTION OF a large number of psalms to David and Solomon, and the special reverence in which the Davidic Dynasty was held by the inhabitants of Jerusalem and of Judah (where the psalms were composed and transmitted), have led to the inclusion in the Psalter of a series of odes composed in honor of the king, God's anointed and the living reminder of the covenant made by God with David, the king's great ancestor.

Thus in Psalm 21 the king's victory over his foes is ascribed, after the regular manner of ancient oriental poetry, to his personal, single-handed achievement, the part played by the army being totally disregarded. The king's own right hand has "found" all his enemies, all

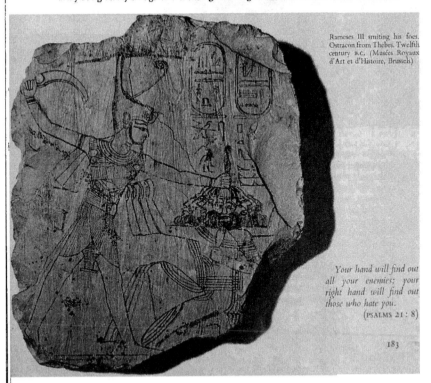

Rameses III smiting his foes. Ostracon from Thebes. Twelfth century B.C. (Musées Royaux d'Art et d'Histoire, Brussels)

Your hand will find out all your enemies; your right hand will find out those who hate you.
(PSALMS 21 : 8)

183

There I will make a horn to sprout for David; I have prepared a lamp for my anointed. His enemies I will clothe with shame, but upon himself his crown will shed its luster.

(PSALMS 132: 17–18)

Naram-Sin king of Akkad on his victory stele. Twenty-third century B.C. (Louvre, Paris)

those that hate him. This highly individualized conception of a battle is also common in the paintings and reliefs of the ancient East, in particular those of Egypt. There the king is portrayed as a being of superhuman size who holds a kneeling foe by the hair with his left hand while he despatched him with a swinging blow from the sword held in his right.

Psalm 72 is a coronation ode sung on the accession of a new king. The court and the people invoke three blessings on their newly crowned ruler: a reign without end, "till the moon be no more"; success in his high office of righteous judge and savior of the down-trodden; and dominion over the whole world "from sea to sea and from the River to the ends of the earth", with all nations doing obeisance to him and bringing him tribute and gifts. This formula of address to a reigning monarch is derived from the traditional court-language current in the ancient East. The motif of world-dominion can hardly have been a characteristically Israelite conception, since the actual limits of Israelite sovereignty only rarely reached even the boundaries delineated in the Bible—the two seas and the River Euphrates. It is more in keeping with the large empires of the ancient Orient, such as those of Akkad and Egypt.

At the end of Psalm 132, God's assurance to David that his descendants will reign forever and that they will have absolute dominion over their foes is poetically given the form of a promise "to make a horn sprout" for him on the royal throne in Zion. This image, like many other figures of speech in the psalms, seems to have belonged to the traditional repertoire of ancient Oriental symbolism. In the art of the ancient Near East we sometimes find gods, or deified kings, portrayed with horns sprouting from their foreheads. A striking illustration of this is provided by the stele of Naram-Sin, king of Akkad (twenty-third century B.C.), who is shown at the head of his army, trampling on his foes; he is holding a spear, a bow and an axe, and is wearing a helmet with two horns, the symbols of his godlike status.

MUSICAL INSTRUMENTS

IN CONTENT THE Psalms were a poetical medium for the expression of certain religious ideas; but in form they were songs, intended to be rendered to the accompaniment of musical instruments. Hence the frequent descriptions in them of the harp and the lyre used in singing the praises of God. The string instruments most common in Biblical times were the harp (Heb. *nebel*) and the lyre (*kinnor*). The harp was the heavier of the two. It had a hollow, bulging body (to increase the resonance) with strings stretched over it which emitted sounds when plucked. The number of the strings varied according to the size and shape of each particular harp: a "ten-stringer" (Ps. 92: 3, Heb. *asor*) was presumably not a separate kind of instrument, but merely a harp with ten strings. A harp found in the royal tombs at Ur (twenty-sixth century B.C.) has an elongated body shaped like a boat, with a bearded bull's head at one end. The instrument itself is made of wood inlaid with jewels, while the bull's head is of gold inlaid with jewels and shells. This harp from Ur has eleven strings. A representation of a seven-stringed harp occurs on a clay plaque from Khafajah in Mesopotamia.

To declare thy steadfast love in the morning, and thy faithfulness by night, to the music of the ten-stringer and the harp . . .   (PSALMS 92: 2–3)

Musician on clay plaque from Khafajah, Mesopotamia. c. 2000 B.C. (Louvre, Paris)

185

The musical skill of the Judaean exiles was famous: Sennacherib mentions that king Hezekiah sent him male and female musicians. Such accomplished performers of instrumental and vocal music, many of whom had taken part in the divine service in the Temple courts, were in Babylonia invited to perform the "songs of Zion" for the delectation of their captors. But how could they in exile sing the "LORD's song", the sacred music which had once echoed through the courts of the Temple? They preferred to hang their lyres on the willows beside the Euphrates and to sit down and weep "by the waters of Babylon".

THE BOOK OF PROVERBS

THE BOOK OF PROVERBS is a manual of the philosophy developed by the schools of scribes and teachers of "wisdom". As these writers were attached to the royal court, their works were sometimes ascribed to various kings, particularly to Solomon, who was regarded as the personification of all knowledge. The "wisdom" taught in these schools by means of proverbs and parables was of a practical nature: its aim was to make men good and hence happy. The first element in such moral education was the "fear of the LORD", religious righteousness. This included the observance not only of ritual laws, but also of moral injunctions and principles of behavior. Diligence, sobriety, and prudence, together with generosity, good will, and unselfishness, characterized the conduct of the wise man. The pitfalls which he had to avoid were indulgence in drink, dishonesty in business, and association with loose women. The rewards of such "wisdom" were social success, well-being, and long life. The philosophy of the Proverbs is therefore distinguished by an optimistic and robust outlook on the world and is intended to give practical guidance to the young and inexperienced.

The "wisdom" literature of the Old Testament drew its inspiration from the traditional gnomic aphoristic writings in circulation throughout the whole ancient East, and in particular from Egypt, where this kind of literary compilation first made its appearance in the Old Kingdom (middle of the third millennium B.C.) and continued to appear down to the Ptolemaic era. From this long period of time there are extant about a dozen Egyptian "wisdom" collections offering interesting parallels to the Biblical "wisdom" books. But in spite of the many points of resemblance, the Book of Proverbs is quite different in spirit and intention from the Egyptian manuals of instruction. In contrast to Egyptian "wisdom", the main purpose of which was to fit the sons of aristocratic families for high office in the royal service, the gnomic literature of the Old Testament is essentially classless and non-professional; the Biblical philosopher-scribe was ready to give instruction to all who asked for it. The royal scribes trained in the Egyptian schools of "wisdom" are frequently represented in Egyptian sculpture. They are shown squatting on their haunches, legs crossed and ready to write, with a partly unrolled papyrus scroll on their knees.

The "wisdom" that the Book of Proverbs sets out to inculcate is metaphorically depicted as an independent entity which existed even before the creation of the world. Before even the mountains and the deeps, the heavens and earth were brought into being, "wisdom" was already the "nurseling" of God, i.e. was reared by God like a child in its foster-father's arms

That prudence may be given to the simple, knowledge and discretion to the youth . . . to understand a proverb and a figure, the words of the wise and their riddles.

(PROVERBS I : 4–6)

Egyptian scribe, Fifth Dynasty. From Sakkarah, Egypt. (Louvre, Paris)

and was His constant delight. Later it played on earth, disporting itself with the sons of man who were created after it. This figure of speech is taken from the custom prevailing in aristocratic circles in antiquity of placing children, soon after their birth, in the charge of nurses and guardians who reared and educated them.

The Israelite author of Proverbs evidently based the collection of aphorisms about "wisdom" in chapters 22: 17–24: 22 on originally Egyptian literary patterns, such as the "Instruction of Amenemopet son of Kanakht", the vizier-scribe of the king of Egypt (extant on a papyrus from the first half of the first millennium, but composed in the twelfth century B.C.). But what we have here is no mere case of mechanical plagiarism. Even the essentially non-Israelite elements have been so well adapted to the beliefs of the scribe's own people and thought and to the special conditions of their country as to receive a thoroughly Israelite stamp.

Another collection of aphorisms in chapters 25–9 includes sayings of Solomon's as copied out by the scribes of Hezekiah, king of Judah. The political and economic prosperity of Hezekiah's reign has left its marks on the literary activity of the time. Like the Assyrian king, Ashurbanipal, who formed a library of ancient works in his archives, Hezekiah too made a collection of old wise sayings. Israelite scribes wrote on sheets of papyrus or parchment. In Assyria and Babylonia, however, writing was done not only on parchment but also on clay tablets, on which cuneiform impressions were made with a stylus.

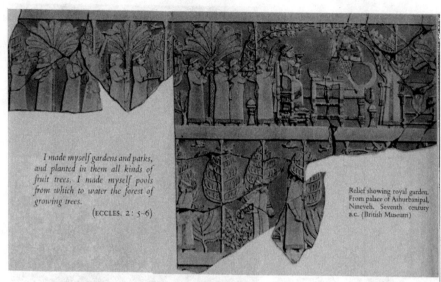

*I made myself gardens and parks,
and planted in them all kinds of
fruit trees. I made myself pools
from which to water the forest of
growing trees.*

(ECCLES. 2: 5-6)

Relief showing royal garden.
From palace of Ashurbanipal,
Nineveh. Seventh century
B.C. (British Museum)

Proverbs end with a collection of the sayings of Agur the son of Jakeh, and a poem in praise of the virtuous woman placed in the mouth of the mother of King Lemuel. The latter passage was probably intended as an antidote to the many aspersions cast upon women in the earlier chapters.

ECCLESIASTES
OR THE PREACHER

ALL IS VANITY

THE PREACHER, WHO calls himself the son of David and declares that he once ruled in Jerusalem, was naturally identified by Jewish tradition with king Solomon. His book is the record of a single-minded endeavor: the search for lasting values to give meaning to life. To this end the Preacher embarked first on a quest for practical "wisdom"; then, and more characteristically, he turned to pleasure. But pleasure here is conceived in the tradition of great kings and aristocrats: no mere vulgar sensual indulgence, but the more temperate delights afforded by the construction of palaces and the planting of vineyards, gardens, and orchards. Shady pleasances of this kind, in which delectable banquets could be held in comfort even in the torrid heat of the oriental summer, are represented in Egyptian and Assyrian art, as, for example, on a relief from the palace of Ashurbanipal

A living dog is better than a dead lion.
(ECCLES. 9: 4)

at Nineveh. The king is shown reclining on a couch, with the queen sitting beside him. Slaves and attendants, in a long line, are bringing a rich assortment of foods to their royal master, while beyond them stand musicians playing soft strains on their instruments. Below is the varied vegetation of the garden—ornamental and fruit trees, palms and vines. Walking among the trees are princes belonging to the royal entourage.

From the pursuit of his refined pleasures the Preacher returns to his philosophical reflections. He begins to doubt man's ability to comprehend the purpose of the things that are done under the sun and eventually comes to the conclusion that everything has been predetermined by divine decree and that nothing can ever be changed. The constantly shifting kaleidoscope of events is largely beyond man's control, since God has already determined all that can happen from the beginning to the end of time. This fatalistic approach, which marks out the Preacher from the rest of the wisdom writers of the ancient Orient, has been interpreted by some scholars as showing that Ecclesiastes was composed under the influence of Greek philosophy, in particular that of the Stoic school. The Stoics also taught that man should live in accordance with nature's laws and patiently accept the ceaselessly changing flux of events, since he is powerless to change his fate.

In his list of human activities that have pre-ordained times the Preacher mentions mourning and dancing. Mourning is represented on Attic vases, occasionally in the form of a funeral procession of men and women. The men's arms are stretched out in front of them, while the women are beating their shorn heads. Dancing is illustrated by many Greek statuettes in which dancers are portrayed swaying rhythmically, with their arms raised and head thrown back.

Since death is also pre-ordained and inescapable, the Preacher, who does not believe that men are destined for a better fate than the animals, clings passionately to life, regarding it as the be-all and end-all of human experience. This attitude of his finds expression in the telling aphorism: "A living dog is better than a dead lion." The dog, the Biblical symbol of the

Relief from palace of Ashurbanipal, Nineveh. Seventh century B.C. (British Museum)

most abject degradation, is while still alive to be preferred even to the lion, the symbol of majestic courage, when dead. The lion aroused the awed admiration of the ancients, even in its death-throes. One of the finest achievements of Assyrian sculpture is the relief, found in Ashurbanipal's palace at Nineveh, of a lion mortally wounded in a royal hunt. The arrow has entered its body between the right shoulder and mane and has evidently come to rest in, or close to, its heart. Blood is pouring from the dying animal's mouth, but even in the face of death the "king of the beasts" still keeps its majesty and pride.

As a result of this attitude to life, the Preacher finally arrives at the philosophy of enjoying to the full the good things of this world. Man should make the most of his all too brief youth, because soon old age will come creeping on and "the dust shall return to the earth as it was"; "Vanity of Vanities saith the preacher; all is vanity."

THE SONG OF SOLOMON

THE SONG OF SOLOMON is a collection of ancient love poems, the authorship of which was attributed to king Solomon. The religious prestige attaching to the name of its supposed author, and its subsequent interpretation as an allegory of the relations between God and His people, Israel, led to its inclusion in the Old Testament canon, although on the surface these poems of courtship and passion contrast strongly with the austere moral tone of most of the other canonical works. The whole poetic sequence, in which there is a strong folkloristic element, depicts the various stages of a happy love affair, including the wedding itself with its traditional sword dances; these latter explain the military metaphors used in some of the poems.

The work opens with the yearning of the love-intoxicated mistress for her beloved, whose passion for her is better than wine.

O that you would kiss me with the kiss of your mouth! For your love is better than wine.

(SONG OF SOL. I : 2)

Ivory plaque from Ugarit. Fourteenth century B.C. (Louvre, Paris)

190

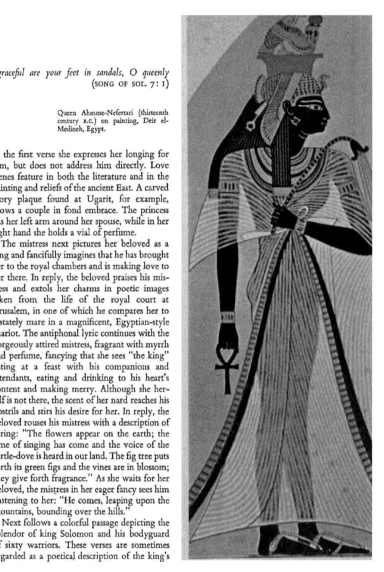

Queen Ahmose-Nefertari (thirteenth century B.C.) on painting, Deir el-Medineh, Egypt.

In the first verse she expresses her longing for him, but does not address him directly. Love scenes feature in both the literature and in the painting and reliefs of the ancient East. A carved ivory plaque found at Ugarit, for example, shows a couple in fond embrace. The princess has her left arm around her spouse, while in her right hand she holds a vial of perfume.

The mistress next pictures her beloved as a king and fancifully imagines that he has brought her to the royal chambers and is making love to her there. In reply, the beloved praises his mistress and extols her charms in poetic images taken from the life of the royal court at Jerusalem, in one of which he compares her to a stately mare in a magnificent, Egyptian-style chariot. The antiphonal lyric continues with the gorgeously attired mistress, fragrant with myrrh and perfume, fancying that she sees "the king" sitting at a feast with his companions and attendants, eating and drinking to his heart's content and making merry. Although she herself is not there, the scent of her nard reaches his nostrils and stirs his desire for her. In reply, the beloved rouses his mistress with a description of spring: "The flowers appear on the earth; the time of singing has come and the voice of the turtle-dove is heard in our land. The fig tree puts forth its green figs and the vines are in blossom; they give forth fragrance." As she waits for her beloved, the mistress in her eager fancy sees him hastening to her: "He comes, leaping upon the mountains, bounding over the hills."

Next follows a colorful passage depicting the splendor of king Solomon and his bodyguard of sixty warriors. These verses are sometimes regarded as a poetical description of the king's nuptials which were imitated in the far humbler village wedding. Everything is ready for the regal ceremony, and the daughters of Jerusalem eagerly jostle each other to obtain a view of the magnificent spectacle. The poet dwells with particular pride on the cedar-wood palanquin, with its silver posts, gilt work, and high seat spread with purple stuffs, in which the bridegroom was carried to the nuptial feast. Then the poem goes on to praise the beauty of the bride, one of whose physical charms is her long neck which reminds the poet of the lofty tower of David.

The whole setting of the Song of Solomon—despite all the lovers' longing for nature, for the trees, the villages, and the fields—breathes the atmosphere of an ancient city. Here is Jerusalem with its towers, markets, busy streets, and the watchmen on its walls. The mistress decks herself out like a typical daughter of Jerusalem: her necklace is studded with jewels; the fragrance of her raiment is like the scent of Lebanon; and in her bosom she always carries a bag of perfumes, including myrrh, the choicest of them all. While the mistress is asleep, dreaming that her beloved is knocking at the door and that she rises to open it for him, myrrh drips from her hands and "liquid myrrh" from her fingers, since she has perfumed her body before lying down on her couch, as do the women of the city.

The application of perfume was, in the ancient Orient, always a privilege of ladies of noble birth. On a relief from the sarcophagus of the Egyptian queen, Kawit, she is shown seated on her throne, holding a lotus flower in one hand and taking a little cosmetic cream or perfume with two fingers of the other from a pot held by a waiting woman.

The beloved continues to descant on the beauties of his mistress—her hair, teeth, cheeks, and veil—in a series of vivid natural images. In these verses nature not only provides the metaphors for the mistress's striking looks, but is also the setting for the whole romantic scene. The lover, who from afar beholds his loved one shining forth like the dawn with its miracle of cosmic rebirth, also goes down into the garden in the heart of spring, to feast his eyes on the trees which are burgeoning again after the winter rains. Nature's spring, with all its primal joy, is here a fitting symbol for youth, the springtime of life. Another of the signs of nature's rebirth mentioned here is the pomegranate blossom, a prominent feature of the Judaean landscape in the spring. When the buds first open, the young foliage is reddish in color, so that an orchard of budding pomegranate trees seems to be enveloped in a thin red veil. Then, in the early summer, there appear the characteristic large red flowers with their intense, flaming color.

In the description of the wedding ceremony the bride is described as joining in the dance and being lost for a moment among the many other girls dancing with her. The onlookers wait for her to reappear when the circle of dancers comes round to them again, urging her on in the meanwhile with rhythmical shouts of "Return, return O Shulamite return, return that we may look upon you" (6:13). As she dances she displays her elegant sandal-clad feet. The girls of the lower classes in Israel mostly went barefoot, the use of footwear being confined to the daughters of the nobility; but we may assume that on this festive occasion the bride wore sandals, as was common in aristocratic circles throughout the ancient East. The artistic representations of the queens of Egypt, such as that on the preceding page, show them with elegant sandals of a style similar to those worn by the Pharaohs also.

The Song of Solomon ends in the vein in which it began, with the mistress's eager call to her beloved to come to her with the fleet-footed swiftness of a young stag.

Prophecy

View of the Temple Mount, Jerusalem, from the southeast

It shall come to pass in the latter days that the mountain of the house of the LORD
shall be established as the highest of the mountains . . .   (ISA. 2: 2)

THE BOOK OF THE
PROPHET ISAIAH

ISAIAH THE SON of Amoz, whose prophecies open the series of the prophetical books of the Old Testament, was born probably at Jerusalem, in the reign of king Uzziah. His prophetic vocation was revealed to him in a great vision which he saw in the year of Uzziah's death (734 B.C.—see Isaiah ch. 6). The political standpoint adopted by Isaiah was determined by his realistic understanding of the decline in the strength and fortunes of Judah and Israel in the period following the great days of Jeroboam II and Uzziah, while the menace of Assyrian power was looming steadily larger and larger on the horizon of the small kingdoms of the Orient. The prophet therefore seems to have supported Ahaz in his refusal to be drawn into the anti-Assyrian alliance of Pekah of Israel and Rezin of Damascus; but he opposed his sovereign's subsequent abject submission as a vassal to Tiglath Pileser III and his idolatry. In the reign of king Hezekiah, Isaiah opposed Hezekiah's Egyptian and Babylonian alliances and warned him of the disaster to come. But when his prophecies actually came true and the conquering Assyrians appeared before the walls of Jerusalem, he placed his trust in God and spoke of God's protecting of his city, decrying man's lack of faith. The armies of Sennacherib suddenly retreated, but Judah remained subservient to Assyria. Isaiah lived all his life in Jerusalem, where he married and had several sons to whom he gave symbolical names. He must have been violently opposed to the pro-Assyrian policies, including the worship of foreign gods, inaugurated by Hezekiah's son and successor Manasseh, in whose reign, according to later legends, he suffered a martyr's death.

The prophecies of Isaiah are written in a lofty and powerful poetic style which has served as a model for later Hebrew literature.

Instead of perfume there will be rottenness . . . ; and
instead of well-set hair, baldness . . .   (ISA. 3 : 24)

Terracotta bust from Spain. Fifth–fourth
century B.C. (Ibiza, Spain)

THE SINS OF JERUSALEM

ISAIAH'S PROPHETIC INDIGNATION
was first aroused by the glaring religious,
moral, and social evils that he saw in his own city—
the idolatry, the oppression of the poor, the arrogance
and sensuality of the rich and aristocratic, the empty
formalism of the Temple ritual which was regarded
as sufficient expiation of all moral failings. This
blatant corruption was all the more painful for him
to behold because of the contrasting idea of Jerusalem
as God's holy city which lived in his heart. At the
center of his prophecy stands a vision—found also in
the prophecies of Micah—of all the nations congre-
gating in harmony on the Temple Mount, the germ
of the still inspiring conception of the millennium
of universal peace and righteousness. The setting of
this vision is the northern spur of the more easterly
of the two hills on which ancient Jerusalem was built. This spur was included within
the confines of the city under king Solomon, who chose it as the site of his Temple and
of the adjacent royal palace and treasuries. It is bounded on the east by the Kidron valley
and on the west by the cleft separating the two hills of Jerusalem. The configuration of
the terrain here has been radically changed since the time of Isaiah by the great esplanade
built by king Herod to support his reconstruction of the Second Temple. The outer wall of
the Temple Mount now rests on the Herodian walls, while the Dome of the Rock (built
A.D. 691 by the Moslem caliph Abdulmalik) stands on the site of the sanctuary itself.

The religious and moral decline of Judah in the reigns of Ahaz and Hezekiah is starkly
revealed in Isaiah's description of the dissolution of the bonds of society, resulting from the
breakdown of the social hierarchy in which every individual had his appointed place and
function.

One of the striking signs of this social dissolution was the decline in the traditional
standards of austerity, especially in the case of women. Isaiah denounced the ostentatiousness
of the women of Jerusalem, whose passion for material comfort and personal adornment
drove their fathers and husbands to amass ill-gotten wealth, pervert justice, and oppress the
poor. Since the conduct of these women was hastening the downfall of Jerusalem, they

would be the first to suffer from its destruction, which would be followed by their utter destitution. Stripped of their gorgeous raiment and jewelry, the once pampered ladies of the city would go into exile barefooted and with heads shorn. The upper-class Israelite woman, like other oriental women of some position, paid no less careful attention to her coiffure, than she did to her dress and adornment. City ladies used to bind up their hair, curling and fixing its ends until their coiffure was "well set". An illustration of this fashion is provided by the terracotta bust of a lady found in Spain and dating to the fifth or fourth century B.C., the period of Phoenician expansion. Her hair is swept upwards and enclosed in a miter-shaped head-dress the ends of which hang down over her shoulders. A similarly formal coiffure is also found on the statuettes of the goddess Ashtoreth excavated in Palestine.

Ultimately Israel will be compelled to submit to the yoke of the Assyrian oppressor. This comparison of the captive's harsh lot to the yoke in which farm animals worked is commonly used in the Old Testament to depict the enslavement of Israel to the great powers of the ancient world. Isaiah's words here give us a vivid and exact picture of what actually happened in those countries where prisoners of war were set to hard labor. Their animal-like toiling at back-breaking tasks is also frequently represented in the art of the ancient East. An Assyrian relief from Dur-Sharruken (Khorsabad), for example, clearly shows captives straining in the yoke as they drag heavy burdens under the watchful eye of a taskmaster. Conversely, Isaiah likens the liberation of Israel from its Assyrian bondage to the breaking of a yoke and the lifting of a burden from the shoulders.

For the yoke of his burden and the staff for his shoulder, the rod of his oppressor, thou hast broken as on the day of Midian. (ISA. 9: 4)

Assyrian relief from Dur-Sharruken. Eighth century B.C. (Louvre, Paris)

An oracle concerning Moab . . . because Kir is laid waste in a night, Moab is undone. (ISA. 15 : 1)

View of ruins of Crusaders' castle at el-Kerak (Kir of Moab).

THE ORACLES AGAINST THE NATIONS

NOT ONLY ISRAEL but the various nations of the ancient Orient too are threatened with doom in the collection of dire predictions traditionally attributed to Isaiah but containing later material too. The prophecy of the coming destruction of Babylon is probably in parts at least of later origin. It vividly illustrates the prophet's central conception of the working out of the God of Israel's design in human history. The punishment to be inflicted on the sinful empire is an exact recompense for its own crimes. When the day of reckoning for the iniquity of the wicked and the arrogance of the ruthless comes, the would-be lords of the earth and masters of the heavens will be annihilated. A remote nation dwelling beyond the ken of the peoples of Mesopotamia will destroy them and their land and make their king bite the dust. A parallel to this prophecy can be found in Babylonian texts, in particular in the stele of Nabonidus, the last king of Babylon (556–539 B.C.). There the overthrow of the Assyrian empire is explained as the god Marduk's wrathful revenge for the destruction of Babylon by the Assyrians. Marduk sent against Assyria a foreign and barbarous nation which came from afar and avenged the Babylonians by plundering and destroying and breaking down the Assyrian temples. In the prophetic vision, however, the punishment of a ruthless imperial power is not merely a turn in the wheel of political fortune, but an integral part of the conception of a universal, all-embracing Day of the LORD "against all that is proud and lofty".

Another nation to suffer grievously will be Moab. The oracle concerning this country, which is a prophetic lament in the style of an ancient ballad, describes the destruction which will fall with appalling suddenness on the cities of Moab and first of all upon Kir, the most important of its fortresses. Kir Moab, known to the Arabs as el-Kerak, was built on a rocky ridge overlooking the main highway that ran from Egypt to northern Mesopotamia, along the Trans-Jordan plateau. On the site of the ancient city potsherds have been found dating back to the times of Joshua and the Judges, as well as the remains of a tunnel connecting the citadel with the water-source which lay outside its walls. Because of its central position and powerful fortifications, Kir-Moab was the keypoint in every invasion of Moab; once this city fell, the rest of the country was doomed. In later times Kir-Moab was inhabited by the Nabataeans. The Romans knew it as Charach-moba, a posting station and a strongpoint on the imperial road built by Trajan. Centuries later the Crusaders erected there one of the strongest of their castles in the Middle East.

After the burden of Moab comes a short description of the fate in store for Damascus and a hint at an unsuccessful attack upon Jerusalem by an army of many nations. The main theme is then taken up again in the burden of Ethiopia, followed by the oracle against Egypt, still one of the most powerful nations in the Orient.

Here too the prophet has suited his prophecy of doom to the particular land against which it was uttered. Egypt was to be smitten at its most vulnerable point, its absolute dependence on the Nile river, the main source of the country's life and livelihood, which provided its inhabitants with abundant supplies of fish and with the water needed for the irrigation of their fields. The punishment in store for Egypt will take the form of attacks by enemies from outside the country and of social anarchy within it; but above all it will be felt in the horrors of a failure of the Nile's annual flooding. The level of the river's waters will fall until the irrigation canals running off it dry up and all the cultivated fields are parched. Finally the reeds along the river bank will wither, and even the fish will die, thus depriving the fishermen of their subsistence. The methods of fishing in the Nile referred to by the prophet are also represented in Egyptian art. In the bottom row of the relief reproduced here two teams of fishermen are hauling full nets out of the river, while at the right the fishing is being done with a hand net manipulated by a single fisherman or with fixed nets spread under the

The fishermen will mourn and lament, all who cast hook in the Nile; and they will languish who spread nets upon the water.

(ISA. 19: 8)

Fishermen on relief from tomb of Meretuka, Sakkarah, Egypt. Second half of third millennium B.C.

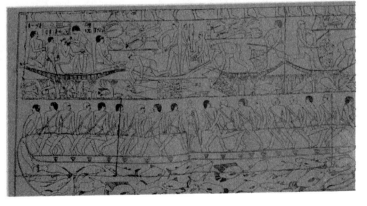

surface of the water. The fish enter the net by its wide, open end, while the other narrower end is kept closed by a rope held by the fishermen. At the top left other men are fishing with line and hook.

The drying up of the Nile will ruin both the flax-growers and the spinners and weavers who earn their livelihood by processing the flax. The growing and processing of flax played an important part in the economy of ancient Egypt, and the exquisite Egyptian cloths were famed for their quality throughout the ancient East. The various stages in the processing of

The workers in combed flax will be in despair, and the weavers of white cotton. (ISA. 19: 9)

Working flax—tomb of Amenemhet, Beni Hasan, Egypt. Nineteenth century B.C.

flax, as portrayed in Egyptian art, included the growing of the plant, the soaking of the sheaves (for which large quantities of water were required; hence the connection between the disaster to the weaving industry and the drying up of the Nile), followed by the pounding, the spinning of the threads, and finally the manufacture of cloth.

Further oracles against the nations predict the swift victories of the Assyrians in their campaigns against Philistia, the "desert of the sea", and Arabia. The prophet then pronounces the doom of Tyre and Sidon, after having first vented his wrath on the chamberlain of the Judaean court, a certain Shebna who was possibly himself a Phoenician residing in Jerusalem.

Tyre, "the bestower of crowns" (Isa. 23: 8), one of the most important ancient cities at the eastern end of the Mediterranean, was originally built on an island about one-third of a mile off the coast. From this island base the Tyrians conducted a flourishing overseas trade, venturing forth to establish their colonies in distant parts of the Mediterranean Sea. Wherever they went the Tyrian traders carried with them the Canaanite culture of their mother city, which thus spread as far afield as Greece, North Africa, and Spain. Since Tyre was entirely surrounded by sea it was virtually unconquerable from the mainland. The armies of both Assyria and Babylonia besieged it for long years but were unable to reduce it for lack of powerful enough sea forces. It was not until Alexander the Great in 332 B.C. constructed a causeway out to the island that the city was stormed and the prophet's prediction came true. In the course of time this causeway gradually grew wider and higher, until it turned the island of Tyre into a peninsula.

After pronouncing the judgment of God on all the nations of the world in the form of a devastating earthquake, the prophecies of doom conclude with another reference to Moab whose downfall, with the total destruction of its fortresses and strongholds, typifies for the prophet the divine retribution in store for all the other enemies of Israel. The cities of the ancient Near East usually stood on a hill or mound and were surrounded by a strong outer wall with a heavily fortified gateway flanked by protecting towers. In the heart of the city, usually at its highest point, towered the royal citadel which was encircled by an inner wall. In the time of Isaiah, however, even such strongly protected cities were often reduced to ruins by Assyrian siegecraft. Assyrian reliefs show how this was accomplished. While bowmen harassed the city's defenders with their arrows, a team of battering-rams pounded its way through the wall close to one of its protective towers and then proceeded to pulverize its defenses.

SENNACHERIB'S CAMPAIGN AGAINST JERUSALEM

SENNACHERIB'S FORCES THREATENED Jerusalem with a similar fate. After the disastrous battle of Eltekeh (701 B.C.) at which the anti-Assyrian confederacy—including Hezekiah of Judah—was routed, the victorious Assyrians advanced inland into Judah, capturing one city after another. The battle for Lachish, which was particularly fierce, is represented in detail on the reliefs of Sennacherib's palace at Nineveh.

From Lachish, Sennacherib sent an army against Jerusalem, commanded by Rabshekeh, one of his generals, who negotiated with the ministers of Hezekiah on the walls of Jerusalem and even made an appeal directly to the people of the city over the heads of their rulers, by speaking to them in their own language. He significantly reminded them of the many cities in Syria which the Assyrians had captured and whose gods had been powerless to save them from the might of Sennacherib, clearly implying that the God of Israel would be equally

*And the high fortification of his walls he will bring
down, lay low, and cast to the ground, even to the dust.*
(ISA. 25 : 12)

Assyrian battering-ram. Balawat palace gates.
Ninth century B.C. (British Museum)

Surrender of king of
Hamath. Balawat palace
gates. Ninth century B.C.
(British Museum)

powerless to prevent the destruction of His city. The wars referred to were all fought during
the ninth and eighth centuries B.C., when the Assyrian empire was expanding westwards
into the Mediterranean coastlands. Even Hamath, one of the most powerful of the Syrian
kingdoms, had in 848 B.C. to submit to Shalmaneser III. The Assyrian monarch depicted
this victory on his palace gates at Balawat. In the upper row the aged ruler of the city is being
carried out of it on his litter, his hands held up in supplication as a sign of surrender to the
Assyrian forces arrayed in front of the city walls. Below, Assyrian soldiers are leading some
of the captured inhabitants off into exile.

When Hezekiah was informed of Rabshakeh's threats he went to the Temple to pray
for deliverance. There he recalled the many atrocities committed by the Assyrians in the
course of their military campaigns, the brutality with which they had tortured all the
conquered nations, laid waste their lands, and cast their gods into the fire. Far from being
ashamed of such barbarities, the Assyrians actually boasted of them. The fate in store for
Jerusalem, should it fall to the Assyrian army, is vividly illustrated by the relief showing the
destruction of Muzazir. This relief, found at Dur-Sharruken, the modern Khorsabad, dates
from the reign of Sargon II (721–705 B.C.). The city, one of the most important of the land
of Ararat, was taken by the Assyrians, who are seen destroying one of its temples. The
soldiers climb on to the roof and from there force their way inside. The shields and spears
hung in the Temple as war trophies are being carried away by the victorious troops, who
are systematically looting the whole building.

In this terrible crisis, when the fate of the kingdom of Judah hung in the balance, Isaiah
strengthened Hezekiah's will to resist; the blasphemies of the Assyrians had convinced him
that their onslaught would fail. According to one Biblical account, an angel of the LORD
miraculously laid low 185,000 of the besieging Assyrian army, thereby forcing Sennacherib

to retreat. The Assyrian version of the story is given on one of the inscribed prisms of clay recording the king's battles in chronological order. There he boasts of having taken forty-six of the walled cities of Judah, of having deported 200,150 of the country's inhabitants, and of having made Hezekiah "prisoner in Jerusalem, his royal residence, like a bird in a cage". The inscription ends with a list of the tribute paid by Hezekiah to Assyria: "30 talents of gold and 300 talents of silver, and precious stones, antimony, couches and arm-chairs inlaid with ivory, elephant hides, ivories, ebony wood, box wood, and all kinds of treasures; as well as his own daughters and concubines. And his personal messenger he sent to me to deliver tribute and to do obeisance." However, in spite of these boastful Assyrian claims, the fact remains that Jerusalem's resistance, inspired by Isaiah, was temporarily successful; it saved Judah from immediate destruction and its population from exile; it allowed time for the spiritual consolidation of the Davidic monarchy; and it enabled little Judah to outlive the mighty Assyrian empire and to escape for a time the fate of the kingdom of Israel.

THE MESSAGE OF SALVATION

THE MAJOR PORTION of the second part of the Book of Isaiah (chs. 40–55) is now attributed to another prophet, who lived at the time of the Return from the Babylonian Exile (second half of the sixth century B.C.) and who delivered a message of consolation to his people. (Chs. 56–66 contain yet other and probably later prophecies.) The prophecies of the "Second Isaiah" open with the declaration that the past iniquities of the people of Israel have been pardoned and that their term of slavery is about to be ended. Their deliverer, sent and supported by God, is to come from the northeast. While expecting

Of a truth. O LORD, the kings of Assyria have laid waste all the nations and their lands, and have cast their gods into the fire . . .   (ISA. 37: 18–19)

Looting the temple of Muzazir. Relief from Dur-Sharruken. Eighth century B.C.

Tomb of Cyrus at Pasar-
gadae, Persia. Sixth cen-
tury B.C.

immediate succor by human means, the prophet's vision spreads out from Israel's redemption and far beyond the narrow confines of the historical hope of a national revival till it
embraces a renewal of the whole universe. The idolaters who worship the work of human
hands shall be utterly confounded. The prophet holds them up to derision in a satirical
description taken from the realities of everyday experience: they place their trust in statues
made from the selfsame tree-trunks whose branches they use for roasting meat and baking
bread.

The hope of redemption cherished by the Prophet of Consolation finds its political
expression in the glorification of Cyrus, the founder of the Persian empire. Cyrus was
originally (557–553 B.C.) the king of Anshan, a city of Elam. In 553 he revolted against his
overlord, Astyages, king of Media, and captured Ecbatana, the Median capital. In 547 B.C.
he overcame Croesus, the king of Lydia in Asia Minor; and in 539 B.C. Babylon opened its
gates to him without offering any resistance. After his conquest of Babylon, Cyrus boasts of
restoring all the gods of the various nations conquered by the Babylonians and he authorized
the rebuilding of the Temple in Jerusalem and so the re-establishing of the Jewish community
there. Having thus extended the dominion of Persia over all the lands of the ancient Orient
formerly ruled by Babylon, Cyrus died in 529 B.C., leaving his empire to his son Cambyses.
His traditional tomb is still shown at Pasargadae in Persia, about 40 miles north of Persepolis,
towering high above the surrounding countryside at the top of seven tiers of steps.

After describing the destruction of the idols of the Babylonian gods, Bel and Nebo, and
the total downfall of a people used to arrogantly lording it over the others, the prophet
turns to a glowing description of the triumphant Return to Zion. The redeemed city will be
like a bereaved mother whose children have been miraculously restored to her. The same
foes that had deported her children with such brutal ferocity will, in the days that are to
come, be compelled to restore them with all due care for their well-being and comfort. The
kings and tyrants of the nations will conduct the people of Israel on their hazardous journey
as a nurse bears an infant in her bosom, or as a mother carries her young child on her
shoulders. The latter method of carrying children was particularly common on long
journeys by foot, such as the Return to Zion would be. Mothers also carried their little ones

on their backs, wrapped in a large kerchief or in the ample folds of a garment and fastened to their bodies, so as to leave their hands and arms free for the performance of their domestic tasks. A wooden statuette of a non-Egyptian woman from the Middle Kingdom (nineteenth century B.C.) shows her carrying a child in this way.

The central figure of the prophecy in the latter part of the Book of Isaiah is the "servant of the LORD", perhaps to be interpreted as the prophet himself or as a symbol of the people of Israel, who by his sufferings is to redeem the nations of the world. When the time of Israel's revival comes, beginning with the redemption of Jerusalem, no enemy will be able to harm the returning nation any more; indeed, Israel's deliverance from the Babylonian captivity will be a miracle comparable to the renewal and transformation of the whole creation. The leaders of the people who have betrayed their trust and all those who have obstinately clung to strange gods, who have perverted justice and sworn false oaths, shall be utterly destroyed while the rest of the nation in reward for its return to God shall be gathered from all the lands to which it had been dispersed, like pigeons homing to their nest.

At the end of his message of consolation the prophet returns to his opening theme. All the nations will praise the God of Israel and will do homage to His chosen people, whose scattered sons they will reverently restore to Jerusalem with all due pomp, borne on the backs of mules and horses or transported in carriages. Wagons drawn by oxen, similar to those shown on a relief of Ashurbanipal at Nineveh, had been used in the deportation of the captives from Judah. Now vehicles of the same kind, in addition to swift and light covered carriages for long distance travel, will be used to effect their triumphant return.

Thus says the LORD God: "Behold, I will lift up my hand to the nations, and raise my signal to the peoples; and they shall bring your sons in their bosom, and your daughters shall be carried on their shoulders."

(ISA. 49: 22)

Mother carrying child. From tomb of Useri, Beni Hasan, Egypt. Nineteenth century B.C. (Royal Scottish Museum, Edinburgh)

THE BOOK OF
THE PROPHET JEREMIAH

JEREMIAH CAME FROM a priestly family of Anathoth. He was probably related to the Abiathar expelled by Solomon from Jerusalem (2 Kings 2 : 26–7), and therefore belonged by heredity to the opposition to the ruling class in Jerusalem. He was born about 650 B.C., and received the call to prophesy in the thirteenth year of Josiah's reign (627 B.C.), while still in his native town. He subsequently lived in Jerusalem; till the destruction of the city, in bitter and lonely conflict with kings, ministers, priests, and other prophets. Jeremiah was able to survive these years of persecution, thanks to his unusual strength of character. His courage and conviction were only strengthened by his almost complete isolation, though he did have a few faithful disciples, chief amongst them Baruch the son of Neriah.

In his early teaching Jeremiah proclaimed that the cultic reforms of Josiah were not enough; a thorough moral regeneration was needed. In the valley of Ben-Hinnom, Jeremiah uttered a dire prophecy of woe against Jerusalem and denounced the king of Judah and his subjects for the most heinous of all idolatries. In that same spot the hideous practice in which children were passed through the fire, perhaps introduced by Ahaz and encouraged by Manasseh, had been practiced by the people until the reform of Josiah, and may have been revived after Josiah's death. As a result of the ghastly scenes of human sacrifice enacted in the valley of Hinnom, its Hebrew name *Gehinnom* (or Gehenna) eventually came to signify the place of torment reserved for the wicked in the next world. Known to the Arabs today as Wadi er-Rababah, the valley runs southwards from the Jaffa Gate through the Serpent's Pool (Birket es-Sultan) and then turns eastwards toward the Kidron valley. In ancient times it marked the western and southern limits of Jerusalem and formed the border between Judah and Benjamin.

Jeremiah lived at a time of profound changes in the balance of power in the Near East. As the Assyrian empire waned, its place in the political firmament was taken by the rising star of Babylon which reached the zenith of its greatness in the reign of Nebuchadnezzar II (605–562 B.C.). For the prophet these epoch-making events were a sign of divine providence and Nebuchadnezzar the instrument of God's purpose. This being so (and future events were to confirm the prophet's judgment of the political and military situation), it was folly to attempt any resistance to Babylonian rule. Jeremiah was therefore consistently opposed to the policy of that party at the royal court which favored rebellion against Babylon and an alliance with Egypt. This policy led in 597 B.C. to the exile of king Jehoiachin and his court.

Jehoiachin's successor, Zedekiah, the last king of Judah, began to rule in 597 B.C. as a vassal of Babylon, but within ten years he also rose against his overlord. Jeremiah who, like the other prophets, took an active part in political life, tried to influence the course of events by admonitory utterances and symbolical actions. He firmly believed that any attempt at revolt against Babylon was utterly pointless. Had not nations and kingdoms been commanded by

God meekly to place their necks in the yoke of the Babylonian king? To give greater force to his contention, the prophet illustrated the necessity of subservience to Nebuchadnezzar by a piece of symbolism. After first tying thongs and bars—the components of a yoke—on to his own neck, he sent them to the kings whose envoys had met at Jerusalem at the beginning of Zedekiah's reign to plot a revolt against Babylon. To the king of Judah, Jeremiah addressed a peremptory demand that he submissively place his neck under the yoke of the king of Babylon and serve him and his people. The figurative expression used here is taken from the practice in antiquity of sometimes placing captives in a yoke, partly as a sign of their abject surrender and partly to ensure that they should not escape. Thus male prisoners of war are shown naked, with their necks tightly fastened in a yoke, on the bronze relief from the gates of Balawat (ninth century B.C.).

During most of his reign Zedekiah wavered between following Jeremiah's council and disregarding it, but in the end the war party at the court prevailed. When the prophet tried to leave doomed Jerusalem for his native Anathoth, he was arrested at the city gate and charged with intent to desert to the approaching Babylonian army. At first he was flung into a cistern and almost left to die there; but then, through the intervention of friends at court, the king placed him in less rigorous confinement in one of the courts of the royal palace. There Jeremiah remained till the city fell to the Babylonians. Zedekiah was caught

Thus the LORD said to me: "Make yourself thongs and yoke bars, and put them on your neck."   (JER. 27: 2)

Captives under yokes, Balawat palace gates. Ninth century B.C. (British Museum)

They went to
Gedaliah at Mizpah
—Ishmael the son of
Nethaniah, Johanan
the son of Kareah,
Seraiah the son of
Tanhumeth, the sons
of Ephai the Neto-
phathite, Jezaniah
the Maacathite, they
and their men.

(JER. 40: 8)

Seal of Jezaniah, found at
Tell en-Nasbeh. Sixth
century B.C. (Palestine
Archaeological Museum)

trying to escape and blinded at Riblah. Most of the upper classes and the craftsmen of
Jerusalem were exiled, leaving behind only a poor remnant of the population, consisting
mainly of husbandmen and vinedressers. The governor set over them was Gedaliah the son
of Ahikam, a former high court official and one of the leaders of the peace party. He took up
his residence at Mizpah, whither Jeremiah went to join him.

GEDALIAH AT MIZPAH

ARCHAEOLOGICAL EVIDENCE FOR the high position occupied by Gedaliah
at the royal court has been found in the excavations at Lachish, in the form
of an impression of what was probably his seal. Engraved on this seal there were two rows
of letters separated by a double line: at the top was written "belonging to Gedaliahu", and
at the bottom "who is over the house", i.e. the holder of the office of royal steward, one of
the highest dignities at the court of the king of Judah.

Gedaliah's official residence at Mizpah became a rallying point for the military commanders and refugees who had fled during the war to Moab, Ammon, and Edom. Mizpah
is generally identified with Tell en-Nasbeh, 7 miles north of Jerusalem, which has been

And said to him, "Do you know that Baalis the king
of the Ammonites has sent Ishmael the son of Nethaniah
to take your life?"   (JER. 40: 14)

Statuette of Ammonite ruler. Eighth–
seventh century B.C. (Amman Museum)

excavated in recent years. The city was
surrounded by a high wall, as reconstructed
in the accompanying drawing. Although it
was settled at the time of the Babylonian
conquest, it bears no signs of destruction from
that period; hence the town was probably
spared by the victorious Babylonians and
could therefore serve as a provincial capital.

Among the military commanders who
joined Gedaliah at Mizpah was a certain
Jezaniah the Maacathite. This particular officer
may have been the owner of a seal inscribed
"Jaazaniahu servant of the king" which was
found in a grave at Tell en-Nasbeh. At the
bottom of the seal there is a representation of
a fighting cock tensed for combat, a fitting
emblem for any warrior and one most appropriate to an officer of Jaazaniah's rank. This
artistic portrayal of a cock (from the beginning of the sixth century B.C.) is the earliest
that has yet been found in Palestine.

The hopes placed in Gedaliah's peaceful rule
from Mizpah were quickly and cruelly
disappointed. Judah's hostile neighbors, seeing
an opportunity to realize their designs on its
conquered territory, stirred up trouble against
the governor. The chief instigator of this plot
was Baalis, the king of Ammon, who must
have looked very like the potentate portrayed
in a statuette of the eighth or seventh century
B.C., found at Rabbath-Ammon. This figure
of a man, holding a lotus flower—the symbol
of royal power and dignity—in his left hand,
is bearded and has side-curls hanging over his
temples, but his upper lip is clean-shaven.

Incited by Baalis, Ishmael the son of Nethaniah, a royal prince of Judah and the leader of the party still bent on continuing the war, assassinated Gedaliah, together with his officials and the Babylonians who were stationed at Mizpah. The remaining Judaean forces commanded by one Johanan the son of Kareah thereupon fled to Egypt to escape the certain wrath of the king of Babylon, taking Jeremiah with them, much against his will.

THE EXILES IN EGYPT

ALTHOUGH JEREMIAH HAD prophesied that Nebuchadnezzar would overrun Egypt, dealing out slaughter and destruction and desecrating the temples of the Egyptian gods, and although the Babylonians actually invaded Egypt in 568–567 B.C., they did not conquer the whole of the country. The refugees from Judah could, for the time being, feel safe in the Nile valley. In fact, they were not the first Judaeans to live there. By the time of the destruction of the First Temple, Jews were already settled in many parts of the country: near Migdol (Tell el-Kheir) and Tahpanhes (Tell Dafna) in the northeastern frontier districts, at Memphis, and even in the region of Pathros, i.e. in Upper Egypt. The existence of a Jewish community at Memphis is attested by Aramaic papyri of the fifth century B.C. found there, containing such patently Jewish names as Jonathan and Jehoram. Other Jewish names such as Benaiah and Nathan also occur in papyri from Hermopolis in Middle Egypt. In addition the letters found on the island of Elephantine (Yeb), and one from Abydos, suggest that Jewish communities existed in Upper Egypt.

Why do you provoke me to anger with the works of your hands, burning incense to other gods in the land of Egypt where you have come to live . . .

(JER. 44: 8)

Stele from Tell Dafna. Sixth century B.C.
(Cairo Museum)

since early times. All these indications add up to a clear proof that at the beginning of the period of the Second Temple there were in many Egyptian cities Jewish settlements (apparently first founded as military outposts), perhaps going back even to the time of Jeremiah.

The Judaean refugees in Egypt continued even after their exile to worship pagan gods, especially the "queen of heaven", just as they had done in Judah and Jerusalem. In this they conformed to a common contemporary Egyptian practice. Ever since the time of the New Kingdom the cults of foreign, and particularly Semitic, deities had been widespread in that country. The form taken by the cult of the Semitic gods in Egypt is illustrated on a stele of the sixth century B.C., found at ancient Tahpanhes, one of the cities in which refugees from Judah settled. On it we see a Babylonian-Assyrian god, apparently Marduk, wearing a high cylindrical cap and standing on the back of a lion in the manner of the Mesopotamian deities. Only the staff which he holds in his left hand is Egyptian. In front of him there is an altar on which a priest is presenting offerings. Emblems characteristic of the gods of Mesopotamia appear at the top of the relief.

When Jeremiah went into exile in Egypt that country was ruled by a Pharaoh of the Twenty-sixth Dynasty called Hophra (588–568 B.C.). His reign was, on the whole, a period of prosperity for Egypt, although his attempts to incite the people of Phoenicia and Palestine to revolt against Babylon, and his interventions on their behalf, ended in failure. Eventually, however, when his own armies were also defeated in Cyrenaica, he was obliged to appoint his commander-in-chief, Amasis, as his co-regent. In the third year of their joint rule their rivalry flared up into open war in which Hophra was killed, exactly as Jeremiah had predicted.

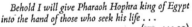

Behold I will give Pharaoh Hophra king of Egypt into the hand of those who seek his life . . .
(JER. 44: 30)

Hophra on relief from Abydos. Sixth century B.C. (British Museum)

THE DOOM OF PHILISTIA AND THE FALL OF BABYLON

NOT ONLY JUDAH was destroyed by Babylon's imperial might. Before the end of the seventh century Philistia too had begun to feel the weight of Nebuchadnezzar's war machine; indeed, being situated on the coastline, on the main road running from Mesopotamia into Egypt, it had a particularly full measure of afflictions. In Jeremiah's lifetime Ashkelon (then, with Gaza, one of the principal Philistine cities) was sacked twice: once by the Scythians, a northern people which, pouring southwards from its steppes near the Black and Caspian Seas, had swept through the whole ancient Orient; and again in 604 B.C. when it was razed to the ground by the Babylonians. Such repeated destruction was Ashkelon's fate throughout antiquity because of its strategic position on one of the great international highways of the Near East. Its capture and sacking are therefore often represented on ancient reliefs.

Though for the present God allowed Nebuchadnezzar to subdue the whole known world, wreaking destruction wherever he conquered, Jeremiah believed that Babylon too would meet with total defeat on its appointed day of doom, as its just punishment by the God of Israel. Babylon, the queen of cities, the impregnable fortress of the land of the Chaldaeans, would in a moment be laid low, while the nations looked on in incredulous amazement. It could not escape its doom, even though Nebuchadnezzar had made it so famous throughout the ancient world for the splendor of its buildings and the massiveness of its fortifications that its walls were considered one of the seven wonders of the world. Among the relics of the ancient city laid bare by the excavator's spade are the remains of the outer walls from the time of the Neo-Babylonian empire, enclosing the immense area of 320 square miles. Within them were the inner walls, in the eastern section of which stood the Gate of Ishtar with its facing of colored glazed bricks, arranged to form representations of wild oxen and legendary serpents.

In his last utterances the prophet predicted not only the fall of Babylon but also the events which were to follow it. The news of the city's fall would spread like wildfire throughout the country. After the capture of the capital, fighting would spread to the outlying parts of the kingdom: the fords of the Euphrates would be seized and the reeds set afire. The reference here may be to the thick clumps of reeds that line the banks of the Euphrates, or to the reed-filled marshes in the region of the Persian Gulf, south of Babylon. The military tactics employed in such terrain, which included the seizing of the fords to prevent the flight of the inhabitants and the firing of the reeds to spread panic and confusion, are represented on Assyrian reliefs from the reign of Sennacherib (704–681 B.C.). Assyrian troops, armed with javelins and shields, are seen boarding the reed-boats of the marsh dwellers. The occupants of the boat on the right are surrendering, while those on the left try to hide with their boat amongst the undergrowth. Such will be the fate of the Babylonians fleeing from their doom.

The Book of Jeremiah ends with a reference to an important event in the life of the exiled king Jehoiachin. The editor's aim in appending this passage was to provide a parable of the future of the Davidic Dynasty which, though temporarily eclipsed after the fall of Jerusalem, would eventually regain its former glory, thereby symbolizing the bright future in store for the whole nation, once it had been purged of its sins. The exiled monarch had evidently

*The fords have been seized,
the bulwarks are burned with
fire, and the soldiers are in
panic.*   (JER. 51 : 32)

River warfare on relief from
palace of Sennacherib, Nineveh.
Seventh century B.C. (British
Museum)

suffered from various ups and downs of fortune during his captivity, depending upon the
constantly shifting political aims of the Babylonian empire. But eventually, thirty-seven
years after Jehoiachin had been carried off captive, Evil-Merodach (561–560 B.C.), Nebuchadnezzar's successor, released him from confinement and decided to treat him with
considerable respect. This Biblical account is confirmed by ration lists, found in the palace
of Nebuchadnezzar, at the head of which stand the names of "Jehoiachin king of Judah"
and his five sons. The privileged status of the king and of his family is evident from the
quantity of the rations they received, which amount to about eight times those received by
ordinary captives.

THE LAMENTATIONS
OF JEREMIAH

THE SUBJECT OF the Book of Lamentations, which has been attributed to Jeremiah since very early times, is the destruction of the kingdom of Judah and Jerusalem, its capital, with the exile of its people and all their consequent physical and spiritual sufferings. The book is a collection of five separate dirges, through each of which runs the same dominant theme: desolate and despised as she is, Zion's only hope of salvation is to throw herself upon God's abundant mercies. The dirges are steeped in the dark atmosphere of that time of grim destruction and anguished soul-searching. The poignant descriptions of the princes of Judah pursued like deer by the huntsmen, and of the looting of the Temple treasures and the invasion of the sanctuary, are all dominated by a single,

*How does the city sit solitary
. . . how is she become a widow!*
(LAM. I: I)

Weeping woman on
relief from Sakkarah,
Egypt. Thirteenth cen-
tury B.C.

Young men are compelled to grind at the mill; and boys stagger under loads of wood. (LAM. 5: 13)

Captives doing forced labor on relief
in palace of Sennacherib, Nineveh.
Seventh century B.C.

somber image—that of the mourning daughter of Zion whose spirit faints at the wholesale slaughter of the vanquished city's inhabitants. Such a mother's grief over her children is strikingly illustrated in an Egyptian relief of a forward-drooping woman's head, the down-turned eyes half closed, and the mouth contorted with sobbing. The expression of the face is one of open but restrained weeping, as becomes a silent grief.

The plight of the captives and the prophet's own affliction were more than enough to justify such sorrow. Chapter 5 of Lamentations describes in detail the physical suffering and spiritual anguish of what was left of the nation in war-ravaged Judah after the downfall of the kingdom. The victorious Babylonians gave free rein to their savage brutality, having apparently taken over from the Assyrians the methods of torture which the latter had been in the habit of employing on their conquered foes. Far from attempting to gloss over such atrocities, the Assyrians proudly commemorated them in stone. Reliefs excavated in the palace of Ashurbanipal at Nineveh show how Assyrian soldiers, acting upon the king's orders, subject prisoners of war to a horrible series of systematically planned tortures: some of the victims are pegged down and flayed alive; others are maimed with iron bars; while others have their tongues torn out.

While the princes and elders of Judah were thus savagely tortured, the rest of the nation was carried off into exile. As usual in antiquity the captives, especially the young men and boys, were put to work in the royal labor gangs. Sennacherib's reliefs at Nineveh illustrate very clearly the kind of forced labor to which they were subjected. In one of them rows of men, no doubt captives, are seen carrying beams on their shoulders, closely watched by special overseers, two of whom are beating some of the laborers with a stick to make them work faster. Other captives are shown making a fill or an embankment: tied to their backs are baskets full of small stones and gravel prepared for the purpose. Both groups are being given no respite.

The Book of Lamentations ends with the nation's confession of the sins which had brought its present affliction upon it. Suffering led to repentance, and repentance would be followed by divine forgiveness and the people's hope of a return to freedom in its own land.

And you, O son of man, take a brick and lay it before you,
and portray upon it a city, even Jerusalem. (EZEK. 4: 1)

Map of Nippur on a clay
tablet. c. 1500 B.C.

THE BOOK OF THE
PROPHET EZEKIEL

EZEKIEL, THE SON of Buzi, was a priest and apparently a member of a noble
Jerusalem family which was exiled in 597 B.C. with king Jehoiachin. His
prophetic activity began in the fifth year after the exile of Jehoiachin, i.e. in 592 B.C., and
he prophesied in Babylonia, though some scholars think that he may have been active in
Palestine too. His first vision came to him near the River Chebar while he was living in the
Babylonian city of Tel-Abib. He continued his mission for many years after the fall of
Jerusalem, an event which marked a turning-point in his prophetic message. In some respects
Ezekiel was the Babylonian counterpart of Jeremiah. Like his fellow-prophet from Anathoth,
he first devoted his inspired utterances to denouncing the sins of Jerusalem, especially that of

idolatry, and to proclaiming the inevitable divine punishment of the city through the medium of a foreign conqueror. Like Jeremiah, too, he opposed false prophets who promised deliverance, and he ridiculed the views of those who confidently placed their trust in their possession of the Temple. Nor did he expect any good to come from an alliance with Egypt.

However, once the events foretold by him had actually taken place and Jerusalem had fallen, the prophet's message changed. As before, he opposed the popular sentiment of the moment. When the people in Judah and the exiles in Babylonia alike had clung to a facile belief in the help of Egypt and the salvation bound to come from the Temple, deluding themselves with false complacency, Ezekiel had foretold death and destruction. But when Jerusalem fell and the people's mood swung to the opposite extreme of utter despondency, he began to speak words of encouragement to them. Release from this despondency was proclaimed in his affirmation that the sins of the fathers were not visited on the sons, but that every individual had to bear the full and sole responsibility for his own sins and to expiate them in his own lifetime. The fathers who had sinned had been punished with death or exile; the sons could now make a clean start and hope for divine mercy. The real basis for this more hopeful message lay in Ezekiel's belief that God would act to save his people so that the glory of his nature would be proclaimed.

The visions of Ezekiel bear unmistakable marks of the influence of his Babylonian environment. Thus, his book opens with a detailed description of the chariot of God seen by the prophet in his initiatory vision. The central structure of this chariot is a platform supported by four living creatures, each of which has at its feet a wheel within a wheel. Each of these creatures has a human trunk, with four faces facing the four points of the compass, four wings on either side of their body, and the feet of a bull. Thus each of them is a combination of man, bird, and beast. Composite figures of this kind occur frequently in the mythology and plastic art of the ancient East. Such creatures, called in Akkadian *lamassu*, were found in the palace of Sargon II (721–705 B.C.), flanking the entrance to the throne room. They have the face of a man and the wings of an eagle, with a bull's trunk, legs, and horns. Their function was apparently to protect the palace from evil spirits.

Ezekiel made more use of symbolic acts than any other of the major prophets. Some of these, performed by him at the beginning of his prophetic activity, proclaimed the coming siege of Jerusalem. In one such case the prophet was commanded to draw Jerusalem—obviously meaning a plan of the city—on a brick and to lay symbolical siege to it. Excavations in Babylonia have brought to light many such plans, all surprisingly accurate, drawn on the usual writing material of the country, clay bricks. One of them, a map of the city of Nippur from the middle of the second millennium B.C., shows the city's walls and gates, its main temple ("the House of Enlil"), the water channels traversing it, and the River Euphrates by which it was encircled. As a native of Jerusalem, Ezekiel could undoubtedly have produced a similarly accurate plan of the Holy City.

Another of Ezekiel's symbolic acts was intended to bring home the stark reality of the exile in store for the people of Judah and their king. The prophet, complete with "exile's baggage", publicly enacted the fate of the deportees. The "exile's baggage" consisted of a bundle of personal possessions carried by exiles on their backs. Such bundles feature prominently on Assyrian reliefs, since it was the Assyrians who first introduced systematic mass deportations as an instrument of policy. Thus on a relief from the palace of Ashurbanipal (668–630 B.C.) at Nineveh depicting a group of three deportees—two men and a boy—pack-like objects are being carried by both men on their backs and in the right hand of the one in front. An Assyrian soldier is urging the deportees along with a staff in his hand.

The deportation of the inhabitants of Judah was, for Ezekiel, the inevitable result of the idolatry practiced by them. But the final sin which brought about the fall of Jerusalem was only the last link in a long chain of similar acts of apostasy. In fact, the prophet regards the whole past history of Israel as a long series of such acts, beginning even before the Exodus from Egypt. While still slaves in the Valley of the Nile they had already defiled themselves with idol-worship and other abominations. This was especially damnable in view of the absurd and repulsive form of the Egyptian idols. That of the Goddess Taweret, for instance, has a heavy, sagging woman's body and the head of a hippopotamus on which there is a wig and a cylindrical head-dress, such as was worn by Egyptian ladies of rank; the arms and legs end in lion's claws. A similarly grotesque figure was the dwarf-like demon called Bes. His

Therefore, son of man, prepare for yourself an exile's baggage, and go into exile by day in their sight . . .
(EZEK. 12:3)

Deportees on relief from palace of Ashurbanipal at Nineveh. Seventh century B.C. (Louvre, Paris)

218

And I said to them, Cast away the detestable things your eyes feast on, every one of you, and do not defile yourselves with the idols of Egypt . . .   (EZEK. 20: 7)

(*Left*) Statue of Taweret, from Karnak. Seventh–sixth century B.C. (Cairo Museum)

(*Right*) Figurine of Bes. (University Museum, Philadelphia)

broad, bearded face is shown contorted into a hideous grimace, with his tongue sticking out. On his head there is a crown of feathers, in his arms a child-dwarf with similar features to his own, and all around him are the figures of twelve monkeys and two geese. Yet on such "detestable things" did the Israelites "feast their eyes".

THE SINS OF JERUSALEM AND SAMARIA

IN A GREAT allegory (ch. 23) Ezekiel castigates the idolatry of Judah and Israel by comparing the two nations to two lewd sisters—Ohola and Oholibah—who lusted for foreign paramours from Egypt and Assyria. When Oholibah, who represents Jerusalem, sees portraits of Chaldaeans painted on the wall, she becomes so inflamed with passion for them that she sends messengers to Babylon to entice them to come to her. This detail of the prophet's allegory is taken from the common practice in ancient Mesopotamia of decorating the walls of large chambers with painted reliefs in a variety of colors, including the vermilion mentioned here by Ezekiel.

THE ORACLE AGAINST TYRE

LIKE THE OTHER great prophets, Ezekiel devoted part of his prophecy to fore-telling the doom of the various nations bordering on Judah. The longest of his oracles concerning the nations is that uttered against Tyre, the great merchant city which, because of its unique strategic position on a rocky island, was able to resist the Babylonians for thirteen years. It was Tyre's overweening confidence in its impregnability that provoked the prophet into pronouncing its impending doom. Perhaps he obtained his detailed information about the Phoenician city from Tyrian exiles living in Babylon side by side with the Judaeans. In his twenty-seventh chapter Ezekiel gives a sweeping survey of the far-flung commercial empire which Tyre had created for itself by taking full advantage of its unique geographical situation. This empire extended from the Persian Gulf to the Straits of Gibraltar, and from southern Arabia to the shores of the Black Sea. Some of the articles traded were produced in the factories of Tyre, but most of them were raw materials obtained from the natives of various countries in exchange for other materials brought from far off lands. Tyre owed its centuries' long success as the great middleman in the international trade of antiquity mainly to its far-ranging fleet of merchant ships. Hence the prophet likens the city's downfall to the shipwreck of a surpassingly beautiful vessel on the high seas. In so doing, he describes in detail the various fittings of the ship, the choice materials that were imported for its construction, and the allocation of nautical tasks among the sailors pressed into service from the neighboring countries of the Phoenician seaboard, the inhabitants of which were renowned far and wide as shipbuilders and seafarers.

All this maritime splendor would be of no avail when the day of Tyre's doom came. Until then the king of Tyre could vainly vaunt himself as a more than mortal being, dwelling in the "garden of God". Traditions of such a "paradise" are found not only in the Bible but also in the art and literature of the other nations of the ancient East.

THE VISION OF THE DRY BONES

IN CHAPTER 37 Ezekiel gives an impassioned description of his great vision of consolation and revival. He sees himself borne by the spirit of the LORD to a valley full of dry bones and ordered to prophesy to them that they will be restored to life. "And the bones came together, bone to bone . . . and the sinews and the flesh came upon them . . . and the breath came into them and they lived and stood up upon their feet, an exceeding great army." The primary symbolical meaning of this vision, which contains the germ of the later Jewish belief in the resurrection of the dead, is the redemption and eventual restoration of Israel and Judah. The profound influence it exercised on later generations is

The hand of the LORD was upon me, and he brought me out by the Spirit of the LORD, and set me down in the midst of the valley; it was full of bones . . . (EZEK. 37: 1)

Fresco showing the vision of the dry bones in the synagogue of Dura-Europus. Third century A.D.

exemplified in the fresco on the wall of a synagogue excavated at Dura-Europus and dating to the third century A.D. The fresco depicts the vision in a consecutive series of episodes linked together by the central figure of the prophet who is portrayed first in a short Parthian garment and then in the dignified long Greek cloak, as he joins with the resurrected dead, similarly clothed, in the praises of God.

The last chapters of the book give a detailed account of how the Temple was to be rebuilt and the land resettled with holy people fit for the worship and service of God.

THE BOOK OF DANIEL

THE BOOK OF DANIEL is believed by most modern scholars to have been compiled in the time of Antiochus IV Epiphanes (175–164 B.C.), using older stories and giving an exilic setting to a figure whose visions and actions are designed to encourage the faithful and to explain the distresses of the time.

The hero of the book is one of the young Jewish deportees from Judah who, together with his companions, was brought up at the Babylonian court of Nebuchadnezzar. All these youths steadfastly remained true to the God of Israel and His Law, despite the constant danger in which they placed themselves by their uncompromising monotheism. Daniel himself rose to a position of high authority after he had successfully described and interpreted a dream of the Babylonian king. In his dream the king had seen a large statue with a head of gold, chest and arms of silver, stomach and thighs of bronze, legs of iron, and feet partly of iron and partly of clay. Suddenly this image was pounded into fine dust by a stone which grew larger and larger until it was a huge mountain, filling the whole earth. The dream was interpreted by Daniel as follows: the head of gold was Babylon, which was to be followed by a succession of empires, until finally God raised up a ruler who would destroy all these and reign forever. In the opinion of most Biblical commentators the silver empire is that of Media and the bronze that of Persia (the official emblem of which was the god Ahura-mazda, portrayed standing inside a winged ring with his right hand raised in blessing and his left holding a lotus flower); the iron empire is that of Alexander the Great, who is portrayed on later coins as a god, with a covering of elephant's hide over his head and "horns" protruding from his forehead, as from the foreheads of Babylonian gods: the mixed iron and clay symbolize Alexander's successors, the Diadochi, some of whom were strong rulers and some weak. The god Apollo, seated on the omphalos (earth's navel) at Delphi, was the emblem of the empire ruled by one of these dynasties, the Seleucids.

DANIEL IN THE LION'S DEN

EVEN HIS ELEVATION to high office under the Babylonians did not put an end to the tribulations of the faithful believer in God living in the midst of an idolatrous court. When Daniel's companions refused to bow down to an image of Nebuchadnezzar, set up in the plain outside Babylon and inaugurated with great public pomp and

This was the dream; now we will tell the king its interpretation. (DAN. 2: 36)

(*Left*) Head of Alexander the Great. Fourth century B.C. (Münzkabinett, Berlin)

(*Below*) Seleucid coin. Second century B.C. (Hebrew University, Jerusalem)

mass obeisances, they were condemned to be thrown into a fiery furnace. The musical instruments used in these inauguration ceremonies are described in detail in the Book of Daniel. They included three kinds of wind instrument (the horn, the pipe, and the bagpipe) and three kinds of string instrument (the lyre, the trigon, and the harp).

On the death of Nebuchadnezzar his empire (according to the Book of Daniel) passed to his son Belshazzar. There actually was a Babylonian ruler of this name, who governed the city on behalf of his father, Nabunaid (Nabonidus), the last king of Babylon, and who was killed when the city fell to Cyrus and the Persians in 539 B.C. In the Book of Daniel, Belshazzar is represented as desecrating the holy vessels looted from the Temple of Jerusalem by putting them to profane use at a royal banquet. Suddenly in the midst of the revelry a mysterious hand appeared and wrote four words on the palace wall: *Mene, mene, tekel, upharsin.* No one could interpret this mysterious message till Daniel was sent for. He at once explained its true meaning: "God has counted out (the days of the Babylonian kingdom), weighed (its king) in the scales (and found him wanting), and divided up (his dominions among the Medes and the Persians)." In their literal sense, the words denote a series of common ancient weights, called *maneh, shekel,* and *peres,* which were employed as units of silver in commercial exchanges before the introduction of coinage, and subsequently gave their names to the coins themselves. The Babylonian *minah* was a weight of sixty shekels; weights marked thus have been found dating from the reign of Nebuchadnezzar II.

After the fall of Babylon to the Persians, Daniel is described as retaining his high office

Then the king commanded, and Daniel was brought and
cast into the den of lions . . . (DAN. 6: 16)

Bronze support from Persepolis.
Fifth century B.C. (Oriental
Institute, Chicago)

under the new rulers, a reflection of the historical fact that the empire of Babylon passed
without resistance from Nabunaid to Cyrus. While continuing to perform his duties at the
court of Cyrus' successor, Darius I, Daniel still remained true to the faith of his fathers, and
despite the king's stern interdiction regularly turned to Jerusalem three times a day in
prayer. This provided the other courtiers with an opportunity to denounce him to the king
and thus have him thrown to the wild beasts, as decreed in the royal law which could not
be changed. So Daniel was cast into a lions' den but emerged from this ordeal also unscathed,
because God sent an angel and closed the lions' mouths.

The presence of lions at the Persian court explains the fact that lions are a favorite subject
of Persian art. The bronze stand in the form of three lions reproduced here was found at
Persepolis and dates to the time of Darius' successors in the fifth century B.C. The artist seems
to have based his work primarily on direct observation of the animals kept at the royal court
of Persia, despite the obvious signs of Assyrian influence.

THE VISION OF THE FUTURE

STANDING ON THE banks of the river Ulai in Elam, not far from the Persian
capital, Susa, Daniel had a vision of the struggle between Persia and Greece.
Persia was symbolically represented by a ram with two horns, one of which stood for
Media and the other, "higher" one, for Persia proper. The ram had once been vigorous and

Then the king of the south shall be strong, but one of his princes shall be stronger than he and his dominion shall be a great dominion. (DAN. 11: 5)

(*Top*) Bust of Seleucus I. (Museo Nazionale, Naples)

(*Bottom*) Head of Ptolemy I. (Nij Carlsberg Glyptothek, Copenhagen)

strong, but now its valorous days were past and it was no longer a match for the he-goat that came furiously charging at it. The goat is an allusion to Alexander the Great, who is portrayed in his statues with the horns of his supposed father, Zeus Ammon.

The ram was apparently in antiquity a generally accepted symbol of the Persian empire. Rams' heads made of gold are among the archaeological finds dating to the Persian period; and indeed, the ram was a favorite subject of Persian art, so much so that its shape often adorns purely functional objects such as jar handles.

In the continuation of his vision Daniel foretells the later history of the Hellenistic empires: Alexander the Great's empire will be broken up "and divided towards the four winds of heaven". For a time "the king of the south" will be supreme; this is a reference to Ptolemy I Lagos, one of Alexander's generals, who, after his master's death, seized control of Egypt and Palestine. However, "one of his princes shall be strong above him"; this was Seleucus I, another of Alexander's generals and for a time one of Ptolemy's commanders. Acting in alliance with Ptolemy, Seleucus conquered Mesopotamia for himself and made himself master of the greater part of Alexander's empire, from the Aegean Sea to India. This was the beginning of the conflict between the Seleucid and Ptolemaic dynasties that lasted until both fell to the stronger power of Rome.

After the struggles between the kings "of the north" (the Seleucids) and "of the south" (the Ptolemies), which continued throughout the third century B.C., Daniel next saw in his vision two great battles that were fought by them for the control of Palestine. When Antiochus III, called "the Great" (223–187 B.C.), tried to conquer Palestine at the battle of Raphia (217 B.C.), his large army was defeated by the Egyptian king. However, in 198 B.C. he made another attempt and this time defeated the Egyptian general, Scopas, near Paneas. The rule of the Ptolemies was further weakened by revolts which broke out inside the country and in which some of the Jews apparently took part. Within one year all Palestine passed under Seleucid control and remained part of their empire till the time of Antiochus's successor, Antiochus IV (175–164 B.C.). This ruler, who tried to increase the power of his kingdom in face of the growing menace of Rome (for the Romans had already defeated Antiochus III in 188 B.C. and imposed a heavy tribute on his kingdom), was vaingloriously boastful of his own might, even to the extent of attributing divine powers to himself. This self-aggrandizement had a primarily political purpose: the unification of the medley of peoples comprising the Seleucid empire. Antiochus sought to introduce a degree of uniformity into the multiplicity of faiths existing throughout his empire by establishing the supremacy of the cult of the Olympian Zeus. To this end, he identified his "Zeus of the Fortresses" with the Semitic gods "Baal of the Heavens" and "Hadad". The head of Zeus appeared henceforward on the coins of the Seleucid empire in place of the image of Apollo, the traditional protector of the dynasty. However, Antiochus' attempts to include the Jews in his grandiose schemes of religious unification met with fanatical opposition, culminating in the Maccabean revolt which, after several years of bitter struggle, set Judah free from Seleucid rule.

And in those times there shall many stand up against the king of the south . . .

(DAN. 11 : 14)

Coin of Ptolemy III.
(Louvre, Paris)

The LORD said to Hosea, "Go, take to yourself a wife of harlotry and have children of harlotry, for the land commits great harlotry for forsaking the LORD". (HOS. 1 : 2)

Papyrus. Second half of second millennium B.C. (Torino Museum)

HOSEA

HOSEA THE SON of Beeri prophesied in the dark days that came upon the kingdom of Israel after the glorious reign of Jeroboam II (784–748 B.C.). He thus saw Israel in the period of its moral decline, its eager adoption of pagan creeds, and its social and political demoralization. Paradoxically, it was the prophet's bitter experience with a dissolute and faithless wife, Gomer the daughter of Diblaim, which led him to conceive of Israel's association with its God primarily in terms of marriage and of the mutual love which a healthy marital relationship necessarily involves. Pondering the lessons of his own unhappy domestic life, Hosea was able to contribute to Biblical thought the conception that God is the husband and lover of his people rather than merely their sovereign and judge. Unfortunately, the Israel which Hosea knew was a faithless wife, a harlot, and this may suggest a love of luxury and wanton sensuality expressed in ostentatious self-adornment and heavy use of eye-paint and rouge as was common to such women. Cosmetic preparations of this kind are depicted on Egyptian papyri from the time of the New Kingdom. One of these shows an Egyptian woman painting her lips with a brush held in her right hand, while in her left she is holding a mirror and what may be a tube of kohl for touching up her eyes.

227

Her hair is elaborately groomed and her eyes appear enlarged. Around her neck she is wearing a double necklace.

In consequence of this religious apostasy, coupled with the persistent malevolence of Judah toward her weakened northern sister, the kings of Israel were forced to become vassals of Assyria and sought to placate their overlord by introducing the worship of his gods. Hosea opposed such an abject policy as neither sound nor practical and bound to end in disaster for the whole nation. No good could come of trying to curry favor with the "great king", since the gifts lavished upon him would only impoverish the country, without bringing it any guarantee of security. The attempts made in their brief reigns by two successive kings of Israel, Menahem the son of Gedi and Hosea the son of Elah, to gain the support of the Assyrian monarch by "gifts" and protestations of loyalty merely succeeded in postponing their doom, as did those made by Ahaz and Hezekiah of Judah. Scenes of tribute being brought to Assyrian kings by the emissaries of various subject nations are very common in Assyrian art. On one of the four sides of the "Black Obelisk" of Shalmaneser III (857–824 B.C.) a deputation sent by Jehu, king of Israel, is shown. The bearded Israelites wear long tunics covered by fringed cloaks; their heads are covered by the characteristic Syrian head-dress, and their feet protected by the pointed shoes of the mountain peoples. They are carrying various objects, including stamped bars of metal, vessels, and staves.

Then Ephraim went to Assyria, and sent to the great
king . . .   (HOS. 5 : 13)

Relief from "Black Obelisk" of Shalmaneser III of Assyria. Ninth century B.C. (British Museum)

JOEL

THE PROPHECY of Joel the son of Pethuel, which cannot be dated with certainty, is dominated by the indelible impression made on the prophet by a particularly disastrous invasion of locusts. Of the many kinds of locust known in Biblical lands only three multiply enormously and invade regions far removed from their breeding-grounds. Foremost of these in its visitations of Palestine and Egypt is the desert locust (*Schistocerca gregaria* Forsk.), which breeds in the wastes of Arabia and Sahara and, when climatic conditions are favorable, increases a myriad-fold. In such years huge swarms unite to spread over vast areas, from the Atlantic Ocean to India. The locust moves mainly by day, resting at night on plants and hedges. In a twinkling of an eye and with a mighty beating of wings, swarm upon swarm of the insect spreads over the land, moving in orderly array like an invading army. They darken the sky in their millions and strip the trees bare of foliage. Only divine intervention can avail against this plague, and it is this that the prophet calls upon his contemporaries to pray for.

AMOS

AMOS, THE FIRST of the prophets of Israel whose words were committed to writing, delivered his message in the days of Uzziah king of Judah and of Jeroboam II king of Israel, i.e. in the first half of the eighth century B.C. Unable to resist God's summons, he was forced to give up "following the flock" at Tekoa in Judah, and was sent to Israel to preach the LORD's word. Israel was then at the height of its prosperity; but all its wealth and material splendor could not conceal the social injustice and moral corruption which would inevitably bring about its downfall. Amos tried to warn the people of the northern kingdom to reform before it was too late. Though he also denounced the sins of the various other small nations in the region (Damascus, the Philistines, Tyre, Edom, and Moab), the main target of his admonitions, to which he returns again and again, is the luxury and sinfulness of Samaria, the capital of Israel. His bitterest reproaches are reserved for its pampered and self-indulgent citizens. Enjoying the fruits of a wealth gained largely by oppression and extortion, the pleasure-loving inhabitants of the capital let themselves be lulled by their material comfort into a false sense of security. The social injustice and lax morality prevailing in Samaria were regarded by the prophets as largely due to the women of the city with their unrestrained sensuality, gluttony, and intemperance. Hence his abusive reference to them as "kine of Bashan", a specially fattened breed of cows. Nor were matters much different in the other countries of the ancient East.

The indolent and dissipated lives lived by the rich, combined with their oppression of the poor and their overweening pride, will inevitably bring stern retribution upon Israel on the LORD's Day of Judgment. The nation, overwhelmed by natural calamities and beset by human foes on all sides, is likened to a man who flees from one danger only to fall victim to another scourge and eventually meets his doom where he least expects it, just when he

Nubians on fresco from tomb of Huy,
Thebes. Fourteenth century B.C.

"Are you not like the Ethiopians to me, O people of
Israel?" says the LORD, "Did I not bring up Israel from
the land of Egypt, and the Philistines from Caphtor and
the Syrians from Kir?" (AMOS 9: 7)

thinks that he has escaped and is safe: "As if a
man fled from a lion and a bear met him; or
went into the house and leaned with his hand
against the wall and a serpent bit him"
(Amos 5: 19).

For Amos, God's choice of Israel has
meaning only in terms of the nation's right
conduct. He is therefore entirely opposed to
the belief, which was widespread among his
contemporaries, that Israel is the chosen race
by virtue of certain inborn natural qualities.
On the contrary, all the nations are intrinsic-
ally equal in God's eyes. Hence, if the
Israelites violate the covenant made with
them by God, there is no longer any difference
between them and a far-off, strange people
like the Nubians. These black natives of
Africa frequently appear in the art of ancient
Egypt. Thus in the tomb-painting of prince
Huy, who was Tutankhamon's viceroy in the
south, we see the dark-skinned escort of a
Nubian princess presenting gifts to the
Pharaoh (fourteenth century B.C.).

As in many other prophetic books, the last words of the Book of Amos are words of
consolation. The sinners of Israel shall die by the sword, but the righteous remnant of the
people shall again be firmly planted in its soil.

JONAH

THE BOOK OF JONAH is unlike the other prophetic books. In the form of a
story about the prophet, it conveys teaching about God and His purpose to
the whole people.

Jonah, the son of Amittai, is described as living at some time when Nineveh was still the
capital of the Assyrian empire. When ordered by God to go there and call its inhabitants
to repentance he sought to escape. Other prophets too had at first shrunk back from the
mission imposed on them, but they had in the end submitted to God's command, whereas
Jonah persisted in his rejection of God's summons, perhaps because he found it distasteful to

call a Gentile city to repentance. He went down (presumably from his home in the mountains of Judah, or Jerusalem) to Joppa, with the intention of sailing across the sea to Tarshish (Spain, Sardinia, or Etruria?). In Biblical times Joppa was one of the principal ports of Palestine. At the end of the second millennium B.C. it came under Philistine control and remained so throughout the period of the Old Testament. In the time of Sennacherib it was apparently within the confines of the kingdom of Ashkelon. After Sennacherib's campaign against Judah in 701 B.C. it passed under Assyrian control; the Phoenician elements amongst its population now became so numerous that, in the Persian period, it was considered a Tyrian city. The presence of these Phoenician sea-farers at Joppa explains why Jonah could expect to find a ship there to take him to one of the distant shores of the Mediterranean.

The vessel on which Jonah embarked was no doubt one of the large type which, in Biblical times, ventured out into the open seas. Ships of this kind, usually manned by Phoenician crews, were propelled by sails, with as many as sixty rowers in reserve in case of need. In their voyages across the length and breadth of the Mediterranean the Phoenicians hugged the shores wherever possible, as did all sailors in antiquity. Owing to the absence of navigational aids the ships had nothing to steer by on clouded nights. In a sudden storm the crew would hurriedly furl their sails and row with all their might for the nearest point of land. A relief found at Karatepe in southeastern Asia Minor (eighth century B.C.) shows a ship with a rounded hull, like the Phoenician merchantmen. The two rowers represent a

*The men rowed hard to bring
the ship back to land . . .*
(JONAH I: 13)

Ship on Karatepe relief. Eighth
century B.C.

larger crew; the steersman is sitting in the stern, holding a goblet in his hand; while the captain is scanning the surface of the sea from the prow. The figures of men and fish in the sea underneath recall the story of Jonah.

For the prophet was not permitted to escape God's call by flight. A great storm blew up and threatened to wreck the ship on which he was sailing. When all efforts to save the vessel proved of no avail, the crew cast lots to discover who was responsible for their desperate plight. The lot fell on Jonah who, realizing that his attempt to flee from the LORD's presence was in vain, confessed the whole truth about himself to the sailors and told them to throw him into the raging sea. After one last, unsuccessful attempt to row to land the sailors reluctantly did as he had told them and the storm immediately abated. But Jonah did not perish, for the LORD "appointed a great fish to swallow up Jonah; and Jonah was in the belly of the fish three days and three nights".

The now humbled and contrite prophet's prayer from the belly of the fish was answered and he was cast out on dry land. When commanded again to go to Nineveh, he at once did so and preached there with such success that the inhabitants repented of their sins and were pardoned by the LORD. Embittered by this unexpected outcome of his mission, which seemed to make a mockery of his prophecy, Jonah left the city and made himself a booth outside its walls: "And the LORD God appointed a castor oil plant (A.V.: gourd) and made it come up over Jonah, that it might be a shade over his head." The castor oil plant (*Ricinus communis* L.), a bush that sometimes attains the height of a tree, is extremely fast-growing and has leaves large enough to provide shelter from the burning rays of the sun. But hardly had Jonah begun to enjoy the coolness of its shade when the plant was attacked by a worm and withered; and the next day a hot east wind so greatly added to the prophet's discomfort that he prayed to die. Then it was that God pointed the moral of Jonah's plight: if the discomfort caused by the withering of the castor oil plant had so distressed him, how much more would God be grieved by the destruction of so great a city as Nineveh? Thus Jonah —and through him his own people—received a much needed lesson in tolerance and learned that wholehearted contrition may make atonement even for the worst sins and that God makes no difference between Gentiles and Jews as far as His mercy is concerned.

MICAH

MICAH'S BIRTHPLACE, MORESHETH GATH, was one of the cities of the Shephelah in the region of Lachish and Mareshah. It is most probably to be located at the artificial mound known in Arabic as Tell el-Jedeideh, which dominated the road running up from Lachish into the Judaean hills. The prophetic activity of Micah covered the reign of Jotham, Ahaz, and Hezekiah in Judah; that is to say, the second half of the eighth century B.C. Like his contemporary Isaiah, Micah sternly censures the perversions of justice and the social oppression which were rampant in the kingdom. He denounces the nobles and the judges who batten upon the simple folk, blandly confident that the mere existence of the Temple in Jerusalem would absolve them from all sin. Their doom would therefore be all the more terrible: "Zion shall be plowed as a field and Jerusalem shall become a heap of ruins."

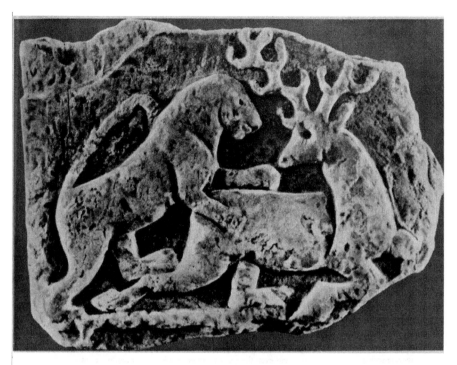

And the remnant of Jacob shall be among the nations, in the midst of many peoples, like a lion among the beasts of the forest, like a young lion among the flocks of sheep, which, when it goes through, treads down and tears in pieces, and there is none to deliver. (MIC. 5: 8)

Kish relief, showing lion and stag. Third millennium B.C. (Baghdad Museum)

Like the other prophetic works, Micah's book contains the promise of ultimate redemption after the punishment has run its full course. The nation's future deliverance from the might of Sennacherib is depicted in a simile taken from animal life. Not only will Judah be saved from its foes, but the remnant of Jacob will actually go over to the attack against Assyria. The prophet then likens Zion triumphant to a lion and its cub preying upon both the wild life of the forest and upon domestic animals. Such scenes were amongst the most common themes of oriental literature and art. Thus a relief found at Kish in Mesopotamia, and dating back to as early as the third millennium, shows a lion pouncing upon a stag; the victim is sinking to the ground under the weight of its attacker whose claws are already firmly fixed in its flesh, as described by Micah: "It tears in pieces, and there is none to deliver" (Mic. 5: 8).

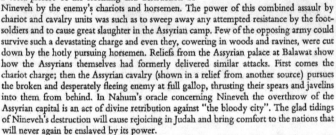

Chariots on Balawat palace gates. Ninth century B.C. (British Museum)

NAHUM

NAHUM OF ELKOSH preached in Judah at the end of the seventh century B.C. He thus lived in one of the most critical periods in the history of the ancient East when the Assyrian empire, which had been founded two hundred years before on the spoliation and oppression of the countries it had conquered, was tottering to its fall. Its magnificent capital, Nineveh, was sacked in 612 B.C. by nations that only a few years before had been its vassals.

With a few powerful strokes the prophet paints a vivid picture of the storming and destruction of Nineveh by the enemy's chariots and horsemen. The power of this combined assault by chariot and cavalry units was such as to sweep away any attempted resistance by the foot-soldiers and to cause great slaughter in the Assyrian camp. Few of the opposing army could survive such a devastating charge and even they, cowering in woods and ravines, were cut down by the hotly pursuing horsemen. Reliefs from the Assyrian palace at Balawat show how the Assyrians themselves had formerly delivered similar attacks. First comes the chariot charge; then the Assyrian cavalry (shown in a relief from another source) pursues the broken and desperately fleeing enemy at full gallop, thrusting their spears and javelins into them from behind. In Nahum's oracle concerning Nineveh the overthrow of the Assyrian capital is an act of divine retribution against "the bloody city". The glad tidings of Nineveh's destruction will cause rejoicing in Judah and bring comfort to the nations that will never again be enslaved by its power.

Nahum compares the downfall of Nineveh to the fate of Thebes, the capital of Egypt and one of the greatest and most famed cities of the ancient East. Esarhaddon of Assyria had succeeded in conquering Lower Egypt in 671 B.C.; but it was not till 663 B.C. that his son, Ashurbanipal, advanced on the capital of the kings of the Twenty-fifth Dynasty and took it by storm.

Nahum ends his song of triumph over the downfall of the hated enemy with the gloating taunt that it is the people of Assyria that are now "scattered upon the mountains", and that the destruction of their empire is final and complete: "There is no assuaging your hurt, your wound is grievous. All who hear the news of you clap their hands over you. For upon whom has not come your unceasing evil?"

The crack of whip, and rumble of wheel,
galloping horse and bounding chariot!
Horsemen charging, flashing sword and
glittering spear . . . (NAHUM 3 : 2–3)

Assyrian cavalry charging. Relief in British
Museum.

HABAKKUK

HABAKKUK PROPHESIED IN the days when the Chaldaean (Babylonian) empire was at the height of its power. The hopes raised throughout the ancient East by the fall of Nineveh were quickly dashed when the conquering Babylonians themselves adopted the Assyrian methods of power politics and established a great empire of their own, also based on the oppression of subject peoples. In his oracle, Habakkuk expresses his perplexity at the doom in store for these nations. On the one hand, like Isaiah and Jeremiah, he regards the Chaldaeans as sent by the LORD to deal out divine retribution to sinful peoples. But unlike them he cannot resign himself to the dominion of Babylon and bitterly complains to the LORD: "Why dost thou make me see wrongs and look upon trouble? Destruction and violence are before me."

The Chaldaeans of Habakkuk's description came to be the name used symbolically by later

235

generations of Jews of any merciless enemy. Thus among the writings of the sect which has left us the Dead Sea Scrolls, there is a commentary on the Book of Habakkuk in which the prophet's words are applied to contemporary history. The "Chaldaeans" are there interpreted as "Kittim"—apparently meaning the Romans—who come from afar, "from the isles of the sea to devour all the nations like vultures that are never sated".

Habakkuk compares all-conquering Babylon to a fisherman who hauls up catch after catch in his net, till he is drunk with pride in his own prowess. So Babylon, intoxicated by the dizzy speed of its victories and conquests, bows down in worship to its own military power. Faced with this spectacle of sinfulness and idolatry triumphant, the prophet is sorely perplexed by the workings of divine providence. God's reply to his anxious questioning is given in the form of an obscure vision indicating that he must simply hold fast to his faith in the eventual downfall of Babylon. At the same time Habakkuk is commanded to write down his vision on a tablet as a testimony for the days to come, when the prophecy about the overthrow of the idolatrous empire has been fulfilled. Writing on tablets formed of cleaned and smoothed lumps of clay was practiced in Mesopotamia and other oriental countries from very early times. Impressions were made on the tablet with the triangular-shaped end of a wooden stylus. By a downward pressure of this stylus, with its point resting in the soft clay, wedge-shaped marks were produced running vertically, horizontally, or diagonally. Groups of such wedges formed the various signs of the script. When the writing was completed the tablet was fired in an oven to make it resistant to damp and salinity so that it could be preserved for future reference—as indicated here in God's command to the prophet.

ZEPHANIAH

ZEPHANIAH IS TRADITIONALLY regarded as a member of the royal Davidic house, a descendant of king Hezekiah in the fourth generation. He was active in the seventh century, the time of Josiah. His prophecy opens with a proclamation of the coming Day of the LORD when both the idolatrous nations and the sinners of Israel will meet their doom. Then follows a message of consolation to Judah into which the prophet has inserted a pronouncement of the coming destruction of the four Philistine cities of Gaza, Ashkelon, Ashdod, and Ekron. The omission of Gath is explained by the fact that it had ceased to be an independent kingdom in the ninth century B.C. The remaining Philistine cities underwent various fluctuations of fortune in the eighth century. Gaza and Ashdod were punished by Sargon, while Ashkelon and Ekron suffered for their revolt against Sennacherib. However, after Sennacherib's campaign against Judah both Gaza and Ekron were allowed to enlarge their territories at Judah's expense.

The capture of Ekron is represented on a relief from the palace of Sargon II. The city's defenders are seen on its towers, shooting with their bows at the advancing Assyrian soldiers. In the center of the picture two of the Assyrian auxiliary troops are seen crouching on one knee and aiming their arrows at the defenders. Inscribed in cuneiform characters on the wall is the name of the city: "Amqaruna" (i.e. Akkaron).

And they answered the angel of the LORD who was standing among the myrtle trees, "We have patrolled the earth and behold, all the earth remains at rest."

(ZECH. I: II)

Relief at Behistun, Persia, showing Ahuramazda leading the enemies of Darius to surrender.

ZECHARIAH

ECHARIAH, THE SON of Berechiah the son of Iddo, was one of the heads of the priestly families that returned to Jerusalem from the Babylonian Exile with Zerubbabel. Like his contemporary and fellow-prophet Haggai, Zechariah expresses his confidence in the restoration of Judah and the annihilation of its enemies, in the rebuilding of Jerusalem and the removal of the wicked nations from its midst. In his vision of the four horses an angel of the LORD appears and proclaims that the earth is now at rest. This seems to be an allusion to the suppression of the revolts in the Persian empire against Darius I. The surrender of this king's enemies is represented on a rock-cut relief at Behistun, with an accompanying inscription in three parallel versions (in Persian, Elamite, and Babylonian) which recounts the story of the political unrest in Persia during the two first years of Darius' reign. In the course of a detailed chronological record of these events, Darius boasts that from the day of his accession he has waged war against nineteen countries and subdued all his enemies. According to the text of Zechariah (I: 7), the pacification of the empire was completed by February 519 B.C.

Judah may have been involved in the general turmoil. Some scholars think that both Zerubbabel and the high priest Joshua, the son of Jehozadak, were implicated. The former is not again mentioned in this context, the high priest was acquitted and retained his office. Zechariah describes the trial of the high priest as taking place before the heavenly host; at its conclusion Joshua is cleared of guilt, and his filthy garments, the symbol of sin, are taken off him and replaced by splendid raiment and a clean turban.

The second portion of the Book of Zechariah is of a later date. Here we are told how the Messianic Age will dawn and the Israelites, with God fighting at their side, will wreak vengeance on their foes. At the end of the apocalyptic war God will gather in the widely scattered exiles of His people. The House of Judah and the House of Joseph will be united as of old and their combined military might will be invincible. In the prosperity that follows, the rapidly multiplying population will spread till it reaches the Lebanon and

Gilead. The former is often referred to in the Old Testament as a symbol of strength, dignity, and splendor. The combined reference to the Lebanon and Gilead may be intended to show the future power and glory of the Messianic kingdom of Israel.

On the Day of the LORD—the day on which God will take vengeance on the nations that have ravaged and oppressed Israel—the LORD of Hosts will appear in His glory on the Mount of Olives, the mountain that rises high above Jerusalem, to war against the nations and to mete out retribution to them. At this awe-inspiring theophany, the whole mountain will shake and be cloven asunder, as the earth was convulsed in the great earthquake that occurred in the reign of Uzziah.

MALACHI

MALACHI, "MY MESSENGER", an anonymous work stands last in the prophetic canon, and belongs to the beginning of the fifth century B.C., when the fortunes of Judah were at a very low ebb. The returning exiles' hopes for the restoration of Judah, to be brought about by the rebuilding of the Temple, had been dashed; instead there was general disillusionment and apathy. Taking issue with this prevailing mood, the prophet tried to raise the people's spirits by assuring them of the everlasting and unchanging character of God's promises to Israel.

Bitterly disappointed in the high hopes they had placed in the rebuilding of the Temple, the returning Judaeans began to be remiss in the observance of the ritual commandments. The priests accepted from the people animals which had some physical defect and were therefore unfit for sacrifice. This gross disrespect for their divine ruler was in glaring contrast to the great honor shown by the people to their temporal governor, the representative of the Persian king, for whose "allocation of food" only the best was good enough. This almost religious awe in which the governor (peha) of the province called Judah (Yehud) was held stemmed from his virtually absolute control of the affairs of the nation. He was responsible only to the satrap of the province called "Beyond the River" (Euphrates, one of the twenty great satrapies of the Persian empire) into whose care was entrusted the administration of an immense area stretching from Asia Minor to Egypt.

The noble vision of consolation with which the Book of Malachi ends forms a serene conclusion to the prophetic canon of the Old Testament. Out of the political despondency and spiritual darkness of his own days the prophet looks confidently forward to the Messianic second appearance of the prophet Elijah in whose person the traditions of revelation and prophecy will be renewed; for the spirit of God will not depart from His people. The profound influence of this vision of Elijah's second coming can be seen not only in the Gospels and in Jewish legend, but also in early Jewish art. In one of the wall-paintings from the synagogue at Dura-Europus on the Euphrates (c. A.D. 255) we see Elijah in contest with the priests of Baal on Mount Carmel. Thus the author of the Book of Malachi, one of the last of the prophets who fought to make the word of God prevail, is directly linked to Elijah, the first of that devoted band who, as the performer of miracles and the great harbinger of the Messianic Age, became the hero of later Jewish legend.

Between the
Testaments

BETWEEN THE
TESTAMENTS

FIVE GENERATIONS SEPARATE the events foreseen by Daniel in his concluding vision and the beginning of the Gospel story. In this interval momentous developments took place in Judaea and the whole of the Mediterranean world. The attempt of the Seleucid king, Antiochus IV Epiphanes (175–164 B.C.) to Hellenize the Jews and introduce a pagan cult (167 B.C.) provoked a rebellion on the part of those who clung devotedly to their ancestral faith. This movement, led by Judas Maccabeus ("the hammer-like one") and his brothers, finally resulted in the creation of a kingdom ruled by the Hasmonaean dynasty (Hasmon being the ancestor of the Maccabees). Profiting from the disintegration of the Seleucid rule, the Hasmonaeans gradually extended their territories until under Alexander Jannaeus (103–76 B.C.) almost the whole of Palestine was under their control.

In this process, however, the Hasmonaeans themselves evolved into rulers of the Hellenistic type, much like other dependent kings of the time. They now relied on mercenaries, and could on occasion use these against their own subjects. The very people who had been their main supporters disapproved of their acceptance of the high priesthood at the hands of the Seleucids, for was not that office reserved by God for the descendants of the house of Zadok, to which the Hasmonaeans, though priests, did not belong? Furthermore by arrogating to themselves the regal title they obstructed the fulfillment of the promise of God to the house of David. In this situation of cleavage a party known as the "Pharisees" or "separated ones" arose, and opposed Alexander Jannaeus. At an opportune time a revolt broke out, which was put down only with great difficulty. Eight hundred Pharisees were crucified by Alexander and thousands of people fled the country. So great was the tension between king and subjects that Alexander on his death-bed advised his queen, who was to reign after him, to make peace with the Pharisees. In the decade of her rule they exercised great influence.

The same events that had led to the rise of the Pharisees may also have given birth to (or augmented the numbers of) the sect that produced the Dead Sea Scrolls; it was in opposition to a "lying priest" and stayed away from the Temple. Its "teacher of righteousness" seems to have suffered death—perhaps under Jannaeus. The sect's devotion to his memory parallels that which Christians were to show to Jesus after he had been taken from them. The Qumran sect continued to exist until queen Salome Alexandra (76–67 B.C.) appointed her elder son, Hyrcanus, high priest, for it was unthinkable that a woman should hold this office among the Jews. After her death, Hyrcanus' younger brother, Aristobulus, sought to become king, and this led to strife in which Hyrcanus invoked the aid of the Nabataeans.

Meanwhile Rome was asserting its power more actively in Eastern affairs. In 65 B.C. Pompey came to Syria. He deposed the last Seleucid ruler, and therewith Rome assumed the right to regulate the affairs of its dependencies. The rival Hasmonaean brothers appeared before Pompey for an adjudication of their claims. He terminated the kingship, stripped Judaea of its military acquisitions, recognized Hyrcanus as high priest and ethnarch, and put Aristobulus under arrest. The latter's supporters had control of the Temple at the time and resisted Pompey when he came to Jerusalem. It was necessary for him to besiege the Temple. After three months its defenders were overcome and slaughtered, and Pompey entered the Holy of Holies. He did not, however, despoil the Temple treasure. Judaea now was tributary to Rome. Hyrcanus had an able political *aide* in the person of the Idumaean Antipater. The Idumaeans had been converted to Judaism under John Hyrcanus.

A Parthian invasion of Syria and Palestine brought about a change in the status of Judaea. A Hasmonaean kingship was established under Antigonus, the son of Aristobulus (40–37 B.C.). Herod, Antipater's son, who had governed Galilee, managed to escape and went to Rome, where the Senate named him king of Judaea and encouraged him to win the position by his efforts. This Herod succeeded in doing.

While the siege of Jerusalem was in progress Herod wed Mariamme, the granddaughter of Hyrcanus at Samaria, thus gaining a valuable marital connection with the Hasmonaean family. When Gaius Octavius prevailed over Mark Antony, Herod obtained the former's recognition and in the course of time his territory was greatly increased, so that he ruled not only Judaea but non-Jewish areas. A great builder, his foremost achievement in that respect seems to have been the rebuilding of the Temple at Jerusalem, which allegedly took forty-six years (John 2: 20). But no matter what he did law-abiding Jews regarded his kingship as illegitimate, and it made matters even worse that he was of Idumaean origin. The horrors that occurred in the royal house, above all the execution of his wife Mariamme, gave him an evil reputation in his later years.

In his testament Herod named his son Archelaus king, the latter's brother, Herod Antipas, tetrarch of Galilee and Peraea, and another son, Philip, tetrarch of the regions in northern Transjordan and beyond. Augustus had to confirm the arrangement, however, and denied Archelaus the title of king. He was to have the title ethnarch, which ranked slightly above that of tetrarch. After nine years of his unpopular government the Jews brought complaint against him before Augustus, who summoned him to Rome and banished him to Gaul (A.D. 6). His territory was put under direct administration by an imperial governor who resided at Caesarea. This governor, called a procurator because his primary concern was financial, was subordinate to the governor of Syria. Pontius Pilate, who held office A.D. 26–36, was the fifth in the series of procurators.

In the course of the first century B.C. the political activism of the Pharisaic party had waned. The Scribes had come forward in it as expounders of the written Law. The party's interest was centered on bringing about obedience to the Law and the rapidly accumulating interpretative tradition of the elders. They believed that God in his own time would make an end to foreign dominion and illegal kingship, and accepted the present state of affairs as under his sufferance. The Pharisees had as their chief opponents the party of the Sadducees. This group, which included the priestly aristocracy, did not accept the Pharisaic innovations, but insisted that the letter of the Old Testament Law alone was valid.

After the death of Herod revolts sprang up in various parts of his kingdom. The Roman governor of Syria, Varus, was forced to come down and quell them. Another outbreak took place when Archelaus was deposed, and Judaea placed under direct Roman rule; for a census was ordered by the governor of Syria, Quirinius, to register the inhabitants for tax purposes. Judas the Galilean, the founder of the Zealot party, perished at this time (Acts 5: 37); the center of his activities, Sepphoris, not far from Nazareth was destroyed and its inhabitants sold into slavery. This event must have made a deep impression on the people among whom Jesus grew up.

In the midst of the harsh realities of the present the common people carried with them inspired visions of the future, thanks to the canon of the prophets, which had come to be read in the synagogue in addition to the Law.

There were other books too, which perhaps were not yet received for public reading, but circulated privately. Among these was the Book of Daniel, that product of the time of the great crisis under Antiochus IV Epiphanes. It nurtured the hope of the downfall of world powers and of the coming of God's kingdom, and it taught a new doctrine that had arisen in that age of martyrdom and that the Pharisees made one of their cardinal tenets: the belief in a resurrection of the dead and world judgment. The impact of this book and of other apocalyptic writings created an attitude of expectancy: people felt that the turning-point of history was at hand.

It was against this background that Jesus saw the light of the world.

The New Testament

The beginning of the gospel of Jesus Christ, the Son of God, as it is written in the prophets, Behold, I send my messenger before thy face, which shall prepare thy way before thee.   (MARK I: 1-2)

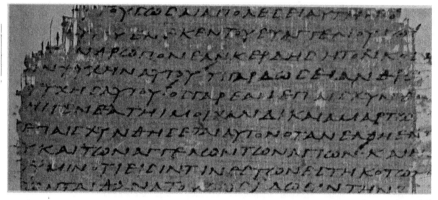

Papyrus fragment of Gospel of St. Mark. Third century A.D.

THE FOUR GOSPELS

IN THE SECOND CENTURY A.D. the Christian Church set up a collection of its own writings to supplement the sacred scriptures of the synagogue, which previously had alone been considered authoritative. The four Gospels—Matthew, Mark, Luke, and John—were the first nucleus of this so-called "New Testament canon". The apostle Matthew was reported by Early Christian tradition to have been the first to write down the sayings of Jesus, but in the "Hebrew" language (presumably the Aramaic speech used by Jesus, as evidenced by the scraps of quotation preserved in the Gospels). The Gospel named after Matthew is, however, a Greek work and is more than a compilation of sayings of Jesus, though it is a particularly rich repository of these.

Gospel research of the last century-and-a-half has shown that the Gospel according to Mark must be the oldest of the four books. Indeed, it has persuaded the majority of open-minded scholars that Matthew and Luke are largely dependent on Mark for their narrative of the life of Jesus, except for their infancy narratives. In effect, then, Matthew and Luke constitute revised and amplified versions of the Marcan story.

The ancient tradition about Mark's Gospel is more explicit than that about any other. It asserts that he was the interpreter of Peter, and wrote down what he remembered of Peter's preaching of what Jesus said and did. He allegedly did his work at Rome, at the request of Roman Christians. If Peter perished in Nero's persecution of A.D. 64, Mark's Gospel must have been written at some time in the sixth decade. Internal evidence suggests that it appeared before the fall of Jerusalem in A.D. 70. While direct dependence on Peter's reporting is not certain, this Gospel is composed from the viewpoint of those who held Peter to have been the most important of the disciples of Jesus, and gives him more prominence in the narrative than the other three Gospels.

The Gospels of Matthew and Luke must then have arisen subsequently, and a certain amount of time must be allowed for a desire to revise and supplement Mark to develop. There is no evidence that either Gospel presupposes the other, and hence no way of knowing which of the two was written first. They may have arisen at about the same time. The Gospel of Matthew was apparently written for Jewish Christians, Luke for Gentile Christians as well as for outsiders interested in learning something about Christianity. The Book of Acts is patently by the same author as the Gospel of Luke and early ecclesiastical tradition thought of Luke as presenting a Gospel buttressed by Paul's authority, as Mark's was by Peter's.

Gospel study for the last century has inferred for the time of Matthew and Luke the existence of another common source besides Mark—a collection of sayings of Jesus on which both drew in composing their revised versions of Mark. Some think that this source was originally the work of the apostle Matthew of which tradition speaks. In addition to this source, each of the two evangelists had special materials of his own.

Luke alone among the evangelists has a historian's interest. He makes certain important chronological allusions. However, for his actual narrative material of the ministry he is largely dependent on Mark, just as is the case with Matthew. Mark thus remains the primary source, and in any telling of the story of Jesus deserves to be given the preference.

The fourth Gospel, according to ancient tradition, was the last to be written and was ascribed to John the son of Zebedee. The latter claim was disputed at first but by the end of the second century enjoyed general acceptance. The author is not so much interested in the external events of that life as in the words of Jesus, and relates events chiefly to provide occasions for his discourses. These are very different in style from those reported in the other Gospels. It is evident, therefore, that John is not reproducing literally what the historical Jesus had said but is rephrasing freely. The Dead Sea Scrolls finds have shown that John must have been at home in a sectarian environment similar to that of the Essenes before becoming a Christian. In his narrative he sometimes differs in a perplexing manner from the other Gospels, for example in having the Crucifixion take place before the Passover.

The ancient churchmen who set up the canon did not regard any one Gospel as all-sufficient. Each had its own contribution to offer which the Church could not afford to miss, and therefore they coordinated them and spoke not of four Gospels but of "the gospel according to the four"—Matthew, Mark, Luke, and John. There was only one Gospel but there was a fourfold portrayal of it, each exhibiting it in a different light. The churchmen were evidently not troubled by the divergencies in the narratives, for their minds were not on biographical accuracies but rather on the workings of the Holy Spirit in the lives of men.

None of the Gospels was written with the objective biographical interest of a Plutarch. They were all composed out of faith in Jesus as the Saviour and to present him in that light to fellow-believers of the authors. The faith of the Church is thus antecedent to all written

And it came to pass in those days, that there went out a decree from Caesar Augustus, that all the world should be taxed. (And this taxing was first made when Cyrenius was governor of Syria.)

(LUKE 2 : 1–2)

Statue of Augustus, found at Rome. Inscription thought to relate to Quirinius.

Gospels. In their individual remolding of the received traditions the Gospel authors reflect their own viewpoints as well as the needs of the congregations for which they wrote. When studied from this angle they reveal much forgotten Early Christian history.

However inadequate the Gospels may be as source-material for the biographer, they are deeply satisfying to a Christendom that worships Jesus as its Lord and finds this reporting of what he said and did a source of inspiration and instruction in the conduct of life.

THE BIRTH AND EARLY YEARS OF JESUS

MATTHEW AND LUKE agree amazingly with Mark where they have him to follow. But Mark told nothing of the birth of Jesus. His purpose was not to write a life of Christ but to present in narrative form the Christian message of the Messiahship of Jesus and his atoning death. Matthew and Luke, especially the latter, show a trend in the direction of the biographical. They want to tell also of the background and birth of

Jesus. Having no help from Mark they go their separate ways in this respect and present
independent infancy stories.

Matthew provides the historian only such chronological toe-holds as that Jesus was born
at Bethlehem under Herod (37-4 B.C.), and that his parents returned from Egypt after the
death of Herod and, on hearing that Archelaus had succeeded Herod in Judaea (4 B.C.–
A.D. 6), went to Nazareth in Galilee and settled there.

Luke proceeds more "historically". While presupposing the birth of Jesus in the time of
Herod (Luke 1 : 4), he links the event more particularly with a world census under "Caesar
Augustus", i.e. Gaius Octavius, a nephew of Caesar, whom the latter had adopted by
testament and who in the turbulent times after Caesar's assassination had succeeded in making
himself the master of the Roman Empire (30 B.C.–A.D. 14). As such he received the title of
Augustus which was equivalent to "Imperial Majesty". Caesar was the *cognomen* or third of
the three customary names of his father by adoption (Gaius Julius Caesar). Luke offers no
dating for the event of the census, but knows only that it took place when Cyrenius was
governor of Syria. Only the man's *cognomen* is given. From Roman sources, however, his
full name is known: P. Sulpicius Quirinius. He was governor of Syria in A.D. 6/7 and at this
time—after Archelaus was deposed—a Roman census was conducted in Judaea. There is a
possibility of an earlier incumbency of the governorship by Quirinius in 3/2 B.C. but since
Herod died in 4 B.C. the two men were not on the world stage at the same time. Furthermore
there is no knowledge of a census having been held then, nor was one appropriate for Judaea
under Roman law, since the country was not under direct Roman administration. Luke's
attempt to date the birth of Christ thus creates problems of chronology which archaeological
discoveries may yet resolve.

Matthew has associated the birth of Jesus with the story of the Magi and of the marvelous
star. This has been used since Kepler for an astronomical calculation of the time of the birth
of Christ. But it is arbitrary to identify the star of the Messiah with a conjunction of planets,
or even with a known comet. In any case only hypotheses, not facts, can be obtained by
this approach.

Perhaps Luke's estimate of Jesus' age at the beginning of his ministry—"about thirty years
old" (Luke 3: 23)—is the most reliable indication available, for this could have been
remembered by men who had known Jesus. It would confirm the tradition that he was born
under Herod. It seems unlikely in any case that he was born at the time of the census in
A.D. 6/7, for this would have exposed him to derogatory remarks about his youth such as
were never brought forward in the Gospels. It must always be remembered, however, that
our historical information, outside the Gospel record, is severely limited.

Matthew and Luke agree in making Bethlehem the birthplace of Jesus. Since they believed
that Messianic prophecy was fulfilled in Jesus, this was a necessary assumption, in view of the
enthusiastic prophecy of Mic. 5: 2: "And thou, Bethlehem Ephratah . . . from thee shall
come forth for me one who is to be ruler in Israel." The town was of minor importance in
those days, but was nevertheless still of a considerable size, as the first convenient halting-
place for caravans going from Jerusalem southward. In the fourth century Bethlehem became
an objective of Christian pilgrimage, especially after Constantine had erected the Church of
the Nativity over the grotto where it was said Jesus was born.

The flight of the Holy Family to Egypt is reported by Matthew only, and is difficult to

*Now when Jesus was born in Bethlehem of Judaea in
the days of Herod the king, behold, there came wise men
from the east to Jerusalem.*　　　(MATT. 2: 1)

View of Bethlehem.

harmonize with Luke's traditional account that the infant Jesus was presented in the Temple.
Both evangelists, however, are in accord on the essential fact that Jesus grew up in Nazareth
in Galilee. The region was ruled by another of Herod's sons, Herod Antipas. Nazareth is not
mentioned in the Old Testament or by Josephus, and appears for the first time in a Jewish
poem of about the sixth century A.D. It owes its prominence exclusively to the fact that
Jesus grew up there. Its name may mean "guard-place". Nazareth stood like a sentinel on
the southern slopes of the mountains of Lower Galilee, with a wide view over the valley of
Jezreel. Jesus grew up in the quiet and peace of this semi-rural retreat, nurtured in the
beautiful piety and stern morality of Israel. Because it was his home it has been a place of
pilgrimage through the ages, and many churches, of which the greatest is the Church of the
Annunciation, have been built there. Today it is a town of 40,000 inhabitants and the capital
of the northern district of Israel.

Luke alone has preserved the story of the twelve-year-old boy's first visit to Jerusalem and
the saying that reveals the complete concentration of his youthful mind on the things of
God (Luke 2: 41-52).

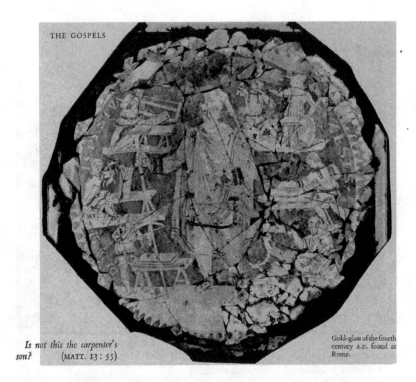

Is not this the carpenter's son? (MATT. 13 : 55)

Gold-glass of the fourth century A.D. found at Rome.

It is stated later and only in passing that Jesus was a carpenter (Mark 6:3). This determined his social status in the eyes of the people of his own town. In the fairly rigid social hierarchy of antiquity, artisans, being engaged in manual labor, were regarded with little more respect than peasants and slaves; and indeed, much of the work done by free craftsmen was also done by trained slaves. The contempt expressed for the "carpenter" thus agrees well with what we know of ancient society, which reserved the higher political and intellectual activities for "gentlemen of leisure". However, despite the low opinion held of them, ancient carpenters were most skillful, as we see from the extant specimens of their work. They were not as with us builders of houses, but rather makers of yokes, plows, carts, and furniture.

JOHN THE BAPTIST, THE BAPTISM AND TEMPTATION

AFTER RELATING THE childhood stories, both Matthew and Luke continue in dependence on or reaction to the pattern set by Mark, whose narrative thus is primary and must serve as the thread to be followed. Mark had recorded the ministry of the Baptist as the beginning of the Gospel about Jesus Christ. In reworking Mark at this point Luke again provides a chronological setting: he dates John's appearance as a prophet in the fifteenth year of the reign of Tiberius Caesar (A.D. 14–37). Counting the first year of Tiberius as beginning with the date of the death of Augustus on August 19, A.D. 14, the fifteenth year would have begun August 19, A.D. 28. The Jewish coins of the time of Tiberius support this manner of counting his regnal years. Luke buttresses this date further by a series of rough synchronisms, mentioning the contemporary rulers of the three regions into which the realm of Herod had been divided; Pontius Pilate, who was governor of Judaea (A.D. 26–36); Herod Antipas, Herod's son, who ruled Galilee from 4 B.C. until he was deposed in A.D. 39; his brother Philip who ruled the Herodian lands in the Golan, Bashan, and Hauran from 4 B.C. to his death in A.D. 34; and finally Lysanias, who ruled over the principality of Abilene north of Mount Hermon.

Extant literary history knows only of a Lysanias who was executed in 36 B.C., but an inscription found near Damascus substantiates the existence of a later ruler of that name. It is a votive offering for the salvation of "the august lords" (probably Tiberius and "Julia", i.e. Livia his mother, the widow of Augustus) in connection with the erection of a sanctuary by a freedman of "Lysanias the tetrarch".

According to Mark's account "all the country of Judaea and all the people of Jerusalem" were attracted to visit the place at the Jordan where John preached and to undergo baptism in the river at his behest. Even from faraway Galilee some came, and among them was Jesus of Nazareth. When he was baptized and came up out of the river he saw the heavens opened and the Spirit descending upon him like a dove, and he heard a celestial voice declaring him to be God's beloved Son, with whom God was well pleased. Thus the birth of the Messianic consciousness of Jesus is described and made vivid.

The baptism is followed by the temptation. The Spirit leads Jesus into the wilderness and there it must be shown whether the "Satan"—or "adversary"—can damage his righteousness and prove God's expression of approval premature. Mark does not elaborate on the temptations, which were

Now in the fifteenth year of the reign of Tiberius Caesar, Pontius Pilate being governor of Judaea, and Herod being tetrarch of Galilee, and his brother Philip tetrarch of Ituraea and of the region of Trachonitis, and Lysanias the tetrarch of Abilene.
(LUKE 3 : 1)

Statue of Tiberius Caesar.

Then the devil taketh him up into the holy city, and setteth him on a pinnacle of the temple. (MATT. 4: 5)

continued for "forty days" (i.e. a considerable period). According to this source, Jesus lived in the habitat of the wild beasts, receiving food at the hands of the angels. The wilderness meant is the wilderness of Judah which extends along the entire descent from the high plateau of Judaea into the Jordan valley. The floods of winter have cut deep canyons into the limestone hills. The many caves formed in this rocky desolation by the action of water on the soft cliffs served as refuges for fugitives, exiles, and in Christian times for hermits. Jesus presumably was led into the area west of Jericho; a few miles farther to the south near the Dead Sea was the settlement of the Essene sectarians, whose scrolls have been recovered in nearby caves.

Matthew and Luke give a more elaborate story of the temptation than Mark. Particularly striking is the incident in which the devil takes Jesus to the "pinnacle" (literally "wing") of the Temple and dares him to cast himself down, in reliance on Ps. 91: 11-12. Tradition sought the spot in the southeastern corner of the Temple esplanade, where the great retaining walls built by king Herod to carry the flat surface for his Temple and the colonnaded porticoes surrounding it jutted into the Kidron valley. These walls were highest at the southeast corner where even today the wall is 50 feet high. In the time of Jesus it dropped a sheer 130 feet to the slope of the rock, a dizzy height indeed.

THE BEGINNINGS OF JESUS' MINISTRY

MARK GIVES NO indication of what Jesus did after the temptation. He connects his return to his homeland with the arrest of John (a more detailed report of which he defers until 6 : 17 ff.). Jesus then went to Galilee preaching "the gospel of God"—the announcement of the imminence of the kingdom—demanding repentance and faith.

Mark makes no mention of a visit to Nazareth at this time. Jesus went to the Sea of Galilee, and on its shores called his first disciples—two pairs of brothers, Simon and Andrew, James and John, all professional fishermen. The first pair, when he approached them, were casting nets into the lake. This is one of the methods of fishing still used to this day on the shores of the Sea of Galilee. The fisherman wades into the water and with a skillful swing throws out a circular fishing-net, 9 to 15 feet wide, so that it falls outspread on the surface. After a time it is drawn back by a rope attached to its center. Other methods employed in antiquity were the casting of a dragnet from a boat and drawing it to the shore (John 21 : 6 f.) or plunging a deep-sea net into the water. There were particularly good fishing-grounds near Capernaum, where warm springs issuing into the sea still draw fish to the shore. Of course nets were often fouled on rocks and had to be mended. James and John were sitting in their father's boat mending nets when Jesus called upon them to follow him.

Jesus went with the men to Capernaum, *Kefar Nahum* or "the village of Nahum"—a place named not after the Old Testament prophet, but rather an unknown Nahum. It has been identified with the site called *Tell Hum* by the Arabs. The first thing Jesus and his companions did was to attend a synagogue service, at which he preached (cf. below on the visit to Nazareth) and at which he healed a man possessed by an unclean spirit. Both his preaching and his healing made a tremendous impression and raised questions as to his message and the source of his power.

The remains of a Jewish synagogue at Capernaum survive and the building has been partly reconstructed by the Franciscan fathers who have acquired the site. This synagogue does not date from the time of Jesus, but rather from the end of the second century A.D. but it probably occupied the same site as its predecessor. It was built in the prevailing style of Graeco-Roman architecture and its façade faced Jerusalem. When the ornamentation of this and other Palestinian synagogues of the same period was first brought to light and studied, scholars were astounded, because it was believed that Judaism was uncompromisingly hostile to a decorative art featuring representations of animate things. However, by then the original opposition of the rabbis had been relaxed. The third-century synagogue excavated at Dura-Europus in Mesopotamia, with its rich decoration in wall-paintings, shows how far Jews were willing to go in adornment of their places of worship.

After the synagogue service Jesus went to the house of Simon, whose mother-in-law he healed of the fever. The news was spread abroad quickly and at sun-down crowds gathered and sick people were brought to his door. Of these Jesus healed many. On the following morning, however, he rose early and went out to a lonely place to pray. There Simon and his companions found him and informed him that everyone was searching for him. But Jesus desired to go into other towns to achieve his purpose of carrying the message of the

And, behold, they brought to him a man sick of the palsy, lying on a bed . . . And he arose, and departed to his house.   (MATT. 9: 2, 7)

Painting from Dura-Europus.
Third century A.D.

kingdom abroad. Mark knows no details, but states merely that he went throughout Galilee, preaching in synagogues and casting out demons, as in the single characteristic instance described. Only one further important healing is related—that of a leper. It forced Jesus to avoid towns and remain out in the country, for people now flocked to him from all sides.

"After some days" Jesus returned to Capernaum. He evidently considered this his headquarters, perhaps because the hospitable house of Simon provided him a place of rest. There he healed a paralytic. Paralysis, i.e. the loss or impairment of the motor or sensory function of the nerves, as we now know, may result from a variety of causes, some connected with organic changes, some with lesions, some with poisonous substances, and some with virus diseases. In the state of medical knowledge in antiquity no proper diagnosis was possible, and recovery from this terrible affliction was generally despaired of. The patient was kept lying on his bed until he died, or in a few rare instances, actually regained the use of his limbs. Hence the fact that in this particular case the paralytic was suddenly able to arise from his bed and pick it up and carry it to his house made a tremendous impression on the people of Capernaum and on future generations.

This miraculous act of healing consequently became a favorite subject of Early Christian art. It is depicted on the walls of the oldest known Christian church, found in a private house in the city of Dura-Europus on the banks of the Euphrates and dating to the first half of the third century A.D. In this painting we see the formerly paralyzed man, now healed, carrying on his back a typical ancient bed (*klinē*) consisting of a metal or wooden framework and a mattress formed by a criss-cross of ropes.

Jesus caused amazement by this act of healing, but at the same time laid the basis for a conflict with the Pharisees by assuring the sufferer of the forgiveness of sins and demonstrating his authority to forgive as well as his power to heal.

A fifth disciple was then acquired by Jesus in the person of Levi the son of Alpheus who was sitting at "the receipt of custom" (in Greek *telonion*). He thus was a publican (Greek *telones*). In Matthew's Gospel the man's name is changed to Matthew, while Luke preserves the Marcan "Levi". The word "publican" denotes a person concerned with two different kinds of fiscal activity: the levying of customs or tolls paid on merchandise passing from one country to another, and the collection of taxes due to the State. Levi was presumably engaged in collecting customs dues rather than taxes, as Capernaum was not an important administrative center but was close to the frontier (which followed the line of the Jordan) between the territories of Herod Antipas and his brother Philip.

The "publicans" were tax-farmers bent on extorting from the people not only the sums that they themselves had paid to the State treasury, but as much as possible over and above it, the excess constituting their profits. They were, therefore, universally hated and usually classified with other despised "sinners". But it was just these "lost sheep of the house of Israel" who were the object of Jesus' mission. Hence—despite the scorn and disgust of the puritan Pharisees—he even shared their meals. Jesus defended his conduct with a proverb: "Those who are well have no need of a physician, but those who are sick."

Jesus also departed from the ways of the Pharisees by not doing extra fasting (beyond that required by Old Testament Law), therein differing even from the disciples of John the Baptist. But above all he rejected Pharisaic rules about the Sabbath. He allowed his disciples to pluck ears of grain as they went through a field on the day of rest, and he defended this by citing David's taking the shewbread when hungry; and at a synagogue service at which a man was present who had a withered hand, he challenged the Pharisees to say whether it was lawful on the Sabbath to do good or to do harm? When they remained silent he boldly healed the man. This marked the beginning of a conspiracy to destroy Jesus. Allegedly Pharisees and Herodians cooperated toward that end.

Jesus now withdrew to the shore of the sea, and multitudes of people came to him. He told his disciples to have a boat ready for him that he might escape the pressure of the crowd,

And seeing the multitudes, he went up into a mountain . . . And he opened his mouth and taught them, saying, Blessed are the poor in spirit: for theirs is the kingdom of heaven. Blessed are they that mourn: for they shall be comforted.

(MATT. 5: 1–4)

View of the Mountain of the Beatitudes, above Capernaum.

255

but apparently he made no use of it. We hear only of his healings in this connection (Mark 3 : 7–12)—later in the identical situation (4 : 1 f.) we hear only of his teaching.

Jesus then interrupted his healing activity to go up into the hills above the Sea of Galilee. He called to him those he desired and appointed twelve disciples as companions and co-workers. A name list of these is given by Mark (3 : 16 f.). A James son of Alpheus is mentioned, but not the Levi son of Alpheus of 2 : 14, and a Matthew is included. Andrew is separated from his brother. The list gives Simon's surname as Peter, using the name by which Simon was known to Mark's readers; the Aramaic-speaking Palestinian Christians had called him *Cephas* ("rock"). Peter (Greek *Petros*) is a short form of a name which is related to the Greek word for rock (*petra*). The two brothers, James and John, also receive a characterizing name: Boanerges, "sons of thunder". Both Matthew (10: 2 f.) and Luke (6: 14 f., cf. Acts 1: 13 f.) make minor readjustments in Mark's list.

Matthew was stimulated by the staging Mark gives the appointment of the disciples to introduce into it the Sermon on the Mount; he defers reference to the twelve until 10: 2 f. The Sermon on the Mount is not a sermon in the real sense, since it is composed of pithy sayings, many of which appear in Luke in very different contexts. As it stands it is a remarkable piece of editing and presents the message of Jesus in a powerful and systematized manner, beginning with the beautiful beatitudes, pronounced over various kinds of people who shall inherit the kingdom of heaven. It must, however, be remembered that Jesus may have uttered the same or similar words on different occasions, thus creating difficulties for tradition.

In Mark's basic version Jesus goes home (i.e. to Capernaum) after appointing the twelve, and is so busy with the assembled crowd that he and the disciples are not even able to eat. He is forced to reject a twofold attack on his activity: one from the Scribes, who had been sent from Jerusalem, whither a report of his activities must have been carried, and the other from his own immediate family. The latter regarded him as "beside himself" (3 : 21), while the Scribes declared that he was possessed of Beelzebub, "the prince of demons", and hence could drive out demons (3 : 22). Jesus refutes the second assertion with his famous "a house divided against itself cannot stand", and speaks sharp words about blaspheming the Holy Spirit. When his mother and brethren seek to interrupt him in the midst of his teaching, he rejects their special claim upon him; by his answer to the Scribes he has refuted their assault as well. With a glorious flash of insight he transcends the ties of blood and exalts those of the fellowship of moral striving. The ultimate consequence of this had to be the transcending of nationality also.

Mark now reverts in chapter 4 to the seaside scene of 3 : 9. Jesus, here in the boat off-shore, teaches the crowd. He teaches in "parables"—which sometimes are stories, sometimes only figurative sayings. The former require interpretation, but Jesus leaves his hearers to guess the meaning; to his disciples he explains them in private. In this connection Mark has Jesus declare that to the disciples alone has been given the secret of the kingdom of God, but that for those outside everything is in parables lest they understand and be forgiven—a stern thought derived from Isa. 6: 9–10.

The leading parable given in this connection is that of the sower, who distributes his seed evenly but with varying result, depending on the nature of the ground. The good soil bears thirtyfold, sixtyfold, and a hundredfold. A thirtyfold yield is attested to in antiquity for the mountain lands of Judaea, while crops of sixty to one hundred times the original sowing were obtained in countries with great alluvial plains such as Babylonia and Egypt, and also occasionally in the most fertile parts of the land of Israel.

Matt. 13 not only repeats the parables of Mark 4 but adds a few new ones. An especially appealing one is that comparing the kingdom of heaven to a treasure hidden in a field. The unstable political conditions in the Orient during the Hellenistic and the Early Roman periods, with their frequent wars and revolutions, led many people to safeguard their fortunes by converting them into coins and burying these in some place where they could remain unsuspected till reclaimed. If, as often happened, the original owner of the coins perished suddenly, all knowledge of his treasure was lost, except for the few cases of accidental discovery at a much later time. Such a hoard, found in 1960 on Mount Carmel, consists of nearly five thousand pieces, mostly Tyrian shekels, half-shekels, and Roman coins of the first centuries B.C. and A.D. This great "treasure hidden in a field" was a lucky windfall for the man who chanced on it.

On the evening of this day of parable-preaching Jesus suggests a crossing to the eastern shore of the Sea of Galilee (Mark 4 : 35).

And when they had sent away the multitude, they took him even as he was in the ship: and there were also with him other little ships.
(MARK 4 : 36)   Boats on Pompeian painting.

And when he was come to the other side, into the country of the ˙ Gergesenes, there met him two possessed with devils, coming out of the tombs, exceeding fierce, so that no man might pass by that way.

(MATT. 8: 28)

Rock-cut tomb near Jerusalem.

Sailing and fishing, even in the waters of an interior lake like the Sea of Galilee, involved the use of various kinds of vessels, some large and able to withstand the storms, others small and suitable for plying to and from the big ships. In general, the ancients developed many different types of shipping, adapted to the various purposes of navigation. On a mosaic found at Altiburus in Africa no less than twelve different kinds of ships and boats are represented, each designated by its distinctive name. They include heavy cargo boats, light passenger transport vessels, and fishing and river craft. On a painting from Pompeii, reproduced on the preceding page, we see several such ships sailing the sea.

The boat used in the lake crossing must have been large enough to carry Jesus and his disciples. But it was not large enough to be safe in the sudden wind-storms that may sweep down upon the Sea of Galilee from the west. Such a one struck and frightened the disciples, who awakened the sleeping Master. He rebuked them for their lack of faith and consequent fear, and commanded wind and waves to be calm. The elements obeyed. The disciples were filled with awe at this display of power, and wondered who this Jesus might be? Had they understood what the demons Jesus drove out were saying they would not have had to wonder.

They came now to the country of the Gerasenes (var. Gadarenes, Gergesenes), and there Jesus is met by a man with an unclean spirit, who lived among the tombs. Rock-cut tombs were a characteristic feature of funerary architecture in the Hellenistic and Roman periods, and—in view of the generally mild climate of the country—could easily provide shelter for any kind of outcast, including the mentally deranged. Tombs of this kind, roughly

258

contemporary with the events recorded in the Gospel, consist of a vestibule and a hall, with chambers branching off from the latter. Not often visited, they made excellent hiding-places. The spirit speaking out of the man addressed Jesus as "the son of the Most High God". The demon whose name was "Legion" was driven out into a herd of swine, which rushed down over a precipice and was drowned in the sea.

The "Gerasenes" or people of the city of Gerasa can hardly have had any land on the Sea of Galilee—the place was too distant. "Gadarenes", people of Gadara—found in some manuscripts and particularly well attested in Matthew (8: 28), seems the more probable reading. This city was situated on a mountain peak south of the River Yurmuk and its territory may well have extended to the lake. As citizens of a center of Hellenistic culture the inhabitants flouted the religious scruples of the Jews by keeping herds of swine. Pig-breeding was a profitable business in antiquity; the pork was not only consumed locally but could be salted and sold to the Roman army. Each herd of swine was naturally looked after by a swineherd. In view of the detestation of this animal expressed in the Mosaic Law swine-raising must have been particularly offensive to the Jews living in the same districts. This Jewish abhorrence is evident in the Gospel story. Those for whom the story was first told no doubt relished the idea that the large herd of swine perished and that the demons were cheated out of their dwelling and forced to rove again (Luke 11: 24). A steep declivity exists on the southeastern shore of the Sea of Galilee where the fate of the swine would have been just as described.

When the swineherds reported the loss of the herd, the people of the city requested Jesus to leave the territory. The healed man begged to go along, but Jesus bade him go home and tell people what the LORD had done for him.

And he said unto them, Go. And when they were come out, they went into the herd of swine: and behold, the whole herd of swine ran violently down a steep place into the sea, and perished in the waters. (MATT. 8: 32)

(*Above*) Bronze pig found at Pompeii.

(*Right*) Southeastern shore of the Sea of Galilee.

On arriving again at the western shore Jesus was met by a crowd. While engaged with them, Jairus, "one of the rulers of the synagogue", came and fell at his feet, imploring him to come and lay hands on his daughter who was at the point of death.

At the head of every Hebrew community there were officials with various titles, the *archisynagogos* usually being the chief amongst them. There could be several officials with this title in one place; on the analogy of the occurrences of the similar term *archiereus*, or high priest, in the plural, we may assume that such "rulers of the synagogue" served for a period and kept their title even after completing their term of office. In the Diaspora, each of the synagogues of a big city usually had its own "ruler", but sometimes there was one *archisynagogos* for a whole province. The body of one such personage was brought to be buried at Beth Shea 'rim, the central Jewish necropolis of the third and fourth centuries A.D. A tablet found there commemorates a certain "Jacob from Caesarea, *archisynagogos* of Pamphylia Peace". As we learn from the Acts of the Apostles (2:10), Pamphylia, a province of Asia Minor, contained many Jewish communities. These were united apparently in one provincial organization presided over by an *archisynagogos*.

On his way to the house of Jairus, Jesus felt someone touch the hem of his garment. This was a woman afflicted with an issue of blood. Moved by her faith, Jesus healed her. When he reached the house of the *archisynagogos*, the child had already been given up for dead and preparations for her funeral were well advanced, with minstrels playing and people wailing. It was a custom of great antiquity in the Orient, especially in Egypt, for a large crowd (including professional wailing women) to accompany the funeral procession, weeping and lamenting. Musical instruments were also used to add to the mournfulness of the occasion. The employment of pipers, who played dirges on flutes over the dead, is mentioned at least twice in the *Mishnah*, the codification of Jewish law and practice from the days of the Second Temple onwards.

But when Jesus entered the house of mourning, he said: "Give place, for the maid is not dead but sleeps." And when he went in and took her by the hand, the maid rose from her bed.

THE VISIT TO NAZARETH

JESUS NOW WENT away from Capernaum to his own "country", followed by his disciples. On the Sabbath he spoke in the synagogue. The people were astonished at his ability to teach and his reported wonder-working. "Is not this the carpenter, the son of Mary, the brother of James and Joses and Judas and Simon?" And they took offense at him. He thereupon spoke the proverb, "A prophet is not without honor except in his own country, and among his own kin, and in his own house."

Luke has put this visit to Nazareth at the very beginning of Jesus' ministry (Luke 4:16f.). That this is not more accurate historically, but is merely a different literary arrangement, is shown by the fact that Jesus speaks of being asked to do there what they have heard he did at Capernaum (Luke 4:23). Luke greatly enriches the story, however, by giving some idea of the nature of a synagogue service, and of what Jesus did on these occasions. However, he neglects to mention the important fact that the Law also was read, dwelling instead on the reading of the "concluding lesson" or Haphtarah, chosen from "the prophets", or second division of the Hebrew Bible.

And there was delivered unto him the book of the prophet Esaias. And when he had opened the book, he found the place where it was written, "The Spirit of the LORD is upon me, because he hath anointed me to preach the gospel to the poor; he hath sent me to heal the brokenhearted, to preach deliverance to the captives, and recovering of sight to the blind, to set at liberty them that are bruised." (LUKE 4 : 17–18)

Jesus stood up and was handed the scroll of Isaiah by the attendant. He opened the scroll and "found" the passage Isa. 61: 1–2, read it, closed the book, and gave it back to the attendant and then sat down to speak. The Haphtarah lesson was evidently not yet prescribed —Jesus was free to choose. In the recently discovered library of the Qumran sect (the Dead Sea Scrolls) manuscripts of Isaiah are more numerous than those of any other book, and the finds include the earliest known complete scroll of the book. The one handed Jesus must have looked very similar to this one.

In Luke's version a more dramatic ending is given the Nazareth episode. The people were so enraged by the discourse of Jesus that they put him out of the city and led him to the brow of the hill on which their city was built, intending to cast him down. Tradition has of course sought to identify the spot: an elevation south of Nazareth 1,200 feet above sea-level and 750 feet above the plain of Esdraelon. The drop to the plain is a steep cliff from which a person could well be cast to his death. The Arabic name *Jebel Qafza*, "the mount of the Leap", commemorates the Gospel tradition. According to Luke, Jesus went away "passing through the midst of them".

In Mark's story Jesus, on leaving Nazareth, went about among the villages teaching. He then sent forth the twelve in pairs to preach repentance in the face of the imminent coming of the kingdom and to perform healings with the power he conferred on them.

Into the interim between the disciples' departure and return Mark has placed the story of how Herod, hearing of the activities of Jesus, superstitiously thought that John the Baptist whom he had beheaded had come to life. This gives Mark the opportunity to include the account of the death of the Baptist—a bit of story-telling of a more worldly kind. Herod Antipas, king Herod's son, had put John in prison but was afraid to take any further action against him. Some extraordinary stimulant was required to rouse him against the prophet, and this was supplied by his stepdaughter, the princess Salome, who agreed to dance before him and his guests.

And they say unto him, We have here but five loaves and two fishes.

(MATT. 14 : 17)

Bread-seller on Pompeian painting. First century A.D.

*And when they were
gone over, they came into
the land of Gennesaret.*
(MATT. 14: 34)

View of the plain
of Gennesaret.

The two principal nations of antiquity, the Greeks and the Romans, differed fundamentally in their attitude to the dance. While the Greeks regarded it as one of the bodily
exercises in which a free man might engage without shame, the Romans, with their customary gravity, judged it unworthy of a person of any social standing and left dancing to
professionals of low class and lower reputation. This derogatory opinion of dancers and
dancing explains the extraordinary effect produced by a dance executed by no less a person
than a princess of the royal house in honor of her stepfather's birthday. Instructed by her
mother, Herodias, who had been deeply offended by John, Salome asked for the Baptist's
head, and Herod, much against his will, had to grant her request.

When the apostles returned, Jesus invited them to come away to a lonely place and rest
a while. The scene suddenly becomes the vicinity of the lake. They crossed in a boat to the
eastern side. However, the purpose of Jesus to get away from the crowd is defeated, because
the people followed by going around the shore. The stage is thus set for the feeding of the
five thousand with five loaves and two fishes. The loaves of antiquity, which were baked at
low temperature, resembled flat cakes rather than the loaves made today.

After this miraculous repast Jesus made his disciples board the boat and precede him to the
other side of the lake, while he dismissed the crowd. He then went into the hills to pray.
From the height he could see that the disciples had hard rowing against the wind. About the
fourth watch of the night he came to them walking on the sea. Thinking him a ghost, the
disciples cried out. Jesus bade them take heart and entered the boat, whereupon the wind
ceased. They landed at Gennesaret, where Jesus was immediately recognized and importuned
to cure sick people.

A renewed clash now took place between Jesus and the Pharisees, led by their Scribes from Jerusalem. These criticized the disciples for not washing their hands before eating, and thus disregarding the tradition of the elders. Jesus accused them of abandoning the commandments of God and of holding fast instead to the traditions of men. How clever a way you have designed to circumvent the obligation of supporting needy parents, Jesus argued, adding that only what comes out of the heart of man can defile him. These were mighty blows struck at Pharisaic Judaism in the spirit of the Old Testament prophets.

Though Mark neglects to state so this clash increased the peril of Jesus. Not only was Herod now dangerously interested in his person, but the Pharisees were irritated to a still greater degree. That Jesus arose and went away to the region of Tyre and Sidon is understandable if we recognize his motive to be similar to that which led Elijah to go to Zarephath: to get away from his adversaries.

"The region of Tyre and Sidon" is a rough designation of the land of the Phoenicians, part of present-day Lebanon, here referred to by the name of its principal cities, both of which controlled territory stretching far inland. The domains of Tyre reached as far as Cydasa (ancient Kedesh) overlooking the Huleh region with its lake and marshes; while

Sidon had a common border with Damascus. In the time of Jesus, Tyre had long recovered from the blows inflicted upon it by Alexander the Great and had again become one of the great marts of the Mediterranean seaboard, especially famous for its purple. Sidon, its rival for the leadership of Phoenicia, was the center of ancient glass manufacture, and exported its products to every part of the Roman Empire. In both cities the Phoenician population had become thoroughly Hellenized. Both had considerable communities.

While sojourning in Phoenicia, Jesus was appealed to for help by a Gentile woman who is described in the Gospels as a Greek, but a Syro-Phoenician by race. Obviously the author intended to indicate that, although not of Greek origin, she was thoroughly Hellenized. It

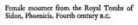

The woman was a Greek, a Syrophenician by nation . . .
(MARK 7 : 26)

Female mourner from the Royal Tombs of Sidon, Phoenicia. Fourth century B.C.

was a cardinal principle that adoption of Greek culture (including, of course, Greek religion) made a person a Hellene, whatever his racial origin, and it was owing to this liberal attitude that Hellenism managed to spread in the Orient so successfully. Of course, Hellenization was only possible in polytheistic nations whose gods could be amalgamated with the Greek deities; it was only partially successful with the monotheistic Jews.

The description of the woman here as a "Syro-Phoenician" is to be explained as follows. From the time of Herodotus, the Greeks, following Persian usage, had extended the term "Syria" (originally "Assyria", Persian *Athura*) from Assyria proper to the whole of the eastern Mediterranean coastland. In order to distinguish between the various nations inhabiting this area they added a qualifying epithet to the general name "Syrian". Thus Herodotus calls the Philistines "Palestinian Syrians". In a similar way this woman is called a Phoenician Syrian; and, indeed, the Phoenicians were among the most Hellenized of the Oriental nations. One of the female mourners portrayed on the Sarcophagus of the Weeping Women, found in the Royal Tombs of Sidon in Phoenicia and dating to the fourth century B.C., is a woman of characteristically Phoenician racial type, though the style and workmanship of the sarcophagus are Greek.

Jesus at first refused the woman's request for help for her sick child, since he felt that his mission was only to his own people, but he relented when she humbly compared her need to that of a dog fed by crumbs fallen from its master's table. Orientals generally held this animal in great contempt, whereas the Greeks, and in particular Greek youths, had a great affection for their hunting-dogs; often we find them represented on the stelae set over their tombs. No wonder, therefore, that the dogs shared their masters' repast, tied under the couches on which the ancients were accustomed to recline while eating. Such a scene is portrayed on a Corinthian *krater* or mixing-bowl (seventh century B.C.,) representing the marriage of Heracles with Iole, the daughter of king Eurytios. Heracles is reclining on the right and Iphitos, a member of the royal family, on the left with Iole standing between them. Two dogs are tied up under the tables bearing the repast, of which they are undoubtedly getting their share.

Mark is vague in his description of the return journey, but brings Jesus via Sidonian territory to the Decapolis, a federation of ten Hellenistic cities east of the Sea of Galilee. There he heals a deaf and dumb man. This incident is followed by a gathering of crowds and another feeding of a multitude—this time four thousand—with seven loaves and a few fishes, perhaps a different version of the earlier story told in Mark 6: 34ff. After dismissing the people Jesus enters a boat with his disciples and crosses to the district of "Dalmanutha".

On landing, Jesus again became embroiled with Pharisees, who argued with him and asked him for a sign from heaven to test him. He rejected this, re-entered the boat, and crossed again to the other side. On the way he warned his disciples to beware of the leaven of the Pharisees and of Herod, and chided them for their lack of perception of the meaning of the miracles of the feedings.

The party landed at Bethsaida in the tetrarchy of Philip. The quick departure from Herod's territory may thus have been caused by a fear of being seized. At Bethsaida, Jesus healed a blind man and then traveled north toward Philip's summer capital, Caesarea. This town had previously been called Paneas, for the most prominent feature of the region was the cave dedicated to the Greek god Pan, the Paneion, situated in a high cliff near the city. The cliff is carved with niches which once contained statues and is inscribed with dedications to

When Jesus came into the coasts of Caesarea Philippi . . .
(MATT. 16: 13)

View of the cave of Pan at
Caesarea Philippi.

And behold,
there appeared
unto them Moses
and Elias talking
with him.
(MATT. 17: 3)

(Left) Elias, (Right)
Moses, on frescoes
from Dura-Europus,
Third century A.D.

Pan and the nymphs, Philip had rebuilt Paneas and renamed it Caesarea in honor of Caesar Augustus, to whom the great city temple was dedicated. It was generally known as Philip's Caesarea (Caesarea Philippi) to distinguish it from Caesarea-by-the-Sea which Philip's father, Herod the Great, had founded.

It was in the area of Caesarea Philippi, perhaps in sight of the great cliff, that Jesus asked the disciples who they thought he was. Peter declared, "Thou art the Messiah." In Matthew's longer version of this event Peter is given the role of being the rock on which Jesus will build his Church.

The Messianic Confession is directly followed by the first Passion announcement. The disciples are not to think that an immediate regal role is in prospect for Jesus. Peter remonstrates with him for entertaining such a conception of the Messianic office, but is rebuffed by the brusque "Get thee behind me Satan." At this moment the tempter seemed approaching with the thought rejected in Matt. 4: 8 f.: to seize power by unethical and hence ungodly means. Jesus now instructs the multitude with his disciples concerning the need of following him in the way of the Cross, yet predicts that some standing here will not taste death before the kingdom of God comes.

Six days later Jesus took Peter, James, and John with him up a high mountain, which tradition since the third century A.D. would identify with Mount Tabor, the most prominent eminence of Lower Galilee. Here he was "transfigured" before them, and Moses and Elias

Go thou to the sea, and cast an hook, and take
up the fish that first cometh up; and when thou
hast opened his mouth, thou shalt find a piece of
money; that take, and give unto them for me and
thee.   (MATT. 17: 27)

(Left) Fisherman on Early Christian sarcophagus.
Fourth century A.D.

(Right) Tyrian stater. First century A.D.

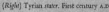

came and spoke with him. He was thus associated with the two great prophetic figures of
Old Testament history, whose removal from the earth was mysterious: Moses, the prophet
without compare (Deut. 34: 10) and Elijah, who saved the true religion from the cult of
Baal. Both these personalities figure prominently in Jewish and Early Christian art. The
disciples were given the revelation by a heavenly voice, declaring that Jesus was God's
beloved son: listen to him. On the descent from the mountain they asked Jesus about the
Elijah prophecy of Mal. 4: 5, and were told that it had been fulfilled (in John the Baptist).

On rejoining the disciples he finds them unable to handle a difficult case of demon-
possession—that of a boy whose father has brought him to Jesus. The latter successfully
exorcizes the demon and later tells the disciples that they have failed because of insufficient
prayer and fasting.

Jesus' further Galilean wanderings were carried on secretly, evidently because of the peril
of being seized by Herod. During these travels the second Passion announcement was given
to the disciples (Mark 9: 30-2). The secrecy motif, however, is not maintained, for Jesus
next returns to Capernaum where his presence would become known immediately.

At this point Matthew in his Gospel introduces the story of the Temple tax (Matt. 17:
24-7). Peter is asked whether their teacher pays this tax. Jesus considers himself and his
disciples exempt from it, but tells Peter that he should go to the lake and cast out a line. He
predicts that he will catch a fish with a *stater* in his mouth. With this coin he shall pay the
tax for Jesus and himself, in order to avoid giving offense.

The obligation which was to be discharged with the money found in the fish was·the
payment of the half-shekel, the annual tax levied from every Israelite for the maintenance
of the Sanctuary (Exod. 30: 13). For two persons this would amount to one shekel, or

a Tyrian *stater* (the word used in the Greek original and translated "piece of money") or *tetradrachma*. There were two kinds of *staters* in antiquity: the one in common commercial use was the light Attic *stater*; this, however, was not regarded by the Temple authorities as the equivalent of the Hebrew shekel. The "holy shekel" was of heavier weight and corresponded to the Phoenician standard. As is proved by the excavated coin hoards, issues of Tyrian money circulated freely in Galilee in Jesus' day and later up to the time of the destruction of the Temple.

In Mark's narrative Jesus now gives instruction to the disciples in their dispute over greatness, forbids intolerance toward a rival exorcist, warns against causing one of these "little ones" who believes in him to sin, and teaches how sin is to be fought radically in oneself. Matthew adds valuable lessons on forgiveness and the powerful parable of the unmerciful servant.

Here the third evangelist, Luke, introduces a whole central section of materials (9:51–18:14) which are not found in Mark, though they have numerous parallels in Matthew. Jesus decides to go to Jerusalem with his disciples, apparently via Samaria. The refusal of a Samaritan village to receive him leads to a question of James and John about calling down fire from heaven (cf. 2 Kings 1:10 and 12), and to their rebuke by Jesus. An important new element is the appointment and sending forth of a group of seventy disciples, who receive instructions as did the twelve when they were sent out (10:1ff.). Another is the brief story

Provide neither gold, nor silver, nor brass in your purses. Nor scrip for your journey, neither two coats, neither shoes, nor yet staves . . .

(MATT. 10:9–10)

Sage on painting from Villa Boscoreale. First century A.D.

269

of Mary and Martha (10: 38–42), who here can hardly be imagined as living at Bethany near Jerusalem. New miracles are added in the healing of the crooked woman on a Sabbath and of the ten lepers (17: 11–19). The latter story, however, is localized "as he was passing along between Samaria and Galilee". There thus has been no real geographical progression since the visiting of the Samaritan village in 9: 52.

If Luke was already concerned with the Samaritans, the Gospel of John on one occasion takes Jesus into the heart of their country. This Gospel makes much of a ministry of Jesus in Jerusalem and Judaea. After baptizing in the Jordan valley for a time, simultaneously with John, Jesus goes back to Galilee via "Sychar" (Shechem), rests there at the well of Jacob, and converses with a Samaritan woman (John 4: 7ff.). She speaks of the fact that their fathers had worshiped on "this mountain" and that the Jews say that Jerusalem is the place where men ought to worship. The mountain she refers to is Mount Gerizim.

This Mountain of Blessings (Deut. 27: 12) was chosen by the Samaritans as the site of their sanctuary after Jerusalem rejected them. In Hellenistic times King Antiochus IV Epiphanes turned the Samaritan sanctuary into the temple of *Zeus Horkios* ("The Zeus who is Guardian of Oaths"), but the Samaritans continued to worship on another peak of the mountain where they had an altar of their own. The sanctity of Gerizim in the eyes of the Samaritans made the mountain obnoxious to the rabbis, who arbitrarily transferred the Biblical mountains of Gerizim and Ebal to the vicinity of Jericho. In this they were followed by some Christian interpreters and the Madaba Map (a mosaic map of the Holy Land made in the sixth century A.D.). Samaritan worship at Mount Gerizim continued till the time of

Our fathers worshiped in this mountain . . . (JOHN 4:20)

View of the city of Nablus, with Mount Gerizim on the right.

And not many days
after, the younger son
gathered all together and
took his journey into a
far country, and there
wasted his substance
with riotous living.

(LUKE 15 : 13)

Wall-painting from
Herculaneum.

the emperor Zeno, A.D. 479; and to this day the surviving Samaritans still perform their
Passover sacrifice on the mountain with the full Biblical ritual.

Reverting to Luke's central section we find it presenting some of the most impressive of
the parables of Jesus. One of the best known is that of the prodigal younger son who, having
obtained from his father his portion of the inheritance, went off to a distant country where
he wasted his substance in riotous living. This conduct was fully in accordance with the spirit
of the times. Hellenistic and Roman literature, and especially the writers of comedies and
satires, have left us detailed accounts of the ways in which young men, amply provided with
money but devoid of any serious purpose in life, squandered their wealth. These usually took
the form of gambling, drinking, and keeping company with women of loose morals, such
as abounded in the great cities of the Graeco-Roman world. As Greek maidens and married
women of good family were kept in strict seclusion at home, cut off from contact with
anyone not of their own family, they were naturally limited in their outlook. If, therefore,
a man wanted to enjoy the society of women of wit and education, he had to seek the
company of *hetaerae*. A wall-painting found at Herculaneum shows a youth banqueting with
such a woman. Various dishes and jugs are set on the table in front of them, while a servant
brings them a box (presumably containing jewels) to which the lady is pointing in an expressive manner; the youth, however, seems to be preoccupied with catching the wine flowing
from the lower end of a *rhyton* held by him at some distance from his lips.

271

And he would fain have filled his belly with the husks that the swine did eat: and no man gave unto him.

(LUKE 15: 16)

Pods of the carob tree.

When the young prodigal had spent his all, the country in which he was living suffered a terrible famine. To such dire straits was he reduced that he accepted the work of feeding husks to swine, and would readily have eaten the husks, had anyone given them to him. The word translated "husks" is the Greek *keratia*, "little horns", a reference to the shape of the pod of the carob (*Ceratonia siliqua*, L.), a tree which grows in very dry soil and reaches a height of 24–30 feet. The pods, up to a foot long, are green at first, but turn brown when ripe; they can also be dried in the sun. Being very rich in sweet syrup they were used in antiquity, and to a certain extent are still used even now, as food for fattening cattle; but they are also quite fit for human consumption. The original habitat of the carob tree, according to botanists, seems to have been in Asia Minor; from there it spread to Cyprus and the Lebanon, and also to Judaea, penetrating deep into the drier parts of the country, including even the Central Negev. By Roman times it was found all over the eastern Mediterranean and had probably reached Italy as well.

Having sunk so low, the young man resolved to return to his father and confess the dire consequences of his riotous living. He was received back into the fold with great affection and given a fine robe, rings, and shoes; a fattened calf was slaughtered, and a splendid feast held in his honor. The elder son, who had stayed at home and never transgressed his father's will, was naturally angered by the wholly unexpected favor shown to the prodigal; but his

Blind Bartimaeus, the son of Timaeus, sat by the highway side begging. (MARK 10 : 46)

Humpbacked beggar, from Alexandria. First century B.C.

father explained that his younger brother had, as it were, suddenly come back from the dead and deserved to be fêted accordingly.

The moral of the story is clear: it is the repentant sinners, returning to God their Father, who specially merit His solicitude.

Jesus then leaves Capernaum and according to Mark, who is followed by Matthew, goes to the region of Judaea beyond the Jordan (Mark 10: 1 ff.). In this setting Mark places a number of incidents in which Jesus gives instruction in such matters as divorce, children and the kingdom, the hindrances of wealth, and the reward in store for those who have left all to follow him. He is imagined as traveling, and in 10: 32 it is disclosed that he is on his way to Jerusalem. Here the third and climactic Passion announcement is given. At this point comes the request of John and James for the places of honor in the coming kingdom and his prediction that they will drink his cup (i.e. of martyrdom). The anger their request provokes among the others is quelled by further instruction on true greatness.

While Luke has given the impression that Jesus went to Jerusalem via Samaria (9: 51 f.) he nevertheless brings him to Jericho, thus regaining agreement with Mark, but introduces as new elements the charming little story of Zacchaeus (Luke 19: 1–10) and the significant parable of the pounds (19: 11–27).

THE ENTRY INTO JERUSALEM

O N LEAVING JERICHO, Jesus healed the blind Bartimaeus, who sat by the wayside begging.

It is indicative of the strong sense of social responsibility in Israel in Biblical times that special provisions were made for the relief of paupers and that their rights were carefully protected. Hence, although the poor are often mentioned in the Old Testament, there is no reference to beggars in the streets. The needy or disabled were taken care of by their family or tribe. It was only in the social disintegration of the Hellenistic period that begging in public places began to be common, and even then it was not regarded as anything but shameful ("To beg I am ashamed," Luke 16 : 3). Almsgiving is first mentioned in Jewish sources in the apocryphal book of Ecclesiasticus or Sirach (4 : 1). Representations of beggars are not common in Greek art; it is only with the advent of the realism and social consciousness of Hellenistic times that we find such statues as the humpbacked beggar of Alexandria (c. 100 B.C.).

After healing Bartimaeus, Jesus went up through the Judaean wilderness and finally drew near the village of Bethany. Preparations were made for a solemn entry into Jerusalem, and two disciples were sent to bring an ass from the village for their Master. Of the two riding animals of antiquity, the horse and the ass, the latter has the longer history, going back long before the patriarchal period. The horse, which was introduced into the Orient by the Hyksos, was at first used for drawing chariots rather than for riding. For the purpose of a triumphal entry into the crowded, narrow streets of an Oriental city, as here envisaged, an ass was far preferable; it was slower, did not endanger the passers-by, and allowed the rider to dismount easily whenever necessary. The ass bred in Palestine, *Equus asinus*, is a sturdy breed and far more intelligent than is popularly believed.

On the way down the Mount of Olives a demonstration was made by the throng accompanying Jesus. Many spread their garments on the way, and others leafy branches which they had cut from the fields, crying "Hosanna" and invoking blessing on the one coming

Then sent Jesus two disciples, saying unto them, Go into the village over against you, and straightway ye shall find an ass tied, and a colt with her: loose them, and bring them unto me.

(MATT. 21 : 1–2)

Ass bred in Palestine (*Equus asinus*).

*And Jesus went into the temple of God, and cast out all them
that sold and bought in the temple, and overthrew the tables of
the money-changers . . .*   (MATT. 21 : 12)

Roman banker on funeral
monument from Neumagen,
Rhineland. Third century A.D.

in the name of the LORD and on the kingdom of David that they hoped would be
renewed.

On entering the city Jesus went directly to the Temple and inspected everything. This
suggests that he had not seen it since his call to his ministry. As it was late in the day he went
out to Bethany. On returning to the city in the morning he sought early fruit from a fig tree,
but on finding it barren pronounced a curse over it. Going to the Temple, he drove out the
various merchants in its courts and overturned the tables of the money-changers, declaring
that God's house was to be a house of prayer for all the nations (Isa. 56: 7), and accusing
them of making it a den of robbers (Jer. 7: 11).

Like most of the business of antiquity, money-changing and banking were conducted in
the open. (The Greek word for "table", *trapeza*, also has the meaning of "bank".) One of
the most important of the many commercial transactions necessitated by the manifold
requirements of the Temple worship was the changing of the money brought by the masses
of pilgrims, who made their way to Jerusalem every year from all over the Jewish Diaspora.
As we have seen, the Temple authorities accepted only the Tyrian coins as equivalent to the
"holy shekel" in which the Temple dues had to be paid. Hence, the various currencies of the
time—Roman *dinars*, Attic *drachmas*, coins from Asia Minor, Egypt, and beyond—had to
be changed into "holy shekels" at the tables of the money-changers. These latter sat in the
Outer Court of the Temple, which was considered less holy than the Temple itself. Next to
them the sellers of doves had their stands, while the purchase of sheep for sacrifices went on
north of the Temple area, near the Sheep Pool. On a funeral monument, found at Neumagen
in the Rhineland (third century A.D.), we see an ancient money-changer, in this case a
Roman banker, sitting at his table with a heap of coins spread before him.

The cleansing of the Temple aroused the hostility of the chief priests, who now sought a way to destroy Jesus. In the evening he again went out of the city with his disciples. Returning the following morning they saw that the fig tree which Jesus had cursed had withered. Jesus made this the occasion of some instruction on faith and prayer, as well as forgiveness.

When they were in the Temple again, Jesus was confronted by the priests, scribes, and elders with the question of his authority (apparently referring to his cleansing of the Temple). Jesus made an answer hinge on their replying to a counter question about John's baptism,

Shew me the tribute money. And they brought unto him a penny. And he saith unto them, whose is this image and superscription? They say unto him Caesar's . . . (MATT. 22: 19–21)

Denarius of Tiberius Caesar.

whether or not it was from God. As they were unwilling to commit themselves he too refused to answer. Instead he told them the parable of the vineyard. Perceiving that it was directed against them they tried to arrest him but desisted, fearing the multitude. However, on departing they sent some Pharisees and Herodians to entrap him in his talk. They asked him whether it was lawful to pay tribute to the emperor. They knew that if he said "No" he could be denounced to the Romans as a rebel; or if he said "Yes" the people, who hated the Roman yoke, would turn against him.

In order to avoid the trap set for him, Jesus asked for a piece of "tribute money" (in the Greek original: "census money"). This, the fixed poll-tax paid by every native of a Roman province (such as Judaea had become after the deposition of Archaelaus in A.D. 6), amounted to a Roman silver *denarius*, the equivalent of a day's wage (Matt. 20: 2). Like all silver and gold currency, these *denarii* were struck by the imperial mint only, the cities and local rulers being restricted to coining in bronze. Therefore, although the emperor's head could have been found also on the local currencies of the cities and on those of most of the Herodian rulers, the reference here is undoubtedly to a *denarius* of the then reigning emperor, Tiberius. On the obverse of such coins we see the head of the emperor with, surrounding it, the Latin inscription (reading from the right) "Tiberius Caesar, son of the deified Augustus, Augustus"; and, on the reverse, the figure of Peace holding an olive branch, encircled by an inscription

Chair of teacher of the Law, from a synagogue at Chorazin.

The scribes and the Pharisees sit in Moses' seat.   (MATT. 23 : 2)

reading: "The High Pontiff". It was such a coin that Jesus must have taken to show the Pharisees the "image and superscription" of Caesar, when he answered them that they should "Render unto Caesar the things that are Caesar's and to God the things that are God's".

Next the Sadducees tried to test Jesus on his attitude to the Pharisaic doctrine of the resurrection of the dead, but he quickly exposed their own ignorance of the after-life.

A sincere Pharisaic scribe, having overheard the dispute between Jesus and the Sadducees, now asked Jesus what he held to be the most important commandment in the Law. Jesus quoted Deut. 6: 5 but coordinated with it Lev. 19: 18. This met the enthusiastic approval of the scribe, and Jesus praised him as not far from the kingdom. This incident terminated further questioning of Jesus, who now asked the populace a question of his own as he taught in the Temple: how can the scribes declare the Messiah to be David's son (and nothing more) in view of the Davidic Psalm 110: 1? Mark notes that the people heard Jesus gladly.

In his teaching he also told the people to beware of the scribes. The brief attack on them given in Mark, castigating them for their quest of public recognition, devouring widows' houses, and for pretense making long prayers, has been greatly expanded in Matt. 23. In this discourse Jesus begins by saying: "The scribes and the Pharisees sit in Moses seat." The "seat (Greek *kathedra*) of Moses" was a specially imposing chair, set up in the synagogue for the principal teacher of the Law or for any other person whom the local community

277

Façade of Catacomb at
Beth Shea 'rim. Third or
fourth century A.D.

wished to honor; the Greek word *kathedra* means specifically the seat (with arm-rests and high back) occupied by a professor when teaching. Chairs of this kind have been found among the remains of several ancient synagogues, notably that at Chorazin. The arm-rests and back of the one excavated there are ornamented in relief with traditional Jewish motifs. To occupy such a seat was the ambition of every aspiring rabbinical student.

In their zeal to propagate their faith the Pharisees were ready, in Jesus' words, to "compass sea and land to make one proselyte" (Matt. 23 : 15).

The decline of the ancient Greek and Roman religions, which had already begun in the Hellenistic period, created a spiritual vacuum and left the way open for the influx of various Oriental faiths. Both Judaism and Christianity were thus able to attract many highly intelligent people whose religious longings remained unsatisfied by the prevailing types of philosophy, whether Stoic or Epicurean. In consequence we find large numbers attracted to the Jewish religion which, before the destruction of the Second Temple, was not yet associated with a defeated and despised nation. The proselytes were of various kinds: some adopted the tenets of Judaism in their entirety, while others (the "proselytes of the gate"), without accepting the full rigor of the Mosaic Law, only followed the moral precepts of a religion to which they felt drawn. To the latter category belonged the "devout and honor-able women" of Antioch of Pisidia who were instigated by the local Jews against Paul (Acts 13 : 50). Greek terms similar to the word used here for "devout" (*sebomenai*) have also been found in inscriptions to denote such sympathizers with Judaism.

After reproaching the Pharisees with ambition and casuistry, Jesus next attacked their ritualism. The laws about ritual cleanness set forth in the Book of Leviticus (chapters 11–15) had been worked into a most intricate system of regulations through the develop-ment of the Oral Law by the scribes or rabbinical scholars. Uncleanness could be conveyed by touch, by carrying, by being in the shadow of an object, by entering an unclean house, and the like. Anyone who wished to keep himself ritually clean had to avoid all contact, direct or indirect, with unclean people or things; otherwise, he had repeatedly to undergo an elaborate ritual of sacrifice and purification. This explains the meticulous care with which the members of the Pharisee sect, who went furthest in their striving for ritual purity, scoured their vessels and strained their wine.

The hypocrisy of the Pharisees was also shown, according to Jesus, in their ostentatious respect for the tombs of the prophets and the righteous, whom their fathers had helped to kill in former days. The custom of commemorating important personages by elaborately built and decorated funerary monuments dates back to Old Testament times. By the period of the Second Temple, the valleys surrounding Jerusalem were filled with rock-cut sepulchers, some of which were subsequently venerated as the burial-places of various prophets and kings. The custom still persisted after the destruction of the Temple by the Romans. Thus, in the Jewish necropolis of Beth Shea 'rim, established in the third and fourth centuries A.D. around the sepulcher of the patriarch Judah I of the house of Hillel (died c. A.D. 217), we find a series of monumental tomb-façades which were intended to make the "sepulchers of the just" more imposing.

The final incident in the Temple given by Mark is that of Jesus sitting opposite the treasury and seeing the poor widow placing her "two mites" in the collection-box. He

And Jesus sat over against the treasury, and beheld
how the people cast money into the treasury . . . And
there came a certain poor widow, and she threw in two
mites, which make a farthing.   (MARK 12 : 41–42)

(*Left*) Coin struck by the procurator
Gratus, A.D. 22.

(*Right*) Syrian temple collection-box.

And as he went out of the temple, one of his disciples saith unto him, Master, see what manner of stones and what buildings are here.

(MARK 13 : 1)

Part of the outer wall of the Temple.

praised her for her devotion, above all those who gave large sums, for out of her poverty she had given her all. This detail accords well with what we know of the Temple finances and of the denominations of money current at that time. Apart from the Temple dues, which had to be paid regularly as a tax, pilgrims and visitors to the Temple were encouraged to make donations for various purposes, a custom dating back to the times of the First Temple. According to the *Mishnah* there were in the Temple thirteen chests, each shaped like a *shofar* (ram's horn), and marked for shekel dues, for bird-offerings, for wood, for frankincense, for gold for the mercy-seat, and six for "free-will offerings". The widow's donation probably belonged to the last class. It consisted of two *lepta* ("mites") which together made up a *quadrans* (the Latin word that is used in the Greek text, and is translated "farthing") or the fourth part of an *as*, the twelfth part of a silver *denarius*. The *lepta* thus represents the smallest denomination of money in circulation, the Hebrew *perutah*, a small bronze coin. Such coins were struck by the Roman governors (procurators) of Judaea. They do not display the head of the emperor, in deference to Jewish objections, but only his title, together with such symbols as a *simpulum* (ladle for purifying water) or a palm branch.

THE DOOM OF JERUSALEM AND THE TEMPLE

ON LEAVING THE Temple, Jesus and the disciples must have passed through the outer wall of the Temple esplanade, which had been built by Herod from huge blocks of stone. Some of these ashlars can still be seen; for example, those used in the western (or Wailing) wall or in the southern and eastern walls of the Temple mount. They average 9–15 feet in length and 3–4 feet in height; the largest one is 36 feet long, and the heaviest (21×6 feet) which is set in the southeastern pinnacle wall weighs nearly a hundred tons. They are all dressed in the manner typical of Herodian times, with a rough boss in the center and a margin around it; as a special refinement the margin is repeated around the bosses. No wonder the massive walls and the splendid buildings of the Temple, which evoked general admiration among Jews and Gentiles alike, made a great impression on the disciples too. But Jesus saw further than they, and prophesied that "there shall not be left one stone upon another that shall not be thrown down".

Peter, James, and John later asked him privately, as he sat on the Mount of Olives opposite the Temple, when this would take place, and what "sign" would precede the catastrophe. Jesus thereupon gave them prophecy and admonition in the so-called "Little Apocalypse" (Mark 13 : 5 ff.). In the course of it he refers to their seeing the "abomination of desolation . . . [RSV, "desolating sacrilege"] set up where it ought not to be"—an allusion to Daniel 9: 27; 12 : 11. The author of Daniel meant the desecration of the Temple by Antiochus IV Epiphanes, who set a pagan altar on the great altar of sacrifice during the persecution that led to the Maccabean revolt in 165 B.C. But most readers of Daniel took it to be an as yet unfulfilled prophecy, or as prophecy to be fulfilled a second time. When Judaea became a Roman province, the term was transferred to other abominated manifestations of the pagan cult; the standards of the legions which were decorated with images of the emperors and of Roman gods; imperial statues in general; and above all to the statue of the emperor himself, which Caligula (A.D. 37–41) intended to have set up in the Temple. The prophecy of Jesus

And as he sat upon the Mount of Olives over against the temple . . .
(MARK 13 : 3)

View of Jerusalem, showing the Mount of Olives.

*For the days shall come upon thee, that thine enemies shall cast a
trench about thee, and compass thee round, and keep thee in on every
side.* (LUKE 19 : 43)

that "the abomination of desolation" would stand in the holy place was fulfilled within forty
years, when the victorious Roman army sacrificed to its gods on the ruins of the Temple.

In connection with the entry into Jerusalem, Luke described Jesus as pausing when he saw
the city from the Mount of Olives, weeping and prophesying the siege of A.D. 70 (Luke 19:
41–4). First, as usual in ancient siege-warfare, the beleaguering forces would make a siege-
wall of earth and stone round the doomed city, thus sealing it off and preventing the escape,
provisioning, or reinforcement of the troops inside. This task completed, the siege-mound
(Latin *agger*) could be thrown up and the siege-engines brought to bear on the defenses.
Such siege-works are still clearly visible round the fortress of Masada on the shores of the
Dead Sea, the last stronghold of the Jews in their first war against the Romans in A.D. 66–73.
Built by Herod on an almost inaccessible rock, 1,000 feet high, Masada defied the Romans

And they shall fall by the edge of the sword, and shall be led away captive into all nations: and Jerusalem shall be trodden down of the Gentiles, until the times of the Gentiles be fulfilled. (LUKE 21 : 24)

(*Above*) Relief showing bringing in of prisoners, from a Roman sarcophagus.

(*Right*) Roman and Dacian fighting, on relief from time of Trajan.

for several months in A.D. 73. The attackers first threw a siege-wall around the fortress at the foot of the rock and put up camps. Then, after they had built a high siege-mound, they at last succeeded in bringing a battering-ram up to the fortress wall and forcing a breach in it. The besieged committed suicide rather than be taken captive. Owing to the dry desert climate and the isolated position of the site, the siege-works around Masada have been wonderfully preserved to this day.

Jesus, according to Luke's version of the apocalypse, predicted that when Jerusalem fell its sons would be either killed or enslaved and their city given into possession of strangers (Luke 21 : 24). His words here are an accurate description of the horrors of ancient warfare. According to the prevailing practice in antiquity (abandoned in the more humane Hellenistic period but revived by the Romans) the vanquished became the property of the victor, to dispose of as he saw fit. He might kill them (the usual fate of the warriors, the old, and the useless); or sell them into slavery; or settle other people in their cities and on their land. All three of these disasters befell the Jews at the end of the first Roman war, a generation after Jesus. The practices enumerated can be seen in ancient artistic representations showing a Roman and a Dacian fighting on a relief from the time of Trajan and on a relief on a Roman sarcophagus showing the rounding-up of prisoners.

*When ye therefore shall see the
abomination of desolation, spoken
of by Daniel the prophet, stand
in the holy place . . .*
(MATT. 24: 15)

Romans sacrificing, on relief of
Emperor Constantine I. Fourth
century A.D.

But in all three versions of this apocalypse (Mark 13: 5 ff., Luke 21: 8 ff., Matt. 24: 4 ff.)
the mind of Jesus went beyond the catastrophe that would befall the Holy City. He thought
of universal catastrophe and of the coming from heaven of the Son of man as judge, as
prophesied by Daniel. And he urged watchfulness and readiness. To this apocalypse Matthew
adds some of the most impressive parables of Jesus, culminating in the powerful scene of the
last judgment (Matt. 25: 31–46).

THE LAST DAYS BEFORE THE PASSOVER

IT WAS NOW two days before the Passover, according to Mark 14: 1 f., and the
chief priests and scribes were seeking to arrest Jesus by stealth and kill him. If
they missed the opportunity of doing it before the festival, they were convinced that they

must wait until after it was over. There was too much danger of a tumult during the holidays, with consequent drastic Roman interference.

When Jesus was sitting at table in the house of Simon the leper at Bethany, he was anointed by a woman with precious ointments, an act which he took as a sign of his approaching death and burial. Some who were present were full of indignation, viewing the woman's act as a waste of ointment worth "more than three hundred pence".

The unguents in general use in antiquity (because of the greater exposure of the body to sunlight and the non-existence of soap) were of various sorts. The most expensive ones—of the kind called "precious"—were prepared with vegetable oils to which were added plant ingredients from distant lands, the spices of southern Arabia, India, and the Far Eastern Isles, brought by way of Ceylon, the Red Sea, and Nabataea. Heavy duties levied on these commodities in transit rendered their price to the consumer hundreds of times dearer than their original cost. Because they were so expensive, such unguents were kept in vessels with very narrow openings, from which they were decanted drop by drop. One of these vessels was the so-called *alabastron* (commonly translated "alabaster box"), actually an elongated drop-shaped juglet, usually made of alabaster, a translucent whitish stone.

There came unto him a woman having an alabaster box of very precious ointment, and poured it on his head, as he sat at meat.

(MATT. 26: 7)

Woman decanting perfumes, on Roman fresco. First century A.D.

Since unguents were used in antiquity mainly for cosmetic and funerary purposes, they were handled chiefly by women. In a fresco probably executed by a Greek artist, found in the ruins of a patrician house near the Villa Farnesina in Rome, we see a young woman, dressed in long violet robes and modestly veiled, decanting perfumes from an *aryballos* or purse-shaped vessel into a narrow *alabastron*. This fresco dates to the Late Augustan period, i.e. to the time of Jesus.

Judas Iscariot, one of the twelve, now went to the chief priests to betray Jesus. They were delighted and promised to give him money. Judas thereupon sought an opportunity to carry out his purpose. On the first day of the Passover—speaking in Gentile fashion, for the Passover day of the Jews only began on that evening—Jesus sent two of his disciples to the city to arrange for a place where they could celebrate the Passover meal and to make the necessary preparations. He instructed them how to find the right house by following a man carrying a jar of water, whom, as he clairvoyantly foresaw, they would meet.

In the absence of cheap metal receptacles, most of the liquids required in ancient housekeeping (water, wine, and oil) were carried on the shoulder in large clay vessels. In this particular case, the jar was used to bring water to the house chosen for the Last Supper. As this was a well-appointed dwelling and therefore probably provided with a cistern, we may assume that the water carried to it was of superior quality, possibly from the aqueduct which Pontius Pilate had had built to bring water to the Temple Mount. This aqueduct skirted round the Upper City, where, according to tradition, the Last Supper took place. Piped water, though common in ancient Rome, was not usual in provincial cities like Jerusalem. On a Byzantine mosaic of the sixth century found at Bethshan, we see a man, symbolizing the month of September,

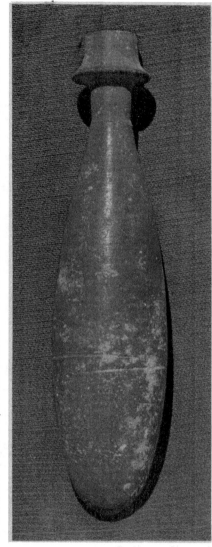

Pottery imitation of an *alabastron*, or alabaster vessel.

287

ΣΕΤΕΜ
ΗΜΑ
ΒΡΗ
ΟC

*Go ye into the city, and there
shall meet you a man bearing a
pitcher of water . . .*

(MARK 14: 13)

Byzantine mosaic, found at
Bethshan. Sixth century A.D.

carrying a cock in his left hand, while with his right he steadies on his shoulder a ribbed
water-jar, typical of the period from Herod to the Byzantines.

The man with the water-jar led the two disciples to the upper chamber of a well-appointed
house. They made the necessary preparations, and when Jesus and the others arrived they all
partook of the Passover, dipping their hands in a communal dish and drinking the wine
from a cup. Jesus revealed at the outset that one of them would betray him and pronounced
a woe over this unidentified individual.

If this was a Passover meal, as Mark claims, it consisted of unleavened bread and herbs,
and at least four cups of wine had to be drunk. The Greek word used here for wine-cup is
potērion. Drinking-cups in antiquity were either shallow bowls with a long stem (*kylix*) or
deep and rounded; the latter were the more usual in the Orient. Such cups, great quantities
of which have been found in the Graeco-Roman strata of the cities of the Holy Land, were
made of pottery, metal, or glass, the first being the most common. As we read, however, in
Mark 14: 15 that the supper took place in the large upper chamber, "furnished and prepared",
we may assume that the service on this occasion was of the best available. In the case of
drinking-vessels this would indicate the use of glassware. The art of glass-blowing had

recently been invented and was practised mainly in the coastal cities of Palestine and Phoenicia. A fine glass cup of this period has handles which show that it was used for drinking.

During the meal Jesus performed a special rite with the bread and wine to bring home to the disciples the meaning of his death. The two material elements were declared to represent his body and his blood—the latter poured out for many. He predicted that he would not drink of the cup again until the kingdom came.

JESUS' ARREST AND TRIAL

AFTER CONCLUDING THE Passover with a hymn (i.e. one of the so-called *Hallel* Psalms, 113-18) Jesus and the disciples went out from the city to the Mount of Olives. On the way Jesus predicted that they would all fall away, but that when he was raised up from the dead he would go before them to Galilee. Peter brushed aside the

And he took the cup, and gave thanks . . .
(MATT. 26 : 27)

Glass drinking-cup. First century A.D.

Then cometh Jesus with them unto a place called
Gethsemane . . .   (MATT. 26: 36)

thought that he would fall away, but Jesus predicted he would deny him three times before the cock crowed twice.

They came to a place called Gethsemane, a name perhaps derived from the Hebrew *gath shemanim*, meaning an oil-press. Its location is not indicated in Mark 14: 32, but two parallel Gospel passages, while not expressly naming Gethsemane, place it on the "Mount of Olives" (Luke 22: 39) or in a garden on the other side of the "brook of Cedron" (John 18: 1). These indications, taken together, have led to the traditional identification of Gethsemane with a spot near the brook of Kidron, at the foot of the Mount of Olives, opposite the Temple Mount. The olive groves which gave the Mount of Olives, or the "Ascent of Olivet" (2 Sam. 15: 30), its name, supplied the raw material for the presses situated at its foot. This spot would usually have been deserted, except for a short period in the late summer immediately following the olive gathering, and would thus, at the spring season of Passover, have been well suited for privacy. Leaving the main group of his disciples there, he took the three most intimate ones with him and went farther.

Confessing to them the sorrow of his soul he bade them wait and watch, and went still farther to be alone. While he prayed to God in the agony of his spirit, the weary disciples succumbed to sleep. Three times Jesus returned and awakened them, the third time declaring that the betrayer was at hand. Indeed, a crowd of people, armed with swords and staves, and led by Judas, now arrived. Singled out by the traitor's kiss, Jesus let himself be seized, sternly forbidding resistance by force, such as one of those standing by attempted. His

Then began he to curse and to swear, saying, I know not the man. And immediately the cock crew. (MATT. 26 : 74)

Roman bronze figurine of a cock, found at Lyons.

followers forsook him and fled, including a youth whose linen outer garment was torn from his body by a would-be captor.

Jesus was first brought to the high priest who, under the supervision of the Romans, exercised supreme jurisdiction over Judaea. Here all the former high priests, the elders, and scribes were assembled. The trial before the high priest's council was concerned with the charge of blasphemy. Difficulties with witnesses, whose evidence could not be made to agree, led the high priest to put the direct question: "Art thou the Christ, the Son of the Blessed [i.e. God]?" To this Jesus answered: "I am", and predicted that they would see the Son of man in the role of Daniel 7: 13. In the eyes of the council, this was sufficient proof of his guilt. Jesus was condemned and mocked as well as abused physically.

Tradition has encased this scene in a story of Peter's penetration into the courtyard of the high priest's palace and of his threefold denial of Jesus, as previously predicted in Mark 14:30.

On the following morning the council met again. Not being allowed to sentence anyone to death, it transferred the prisoner to the Roman governor, Pontius Pilate, apparently to stand trial on a political charge of pretending to be "King of the Jews".

A Roman provincial governor had the right to pronounce judgment in civil and criminal cases brought before him, including sentence of death. As he personified the "majesty of the Roman people", the exercise of his judicial functions was surrounded with ceremonial forms intended to evoke awe and respect. He dispensed justice seated on a raised dais high above the crowd of litigants in front of him. Such a dais was called in Latin *tribunal*, a name applied to the court of justice as a whole; the Greek term here is *bēma*. As the magistrate had to be ready to sit in judgment in any place besides his usual residence, his seat was a special kind of portable chair, called *sella curulis*, with legs which could be folded together. The right to such a chair was equivalent to high office in the Roman commonwealth. The emperor himself, as the chief magistrate of the Republic, distributed his largess from a *sella curulis* set up on a *tribunal*.

When Pilate asked Jesus whether he was the king of the Jews, he replied indirectly, "Thou sayest it", but would not answer charges brought against him by the chief priests.

When Pilate saw that he could prevail nothing, but that rather a tumult was made,
he took water, and washed his hands before the multitude . . . (MATT. 27: 24)

Bronze jug and basin
of the Roman period.

When Pilate therefore heard that saying, he brought Jesus forth, and sat down in the judgment seat in a place that is called the Pavement, but in the Hebrew, Gabbatha.

(JOHN 19: 13)

Stone-paved courtyard, excavated in northwest corner of the Temple esplanade.

(Inset) Inscription on pavement, cut by Romans for playing games of chance.

Pilate tried to save Jesus by making the people choose between his release and that of a condemned robber called Barabbas; but they preferred Barabbas to be freed and demanded the crucifixion of Jesus.

Matthew's Gospel adds some interesting items in this connection: the message from Pilate's wife who had suffered much over Jesus in a dream that night, and the story of how Pilate publicly washed his hands declaring his innocence (cf. Ps. 26: 6, and especially Deut. 21: 6) to disavow responsibility for the death of Jesus.

John's Gospel describes the place where Pilate had his judgment seat as "the Pavement" (Greek *lithostroton*), a term also used for mosaic pavements; and in Hebrew (i.e. Aramaic) "Gabbatha", probably meaning "elevation". The identification of the locality thus described depends on the location of the *praetorium* or temporary seat of the Roman procurator in Jerusalem (his permanent official residence was at Caesarea). Some scholars consider that, while in Jerusalem, Pilate resided at Herod's palace in the northwestern corner of the Upper

City and that the "Pavement" was an open space in front of the palace, facing the market. Tradition, however, places the residence of the procurator in the Antonia fortress, at the northwestern corner of the Temple esplanade. In this area excavations have brought to light a courtyard paved with stone slabs which apparently occupied the center of the Antonia fortress. Marks cut in the stones of the pavement are of the same type as those used by Roman soldiers elsewhere when playing various games of chance. The courtyard of the Antonia would have been a convenient and safe place for the procurator to sit in judgment, and the religious group owning the spot naturally claims it to be the true Gabbatha. But it is doubtful whether the Jewish masses would have been allowed inside the fortress, as is implied in the continuation of the Gospel story.

THE CRUCIFIXION

P ILATE HAD JESUS scourged and delivered him over to the soldiers to be crucified. They led him into the *praetorium*, called together the whole force, and mocked him. They dressed him up as a caricature of a king, with scarlet robe, a crown of thorns, and a reed for a scepter. Then they put his own clothes on him and led him out to

And the soldiers platted a crown of thorns and put it on his head . . .
(JOHN 19: 2)

Branch of *Zizyphus spina Christi* Willd., traditionally used for the crown of thorns.

ישוע דמן וצרת מלכא דיחודיא

JESVS·NAZARENVS·REX·JVDAEORVM

IHCOYC·O·NAZΩPAIOC·O·BACIΛEYC·TΩN·JOYΔAIΩN

And Pilate wrote a title, and put it on the cross. And the writing was, JESUS OF NAZARETH THE KING OF THE JEWS. *This title then read many of the Jews: for the place where Jesus was crucified was nigh to the city: and it was written in Hebrew, and Greek, and Latin.* (JOHN 19 : 19–20)

Reconstruction of inscription over the Cross in Hebrew, Latin, and Greek.

crucify him. A chance passer-by, Simon of Cyrene, was pressed into service to carry the cross-bar for the physically weakened Jesus. The Crucifixion took place in the third hour (9 a.m.). The soldiers cast lots for the possession of his garments. Jesus rejected the wine with myrrh that was offered him.

An inscription was put over Jesus' Cross, in accordance with Roman usage, to deter other possible fomenters of political rebellion; it read, "King of the Jews". According to the fourth Gospel the inscription was longer and was written in Hebrew, Roman (Latin), and Greek.

In the time of Jesus the language most commonly spoken by the Jews in Palestine—and to some extent used also in written texts—was a Jewish dialect of Aramaic; this is the language referred to in the Gospels as "Hebrew". The rabbis continued to use Hebrew proper as a written language, and it was also spoken somewhat by the educated classes, even in later periods; but the average man understood so little of it that it was necessary to translate into Aramaic the inscription over the Cross specifying the crime for which the condemned man had suffered, because Aramaic was the one language understood by all of the population on whom the punishment was intended to make an impression. Greek, too, was

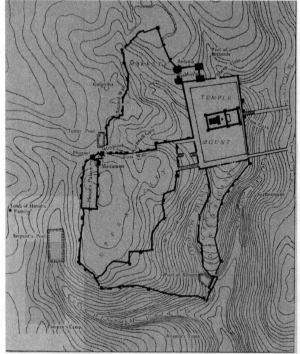

And when they were
come unto a place called
Golgotha, that is to say,
a place of a skull.

(MATT. 27 : 33)

Plan of Jerusalem, show-
ing the presumed site of
Golgotha.

also an obvious choice: becoming the language of cultured people throughout the eastern
Mediterranean in Hellenistic times it remained so under the Romans, and was therefore the
language understood by most of the Jews in the Diaspora, who thronged Jerusalem at
Passover. Latin was, of course, the language of the Roman army and administration. The
scripts shown here in the attempted reconstruction of the inscription are taken from the
Hebrew of the Dead Sea Scrolls and from the Greek and Latin writing found in public
notices painted on walls at Pompeii and elsewhere.

The place of Jesus' execution was Golgotha, "the place of the skull", a locality in the
environs of Jerusalem not mentioned outside the Gospels. It is traditionally identified with
an area now enclosed within the Church of the Holy Sepulcher. Executions in antiquity were
public, and, whenever possible, the spot selected was outside the city gates where passers-by
could be impressed by the spectacle of justice being done. Since there was no suitable flat
area to the west, south, or east of the walls of ancient Jerusalem, we may assume that Jesus
was crucified somewhere outside the then existing north wall. The two walls of Jerusalem
which were in being at that time are described by Josephus in *The Jewish War* (Book V,
chapters 4–5). The First Wall connected Herod's palace (roughly on the site of the present

Citadel), in the northwest corner of the Upper City, with the Temple Mount, and encircled the Upper and Lower Cities to the south of it. The Second Wall began at the "Garden Gate" in the First Wall, close to the towers of Herod's palace, and followed a semi-circular line protecting the commercial quarters of the city, until it reached the Antonia fortress. It was outside this wall that Jesus was crucified between two robbers. They as well as the passers-by and the chief priests mocked him.

At about the ninth hour Jesus suddenly cried out in Aramaic: "My God, my God, why hast thou forsaken me?" This elicited the jest that he was calling for Elijah. Soon afterwards, with a loud cry, Jesus expired. The Roman centurion, seeing him die, exclaimed: "Truly this man was a son of God." A singular portent occurred when Jesus died: the curtain of the Temple was rent from top to bottom. The only witnesses of the Crucifixion from among the followers of Jesus were women, of whom Mark mentions two Marys and a Salome.

THE BURIAL AND RESURRECTION OF JESUS

THE BODY OF Jesus was delivered, by permission of Pilate, to Joseph of Arimathaea, after the centurion had confirmed the death of Jesus. Joseph wrapped it in clean linen, laid it in a tomb hewn out of the rock, and rolled a stone against the opening. The two Marys saw where Jesus was laid. Matthew claims that it was Joseph's own tomb, prepared in advance for himself and his family. This would imply that he had moved from his native Arimathaea to Jerusalem.

The desire to protect one's family vault from robbery, a form of crime very common in antiquity in view of the valuable objects left with the deceased, led to the invention of more or less elaborate methods of guarding the entrances of the tomb-caves which were the usual places of

But one of the soldiers with a spear pierced his side . . .
(JOHN 19: 34)

Tomb-stone of Publius Flavoleius,
a Roman soldier.

And laid it in his own new tomb, which he had hewn out in the rock: and he rolled a great stone to the door of the sepulcher, and departed.

(MATT. 27: 60)

Rolling stone at the doorway of the Tomb of Herod's family, at Jerusalem.

burial among prominent Jews of Jerusalem in the time of Jesus. One such device, of which several examples still survive, was the rolling stone. This was a heavy cylindrical block, placed in a slightly sloping slit cut in the rock across the entrance to a vault and so poised that it remained closed by force of gravity and had to be rolled upwards and secured with a wedge before the tomb could be entered. One such stone has been found in the Tombs of the Kings of Adiabene in Jerusalem; another in the Tomb of Herod's family, a monument mentioned by Josephus as situated opposite the Upper City.

The burial had taken place hastily, on account of the imminence of the Sabbath. There had been no time to anoint the body of Jesus, as was customary with honored and beloved dead. With the expiration of the Sabbath the two Marys and Salome bought spices to go and anoint him.

The Passion story of the fourth Gospel differs from the story of Mark in not having Jesus celebrate the Passover, but rather on being buried before the Passover began. John may have told it thus in order to have Jesus' death take place at the very hour when it was customary to sacrifice the Passover lambs. True, Mark's account raises questions as to how it was possible for the prosecution and execution of Jesus to take place on the day of the festival, but the objections are not insuperable in view of the involvement of the heathen Romans in the matter. The Dead Sea Scrolls, furthermore, have introduced the possibility that some Jewish groups followed a different calendar than the official one and celebrated the Passover two days earlier (Wednesday instead of Friday).

Very early on the morning of the first day of the week the three women went to the tomb, arriving just after sunrise, engaged in the question as to who would roll away the stone for them. Looking up as they drew near they saw that the stone had been rolled away, and entering the tomb they beheld a young man in a white robe sitting there. He bade them be unafraid and gave them the explanation that Jesus was risen; also a message for the disciples and Peter that Jesus would go before them to Galilee where they would see him, as he had said (Mark 14: 28). The women fled from the tomb and said nothing to anyone, for they were afraid.

The present conclusion of Mark's Gospel (Mark 16: 9-20) is a later addition, made on the basis of the other Gospels. That Mark ended at 16: 8 is shown by the fact that from this point on the other three Gospels go their separate ways; they did not have Mark to follow.

Matthew has provided an interesting supplement to the burial story: according to him a guard of soldiers was placed over the tomb in which Jesus had been buried. But an angel of the LORD rolled back the stone, and the sepulcher was seen to be empty. The disciples received the astounding news with awe and rejoicing, while the chief priests tried to persuade the soldiers who had been guarding the tomb to tell Pilate that the disciples had stolen the body of Jesus.

The suggestion that a body might be stolen from a grave has been singularly confirmed by the text of an inscription from Palestine (according to one theory, from Nazareth). This is a partial reproduction of a "decree of Caesar" (probably Augustus). It is written in *Koiné*

And when they were assembled with the elders, and had taken counsel, they gave large money unto the soldiers, Saying, Say ye, His disciples came by night, and stole him away while we slept.
(MATT. 28: 12-13)

Partial reproduction of a decree of Caesar Augustus.

("common") Greek. In his decree the emperor denounces those who damage tombs, exhume the dead, transfer bodies from one tomb to another, or remove inscriptions or other parts of the sepulcher. Such offenders have committed a heinous crime against the gods and one for which, particularly in the case of changing the place of burial, they are to pay with their lives. Although this decree was, in all probability, issued long before the death of Jesus, it bears testimony to the frequency with which, at one time, bodies were removed from their tombs (usually to enable other people to use the ready-made grave).

A new feature in Matthew's account is an appearance of Jesus to the women (Matt. 28 : 1–10). Matthew gives the impression that the women carried the message of the angel to the disciples, and he then relates the appearance of Christ in Galilee, as required by that message. Luke, however, has transferred the Resurrection appearances to Jerusalem and its vicinity, and therein is followed by John, though in the appendix to John (chapter 21) a Galilean appearance is related. According to Luke, Jesus appeared to the twelve at Jerusalem and directed them to await there the coming of the Holy Spirit. He then led them out towards Bethany and was taken from them, while blessing them.

The Gospel story is the most powerful and moving known to man. Within the scope of this book we have been able to follow only the oldest of its four versions, with but an occasional glance at the others. In each "Gospel according to . . ." there is a distinctive

And, behold, two of them went that same day to a village called Emmaus, which was from Jerusalem about threescore furlongs. (LUKE 24: 13)

The site of Emmaus, in the foothills of the Judaean mountains.

viewpoint and spirit. The same incidents are often portrayed differently, and the same sayings may vary considerably in wording, emphasis, or application. These variations, while creating uncertainties, show us the ebb and flow of tradition and the richness of Early Christian thought and sentiment. Each evangelist with his own brush-strokes gives a portrait of the Jesus who stood before his mind and no doubt before the mind of the group of which the evangelist was a member. All four, however, agree in this: they write from the standpoint of faith in the risen LORD.

Mark views the sacred story in the light of the missionary term "gospel" or good tidings, which Paul uses so prominently; it is the message about Jesus Christ, who gave his life as ransom for many, but was raised from the dead and will come again as Messiah and Son of man. He kept his Messiahship secret during his ministry, though it was part of his purpose to bring his disciples to a realization of his office. The evil spirits, minions of Satan, recognized him as Son of God, but he forbade them to make him known. His death on the Cross was part of the divine plan. Before the final revelation of his person as Son of man can take place, the Gospel must be preached to all nations.

For Matthew the term "gospel" is not that of the gospel *about* Jesus, but rather of the gospel *preached by* Jesus. It is the gospel of the kingdom of heaven (the latter noun being a substitute for the sacred word for "God"). Jesus came as the Messiah prophesied in the Old Testament, and many particulars of his life took place that the prophecies might be fulfilled. He did mighty deeds and spoke powerful words. He emphasized the validity of the Law of Moses, but showed that it was to be interpreted in the prophetic spirit. He required a better righteousness than that of the Pharisees, the essence of it being the commandment of love. The Jews under the leadership of the Pharisees rejected him as their Messiah. The mission of Jesus had been exclusively to Israel, and only the risen LORD gives the disciples the command to teach all nations. The belief in the return of Christ is firmly maintained, but the delay in the fulfillment of the expectation is the subject of reflection. The Son of man will come as judge, but only the judgment of professed Christians is described. Matthew alone of the Gospel authors speaks of the Church of Christ. In connection therewith he gives Peter and the apostles great authority.

Luke is more historically oriented than Mark or Matthew. He attempts to fix the situation in which Jesus was born and to date roughly the appearance on the scene of John the Baptist and therewith also of Jesus. He strongly links up the story of John and Jesus with circles among the Jews nurturing the Messianic hope in deep piety. He thinks of the period before Christ as a distinct one that terminated with John the Baptist (16: 16). But he also makes room for a period after Christ—that of the history of Christianity; for though he does not give up the hope of the second coming he postpones it. Luke thus has made the time of Jesus' ministry the central one to which the past pointed and from which the future sprang. Realizing the necessity of Christianity's accommodating itself to a life in the pagan world, Luke is conscious of problems this creates. He also dwells particularly on Jesus as the friend of sinners, has him take a kindly attitude toward the Samaritans and accept women as helpers. Salvation is a thing of the future, but repentance and forgiveness of sins assure participation in it.

The Gospel of John represents the climax of the development, entering into the metaphysical to explain what the other Gospels claim for the person of Christ. The eternal "Word" became flesh in him, and tarried for a while on earth. The world is the sphere of darkness and evil; the Word comes from the sphere of light and good. He who believes in Jesus is no longer "of the world", and after death Jesus will take him to the heavenly dwellings, where he will see the glory of the Son of God. The believer while still in the world must show his love for the LORD by keeping his commandments, and particularly the new love commandment.

The diversity of these viewpoints is perhaps disturbing to a reader who would like to have his witnesses in perfect accord in stating who Jesus was and in defining his message. The matter is made even more difficult when the teaching about Christ and his work found in the Epistles is given consideration. The harmonistic fusions of the Biblical material attempted in former days did violence to the individual standpoints of the authors.

Go into all the world and preach the gospel to the whole creation. (MARK 16: 15)

Hellenistic figure of a fisherman, from Alexandria.

302

And it came to pass, while he blessed them, he was parted from them, and carried up into heaven. (LUKE 24 : 51)

Mosque of the Ascension, on the Mount of Olives.

A simple guidepost may be of help here. The one thing that all the evangelists as well as the other New Testament authors are trying to say, each in his own way, is that Jesus has a unique meaning for mankind and every individual. He cannot be compared to anyone else that ever lived. How were they to express this and make it vivid to their readers who may be symbolized by the Hellenistic figure of a workman on the opposite page? They could only do it in concepts of their own time. The Old Testament, which they read as replete with prophecy of the Messianic Age, provided them with certain helps to this end. Among them were such titles as Messiah or Christ, Son of David, Son of God, Son of man, Servant of the LORD, and even LORD (in the Greek translation of the Old Testament). They found comfort in the belief that the death of the Messiah was foretold and foreordained, as well as his Resurrection and Ascension to heaven and return as judge. Since the Gospels were written in the Greek world some ideas of non-Jewish origin, too, were helpful, e.g. that of the "Word" (Greek *Logos*) in the Gospel of John. By all such means the evangelists made vivid the uniqueness of Jesus. Since the New Testament is the book of the Church, their phraseology is familiar and enduring. No other can be substituted for it. What is clear, however, is that no formulation in words concerning Jesus and his work is more than an inspired effort to bring home his eternal significance to man.

303

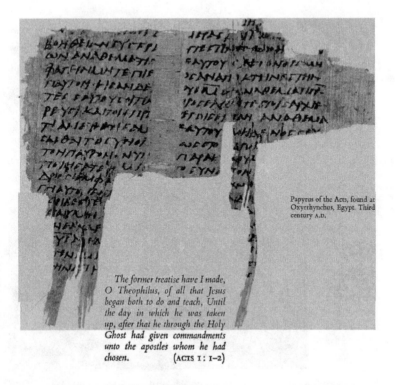

Papyrus of the Acts, found at Oxyrhynchus, Egypt. Third century A.D.

The former treatise have I made, O Theophilus, of all that Jesus began both to do and teach, Until the day in which he was taken up, after that he through the Holy Ghost had given commandments unto the apostles whom he had chosen. (ACTS 1: 1-2)

THE ACTS OF THE APOSTLES

AS STATED IN its opening words, the Book of Acts was written as the continuation of a Gospel and was addressed to a certain Theophilus. Its author was thus evidently identical with the author of the Gospel according to Luke, which also begins with a dedication to Theophilus. The purpose of this second book is to describe the development of the Church after the Ascension of Jesus to heaven. At first the story is concerned only with the events in Jerusalem; then the scope broadens with the missionary work in Samaria and in the coastal plain, and finally with the appeal to the Gentiles in Syria, Asia Minor, and Greece. Acts also recounts the debates within the Church concerning the validity of the Jewish Law as regards both converted Jews and Gentiles who had adopted Christianity.

Parthians, and Medes, and Elamites, and the dwellers in Mesopotamia, and in Judaea, and Cappadocia, in Pontus, and Asia, Phrygia, and Pamphylia, in Egypt, and in the parts of Libya about Cyrene, and strangers of Rome, Jews and proselytes, Cretes and Arabians, we do hear them speak in our tongues the wonderful works of God. (ACTS 2: 9–11)

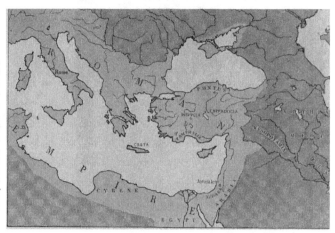

ΙΟΥΔΑΤΟΣ
ΛΑΓΑΝΙΩΝΟΣ
ΠΡΟΣΗΛΥΤΟΥ

(*Above*) Map of the Jewish Diaspora in the first century A.D.

(*Left*) Ossuary inscription relating to a proselyte, found in Jerusalem.

At the beginning Peter stands very much in the foreground, but he disappears from the scene in chapter 12, thereafter to emerge only briefly in chapter 15. From chapter 13 on, Acts is mainly concerned with the missionary journeys of Paul, his arrest at Jerusalem, his long detention at Caesarea, and his final voyage to Rome, where the story ends.

The book opens with an expanded version of the final disappearance of Jesus from this earth; an account of how the apostles and others about them awaited the coming of the Holy Spirit; and the Pentecost empowering the apostles to speak "in other tongues" to the multitude of Jews and proselytes from many nations.

The enumeration of the communities or lands represented by the hearers at Pentecost gives a bird's-eye view of the Jewish Diaspora (literally, "Dispersion") at that time. The list begins with the Jews from the easternmost nations: the Parthians, who had taken over the eastern part of the old Seleucid realm, and the Medes; to these are added the Jews of Elam, and the region around Susa, and of Mesopotamia. All these were outside the Roman Empire. The rest of the list comprises nations subject to the Romans: beginning with Judaea,

And when forty years were expired, there appeared to him in the wilderness of Mount Sina an angel of the LORD in a flame of fire in a bush. (ACTS 7: 30)

Painting of Moses from Dura-Europos. Third century A.D.

we pass to Cappadocia in eastern Asia Minor, Pontus on the shores of the Black Sea, and then to "Asia". (The Roman province of that name included Ionia and Lydia, the western part of Asia Minor.) Phrygia lay to the east of Asia, and Pamphylia was a small province to the south. Egypt had a population of a million Jews in the time of Jesus, but there were also many in Cyrene or Libya. The Arabians meant may be Jews living within the Nabataean kingdom. Crete was a separate province in Roman times. Finally, there were the "strangers" from Rome, the heart of the Empire (no doubt mostly descendants of captives brought there by Pompey). No Jews from countries west of Rome are mentioned, for the Diaspora did not extend so far in the first century A.D. The presence of proselytes in Jerusalem is attested by an ossuary inscription reproduced on the preceding page, found in the city, commemorating one "Judas son of Laganios, a proselyte".

Acts continues with the story of the organization of the Christian community in Jerusalem, the members of which held their property in common. They were faithful in their adherence to the Temple and thus at first regarded themselves and were regarded as part of the Jewish Nation. A healing performed in the Temple led to the arrest of Peter and John. They were released, but soon the entire group of the apostles was arraigned when their activities received too much public attention. The Synedrium refused to condemn them, following the sage advice of rabbi Gamaliel. However, the zeal of Stephen, one of the seven deacons who had been appointed to take care of the needy Hellenistic-Jewish Christians, caused the congregation of one of the numerous synagogues of Jerusalem to prosecute him for blasphemy and to execute him by stoning, as prescribed in the Law (Lev. 24:14). A young man named Saul of Tarsus appears on the scene here, guarding the garments of those who stoned Stephen. Before his death, Stephen defended himself in a speech in which he likened the Church to the burning bush through which the LORD spoke to Moses.

The institution of the synagogue, which apparently came into existence in Babylonia and was then adopted by the provincial communities in the Holy Land, naturally took root last of all in Jerusalem, where the Temple sufficed for the religious needs of the population. It was only the strangers in the city who needed such communal centers. This fact is attested by the reference in Acts 6: 9 to a synagogue of the libertines (i.e. freed slaves, probably repatriated captives who had been carried off by Pompey in 63 B.C.), and various groups of Diaspora Jews from Alexandria, Cyrene, Cilicia, and Asia. A corroborative piece of evidence to the existence of such a synagogue is the inscription found in the "Ophel" excavations in 1914 and which must be dated from the time before the destruction of the Temple. It records the foundation of a synagogue, with a hospice, study rooms, and a water installation, by one Theodotus, son of Vettenius (i.e. a freedman of the Roman family of the Vetti), who, like his father and his grandfather before him, held the office of "ruler of the synagogue".

Then there arose certain of the synagogue which is called the synagogue of the Libertines . . .   (ACTS 6: 9)

Inscription from the tomb of rabbi Gamaliel at Beth She 'arim.

And he arose and went: and behold, a man of Ethiopia, an eunuch of great authority under Candace queen of the Ethiopians, who had the charge of all her treasure, and had come to Jerusalem for to worship, Was returning, and sitting in his chariot read Esaias the prophet. (ACTS 8 : 27–28)

(*Above*) Illustration showing a *rhedae*, or open Roman conveyance.

(*Left*) Relief from a temple in Naga, showing a Nubian queen. First century A.D.

Following the martyrdom of Stephen the Hellenistic part of the Christian congregation was persecuted by Saul and others, and fled from Jerusalem. This led to a spread of Christianity in all directions. The deacon Philip carried on a successful ministry in the city of Samaria, and on the road to Gaza converted the treasurer of queen Candace of Ethiopia, a proselyte to Judaism who was returning from a pilgrimage to Jerusalem. Philip then did missionary work in the coastal plain, settling in Caesarea.

But the most momentous conversion of this period was that of Saul of Tarsus, a Hellenistic Jew who lived at Jerusalem and was the persecutor of the followers of Jesus. Saul saw a vision of Christ on his way to Damascus, where he had intended to arrest and carry off known Christians. Temporarily blinded by the brilliant light, he was led by his companions into the city, to the house of one Judas in the "Street called Straight". There a disciple named Ananias instructed and baptized him. Later, using his Roman name Paul, he was to become perhaps the foremost of Christian missionaries.

Damascus, once the ancient capital of the Aramaean kingdom and later of one of the Assyrian and Persian provinces, was entirely rebuilt in the Hellenistic period according to the principles laid down by Hippodamus of Miletus, a famous Greek town-planner of the fifth century B.C. Traces of this Hippodamic plan are still visible in the Old City of the Damascus of today. It involved the use of straight streets, crossing each other at right angles, with modifications to suit local conditions. In Damascus the city was given the form of a rectangle, the long side running parallel to the River Barada. The royal palace and citadel were situated in the northwest corner, with the great Temple of Jupiter Damascenus (preceded by a temple of the Aramaean god Hadad and followed by a cathedral honoring John the Baptist, now the Umayyad mosque) to the east of them. As a result of this rectangular design the east–west streets of the city were longer than the north–south streets which they crossed. The longest of them all was the "Street called Straight", which to this day serves as the main commercial thoroughfare of the Old City. Like most of the principal thoroughfares of Roman cities, this street was lined by colonnaded porticoes, which offered shade and protection from rain for the passers-by, and also provided space for shops.

Paul began his missionary activity in Damascus with such success that his enemies among the Jews finally resolved to get rid of him by denouncing him to the Nabataean governor of the city (see 2 Cor. 11: 32). To prevent his escape they set a watch at the gates, where surveillance was easy. However, the disciples lowered Paul in a basket through the window

And the LORD *said unto him, Arise, and go into the street which is called Straight, and inquire in the house of Judas for one called Saul, of Tarsus: for behold, he prayeth.* (ACTS 9: 11)

The Darb el-Mustaqin (the "Street called Straight"), at Damascus.

*Then the disciples took him by night, and let him
down by the wall in a basket.* (ACTS 9: 25)

The Gate called Bab Kisan, Damascus.

of a house at the city wall. Thus escaping his persecutors, Paul went to Jerusalem, according
to the Acts account, but his activities there brought him into such peril that the brethren
sent him off to Tarsus.

Acts next deals with the events which induced Peter to take the position that Gentiles
could become Christians without becoming Jews, and that Jewish Christians need not have
dietary scruples in associating with them. He journeyed to Lydda and then to Jaffa, where
he had a vision of various animals brought down from heaven and heard a voice saying:
"What God has cleansed, that call not thou common." Peter thus was prepared to receive
the emissaries of the Roman centurion Cornelius, inviting him to Caesarea, and to proceed
to that city with them. There he preached to those assembled and baptized Cornelius and his
house. Peter is thus given credit for founding the congregation at Caesarea and converting
the first Gentiles.

Caesarea-by-the-Sea was the capital city of the Roman province of Judaea. It was the
normal residence of the Roman governor, who visited Jerusalem from time to time only;
here were stationed the troops under his command, including a cohort called "the Italian".
Caesarea, founded by King Herod on the site of an earlier harbor town called Straton's
Tower, had a mixed population of Jews and Gentiles. Conflicts between these two separate
elements later sparked the first war between the Jews and Romans. At the time of Acts, the
population was evenly divided. The centurion Cornelius evidently was one of the non-

commissioned officers entrusted with the training and command of the troops raised among the allies of the Romans in the Hellenistic cities. As in the legions, these professional soldiers, strict disciplinarians (cf. Matt. 8 : 9), formed the backbone of the allied cohorts. They carried a staff made from a vine stem, with which they are represented on surviving Roman monuments.

Starting at chapter 13, Acts is almost exclusively concerned with the activities of Paul, from the day Barnabas brought him from Tarsus to Antioch until his arrival in Rome. At Antioch a Gentile congregation had been established by some of the Hellenists scattered from Jerusalem in the persecution. Both men labored there for some time; it was here that the so-called "Nazarenes" for the first time adopted the name "Christians", that is, followers of *Christos*, the "Anointed One" or Messiah.

From Antioch Paul and Barnabas began their first missionary journey by going down to Seleucia, the city's port. Seleucia was built at the same time as Antioch, sixteen miles away, to serve as a harbor for the capital of the Seleucid empire. Its plain was the only point at which a city could be built along this strip of coast; even so, it was called Seleucia Pieria, "the stony". From Cyprus they crossed to Perga in Pamphylia, on the south coast of Asia

There was a certain man in Caesarea called Cornelius, a centurion of the band called the Italian band. (ACTS 10 : 1)

View of
Caesarea-by-the-Sea.

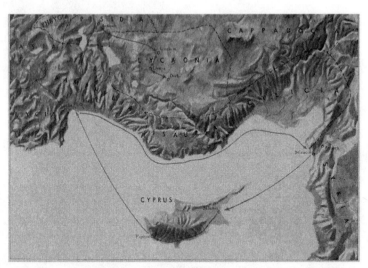

So they, being sent forth by the Holy Ghost, departed unto Seleucia; and from thence they sailed to Cyprus. (ACTS 13 : 4)

Map showing Paul's first missionary journey.

Minor, then proceeded to Pisidian Antioch, farther inland, and to the cities of Iconium, Lystra, and Derbe. Returning to Perga, they re-embarked for Antioch and Attalia.

The miraculous healing of a crippled man at Lystra caused the people there to react in accordance with their pagan views of the supernatural: they accepted Paul and Barnabas as gods visiting their city in human guise. Many stories of such peregrinations of the divinities of the Greek Olympus have been preserved in classical mythology and literature; indeed, the intervention of a god (*deus ex machina*) was the standard denouement of a Greek drama. Acting on this supposition, the Lystrians regarded Barnabas, who probably had the more imposing presence and was no doubt Paul's senior, as the incarnation of Zeus-Jupiter, the chief deity of the Olympian pantheon. Paul, being the more eloquent of the two was identified with Hermes-Mercurius, the herald of the gods. The appearance of gods naturally required the sacrifice of animals, which were first garlanded, as customary. (A relief found at Rome shows a slave leading a garlanded bull to the sacrifice.) Paul and Barnabas had difficulty in stopping such a sacrifice in their honor.

After their return from their journey Paul and Barnabas found the church at Antioch troubled by extremists from Jerusalem who insisted that heathen converts to Christianity should be circumcised and obey the Law of Moses. The two missionaries were sent by the congregation to the apostles and elders in Jerusalem to lay the matter before them. At that occasion Peter reminded the gathering of what had been done in the case of Cornelius (15 : 7f.). After Paul and Barnabas had given a recital of their missionary success, James the brother of Jesus, who was the head of the Jerusalem church after Peter's departure from the city, made the decisive recommendation that Gentiles should not be troubled with the Jewish ritual law in its entirety, but that a letter should be written them stressing four rules which they should obey: to abstain from sacrifice to idols, and from blood, and from what is strangled, and from unchastity (by which here is meant marriage of close relatives). This was adopted and two leading men of the Jerusalem church were sent to Antioch with Paul and Barnabas as bearers of the official letter.

The matter of not eating meat originally sacrificed to idols stands first among the four rules and thus was held to be particularly important. Paul, too, dwells on this subject at length in 1 Cor. 8, though in a more liberal spirit. Gentile Christians, like Jews, were to avoid buying such meat in public markets or accepting invitations to banquets where it might be served. Jewish laws also excluded many kinds of pagan sacrificial victims (such as the pig or wild animals) from permitted foods, but there is no indication here that these were

And they called Barnabas, Jupiter; and Paul, Mercurius, because he was the chief speaker. Then the priest of Jupiter, which was before their city, brought oxen and garlands unto the gates, and would have done sacrifice with the people.

(ACTS 14 : 12–13)

(*Above*) Relief found at Rome, showing a slave leading a garlanded bull.

(*Left*) The Jupiter Veraspi, a Roman copy of a Greek original, now in the Vatican.

That ye abstain from meats offered to idols . . . (ACTS 15 : 29)

Detail from a Roman sarcophagus, showing the sacrifice of a cock to Dionysus. Second century A.D.

forbidden to Christians. A detail from a second-century A.D. Roman sarcophagus shows the sacrifice of a cock on an altar in front of the statue of the bearded god Dionysus.

On his second missionary journey Paul was not accompanied by Barnabas, who instead went to Crete with Mark, but by another companion, Silas. They journeyed on foot through Syria and Cilicia, visiting the congregations previously established in Asia Minor. Led by the Holy Spirit, they came to Troas on the Aegean Sea. In the night Paul had a vision in which a man from Macedonia called him to come over and help them. This meant taking the fateful step of extending his sphere of activity to the continent of Europe.

Crossing the Aegean, Paul disembarked at the harbor of Neapolis, and proceeded thence over the Egnatian Road ten miles to the Roman colony of Philippi, the first place in Europe where the Christian Gospel was preached. Philippi had been founded in 357 B.C. by Philip II of Macedonia, father of Alexander the Great, on the site of an older settlement. Owing to the presence of gold-mines in the nearby Strymon valley, the town prospered until it became the chief city of the district, though not its capital. In 42 B.C. Cassius and Brutus, who had slain Julius Caesar, were defeated there by the army of Mark Antony and Gaius Octavius (the future Caesar Augustus). In gratitude for his victory Augustus later granted Philippi the privileged status of a Roman colony.

Philippi had a Jewish community whose place of prayer was situated near the river. A woman called Lydia, who came from Thyatyra in Asia Minor and was evidently a Jewish convert, accepted Christianity and gave hospitality to Paul and his companions. The healing of a slave girl, who had a spirit of divination, robbed her owners of a source of profit and led them to seize Paul and Silas and accuse them before the Roman magistrates. The two were illegally beaten (as a Roman citizen Paul was theoretically exempt from such rough justice, which was reserved for natives) and imprisoned. Freed from their confinement on the following day, they left the city. Paul's later return to Philippi (Acts 20: 3–6) and the Epistle to the Philippians prove that Christianity took root in the city at the time of his first visit.

Proceeding from Philippi along the Egnatian Road in the direction of Thessalonica, Paul and his companions passed through Amphipolis and, twenty-eight miles farther west, Apollonia. Finally they reached Thessalonica (modern Salonika), the harbor city of Macedonia. From Thessalonica the group traveled to Beroea. In both cities they had some success until driven out by aroused Jews. They then sailed—probably from Pydna, the nearest harbor—to Athens.

Although the Athens visited by Paul was but a shadow of its former glory, it was still the intellectual capital of Greece, celebrated for its splendid monuments, in particular the famous temples on the Acropolis—the Parthenon and the Erechtheion, with the steps leading up to the monumental entrance, the Propylaea, in between—and for its schools of philosophy and of art. Near the Acropolis was the rocky "hill of Ares" (Areopagus), which rises sixty feet

And from thence to Philippi, which is the chief city of that part of Macedonia, and a colony . . .   (ACTS 16: 12)

The ruins of the market place of Philippi.

And they took him, and brought him unto Areopagus . . . (ACTS 17 : 19)

above the valley encircling the Acropolis, with traces of altars, seats, and tiers of steps still visible on its slopes. According to Greek legend it was here that Orestes was tried for and acquitted of the crime of matricide. In classical times the supreme court of Athens sat here. It seems probable, however, that what Paul addressed on the Areopagus was an informal meeting of philosophers, curious to hear the new teaching, rather than a formal session of a court. The Acts do not refer to any charge brought against the apostle during his stay at Athens, and the philosophical tone of the discourse which he delivered on this occasion fits this supposition.

In beginning his address Paul referred to having seen at Athens an altar inscribed "to the unknown god". Of this god, he declared, he was a spokesman. Both altar and inscription have intrigued scholars and invite comment.

The polytheistic beliefs of the ancient world embraced a host of gods, some of them universally known deities residing in their heavenly abode, others personified forces of nature or moral qualities, and still others associated with certain places or natural objects. All these supernatural forces had to be propitiated by offerings at altars or prayers; according to the primitive magical conception which persisted even among the sophisticated Greeks and Romans, the pronouncing of the right name of a god or goddess in prayer gave the worshiper power over the deity and thus made him amenable to his wishes. It was, therefore, very important to know the right names of the god from among the bewildering plethora of appellations handed down by tradition. In order to avoid any possibility of omission of the right name, deities were addressed in such general and comprehensive terms as "whether thou be god or goddess", or "the unknown god". No remains of an inscription exactly like the one referred to by Paul have so far been discovered, but in the excavations of the city of Pergamon in Asia Minor an altar has been found dedicated "to unknown gods".

316

From Athens, Paul proceeded to Corinth, then the capital of Achaia, the Roman province of Greece. As the principal harbor and trading city of that country, Corinth had attracted a Jewish community, which built for itself a synagogue.

As in the other places where Paul's missionary zeal had led to a schism in the Jewish community, the dispute at Corinth ended before the civil authorities; but in this case, since Corinth was the capital of a province, the final arbiter was the proconsul or governor. Gallio's *cognomen* alone is used in Acts; his full name was Marcus Annaeus Gallio; he was the brother of the philosopher Seneca and perished with him under Nero. In Paul's case Gallio's famous judgment. "If it be a question of words and names, and of your law, look ye to it; for I will be no judge of such matters" is a reflection of the prevailing Stoic philosophy of the Roman administration.

An inscription found at Delphi contains a transcript of a letter of the Emperor Claudius in which Gallio is referred to; as the letter was written late in A.D. 51 or in the first half of A.D. 52, it helps to establish the chronology of Paul's travels by fixing the time within which his visit to Corinth must have taken place. The case against Paul was probably brought before the proconsul in the agora, where archaeologists have found a construction which would be

For as I passed by, and beheld your devotions, I found an altar with this inscription, TO THE UNKNOWN GOD . . . (ACTS 17: 23)

Altar dedicated to anonymous gods, found at Pergamon, Asia Minor.

After these things Paul departed from Athens, and came to
Corinth . . . And he reasoned in the synagogue every Sabbath . . .
(ACTS 18 : 1, 4)

View of the agora, Corinth.

a remnant of a proconsular *bema* or *tribunal*; it is also possible, however, that one of the
basilicas adjoining the market place was used for the purpose of the hearing.

From Corinth, Paul left Europe and proceeded to Ephesus, the capital of the Roman
province of Asia (although its proconsul still resided at Pergamon). He visited the synagogue, but soon left for Palestine and thence returned to Antioch.

After spending some time at Antioch, Paul began his third journey, revisiting the Asia
Minor churches, but making Ephesus his main objective. The usual beginnings there in the
synagogue were followed by the inevitable eviction. Paul consequently transferred his place
of instruction to the "school" (*scholē*, "lecture hall") of one Tyrannus, where he continued
teaching for two years.

One of the most striking results of Paul's preaching at Ephesus was the conversion of a
large number of people who had been dabbling in magic arts, a common phenomenon in
times of religious decline. These converts collected and burned their magic books in public.

During Paul's stay at Ephesus he remained unmolested until he came into conflict with
the powerful guild of silversmiths, who were preparing votive reproductions of the temple

And when they heard these sayings, they were full of wrath, and cried out, saying, Great is Diana of the Ephesians! And the whole city was filled with confusion: and having caught Gaius and Aristarchus, men of Macedonia, Paul's companions in travel, they rushed with one accord into the theater.

(ACTS 19 : 28–29)

(*Above*) Remains of the theater at Ephesus.

(*Left*) Image of the Diana of Ephesus.

of the great goddess of the city, the Diana of Ephesus, for the many pilgrims who came to visit her shrine. Diana (or Artemis) of Ephesus was an Asiatic fertility goddess who, though identified with the Artemis of the Greeks, was actually quite different in character. The focal-point of her cult was a stone in the temple supposed originally to have fallen from heaven. Later statues of the goddess, found in many places, show her standing with her arms outstretched, clad in a closely clinging dress, upon which the images of many other gods are drawn in relief. The pendants hanging on her front are held by some scholars to represent many breasts, symbolizing the fecundity of nature; others regard them as merely ornaments. The outraged worshipers of the goddess collected in the theater, the usual place of assembly for the masses in Greek cities. The theater of Ephesus has been excavated: the remains of the stage and orchestra, with some of the seats rising tier upon tier behind them, are still plainly visible.

Thanks to the intervention of some well-disposed officials, the people were calmed and Paul left Ephesus alive.

From Ephesus Paul went to Macedonia and Greece, visiting the congregations he had

And there sat in a window a certain young man named Eutychus, being fallen into a deep sleep: and as Paul was long preaching, he sunk down with sleep, and fell down from the third loft, and was taken up dead. (ACTS 20: 9)

established in those quarters. A plot was made against him by the Jews when he was about to sail from Corinth to Syria, and so he decided to return via Macedonia. He was attended by a number of men who, as we know from his letters, accompanied him on account of the collection he had raised in his churches for the poor at Jerusalem. The group proceeded on to Troas, while Paul lingered to celebrate the Passover at Philippi, catching up with them shortly thereafter. After seven days at Troas, where Paul revived a young man who had fallen from the window of one of the tall blocks of dwelling-houses common in the crowded Roman cities, Paul walked alone to Asos where he rejoined the rest of the party traveling by boat. They sailed past Ephesus to Miletus where Paul summoned and addressed the elders of the church at Ephesus, and thence to Rhodes and Patara in Lycia. Here a different ship was taken to Tyre and on to Ptolemais (Old Testament Acco, the Acre of the Crusaders). A day's foot journey from this port brought them to Caesarea, where they stayed at the house of the deacon Philip. Here the prophet Agabus brought word to Paul from Jerusalem not to go up to that city, since bonds awaited him there. Under a higher compulsion to go, no matter what might befall him, Paul persisted.

View of the city of Ptolemais.

And when we had finished our course from Tyre, we came to
Ptolemais, and saluted the brethren . . .   (ACTS 21 : 7)

At Jerusalem Paul was warmly received at first by James and the elders, but the assembled
elders on the second day quickly took him to task: his attention was called to the fact that
the many thousands of converted Jews, all zealous for the Law, had been told that he was
teaching all the Jews living among the Gentiles to forsake Moses. He must prove to them
that such was not the case. They gave him an opportunity to do so by taking over the
responsibility for four men who had made a vow but were too poor to bear the ritual expense
of fulfilling it. Paul agreed to associate with the men, to purify himself along with them, and
to pay their incidental expenses. This caused him to linger longer at Jerusalem than he
probably had intended, and to go several times to the Temple. On the final visit made
necessary by his undertaking, he was recognized by some Jews from Asia. Having earlier
seen him in Jerusalem in company with a Gentile from Ephesus they raised the false charge
that he had brought this man into the sacred area of the Temple.

Like most ancient temples that of Jerusalem was partitioned into various sectors, with
different regulations governing admission to each. The so-called "house" could be approached
only by priests, and the innermost shrine of the house, the Holy of Holies, could only be
entered by the high priest, and by him only once a year on the day of Atonement. Male
Israelites could enter the Inner Court, in which the "house" and altar stood. Women could
go only as far as the Women's Court, the outer of the two courts of the Inner Temple.
Gentiles were free to enter the Temple esplanade up to the low barrier encircling the Inner

Warning inscription from the
Inner Temple at Jerusalem.

*Crying out, Men of Israel, help: This is the man that teacheth all men every
where against the people, and the law, and this place; and further brought Greeks
also into the temple, and hath polluted this holy place.* (ACTS 21 : 28)

Temple, but might not pass beyond into the Women's Court. Any infringement of these
regulations was by Roman permission punishable by death. In order to prevent incidents,
inscriptions were set up outside the barrier of the Inner Temple warning non-Jews against
trespassing. One such inscription was found in 1870. It reads: "Let no one of the Gentiles
enter inside the barrier around this sanctuary and the porch; and if he transgresses he shall
himself bear the blame for his ensuing DEATH."

Inflamed by the false accusation the enraged worshipers set upon Paul and tried to kill
him. He was saved by the intervention of a troop of Roman soldiers commanded by a
tribune, who arrested him and took him to the "castle". Before being taken indoors Paul
received permission to address the crowds from the steps leading up to this building
(Acts 21 : 40).

The castle referred to was the fortress called Antonia, adjoining the Temple at its north-
western corner. In the time of the Judaean monarchy, the saddle connecting the Temple
Mount with the hills to the north of it was fortified by the towers of Meah and of Hananiah.
In Nehemiah's day a fortress bearing the Persian name *Baris* (*Birah* in Hebrew) stood there.
This was strengthened by the Hasmonaeans and for a time served as a royal residence. When
Herod transferred his palace to the northwest corner of the Upper City, he refortified the
Baris and named it Antonia, in honor of the triumvir Mark Antony (82–30 B.C.), who was
at that time the ruler of the Orient. The renewed fortress consisted of four high towers, not
symmetrical in shape, with an interior court; the latter is sometimes supposed to be the

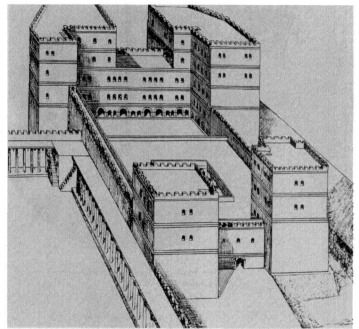

Reconstruction of the
Antonia fortress.

lithostroton mentioned in the Gospel of John (see above, p. 293). Since the Antonia, with its
commanding position and massive walls, dominated the Temple, it was garrisoned with
Roman troops. From it they could intervene quickly in case of any tumult in the Temple
court, as the fortress communicated by stairs both with the court itself and with the roofs
of the porticoes surrounding it.

Receiving information of a plot to assassinate Paul, the Roman commander at Jerusalem
sent him secretly by night to Caesarea, the official seat of the governor. He provided him
with a very strong escort: two hundred soldiers, seventy horsemen, and two hundred
"spearmen". Paul and his escort probably went down by the usual route via Beth-Horon
(called by Josephus the "public road"), and thence by way of Lydda to Antipatris. This city,
the Biblical Aphek, had in Hellenistic times been called "Pegae" (the "Springs"). On its site
Herod built Antipatris, naming it in honor of his father Antipater; the name remained until
the end of the ancient period, although the city had by then lost its importance. It was a
convenient stopping-place on the road from Jerusalem to the coast.

In Caesarea Paul was brought before the Roman governor of the province, Felix, who
held a hearing at which Jews from Jerusalem brought accusation. Felix rendered no decision,
but kept him in custody for two years. While under arrest at Caesarea, Paul was not kept

Coin of Agrippa II.
First century A.D.

And after certain days, king Agrippa and Bernice came unto
Caesarea to salute Festus . . .   (ACTS 25 : 13)

in close confinement and was able to continue his missionary activity. In A.D. 55 (or according to some authorities A.D. 60) Felix was succeeded by Portius Festus, who re-examined
Paul's case. When he sought to have the trial transferred to Jerusalem, Paul appealed to
Caesar. A visit of king Herod Agrippa II and his sister Bernice gave Festus an opportunity
to bring Paul before them and to get Agrippa's opinion.

Agrippa II was the son of king Herod (Agrippa I), of Acts 12: 1f., but on the death
of his father was considered too young to rule. In A.D. 50 he was at last made ruler of
Chalcis, but in A.D. 53 received instead the tetrarchy of Philip. In A.D. 54 parts of Galilee
and of Jewish Trans-Jordan were added to his domain. He was also entrusted with the
supervision of the Temple in Jerusalem, including the right of appointing the high priest.
At the beginning of his reign Agrippa II showed some independence, and even struck coins
with his portrait. At the outbreak of the war with the Romans he tried to pacify his Jewish
subjects. Failing in that, he sided with the Romans and succeeded in keeping his realm; but
he had to witness the destruction of the Temple and of the Holy City.

When Paul stood up to address Agrippa, "he stretched forth his hand to answer for
himself". Gestures played a particularly important part in the studied rhetoric of speakers in
popular assemblies and of preachers, whether philosophical or religious. In the many ancient
works of art representing orators they usually appear with one arm raised, as in the statue
of an Etruscan speaker, one Avle Metle, of about 100 B.C., who is shown addressing a
meeting with hand uplifted. This was evidently the gesture appropriate for the beginning
of a discourse.

Then Paul stretched forth the hand, and answered for himself.   (ACTS 26: 1)

Agrippa's verdict on hearing Paul was that he could have been set free if he had not appealed to Caesar.

The right of appeal to the Roman people against a judicial sentence had been one of the most cherished privileges of Romans in the time of the Republic; and when the Republic was abolished (in fact, although not in theory) the hearing of appeals was transferred from the people to the emperor, who supposedly personified popular sovereignty. As Paul was still a prisoner, he had to be accompanied by an armed guard; besides, we learn from Acts that he was not the only prisoner being sent to Rome.

The officer in charge of the escort was a centurion of one of the cohorts stationed in Judaea which had the honor to bear the appellation "Augustan", probably with some addition indicating its place of recruitment, as in the case of other such units, e.g. "the Augustan cohort of the Sebastenes". The centurions were dependable men to whom such delicate missions could be entrusted; moreover, they were usually Italians, and Julius was no doubt well pleased at the chance of visiting his home town after safely delivering his prisoners. The embarkation took place at Caesarea, but the ship was from the city of Adramyttium, a harbor in Mysia

Hellenistic statue of an Etruscan orator. First century B.C.

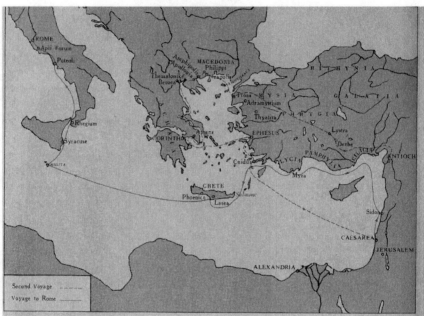

And when it was determined that we should sail into Italy, they delivered Paul and certain other prisoners unto one named Julius, a centurion of Augustus' band. And entering into a ship of Adramyttium . . . (ACTS 27: 1–2)

(Asia Minor, near Troas). Probably there was no ship sailing directly to Italy from Caesarea at the time, which, from the subsequent story, was probably late in the autumn of A.D. 60. As Judaea was not among the provinces sending regular supplies to Rome, westward-bound vessels calling there must have been somewhat rare, especially so close to the approach of winter, when Mediterranean shipping stopped altogether.

Proceeding along the coasts of Phoenicia, Syria, and Cilicia, the ship finally reached the port of Myra on the coast of Lycia; from there it probably sailed along the coast of Ionia to its home town before the onset of winter. At Myra the centurion transferred his charges to another vessel, most probably a bigger one, which was *en route* from Alexandria to Italy. This was one of the principal trade routes of the Mediterranean in Paul's time. The populace of Rome depended for the free distribution of the grain to which it was accustomed on the two great grain-producing countries of the Empire, North Africa, and especially Egypt. The interruption of this supply could provoke riots in Rome and endanger the safety of the emperor and his court. No wonder therefore that, in spite of the late season of the year, ships were still sailing from Alexandria, the great harbor of Roman Egypt, to Italy. Unwilling to risk the open sea, the captain of this ship naturally hugged the coast and so came to Myra, where his new passengers awaited him.

A big merchant ship of antiquity is represented on a sarcophagus from Sidon; in contrast to the naval vessels, which also had oarsmen, such merchantmen used only sail-power. Generous provision was made for storage capacity, the passengers being accommodated, as far as possible, in a cabin on the poop or on the forecastle.

The frail craft of antiquity were an easy prey to the storms which swept across the Mediterranean from time to time. If we bear in mind that the largest vessel of which we hear in ancient times was about 1,500 tons—an Alexandrian wheat-ship driven into port by rough weather—and that a boat of 30 tons is already called a "ship" in the *Mishnah*, we can understand the nature of ancient seamanship. Navigation was entirely by the stars or the sun, without any of the instrumental aids, such as the compass, which were known in the

And there the centurion found a ship of Alexandria sailing into Italy; and he put us therein.
(ACTS 27: 6)

(*Right*) Painting found at Ostia, showing the loading of an Egyptian grain-ship. Third century A.D.

(*Below*) Large merchant ship, represented on sarcophagus from Sidon.

And we being exceedingly tossed with a tempest . . .
(ACTS 27: 18)

Middle Ages; there was no possibility of ascertaining the position of the ship on cloudy
nights. The saying of the Roman poet Horace that "he who dares to cross the sea must have
a heart bound in brass" sums up the whole ancient attitude toward navigation. A Roman
relief of the third century shows a series of ships being tossed by a storm, a predicament
which the ancient seamen tried to avoid at all costs. The ship on which Paul traveled must
have been fairly large, as it had 276 passengers and crew.

Driven helplessly for a long time before a northeasterly gale, Paul's ship was finally
wrecked on the island of Melita (now Malta). Everyone on board was saved, although the
ship itself was a total loss. The traditional place where the passengers came ashore is the
so-called St. Paul's Creek.

But not long after there arose against it a tempestuous
wind, called Euroclydon.   (ACTS 27: 14)

And when they were escaped, then they knew that the island was called Melita. And the barbarous people shewed us no little kindness . . .

                (ACTS 28 : 1–2)

View of St. Paul's Creek, Malta.

Malta is the largest of a group of five islands at the eastern end of the strait between Sicily and Tunis. It has been inhabited since prehistoric times, but the first settlers of whom we have historical information were the Phoenicians of Carthage. Their Semitic language, a dialect of Phoenician, is still spoken on the island and was also written there in antiquity. Evidence of the mixed culture of ancient Melita, which became part of the Roman Empire after the Punic Wars, is provided by the bilingual inscription on the base of a dedicatory obelisk found there. The upper part is written in the Phoenician script; the bottom three lines are in Greek and contain a dedication by two Tyrians to Heracles (Melkarth), the national god of Tyre. The "barbarous" character of the people of Melita, referred to in Acts 28 : 2, applies to their language and culture (which were non-Hellenic and therefore uncouth in the eyes of the Greek-speaking people of Paul's time), but by no means to their manners, which are attested here to have been surprisingly gentle.

In Melita the travelers found another wheat-ship, also from Alexandria, which was luckier than their own vessel—or perhaps had a more prudent captain—and which had remained in harbor there, awaiting the passing of the winter season. Its captain no doubt judged it better to deliver his cargo late than to risk its total loss at sea. After three months, he ventured out and completed his voyage successfully.

Dedicatory obelisk, found in Malta.

The port of Puteoli, from
a Pompeian painting.

*And we came the next day to Puteoli . . .
they came to meet us as far as Appii forum, and
The three taverns . . . And when we came to
Rome, the centurion delivered the prisoners to
the captain of the guard . . .*

(ACTS 28 : 13, 15, 16)

View of the Appian Way.

Paul's journeyings ended safely at
Puteoli (modern Pozzuoli), the harbor
of ancient Rome, north of Naples. A
landscape on a Pompeian painting is
presumed to show the port of Puteoli,
with its moles and shipping. From
Puteoli the party traveled to Rome by
the Appian Way, the "Queen of the
Roman Roads". The hamlet of the Forum
was forty miles from Rome, about
one-third of the whole distance from
Puteoli. Nearer Rome both sides of the
road were lined with funerary monuments. In Rome, Paul was able to live in
his own rented dwelling for two years,
with one soldier guarding him, and
could establish contact with the local
Jewish community and receive visitors,
thus continuing his apostolate. At this
point the story of Acts terminates.

Roman relief showing members
of the Praetorian Guard.

THE EPISTLES

THE TWO GROUPS OF LETTERS

THE FOUR GOSPELS, giving an account of the life, teaching, and death of Jesus, are followed as we have seen by the Acts of the Apostles, which relates the story of the early days of Christianity up to Paul's ministry in Rome. The New Testament then spreads before the reader fourteen Epistles attributed to Paul and another seven attributed to leaders of the Primitive Church, two of them disciples (Peter and John) and two of them "brethren" of the Lord Jesus (James and Jude).

The Epistles of Paul are put at the head of the list in our modern Bibles, and the one to the Romans, his supreme effort in Christian thinking, stands first. The two Epistles to the Corinthians rank next because of their length and importance, and are followed by the one to the Galatians which, though short, is of great weight. The so-called Epistle to the Ephesians, a remarkable Early Christian document, is controversial in that many doubt its direct authorship by Paul. Philippians and Colossians were written in captivity. The Epistles to the Thessalonians reveal Paul's message at an earlier stage of his ministry than the others. The Epistles to Timothy and Titus—which are called the Pastoral Epistles—are again controversial as to authorship; many scholars believe the writer is using Paul's name as a pseudonym, according to a custom very common in antiquity. If they were authentic one would have to suppose that Paul was freed from his Roman captivity and traveled about again, for the allusions to his journeys cannot be reconciled with the Book of Acts. Philemon is a brief personal letter, written at the same time as Colossians. The Epistle to the Hebrews

Paul, a servant of Jesus Christ, called to be an apostle, separated unto the gospel of God.
(ROM. I: I)

Part of a codex of the Pauline Epistles. Third century A.D.

is attributed to Paul in the title of some manuscripts (such as those used in the King James Version) on the strength of Eastern tradition which originally was disputed in the West. But the thought and the literary style are so un-Pauline that the claim is untenable; the author is unknown. It is, however, the most eloquent piece of writing in the New Testament and has had a great influence.

The other seven Epistles are called "General" (literally "Catholic"). This was probably due to the fact that such important ones as the Epistle of James and the First Epistle of Peter were addressed to a widespread audience, and were like "encyclicals". In the Second Epistle of Peter the address is vague and purely a matter of form. The First Epistle of John is anonymous and begins more like a tract than a letter. The Second and Third Epistles of John, however, are addressed respectively to a congregation, which is not named, and to an individual; the author identifies himself only as "the Elder". The Epistle of Jude has an address similar to that of 2 Peter. The use of the names of authors in James, 1 and 2 Peter, and Jude is regarded by many as pseudonymous.

The Epistles, particularly those of Paul, contain much that reflects the Hellenistic-Roman world. The points picked out here and topically discussed have been chosen largely because they lend themselves to helpful illustration.

Paul, called to be an apostle of Jesus Christ through the will of God, and Sosthenes our brother, Unto the church of God which is at Corinth . . .

(I COR. I: 1–2)

View of modern Corinth

*I am debtor both to the Greeks, and to
the Barbarians . . .* (ROM. I : 14)

(*Left*) Head of a Greek, from a mausoleum of
Halicarnassos. Fourth century B.C.

(*Right*) Head of a Cyrenian barbarian. First century
A.D.

SOCIAL STRUCTURE OF THE HELLENISTIC WORLD

WHEN THINKING FROM a Hellenistic-Roman point of view Paul can divide
humanity into two sections: Greeks and barbarians (Rom. I : 14). The term
"Greeks", as used here, is not confined to the Greek or Hellenic nation which produced the
Greek culture, but rather encompasses all who had accepted that culture when it was spread
across the world in the so-called Hellenistic period (from 336 B.C.). One of the factors which
aided this spread of Hellenism was the absence of any racial or religious discrimination in
the Hellenistic world; a man was judged only by the degree of his adoption of Hellenic
culture. Paul himself was, to a great extent, an inheritor of the Greek tradition, as were most
of the Jews living in the Diaspora. The growth of Christianity was, from the first, greatly
helped by the uniform culture, including language and literature, thus created by Hellenism.
Those not sharing the Hellenistic culture were classed as "barbarians". Paul declares himself
a debtor to both Greeks and barbarians (Rom. I : 14). They are represented here by a statue
of a typical Greek from a mausoleum of Halicarnassos, fourth century B.C., and by the
bronze head of a Cyrenian barbarian, the work of a Greek artist in the first century A.D.

All the saints salute you, chiefly they that are of Caesar's household.
(PHIL. 4: 22)

Bust of Salvius,
found near Rome.

But another sharp division ran through that world to an even greater degree than it had run through the ancient Orient: that between slave and freeman. Aristocratic Roman households contained hundreds of slaves, some of whom labored in the personal service of their master and others on his estates. In several cases, slaves were even allowed to set up in a trade or craft, paying part of their profits to their owner. The imperial household was, from the time of Augustus to that of Trajan, constructed on the aristocratic Roman model, but on a vastly larger scale. It contained literally thousands of slaves, some of whom, especially those who succeeded in obtaining their freedom, rose to key political positions. They in fact constituted the civil service of the Early Empire and, as such, wielded almost absolute powers in the emperor's name. In this large community of slaves, many of whom came from Greece and the Orient, early Christianity found a foothold, especially because of its appeal to those of low social status. The bust of Salvius, the emperor Tiberius' official in charge of the silver plate (*"Salvius Caesari servus supra argentum"*), which was found in the Second

Columbarium (cemetery) of the Vigna Codini on the Appian Way, near Rome, gives a fair idea of the dignified appearance of some of these palace slaves.

Indeed, the powerful human appeal of Christianity, as taught by Paul, lay in its complete disregard of the social hierarchy of the Early Roman Empire. To the various new Christian communities, which were composed of mixed groups of people from different nations and different religions, each regarding the other with suspicion and occasionally with contempt, the apostle stresses their unity in the new faith (Col. 3 : 11). Greeks who regarded the rest of the world as barbarians, Jews who drew a sharp distinction between those who had entered the covenant of Abraham and all others, and barbarians who suffered from inferior status because of their lack of Greek culture (including even the most savage of them, the uncouth Scythians)—all could equally hope for redemption. So could even the slaves, who had lost their freedom and had to labor hard in this world but would participate in the salvation of Paradise.

The manual tasks performed by slave labor are illustrated by a Roman relief, showing the placing of blocks on a sumptuous funeral monument in the form of a temple; the work is being carried out with the aid of a machine consisting of a high mast with ropes attached to it

Where there is neither Greek nor Jew, circumcision nor uncircumcision, Barbarian, Scythian, bond nor free . . .
(COL. 3 : 11)

Roman relief showing the building of a funeral monument. From the tomb of the Haterii, Rome. First century A.D.

335

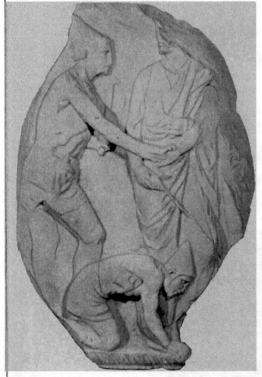

Roman relief, showing slaves
being freed. First century A.D.

*Being justified freely by his grace through
the redemption that is in Christ Jesus.*
(ROM. 3 : 24)

by pulleys, the motive force being
supplied by a treadmill worked by
the exertions of slaves. The relief
comes from the tomb of the Haterii
at Rome, from the first century A.D.

But not all slaves were doomed
to remain in bondage; some were
liberated. In Rom. 3 : 24 Paul
speaks of "the redemption that is
in Christ Jesus", i.e. salvation
through faith in Christ, Paul's
central point. The original meaning
of the Greek word translated
"redemption" (*apolytrosis*) is the
ransoming of a slave. The institution
of slavery is recognized both in the
Old and New Testament, as it was in the whole of the ancient world. However, all ancient
religions, as well as systems of law, conceded that, just as a free man could become enslaved,
so a slave could regain his freedom. Jewish Law did not allow the enslavement of a Hebrew
to continue beyond the sabbatical year (Exod. 21 : 2–6). In Greek religion the setting free
of a slave was regarded as a pious act, as is shown by the many inscriptions at Delphi commemorating such emancipations. Roman law, too, made provision for the freeing of a slave,
either by payment of a sum of money or by the last will and testament of his master. Certain
ceremonies had to be performed to make such a manumission valid; they are portrayed on
a relief from the first century A.D., in which two slaves are being freed. One of them, already
a free man, shakes the hand of his former owner; the other is kneeling to be touched by the
magistrate's rod (*vindicta*) as a sign of his release. Both are wearing the *pileus*, the high cap
worn by freemen.

Roman relief showing a physician.

For I bear him record, that he hath a great zeal for you, and them that are in Laodicea, and them in Hierapolis. Luke, the beloved physician, and Demas, greet you.

(COL. 4 : 13–14)

However, not all early Christians were from the lower classes; the Church included amongst its earliest converts many members of the professions. Foremost among these was "Luke, the beloved physician" (Col. 4 : 14), identified by ancient tradition with the evangelist and author of Acts. Luke's profession was highly esteemed in the Greek and Roman world; some of its practitioners, especially the physicians of the reigning emperor, were able to do great services to their native towns and were honored by them. In a relief on the tombstone of a physician named Jason, who lived in the Roman period, we see him "auscultating" or listening to the body sounds of a patient.

EDUCATION

IN THE COMPLEX world of Hellenistic culture, a man's social status was determined, above all, by his education. It was therefore extremely important to go to the right teachers from the beginning. The rich could engage a special slave, called a "pedagogue" (lit. "leader of children"), to take care of the education of their offspring.

Paul several times speaks figuratively of the pedagogue (1 Cor. 4 : 15, Gal. 3 : 24, "instructor" or "schoolmaster"). Such a teacher is portrayed on a Greek vase of the fifth century B.C.—an oldish, balding man, with a thick beard, wearing a laurel wreath on his brow as a sign of his dedication to Apollo, the god of poetry. He is instructing his (invisible) pupils with outstretched right hand, in

Pedagogue represented on a Greek vase. Fifth century B.C.

An instructor of the foolish, a teacher of babes . . . (ROM. 2 : 20)

337

Fragment of Temple inscription, found at Jerusalem.

Metal ink-pot and pen.

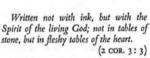

Written not with ink, but with the Spirit of the living God; not in tables of stone, but in fleshy tables of the heart.
(2 COR. 3 : 3)

which he is holding a stylus (a pointed writing implement), his left hand behind his back, and his rod leaning against his chair.

After completing their elementary education, more advanced pupils were entrusted to a teacher of rhetoric, which then included literature and the art of expressing oneself in writing and speech.

In contrasting the pagan and the Christian ways of life Paul uses a metaphor drawn from the sphere of writing. He speaks of what is written in the ordinary way and of what is engraved on the tablets of the heart (2 Cor. 3 : 3). He contrasts the testimony of the spirit with the various kinds of material records common in his time. Writing that was meant to last was done on papyrus or parchment with reed or bronze pens which had split nibs rather like their modern counterparts. The ink was kept in metal or faience ink-pots, with narrow openings or with covers to prevent the contents from spilling. But still more permanent in character was writing engraved on stone or bronze tablets, on which the ancients used to chisel out the dedications of both religious and civic buildings, as well as treaties, laws, and epitaphs; as the metal tablets have mostly perished, the bulk of the surviving specimens of ancient epigraphy is in the form of engraving on stone. A fragment of the Temple inscription found at Jerusalem, forbidding Gentiles on pain of death to pass beyond a certain point in the Temple Court is a fairly good example of this kind of writing, with the guiding-lines and the paint inside the letters still visible.

Religious education of the young is urged in the words addressed to fathers to bring the children up in the discipline and instruction of the LORD (Eph. 6: 4). As Christianity adjusted itself to a prolonged existence of the present order, increasing attention was paid to this matter. No doubt the famous saying of Jesus, "Suffer the little children to come unto me" (Mark 10: 14), had an influence. But the Hellenistic-Roman world was inclined to give children greater attention in connection with worship than was the case with the Jews. A common artistic motif in antiquity is that of children worshiping Greek gods. Another favorite subject of ancient art was the portrayal of children (usually identified with Cupid or Amor, the child-god of Love and son of Venus), practicing the various professions or in general behaving like grown-ups; the contrast between the children's diminutive figures

Little children, keep yourselves from idols . . .   (1 JOHN 5 : 21)

Roman fresco, showing children worshiping Diana.

Prayers . . . be made for all men . . . for kings and for all that are in authority . . .

(I TIM. 2: 1-2)

Roman portrait of
the emperor Nero.

and the mature seriousness of their acts was found especially attractive. The painting discovered at Rome in which children are seen sacrificing to Diana and forming a procession in honor of Dionysus might well have been executed in the same spirit.

GOVERNMENT AND LAW

PAUL, THROUGH HIS experience as a traveler and the protection that had been afforded him in particular instances by Roman law, had an appreciation of the value of the Roman State (cf. Rom. 13: 1-7). He sets forth the belief that existing authority is divinely ordained, and that rebellion against it is rebellion against God. A Christian is to subordinate himself to those set over him. When he wrote in this vein to the Romans *c.* A.D. 58/59 the Roman State had not yet taken a definitely anti-Christian position. Nero had ascended the throne in A.D. 54. For the first five years of his reign his ministers governed well for him; it was only later that he began a career of tyranny and debauchery which rendered his name infamous. Besides liquidating the members of his own family one by one and terrorizing the whole aristocracy, he made himself still more odious to serious-minded Romans by his aspirations to shine as poet and singer. After the great fire in Rome in A.D. 64, during which he appeared as a vocal artist commemorating the fall of Troy, he directed popular suspicion away from himself as the arsonist by persecuting the Christians. Paul seems to have lost his life in this persecution.

In the First Epistle to the Corinthians, Paul asks whether he should come to them with the rod or with love, in a spirit of gentleness (1 Cor. 4: 21). In alluding to the rod he may be thinking of the rod of the magistrates. The use of the rod to enforce judicial sentences, and in general to uphold the authority of magistrates and courts, was common in antiquity. The Mosaic Law had on several occasions (e.g. Deut. 25: 3) prescribed flogging, a punishment Paul himself had undergone (2 Cor. 11: 24). The Roman magistrates also relied on the use of the rod to punish anyone who opposed their authority; indeed, the bundles of rods (*fasces*) carried in front of the magistrates by their attendants, the lictors (usually freedmen), were the symbol of their power, as shown on a relief from the time of the Early Empire, found at Portogruaro near Venice. In Rome, where the magistrates' authority in capital cases was limited by the right of appeal to the people, the lictors carried the rods only; but in the provinces, where the governors wielded absolute power of life and death, they had axes

What will ye? Shall I come unto you with a rod . . .   (1 COR. 4: 21)

Lictors, on a relief found at Portogruaro near Venice.

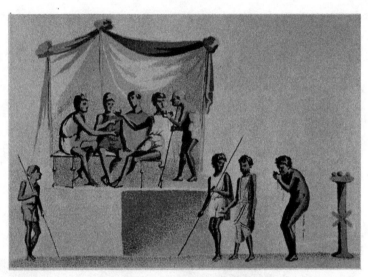

Roman *tribunal*, from a fresco found
in the dyers' quarter, Pompeii.

*Dare any of you, having a matter against another, go to law
before the unjust, and not before the saints?*   (1 COR. 6: 1)

attached to the *fasces*. The number of lictors varied in accordance with the rank of the
magistrate: praetors had six, consuls twelve, and the emperor twenty-four. They walked in
solemn procession in front of the magistrate whenever he went about his official duties.

Elsewhere in 1 Corinthians Paul expressed dissatisfaction over the fact that Church
members had had recourse to pagan tribunals instead of bringing their disputes to the heads
of the community (1 Cor. 6: 1 f.). Although the standard of justice in the Roman courts had
improved under the Empire, in comparison with the unsettled times of the Late Republic,
the various religious communities, such as the Jews, nevertheless preferred to settle disputes
between their own members in their own courts, rather than bring them before the Roman
authorities. Only in the case of outsiders or outcasts, such as Paul appeared to be in the eyes
of the leaders of the organized Jewish communities in the Diaspora, did their opponents
appeal to the Romans or the city rulers. How a Roman *tribunal* functioned we can see from
a fresco found in the dyers' quarter (the *Fullonica*) at Pompeii. The whole fresco depicts a
festivity of the dyers' guild, followed by disputes which end in a brawl. Those accused of
disturbing the peace are brought before the magistrate, who is shown sitting on his tribunal
in unofficial dress (he is wearing a tunic and not a toga), flanked by his assessors. Witnesses
are brought before him, while the court usher hales in two more of the brawlers, one of
whom is bleeding freely.

342

LIFE AND CUSTOMS

As a Roman citizen and a member of a wealthy family living in a Hellenistic city, the apostle was thoroughly familiar with the Greek way of life in which athletics played a most important part. Contests of skill in chariot-riding, racing on foot or on horseback, hurling the spear and the discus, wrestling and boxing, were held in all Greek cities and in those cities of the Orient which had adopted Greek culture. The great games at Olympia, Delphi, Argos, and Corinth drew immense crowds, and the victors, though they received no material reward apart from a crown of leaves, were nevertheless greatly honored throughout Greece. Hence the apostle, to drive home his arguments to the Corinthians, naturally draws a comparison between the self-control practiced by athletes in order to win the coveted prize and the rigorous self-discipline demanded of the Christians to attain the far greater reward of eternal salvation. The sport of boxing, to which Paul refers in 1 Cor. 9: 26, is illustrated on a vase of the fifth century B.C. Two men are seen boxing in the center, with onlookers standing by to encourage the contestants and to judge the result.

Among the subjects touched upon in the Epistles is the insistence on modest attire for

(*Right*) Boxers depicted on Greek vase. Fifth century B.C.

(*Below*) Foot race depicted on Greek vase.

Know ye not that they which run in a race run all, but one receiveth the prize? . . . Now they do it to obtain a corruptible crown; but we an incorruptible. I therefore so run, not as uncertainly; so fight I, not as one that beateth the air.

(1 COR. 9: 24–26)

(*Left*) Portrait bust, supposedly of Julia,
daughter of the emperor Titus.

(*Right*) The lady Bithnaia, on a fresco
from Dura-Europus.

women. This demand was strongly opposed to the female fashions prevailing in Roman
society in the first century A.D. which had entered on a phase of elaborate and fanciful
adornment, contrasting sharply with the simpler habits of the preceding Augustan era and
of the Antonine period which followed. Already in the time of Nero aristocratic ladies began
to pile up their hair in monstrously high, curled coiffures; and under the Flavian emperors
this fashion reached a pitch of absurdity equaled perhaps only in the eighteenth century in
Europe. A portrait bust, supposed to represent Julia the daughter of the emperor Titus,
shows her with her hair towering lock upon lock high over her forehead; such a top-heavy
structure could hardly have been held in position without inside support, probably furnished
by false hair. With such a fantastic style of hairdressing in front of us we can understand how
Roman ladies passed hours in the hands of the slaves who prepared their coiffures. This is the
"braiding of hair" mentioned in I Tim. 2: 9, I Peter 3: 3.

The wearing of costly jewelry and of gorgeous raiment, on the other hand, was not bound up with any special time or place: it has been customary in the Orient since time immemorial, as the strictures of the prophets, especially Isa. 3: 18 f., show. The lady Bithnaia portrayed in a fresco from Dura-Europus, with her high tiara, abundance of jewelry, and purple robe, is but one example of the many that could be given in this connection.

Modest appearance on the part of women, particularly veiling when praying or "prophesying", was insisted on by Paul (1 Cor. 11: 5). The raising up of the hands to heaven was the common attitude of prayer in the East, as contrasted with the covering of the head and folding of the arms in the Roman manner of supplication. In the paintings of the catacombs we find many representations of the early Christians praying with lifted hands. In one such scene we see a woman dressed in long robes, with her head veiled, and without jewels or other ornaments such as are roundly condemned in 1 Tim. 2:9. The woman on the left is wearing the long tunic or *stola* which was the principal female garment among the Romans; it has long sleeves and is adorned solely by two broad stripes of color. Over it she has in addition a mantle, the *palla*, of a darker color. Her head is modestly veiled. On the right is a youth clad in a tunic, also lifting up his hands in prayer. Many similar pictures have

I will therefore that men pray every where, lifting up holy hands, without wrath and doubting. In like manner also, that women adorn themselves in modest apparel, with shamefacedness and sobriety . . .   (1 TIM. 2: 8–9)

Woman and youth praying, from fresco in the catacomb of St. Callixtus, Rome.

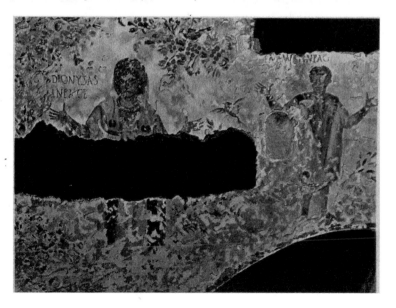

Meats for the belly, and the belly for meats . . .
(I COR. 6: 13)

Roman meal, on border of
mosaic found at Antioch.
Third century A.D,

been found in the catacombs, indicating that the teaching of the apostles bore fruit among the Christians of Rome. It should, of course, be remembered that the early adherents of Christianity were from the lower and middle classes, always more sober in their dress than the aristocracy.

Another vice to be guarded against was indulgence in sensual appetites, especially over-eating. This is probably meant by the "rioting" of Rom. 13: 13, which Paul would have his readers avoid, along with drunkenness and other evils.

The fundamental materialism of the Roman mind found its most grotesque expression in the prosperous times of the Early Empire in a spread of gluttony unparalleled in history before or since. Latin literature abounds in descriptions of the gargantuan and ingeniously devised repasts eaten by wealthy Romans, from Lucullus, whose name became proverbial, to the emperor Vitellius, whose bloated countenance and many chins betray the nature of his favorite vice. A typical Roman meal, and a relatively simple one at that, is represented on the border of a mosaic found at Antioch, dating from the third century A.D. It begins with eggs (hence the Roman saying "*ab ovo*"—lit. "from the egg", meaning from the beginning) and continues, from right to left, by way of a course of fish, ham, and poultry, to its conclusion

346

in the shape of a rich cake. To give some idea of the gastronomical titillations indulged in by many of the highest circles of the Gentile world, this meal would have to be multiplied tenfold.

Paul draws a clear distinction between two kinds of human endeavor: one for the material benefits of this world, and the other for the imperishable rewards which await the faithful in heaven.

BUILDING THE PLACES OF WORSHIP

IN REFERRING TO his work for the development and organization of the young Church, Paul compares himself to a "wise master-builder" (1 Cor. 3: 10f.). As a native of the Hellenized city of Tarsus and a great traveler all over the eastern part of the Roman Empire, Paul was familiar with the immense amount of building which was going on throughout the Roman world in the first decades of the Empire. As soon as the civil wars which had convulsed Rome in the first century B.C. ended with the establishment of the undisputed rule of Augustus, increasing prosperity in the capital and the provinces led to an outburst of constructional activity. Augustus himself boasted that he had found Rome a city of brick and had left it a city of marble, and building on a similar scale was undertaken everywhere in his time. In his simile Paul compares himself to a builder who laid the all-important foundations of an edifice, leaving it to others to complete it. With the enormous increase in the rate and scale of building the actual work of construction naturally became specialized and was divided among various contractors and workmen, one laying the foundations, another erecting the wall, a third adding the decoration. Such cooperation is

The building of the walls of Rome, from a relief found in the Roman forum. First century A.D.

According to the grace of God which is given unto me, as a wise master-builder, I have laid the foundation, and another buildeth thereon. . . .
(1 COR. 3: 10)

(*Above*) Wall-painting from Dura-Europus. Third century A.D.

(*Inset*) Plan of the church excavated at Dura-Europus.

And to our beloved Apphia, and
Archippus our fellow-soldier, and to the
church in thy house. (PHILEM. 2)

seen in the building of the walls of Rome as represented on a relief in the Roman forum, dating from the first century A.D.

An urgent problem facing the apostles and their successors was to find a safe and convenient place of meeting for the faithful. Being small in numbers, despised by the masses, occasionally persecuted by the Roman authorities, and in constant conflict with the local Jewish synagogue, the Early Christian communities were naturally not over-anxious to advertize their existence. Their places of worship were, therefore, mostly located in the interior of private houses which, if built in the then-prevailing Mediterranean style, with the rooms grouped round a courtyard and enclosed on all sides, could not easily be looked into by an unfriendly eye. There was such a church in the house of Philemon of Colossae, a man of standing and the owner of a slave, Onesimus, who ran away to Paul but was sent back to his master with a letter, the Epistle to Philemon. We can form an idea of the external appearance of such a domestic church from one of this kind uncovered in the excavations of Dura-Europus on the River Euphrates, and dating from the third century A.D. This particular church was

348

indistinguishable from a private house; it was entered from the street by way of a colonnaded court and consisted of a chapel, with walls covered by wall-paintings; a large room for the love-feast (*agape*) of the community; and an assembly hall, made by joining together two separate rooms, with a seat for the head of the community, probably a bishop. In the first centuries of the Christian era most Christian worship, even in times of relative quiet, must have taken place in such private churches.

THE CHURCHES OF THE PAGAN WORLD

T HE GREAT DEBATE between Christianity and the pagan world was conducted on all levels and ranged over doctrine, mythology, relations with the "powers that be", and ritual practices.

In his warning against false doctrine Paul (or a writer using his name) refers to the "myths and endless genealogies" of the pagans (1 Tim. 1 : 4). After their early spontaneous and free

For though there be that are called gods, whether in heaven or in earth, (as there be gods many, and lords many) . . . (1 COR. 8: 5)

(*Left*) Representation of Jupiter, from a Pompeian painting.

(*Right*) Statue of the emperor Claudius as a god.

evolution, the Greek myths were systematized by scholars, who linked them together by drawing up a genealogy of the gods in which the inhabitants of Olympus were arranged in generations and related to each other by supposed family ties. Another prolific source of myths and genealogies was the desire of every Hellenized city—and for this purpose Rome could also be counted as one—to have a Greek god or hero as its founder. In Rome especially an elaborate line of descent was fabricated. The founders of Rome, Romulus and Remus, were described as the sons of the god Mars and the Vestal Rhea Silvia; exposed in the Tiber, they were given suck by a she-wolf, till they were discovered by shepherds and brought up among them. This legend is represented on an altar found at Ostia: the she-wolf and the twins are seen below, protected by an eagle; the shepherds with their characteristic crooks are visible above them; while the god of the River Tiber watches over the twins in the lower right-hand corner of the relief. The altar has an inscription giving the date: A.D. 124.

*Neither give heed to fables
and endless genealogies . . .*
(I TIM. I : 4)

Romulus and Remus, on
an altar found at Ostia.
Second century A.D.

Sacrifice to the Egyptian goddess Isis, on a Pompeian painting.

For the time past of our life may suffice us to have wrought the will of the Gentiles, when we walked in lasciviousness, lusts, excess of wine, revellings, banquetings, and abominable idolatries.
(I PET. 4: 3)

The pagan religions of antiquity regarded man and nature as fundamentally one; the gods, men, animals, trees, the sea, and the earth were blended in such a way as to make everything in nature divine. The Hellenes, who were the leading devotees of this pantheistic creed, were enabled by it to rise to the highest peaks of a lofty idealism; but, at the same time, especially when influenced by the ancient Oriental mystery religions, they could sink into natural brutishness. Certain religious festivals in particular, at which heavy eating and drinking were the rule, could end in orgies that released man's worst instincts. In marked contrast to this pantheism both Judaism and Christianity adopted a dualistic attitude, sharply distinguishing God from the evil world, and regarding all forms of sensual indulgence as abominable idolatries to be shunned by all true believers.

Two examples of pagan orgiastic worship are reproduced here. The first is a sacrifice to Isis as depicted in a Pompeian painting. This Egyptian goddess was enormously popular with the Romans of the first century A.D., and was worshiped in particular by women. We see, in the middle, an altar with horns, on which incense is burning; worshipers approach the steps of the temple, while priests with shaven heads play the sistrum and pray on their knees.

THE EPISTLES AND THE OLD TESTAMENT

ALTHOUGH PAUL WAS against imposing ritual law on Gentile converts, the Sacred Scriptures of the Jews were the Bible of the Christian Church. In appealing to the pagan world and the Jews of the Diaspora, the Old Testament (in the Greek version known as the Septuagint) served him and other authors of the Epistles as an inexhaustible source of proof-texts and illustrations by which the faithful could be encouraged, their opponents confounded, and the doctrine of the Church confirmed.

Hellenistic speculation about the origin of sin and evil, led Hellenistic Jews to find great insight about such matters in the opening chapters of Genesis. Paul can allude to Eve's deception by the serpent's cunning as an example of how one can be led astray (2 Cor. 11: 3). But he goes far beyond this when he teaches that Adam's fall brought sin and death upon

As the serpent beguiled Eve . . .   (2 COR. 11: 3)

Adam and Eve, on a fresco
from the catacomb at Naples.

Representation of the Tabernacle, on the frieze of the Capernaum synagogue. Late second century A.D.

A minister of the sanctuary, and of the true tabernacle, which the LORD pitched, and not man.

(HEB. 8 : 2)

humanity (Rom. 5: 12–21) and when he contrasts Christ as the second Adam with the first Adam (1 Cor. 15: 21f. 45f.). Interest in the fall of man is accordingly shown also in Early Christian art, as in a fresco from the catacomb at Naples. Adam and Eve are usually standing on either side of a tree, with the serpent winding around its trunk.

The sacred antiquities of the Jews were not merely of concern to them but also intrigued Christians, especially when capable of being given an allegorical interpretation. Thus the author of the Epistle to the Hebrews compares the entry of the high priest into the Holy of Holies of the Tabernacle with Christ's passing through the greater and more perfect Tabernacle, not made with hands—that is, not of this created world—into the Holy Place, to obtain eternal redemption for man (Heb. 9: 11f.). The Tabernacle, which had been installed at Shiloh after the conquest of Canaan and had then been superseded by the Temple of Solomon, was in late times revered by the Jews as a symbol of their faith. One of the earliest representations of the Tabernacle is that found on the frieze of the Capernaum synagogue, probably from the late second century A.D. Since the discovery of the synagogue frescoes of Dura-Europus on which it is also shown it has become clear that this relief from Capernaum represents the Tabernacle in the desert. In both instances it is in the form of a temple, but here it is mounted on wheels, similar to the carriages shaped like sanctuaries in which the Romans transported the images of their gods from one place to another.

The miracles of the Old Testament also served as a source of inspiration for the early Christians, especially that performed at Rephidim, as related in Exodus (17: 1–7) and again at Meribah (Num. 20: 7–13), when Moses smote the rock and water gushed out. This miracle made a profound impression on succeeding generations; it is referred to again in Deut. 8: 15 as "water brought out of the flinty rock", and also in the poetic and prophetic literature of the Old Testament. Paul gave a symbolic interpretation of the event in 1 Cor. 10: 4, utilizing the rabbinic legend of the rock's following the wandering Israelites, and identifying the rock with the pre-existent Christ. Hence we find Moses' smiting of the rock portrayed in the catacomb paintings more often than any other scene from the Old Testament. There we see the bearded figure of Moses striking the rock in front of him with his staff. As the water gushes out an Israelite bends down to drink from the spring which has appeared so miraculously in the desert. This scene is combined with another to the left: there we see Moses loosing his sandals as commanded by God, who is represented by a hand issuing from a cloud above.

Of the third group of Old Testament books in the Hebrew arrangement, "the Writings", the Psalms were the first to be adapted to the service of the Church; but the other books were not neglected either. Thus the Book of Job, one of the most profound as well as one of the most poetical works of the Bible, recommended itself to the early Christians, and its hero

Scenes from the life of Moses, from a painting in the catacomb of St. Callixtus, Rome. Fourth century A.D.

And did all drink the same spiritual drink . . . (1 COR. 10: 4)

Ye have heard of the patience of Job . . .   (JAS. 5 : 11)

Job, from the sarcophagus of Junius Bassus.
Fourth century A.D.

became the prototype of sufferings meekly and patiently borne. In their own tribulations they found encouragement in the example of Job's steadfastness and his ultimate reward by God. All the greater will be the reward of the faithful at the coming of the LORD. This reference to Job in the Epistle of James 5: 11 has undoubtedly led to his inclusion among representatives of the just in the stock themes of Early Christian art. On the sarcophagus of Junius Bassus, prefect of the city of Rome, who died on August 25, 359, Job is shown sitting on the ash-heap (Job. 2: 8) with his wife and a friend standing by to console him.

Thus the Epistles, too, at many points give us glimpses of the life of the ancient world in which Christianity was seeking to establish itself—a life that archaeological illustrations help to make more real and vivid.

THE REVELATION OF JOHN

THE LAST BOOK of the New Testament is the Revelation of John. Its subject is the unveiling of the future: the Second Coming of Christ, the Day of Judgment, and the End of the World, to be followed by the New Heaven and New Earth. But before this consummation, the wicked are to perish and humanity—save the elect—is

355

to be decimated by the various agencies of divine wrath. Much of this material is traditional and of Jewish origin, as comparison with other apocalypses shows. The Book of Revelation, however, also contains a number of symbolical allusions to contemporary politics, such as the reality of Roman power, the wicked emperor and his predecessors, the danger of invasion from the East and similar subjects.

I am Alpha and Omega ...   (REV. I : 8)

Golden cross, flanked by the letters Alpha and Omega, on a mosaic in the Church of St. Apollinare in Classe, Ravenna. Sixth century A.D.

356

And being turned, I saw seven golden candlesticks.

(REV. 1 : 12)

Jewish ritual objects, on a gold glass found at Rome.

THE VISION OF THE SEVEN CHURCHES

THE REVELATION BEGINS with a message which the author, John, received on the island of Patmos. A voice directed him to write in a book what he was seeing and to send it to the seven principal churches of Asia.

The seven churches are those of Ephesus, Smyrna, Pergamum, Thyatira, Sardis, Philadelphia, and Laodicea. Some of these cities had been connected with the missionary activity of Paul and his helpers. He himself had been active for a long time in Ephesus, the capital of Asia; his disciple, Epaphras, had labored in Laodicea (Col. 4: 12, 13); and his convert, Lydia, was a native of Thyatira (Acts 16: 14). On the other hand the churches of Pergamum, the great trading city of Smyrna, of Sardis, the ancient capital of the Lydian kingdom, and of Philadelphia, situated at one of the main road-junctions in the Hermus valley, are here mentioned for the first time in the New Testament. All seven cities were among the most important centers of the Roman province of Asia in western Asia Minor and, as we learn from this chapter, had Christian communities established in them at an early date.

In his initial vision John sees seven golden candlesticks and in the midst of them one like a Son of man—none other, of course, than Jesus. The single candlestick of the Jewish Temple (cf. Exod. 25: 31f.) is multiplied here to symbolize the seven churches.

In the period following the destruction of Jerusalem in A.D. 70 the candlestick of the Temple became the recognized emblem of Judaism. Ancient representations of this

357

candlestick, beginning with that on the Arch of Titus, are very numerous and the type seems to change with each epoch. It appears sculptured in relief in Galilean synagogues (but not in the predominant position it attains later on), on Jewish lamps both from Palestine and the Diaspora, on gold glasses, on bone and ivory carvings, on the mosaic pavements of later synagogues, on Jewish coffins, and painted on the walls of Jewish catacombs. On the gold glass reproduced here the seven branched candlesticks are accompanied by the full array of Jewish ritual objects: the Ark of the Torah flanked by two lions, and below them the candlesticks, accompanied by ram's horns (*schofar*), citrons (*ethrog*), a palm branch (*lulah*), and an oil jar.

The various churches are addressed by John in terms suited to the special condition of each: Ephesus is urged to repentance: Smyrna is encouraged to stand fast against a persecution instigated by the local Jewish community; Pergamum is warned against heretics in its midst.

This last city had risen to greatness as the capital of the royal dynasty of the Attalids (283–133 B.C.). who founded a powerful kingdom in the northwestern corner of Asia Minor. The last ruler of the dynasty, Attalus III, bequeathed his kingdom to the Romans, and under them it became the nucleus of the province of Asia, the capital of which it remained until the end of the first century B.C., when it was replaced by Ephesus. The Attalids had embellished Pergamum with splendid palaces, temples, and other public buildings. The most

And to the angel of the church in Pergamos write . . . I know thy works, and where thou dwellest, even where Satan's seat is . . .

(REV. 2: 12–13)

(*Above*) Reconstruction of the Temple of Zeus and Athena, Pergamum.

(*Below*) Part of the frieze from the temple, showing Hekate fighting a serpent-legged giant.

*And will give him a white
stone . . .* (REV. 2: 17)

famous of these monuments was the Great Altar in the Temple of Zeus and Athena, erected
by King Eumenes II (197–159 B.C.) in commemoration of Attalid victories over the Gauls.
This building stood on a large terrace overlooking the agora or market place of the city. It
measured 120 feet by 112 feet and consisted of a colonnaded court surrounded by walls on
three sides, without an altar in its center. Around the walls ran the great frieze, 400 feet long
and 7 feet high, depicting the battle of the gods against the giants who attempted to storm
Olympus. This frieze is one of the most magnificent works of Hellenistic sculpture, and the
deep impression that it made on even a hostile beholder is still evident from the appellation,
"Satan's seat", given it in the Revelation (2: 13).

In recompense for their faithfulness the true believers at Pergamum shall be given not
only the hidden manna, but a "white stone" (2: 17). Perhaps the latter may be interpreted
as a token of acquittal. A stone (*psephos* in Greek, also in the sense of a mosaic stone) was used
for voting by the judges of the Athenian courts. To vote with a white stone meant acquittal,
while a black stone called for condemnation. The legendary origin of this custom goes back
to the trial of Orestes, the son of Agamemnon king of Mycenae, in the Areopagus, the
ancient supreme court of Athens. Orestes had avenged his father's murder by killing
Clytemnestra, his mother, and her paramour, Aegistheus. Pursued because of his matricide
by the Erinyes, the goddesses of vengeance, he stood his trial before the Athenian judges.
As the votes were evenly divided, Pallas Athene, who favored him, threw in a white stone
(the *Calculus Minervae*) and thus got him acquitted. On a painted Greek vase, Greek heroes
are seen voting as to who should receive the weapons of the dead Achilles; Athena, standing
behind the altar on which the stones are placed, decides in favor of Odysseus.

359

The church of Sardis, though corrupt, still has a number of the pure and faithful members worthy to wear white raiment (3 : 4–5). White was the hallowed garb of purity among the pagans, as well as among the Christians and Jews. Thus the Israelite priests were dressed in white linen (Exod. 28 : 40–2); and whiteness symbolizes purification from sins in Isa. 1 : 18. In the Gospels, an angel who came to sit by Jesus' tomb (Mark 16 : 5) was clad in a long white garment; and elsewhere in the Revelation the armies of heaven appear in fine, spotless white linen, riding on white horses (Rev. 19 : 14). Representations of saints and martyrs in white raiment abound in Early Christian art. Similarly the priests shown sacrificing on the frescoes at Dura-Europus (third century A.D.) are dressed in long white robes and are wearing a high conical cap of the same material. In the religious philosophy of the Alexandrian Jew, Philo, personages bathed in white light appear endowed with mystic-symbolic significance.

He that overcometh the same shall be clothed in white raiment . . .

(REV. 3 : 5)

Priests, on a fresco from Dura-Europus. Third century A.D.

Column in the synagogue at Capernaum, bearing a dedication in Greek.

Him that overcometh will I make a pillar in the temple of my God; and he shall go no more out: and I will write upon him the name of my God, and the name of the city of my God, which is New Jerusalem . . . (REV. 3 : 12)

Since Philadelphia has stood fast in the hour of temptation, the faithful shall be like a pillar in the temple of God on which God's name shall be written (3 : 12).

The custom of writing upon the pillars of a temple (implied already in 1 Kings 7 : 21) is attested by archaeological evidence from many ancient sites. Sometimes statues of prominent persons were placed against the upper part of a column and their names and titles written on the column underneath. At Palmyra a whole street had been thus adorned; the statues have perished but the inscriptions have remained. In other places the name of the person dedicating the column was written on it. This was especially the custom in the Galilean synagogues of the third and fourth centuries A.D. Since Jewish communities in Galilee had no members rich enough to present a whole building, each separate part was donated by a benefactor whose name was inscribed on it. Thus a column in the synagogue at Capernaum bears a dedication in Greek by Herod, the son of Mokimos, and his descendants. A second column is dedicated in Aramaic. Both prove that the custom of writing on pillars was widespread.

*And I saw in the right hand of him that sat on the throne
a book written within and on the back side, sealed with seven
seals.* (REV. 5: 1)

THE BOOK WITH SEVEN SEALS

THE SECOND PART of the Revelation (4: 1–22: 5) is composed of a series of
dramatic visions of the latter days. In the prelude to the first of these visions a
door is opened in heaven, and the throne of God is seen surrounded by the seats of twenty-
four elders. Four creatures, for whose description Isa. 6 and Ezek. 1 furnished the inspiration,
guard the throne. God holds a book written within and on the back and sealed with seven
seals. The lamb, "standing as though it had been slain", and hence symbolizing Jesus,
receives the book and is acclaimed as alone worthy to break its seals and open it.

The sealing of written documents was intended to protect their contents from unauthorized
eyes and, at the same time, to authenticate them. Prominent personages, such as emperors,
had their own seals executed by engravers skilled enough to make the counterfeiting of the
seal most difficult. Multiple sealings were also used to safeguard signatures. An example of
this is provided by the receipt books of the Pompeian banker, Lucius Caecilius Jucundus.
Each of these consists of six pages, the outer ones (1 and 6) being blank, while 2 and 3 contain the text of the receipt which is sealed on page 4 by a series of seals, with the name of the
witness recorded beside each one. The figure of the book with the seven seals, which were
broken one by one, must have been modeled on some such document, the implication being
that the divine judgment against the world written on its pages was to remain a secret until
the time came to break the seals open.

THE FOUR HORSEMEN

AT THE OPENING of each seal of the heavenly book something dramatic
transpires. In connection with the first four seals, horsemen appear, each
ushering in a different catastrophe. The first, on a white horse, represents the triumph of

foreign foes; the second, on a red horse, stands for civil war; the third, on a black horse for famine; and the fourth, on a pale horse, for pestilence.

The world in which the Book of Revelation was written was that of the Roman Empire at the peak of its tremendous and apparently unshakeable power under the early emperors. The vision therefore dwells on the destruction of the nerve-centers of the existing order by the various enemies which divine omnipotence could raise up against Rome. The first of these are the Parthians, those inveterate foes first of the Hellenistic kingdoms and then of the Romans, who succeeded to the heritage of Hellenism and managed to preserve it at least as far as the River Euphrates. The Parthians, who were the successors of the ancient Persians, gradually drove back the Seleucids from the highlands of Iran and, late in the second century, from Babylonia. In 54 B.C. they defeated a Roman army under the triumvir Crassus at Carrhae (Haran) in Upper Mesopotamia, and thus saved themselves from Roman domination. Wars between the Romans and the Parthians continued throughout the centuries, with now one power gaining the upper hand, now the other. The peoples subject to Rome and restive under its yoke hoped for a Parthian invasion to put an end to Roman rule. Thus one of the anti-Roman Jewish sagas expressed the opinion that the days of the Messiah would come if a Persian (Parthian) horse was seen tethered to the monuments of the Holy Land. The paintings at Dura-Europus contain many representations of mounted Parthian horsemen, usually portrayed as conquerors, holding a bow, the Parthian weapon *par excellence*.

And I saw, and behold a white horse: and he that sat on him had a bow; and a crown was given unto him: and he went forth conquering, and to conquer.   (REV. 6: 2)

Parthian horseman, on a painting from Dura-Europus.

Tombstone of Titus
Flavius Bassus, a
Roman cavalryman.

The Parthians excelled especially in shooting from horseback, and could even fire their arrows behind them when galloping in full retreat. With such tactics they had been able to defeat Roman foot-soldiers who ventured too far into their territory.

The second horseman, on a bright red horse, seems to symbolize civil war. If it is correct to assume that the Revelation was written in the time of the emperor Domitian, the author would vividly remember the convulsion which shook the Roman Empire when Nero by his madness finally provoked a general uprising against his rule. Within the short span of one year no fewer than four emperors were proclaimed, three of whom—Galba, Otho, and Vitellius—perished by assassination, suicide, or execution. The various provincial armies vied with each other in supporting their commanders, conferring on them the title of emperor, each hoping that its own particular claimant would prevail and that it would then enjoy his largesse. In the end Vespasian, the contender chosen by the armies of the East, was victorious and established the Flavian dynasty; but in the civil war of the years 68–69 a seeming instability of the imperial government had been exposed and the enemies of Rome could hope for a repetition of internal uprisings. The rider of the red horse was to cause the Romans "to kill one another"; his "great sword" probably was a typical cavalry weapon, the *spatha* (a broad two-edged sword, as distinguished from the short Spanish sword of the Roman infantry). On the tombstones of cavalrymen the deceased soldiers are seen mounted on their horses, trampling down a fallen enemy. They hold spears in their right hands, with long swords hanging at their sides.

The third horseman, on a black horse, stands for a natural calamity—famine (cf. Acts 11: 28)—which is to overwhelm the organized society of the day. Under the primitive conditions of production, and especially of transport, prevailing in antiquity, a drought and failure of crops in one part of the world could only, with difficulty, be remedied by shipping the produce of another area to the one affected; in Acts two grain-ships bound from Egypt to Rome were delayed or lost.

The rider is enjoined not to touch the wine and oil; that is, he is to confine himself to the spring harvest. He is given a balance called in Greek "a pair", from the pair of scales which, together with the bar and tongue, constituted the usual ancient balance. This instrument was normally used for weighing; here, however, it is largely symbolical, because dearth is expressed not in terms of weight but of measure. The Greeks and Romans employed standard measures, inscribed with the quantity they contained. One measure, found at Carvoran (England) and belonging to the reign of Domitian (the time when the Revelation was probably written), is marked with the date and a line showing a capacity of sixteen

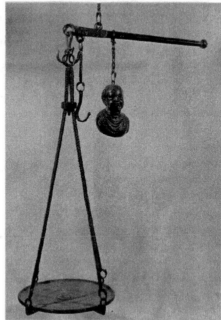

And I beheld, and, lo, a black horse; and he that sat on him had a pair of balances in his hand. And I heard a voice in the midst of the four beasts say, A measure of wheat for a penny, and three measures of barley for a penny; and see thou hurt not the oil and the wine. (REV. 6: 5–6)

(*Above*) Measure, found at Carvoran, England.

(*Right*) Balance, found at Pompeii.

sextarii—equaling one *modius* or "measure". The horseman is to declare: a measure of wheat for a *denarius*, three of barley for a *denarius*. The measure mentioned here in Revelation is the *choinix*, about equivalent to a quart. One *choinix* of grain was sufficient for one day; but the pay for a day's work was only one *denarius* (see Matt. 20: 9), and it was famine price to have to pay a whole day's wage for one measure of wheat. Barley, of course, which was consumed only in time of need and was—except in poor districts—normally fed to horses or donkeys, was three times as cheap as wheat even in times of famine.

The fourth horseman, on a pale horse, is called Death and is followed by Hades. He probably stands primarily for pestilence, though he is also given other means of destruction. The ignorance of bacteriology and hygiene in ancient times resulted in frightful outbreaks of epidemic diseases which periodically ravaged the Roman world, decimating the population and leaving the survivors enfeebled. The physicians of the period were able only to recommend palliatives, the true source of the maladies being unknown.

Clothed with white robes, and palms in their hands.

(REV. 7: 9)

Statue of a victorious charioteer holding a palm branch.

THE REMAINING SEALS

AT THE OPENING of the fifth seal the Christian martyrs, who are imagined as congregated under the heavenly altar, are consoled for having to wait for the judgment over their persecutors. When the sixth seal is broken there is a great earthquake, bringing terror to the kings and mighty men of the earth.

An interlude (ch. 7) retards matters. First the 144,000 from the tribes of Israel are sealed, and then a great host from all nations, clothed in white robes and with palm branches in their hands, acclaim the deity. They are those who have come out of great tribulation.

And another angel came and stood at the altar, having a golden censer . . .

(REV. 8 : 3)

(*Right*) Roman soldiers burning incense, from a painting at Dura-Europus. Third century A.D.

(*Below*) Open incense burner.

The seventh seal of the book is then opened, and there is silence in heaven for half an hour. At this point one expects the climax, the final revelation of God's purpose. But the reader is kept in suspense: what is revealed is another series of harrowing events, announced by trumpets.

THE VISION OF THE SEVEN TRUMPETS

SEVEN ANGELS ARE given seven trumpets, while another angel ministers at the heavenly altar. This angel fills his censer with fire from the altar and casts it upon the earth, causing thunder, lightning, and earthquakes. This is the signal for the trumpet-blowing to start, and each angel blows in turn, bringing on different calamities.

And there was given me a reed like unto a rod: and the angel stood, saying, Rise and measure the temple of God, and the altar, and them that worship therein.

(REV. 11: 1)

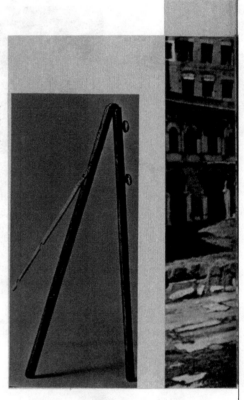

(Right) Roman metal measuring-rod.

(Far Right) View of the ruins of the forum of Trajan.

After the sixth trumpet there is an interlude (10: 1–11: 14), just as there was after the opening of the sixth seal. The visionary sees an angel with a little book or scroll. He is told that when the seventh trumpet is blown the mystery of God, as announced to the prophets, would be fulfilled. He is directed to eat the book and to prophesy to the rulers and peoples of the world. Next he received a measuring-rod and the command to measure the dimensions of the Temple (at Jerusalem) except for its Outer Court, which is to be given over to the Gentiles, who will trample over the Holy City for a period of forty-two months. Two "witnesses" (the returning Moses and Elijah?) are to prophesy for 1,260 days. (The figures are derived from the three and a half times, or years, of Dan. 12: 7.) Then a beast will ascend from the bottomless pit and will kill them, and their dead bodies will lie in the street of the city for

And their dead bodies shall lie in the street of the great city . . . (REV. 11 : 8)

three and a half days. They will then rise up again and ascend to heaven. An earthquake will destroy a tenth of the city, killing seven thousand people.

After the blowing of the seventh trumpet there is advance jubilation in heaven. The elders utter a prayer of thanksgiving, the heavenly temple is opened and the ark of the covenant is seen in it. This leads to the central portion of the book, chapters 12–14, dealing with the Birth of the Messiah, the reign of the Dragon and the Beast, and the Anticipation of Redemption.

A great sign now appeared in the heavens: a woman clothed with the sun (chapter 12). Another sign followed: a fiery dragon with seven heads and seven crowned horns stood before the woman, seeking to devour the babe which she was about to bear. When she gave birth to the child (the Messiah) it was taken away to God and his throne, while the woman fled into the desert. The archangel Michael and his angels now fought with the Dragon and his angels. The Dragon, who is identified with the ancient serpent who is called devil and Satan, was cast to the earth with his minions. Here he pursued the woman who had borne the child, but when he failed in this he turned his attention to the rest of her offspring—those keeping the commandments of God and bearing testimony to Jesus.

The Celestial dragon has a counterpart in an earthly entity—a Beast that comes up out of the sea and that, like the Dragon, has ten horns and seven heads. The Beast is clearly derived from the vision of Daniel (ch. 7); only here it symbolizes the Roman Empire and its vassal States, instead of the Hellenistic kingdoms. The seven heads are apparently the seven emperors (17 : 10); the ten horns are said to be kings that have not as yet received royal power, perhaps the vassal kings of Rome. The number comes from Dan. 7 : 7 and need not be stressed.

The Romans for some time tried as far as possible to avoid direct rule, especially in the countries of the East with their long-established political institutions. A few dynasties which were too big and powerful to acquiesce to Roman overlordship (such as those of the Antigonids in Macedonia, the Seleucids in Syria, and the Ptolemies in Egypt) were deposed;

And I stood upon the sand of the sea, and saw a beast rise up out of the sea, having seven heads and ten horns, and upon his horns ten crowns . . .

(REV. 13 : 1)

Relief from Nimrud Dagh, showing Antiochus I with the god Mithras. First century B.C.

To receive a mark in their right hand, or in their foreheads. (REV. 13 : 16)

Limestone seal of Augustus. A.D. 5–6.

but minor rulers, if sufficiently pliant and well in control of elements inclined to revolt, were left in the possession of their thrones. Only gradually in the course of the first century A.D. were these vassal kingdoms absorbed one by one. They included the Bosporan kingdom in the Crimea, Colchis of the Caucasus, the kingdoms of Armenia, Pontus, Cappadocia, and Commagene in Asia Minor, Judaea under Herod, Chalcis in Syria, the Nabataean kingdom in Arabia, and Mauretania in Africa. One of these vassals, the king of Commagene, Antiochus I (69–34 B.C.), erected a magnificent monument on Nimrud Dagh, adorned with statues and reliefs of himself and his ancestors. On the relief reproduced here Antiochus is portrayed with the god Mithras.

Then the visionary beholds another beast coming up from the land (13 : 11 f.). Its function is to make the inhabitants of the earth worship the first beast. According to later passages (especially 19 : 20) this second beast is a false prophet—probably some leading exponent of the imperial cult of the author's time. The number of the Beast, giving a clue to its name and identity for initiated readers of the author's day, is 666. Many solutions have been offered, but none can be made convincing. A favorite one is that the numbers spell *Nero(n) Caesar*, a theory based on the numerical values of the Hebrew alphabet. Only those bearing the mark or seal of the Beast were allowed to carry on commercial transactions. This was a common practice under Roman rule, when the imperial seal was usually applied to letters of purchase or similar documents.

371

*And the sixth angel poured out his vial upon the great river
Euphrates; and the water thereof was dried up, that the way of
the kings of the east might be prepared.* (REV. 16: 12)

Valerian surrendering to the
Persian king Shapur I, on a
rock relief at Naqsh-i Ruslam.

A brief vision of a comforting and hopeful nature (14: 1–5) relieves the sequence of grim
happenings. The Lamb (i.e. the Messianic child now full grown) stands on Mount Zion with
the 144,000 of 7: 4 who are spotless. Then follow announcements and preparations for the
judgment (14: 6–20) which will terminate the reign of the Beast.

THE VISION OF THE SEVEN VIALS OF WRATH

THE ATTAINMENT OF that goal, however, is again retarded. The seven seals
and the seven trumpets must have still another counterpart: the seven vials or
bowls, which seven angels receive to pour out and bring about a new series of calamities.
Perhaps the most interesting is the next to the last: when the sixth bowl is poured out it
dries up the great River Euphrates (16: 12).

The author of the Revelation here voices the political aspirations of the oppressed Orientals
and their eager desire to see the hated Roman power humbled before the Parthian kings of
the East. The River Euphrates, which formed the boundary between the two empires, will
suddenly dry up, thus in an instant exposing the Roman frontier and clearing the way for

the Parthians to advance deep into the Roman province of Syria or beyond. The latter hope took some time to realize; it was only in the third century A.D. that the reinvigorated Persian empire, under its new Sassanian dynasty, came to serious grips with the Romans. The greatest moment in Sassanian history was the surrender of the emperor Valerian in A.D. 260 to the Persian king, Shapur I, after a defeat in battle, though even before that the Persians had successfully invaded Syria and taken its capital, Antioch, in 255. This moment of triumph is represented on a rock relief showing Shapur I on his horse, with the Roman emperor kneeling at his feet.

The seventh bowl produces an earthquake "such as had never been since men were on the earth". The "great city" (Rome) was split into three parts.

At the time when the Revelation was written, the imperial city had begun to be transformed by the building activities of successive emperors. In particular, the area north of the old Roman forum had been developed by a series of new forums, beginning with that of Julius Caesar, in which stood the temple of Venus Genetrix, the legendary ancestress of the Julian family. Then Augustus built another forum containing the Temple of Mars the Avenger (of the assassination of Julius Caesar); Vespasian constructed a third with the Temple of Peace; and Nerva added a fourth, small forum. Even more impressive than all these was the later forum of Trajan (see p. 369): with its large semi-circular wings. The construction and town-planning activities which were changing the face of imperial Rome justified the title of "the great city" here given it.

And the woman which thou sawest is that great city, which reigneth over the kings of the earth. (REV. 17: 18)

The goddess Roma, incarnation of the city of Rome, on gilt silver bowl, found at Hildesheim.

THE FALL OF ROME

O NE OF THE bowl-angels now invites the visionary to see the judgment of the great harlot. He carries him off to see a woman sitting on a scarlet beast with seven heads and ten horns. The woman symbolizes Rome.

The idea of a woman representing a city was evidently taken from the female statues personifying the great cities of antiquity, or rather their tutelary goddesses or *Tyches.* Once the sculptor Eutychides had created the prototype of such a goddess in his famous work representing the Tyche of Antioch, the personification of cities as dignified females wearing mural crowns (i.e. crowns representing a walled city) became a generally accepted convention. There were local variations: thus Alexandria, the great port of Egypt, is represented wearing a crown made of ships; and Rome, the warrior city, appears with helmet and breastplate, like a second Minerva as shown on the preceding page. A painting found at Pompeii shows another symbolical image of this kind. It is the Venus of Pompeii, majestically draped in blue and crowned with gold, riding on a chariot drawn by elephants, with Cupid

The Venus of Pompeii, on a
wall-painting from the city.

*And I saw a woman sit upon a scarlet colored beast, full
of names of blasphemy, having seven heads and ten horns.
And the woman was arrayed in purple and scarlet color, and
decked with gold and precious stones, and pearls . . .*

(REV. 17: 3–4)

Coins of the Roman emperors. From left to right: (*above*) Augustus, Tiberius, Caligula; (*below*) Claudius, Nero, Vespasian.

The seven heads are seven mountains, on which the woman sitteth. And there are seven kings: five are fallen, and one is, and the other is not yet come; and when he cometh, he must continue a short space. And the beast that was, and is not, even he is the eighth . . . (REV. 17: 9–11)

in attendance on her and winged genii hovering to the right and left. This hieratic figure, which recalls those of the Oriental gods, is of a type not unlike the vision of Rome symbolized by a woman in the Revelation.

The seven heads of the beast on which the woman sat are symbolical of "seven kings: five are fallen, and one is, and the other is not yet come; and when he cometh, he must continue a short space" (17: 10). But room is made for an eighth king by equating him with the beast as such.

The identification of the seven "kings" (emperors) of Rome referred to here depends on the date assigned to the composition of the Book of Revelation. If we assume that the "beast that was and is not" is Domitian, then the five fallen kings will be the five emperors of the Julio-Claudian dynasty: Augustus (31 B.C.—A.D. 14), Tiberius (A.D. 14–37), Caligula (A.D. 37–41), Claudius (A.D. 41–54), and Nero (A.D. 54–68); the "one that is" would be Vespasian (A.D. 69–79) (omitting the three short-lived emperors of the year of civil wars, A.D. 68–69, Galba, Otho, and Vitellius); and the one who "is to come and rule for a short time" would be Titus (A.D. 79–81), to be followed by the "beast", Domitian (A.D. 81–96).

The fall of "Babylon", as Rome is cryptically called here, is then hailed in chapter 18 by an angel. Among those described as bewailing its fate from afar are the shipmasters and sailors.

375

To understand why these are singled out one has to appreciate the basic facts of the imperial city's existence. Its population was swollen by an enormous number of aliens, many of them slaves or freedmen, all of whom relied for their maintenance on the imperial bounty. Any failure of this bounty and the consequent famine would cause rioting and endanger the lives of the emperor and his court. Only by supplies of wheat from Egypt and Africa could the population of Rome be kept quiet. The importance of the wheat-ships can be seen from the references to them in Acts; Paul continued and completed his voyage on Alexandrian ships carrying this cargo to Italy. One of the plans of the Jews who revolted against Rome in the time of Nero was to interfere with this trade and thus rouse the Roman

And every shipmaster, and all the company in ships, and sailors, and as many as trade by sea, stood afar off. (REV. 18 : 17)

Ships being unloaded, from a mosaic found at Ostia. Third century A.D.

proletariat against the imperial government. The importance of these cargoes is also evident from the fact that the emperors most mindful of their duty to the capital, improved its harbor facilities by developing the port of Ostia at the mouth of the Tiber. A mosaic of the third century, found at Ostia, shows two ships being unloaded.

A prophetic illustration of the completeness of the future fall of "Babylon" is given in the act of an angel throwing a great millstone into the sea. In like manner Rome will disappear and not be found.

Again, as after the seventh trumpet, there is celebration in heaven (19 : 1 f.). The imminent marriage-supper of the Lamb is announced.

And he treadeth
the winepress of the
fierceness and wrath
of Almighty God.
(REV. 19: 15)

Laborers working in a
winepress, from a relief
found near Venice.

THE COMING OF CHRIST AND THE FINAL EVENTS

AND NOW THE visionary sees the heaven opened and "Faithful and True"—
the Messiah—comes on his white horse (19: 11f.). Among the things said
of him is that "he will tread the winepress of the fury of the wrath of God the Almighty".

The same metaphor occurs also in the prophecy of Isaiah (chapter 63). The red of the
grapejuice calls to mind the color of blood, and the crushing of the grapes symbolizes the
fate of those who vainly oppose the will of the Almighty. A relief found near Venice shows
two laborers, with hands joined, rhythmically jumping in a vat filled with grapes, while a
third man on the left is bringing more fruit for the winepress.

John now sees an angel standing in the sun and calling the birds to the gruesome feast
after the battle, in which the Messiah smites his foes with a rod of iron. The Beast and its
prophet are not slain, however, but captured and thrown into "the lake of fire that burns
with brimstone".

But there remains the ultimate adversary—the Dragon or Satan himself. An angel bearing
a key and a great chain seizes him and locks him up in "the bottomless pit" for a thousand
years (20: 1-2). The martyrs are now resurrected and reign with Christ for this period, the
millennium. At the end of the thousand years, however, Satan is let loose; then follows the
invasion of Gog and Magog (prophesied by Ezek. 38). It ends with their destruction, and
now Satan too is thrown into the lake of fire and brimstone. The resurrection of the rest of

humanity takes place and the judgment is held. Death and Hades personified are thrown into the lake of fire, as well as all those persons not found written in the book of life.

With the final elimination of Evil the time has come for a complete regeneration of the universe; a New Heaven and a New Earth come into being, and the Holy City of Jerusalem, which has waited in heaven for this time, now descends on earth to take the place of the sinful city which had been destroyed.

This concept of a heavenly Jerusalem as opposed to the terrestrial city is common to both the rabbinical sources and to early Christianity. We find a pictorial representation of it in the frescoes of the synagogue at Dura-Europus. The artist actually intended to depict the Temple of Solomon standing in the middle of the earthly city; but he has encircled the latter with the seven walls of the celestial Jerusalem, each in a different color. The Temple has the form of a Hellenistic sanctuary, and the three gates of Jerusalem are adorned with various images of pagan character, such as were customary on the gates and temples of the cities of the period. These details, so far from seeming incongruous with the general conception of the Heavenly City, served only to augment its splendor.

The Book of Revelation ends with Christ's solemn assurance of his imminent coming, a brief word of prayer for its realization, and with a blessing for all the faithful.

And had a wall great and high, and had twelve gates . . . (REV. 21 : 12)

Pictorial representation of heavenly Jerusalem, from a fresco at Dura-Europus.

He which testifieth these things saith, Surely I come quickly; Amen. Even so, come, Lord Jesus. The grace of our Lord Jesus Christ be with you all. Amen.

(REV. 22 : 20–21)

The last page of the Codex Sinaiticus, one of the earliest manuscripts of the Greek Bible. Fourth century A.D.

CREDITS

This book is based upon the five-volume work entitled *Illustrated World of the Bible Library*, and we wish to express our thanks to the following individuals and institutions not mentioned in the preface:

The Rev. Robert North, S.J., and the Rev. P. Nobler, S.J., both of the Pontifical Biblical Institute; Prof. R. Bianchi-Bandinelli and Dr. E. Nash, both of Rome.

Among the institutions are the Metropolitan Museum, New York; the Oriental Institute of the University of Chicago; the archives of Professor N. Glueck; Professor G. Reed; the collections of the Marburg and Alinari Photographic Institutes; the Museum of Fine Arts, Boston; the Detroit Art Museum; the University Museum, Philadelphia; the Brooklyn Museum; the Baltimore Museum; the British Museum, London; University Library, Cambridge; Chester Museum, Northumberland; the Museum of the Ancient Orient, Istanbul; the Hittite Museum, Ankara; the National Museum, Rome; the Vatican Museum, Rome; Museo civico, Bologna; Archaeological Museum, Florence; Bibliotheca Medicea-Laurenziana, Florence; National Museum, Naples; Museo Concordiese, Portogruaro, Italy; Antiquarium of the Forum, Rome; National Museum of the Villa Giulia, Rome; Capitol Museum, Rome; Museo Nazionale delle Terme, Rome; Museo archaeologico, Venice; Museo civico, Verona; the Staatliche Museen, Berlin; Pergamon-Museum, Berlin; Landesmuseum, Trier; the Archaeological Museum, University of London; the Ny-Carlsberg Glyptothek, Copenhagen; the collection of A. Goitein, U.S.A.; the Louvre, Paris; Bibliothèque Nationale, Paris; the Rijksmuseum, Leiden; Ecole française d'archéologie, Athens; Malta Museum, La Valetta; Kunsthistorisches Museum, Vienna: the staff and library of the Archaeology Department of the Hebrew University; the Department of Antiquities (museum and library) of the Ministry of Education and Culture, and its former director, Dr. S. Yeivin; the National and University Library, Jerusalem; the Bezalel National Museum, Jerusalem; the Haaretz Museum, Tel-Aviv; the James de Rothschild Expedition at Hazor; the collection of Mr. J. Leibovitch; the Clark Collection at the Jerusalem Y.M.C.A.; the collection of Dr. R. Hecht, Haifa; that of the Ben-Zvi Institute for the Study of the Oriental Jewish Communities at the Hebrew University; The Shrine of the Book, Jerusalem; the Tell Qasile Collection, Tel-Aviv; the permanent exhibition on the site of the Megiddo excavations; the Nautical Museum, Haifa; the Pontifical Biblical Institute, Jerusalem; the Israel Aero Club. The Editorial Board also wishes to thank the following authors, editors and publishers for their kind permission to use plates published by them: W. F. Albright, W. Andrae, N. Avigad, D. Baldi, R. D. Barnett, P. Berger, A. M. Blackman, H. Bonnet, E. Douglas van Buren, M. Burrows, E. Chiera, Ch. Chipiez, F. M. Cross, G. Dalman, W. R. Dawson, N. de G. Davies, A. Deimel, J. Dossin, M. Dunand, G. R. Driver, A. Erman, C. S. Fisher, H. Frankfort, A. Furman, S. J. Gadd, K. Galling, A. H. Gardiner, P. C. Gau, A. J. Gayet, H. Gressmann, H. Grimme, L. H. Grollenberg, U. Hölscher, L. Klebs, S. N. Kramer, P. Lemaire, A. Lhote, G. Loud, D. G. Lyon, R. A. S. Macalister, M. J. L. Mallowan, Ch. McCown, B. Meissner, A. Mekhiterian, J. T. Milik, P. Montet, S. Moscati, H. H. Nelson, P. E. Newberry, J. Nougayrol, A. T. Olmstead, M. Oppenheim, M. Pallottino, R. A. Parker, A. Parrot, A. T. Peet, G. Perrot, W. M. Flinders Petrie, K. Pflüger, W. Phillips, H. Ranke, G. A. Reisner, P. Rost, A. Rowe, H. W. P. Saggs, A. H. Sayce, C. F. A. Schaeffer, H. Schmökel, O. Schröder, C. Schumacher, W. Stevenson-Smith, C. Steuernagel, E. L. Sukenik, F. Thureau-Dangin, J. Trever, O. Tufnell, N. H. Tur-Sinai, B. Ubach, C. Watzinger, R. Weill, M. Werbrouck,

J. G. Wilkinson, H. E. Winlock, L. Woolley, W. Wreszinski, G. E. Wright: American Schools of Oriental Research, E. J. Brill, Ltd., British Museum, British School of Archaeology in Iraq, F. A. Brockhaus, Constable & Co., W. de Gruyter & Co., Editions Cahiers d'Art, Editions Ides et Calendes, Egypt Exploration Fund, Egypt Exploration Society, Folkswang Verlag, Fondation égyptologique Reine Elizabeth, M. P. Geuthner, V. Gollancz, Hachette, Harvard University Press, J. C. Hinrichs, Imprimerie nationale, G. Klipper, Mariettim, Metropolitan Museum, J. C. B. Mohr-Paul Siebeck, Monestir de Montserrat, John Murray Ltd., Oriental Institute—University of Chicago, Oxford University Press, Palestine Exploration Fund, Penguin Books, Ltd., Presses universitaires de France, Routledge & Kegan Paul, Ltd., Ferdinand Schöningh, A. Skira, Society of Antiquaries, University Museum—University of Pennsylvania, The Trustees of the Late Sir Henry S. Wellcome, Yale University Press. In addition we have made full use of the comprehensive studies of R. Lepsius, A. Layard and P. E. Botta.

INDEXES

SITES, OBJECTS AND MONUMENTS

REPRODUCTIONS

PHOTOGRAPHS

MAPS

RECONSTRUCTIONS

9 781013 986529